Just XSL

D1409158

ISBN 0-13-060311-2

9 780130 603111
90000

JUST XSL

John E. Simpson

PRENTICE HALL PTR
UPPER SADDLE RIVER, NJ 07458
WWW.PHPTR.COM

A CIP catalog record for this book can be obtained from the Library of Congress.

Editorial/production supervision: *BooksCraft, Inc., Indianapolis, IN*
Acquisitions editor: *Paul Petralia*
Editorial assistant: *Justin Somma*
Marketing manager: *Debby vanDijk*
Manufacturing manager: *Alexis R. Heydt-Long*
Cover design director; *Jerry Votta*
Cover designer: *Design Source*
Project coordinator: *Anne R. Garcia*
Development editor: *Jim Markham*
Technical editor: *Len Bullard*

© 2002 Prentice Hall PTR
Prentice-Hall, Inc.
Upper Saddle River, NJ 07458

Prentice Hall books are widely used by corporations and government agencies for training, marketing, and resale.

The publisher offers discounts on this book when ordered in bulk quantities. For more information contact:
Corporate Sales Department
Phone: 800-382-3419 Fax: 201-236-7141
E-mail: corpsales@prenhall.com

Or write:
Prentice Hall PTR
Corp. Sales Dept.
One Lake Street
Upper Saddle River, NJ 07458

Printed in the United States of America
10 9 8 7 6 5 4 3 2 1

ISBN 0-13-060311-2

Pearson Education Ltd.
Pearson Education Australia PTY. Ltd.
Pearson Education Singapore, Pte. Ltd.
Pearson Education North Asia Ltd.
Pearson Education Canada Ltd.
Pearson Educacion de Mexio, S.A. de C.V.
Pearson Education—Japan
Pearson Education Malaysia, Pte. Ltd.
Pearson Education, Upper Saddle River, New Jersey

To my family:
just right

Contents

Preface

So you're wandering among the shelves of your favorite local or on-line bookstore, looking for a book on the Extensible Stylesheet Language (XSL). These are some things you know about yourself:

First, you already know the Extensible Markup Language (XML) itself. You know that it's a lightweight descendant of the Standardized General Markup Language (SGML), and that it isn't just a single markup language, despite the name, but a standard for creating and managing markup languages. You know that an XML document consists of nothing but text. You know that XML is something like HTML—all those screwy angle brackets, ampersands, and so on —but that it's also something quite a bit more. You know that in XML, the tags that define elements must be either balanced (in start tag/end tag pairs) or empty. Maybe you sometimes get confused whether "DTD" stands for "Document Type *Definition*" or "Document Type *Declaration*," but there's no doubt in your mind at all what a DTD does. And so on.

Second, although you know XML at some level, you're still a little puzzled. It all seems so...so *inert.* What do you do with your documents and data once you've got them locked up inside XML markup? You've heard of XSL (well, you're shopping for a book about it, aren't you?), and you think maybe an answer to the question of what to do with XML might be somehow wrapped up with XSL.

And third—most importantly—you want a book about XSL that helps you *understand* the topic, one that doesn't simply churn out a restatement (however lucid) of the spec's finer points. Sure, you want to be able to refer to the book from time to time once you've learned the subject. But long before you need to refresh your memory, you need to load all that stuff into your memory in the first place.

Welcome to *Just XSL*

If the description of you in the three preceding paragraphs rings true, I think you're in the right place. Here's what I propose to do (and not to do) in the chapters which follow:

What *Just XSL* does

You'll find one introductory chapter laying the groundwork for all that follows. If you've been nosing around XSL for a little while on your own, you can probably skim some or most of the material in this chapter.

After that first chapter, which pretty much stands on its own, the book is broken up into two main parts, the first on XSL Transformations (XSLT) and the second on XSL Formatting Objects (XSL-FO). In each main section, you'll encounter a carefully organized explanation of the relevant standards from the World Wide Web Consortium, or W3C. If something in the standard is ambiguous, confusing, or outright mysterious, I'll say so. But by far, to understand most of this stuff you just need a little patience and a certain amount of guidance. I'll provide the guidance, in the form of explanations, examples, and metaphors. (As for the patience, well, you're on your own there.)

Each chapter in the two main sections of the book includes (in addition to numerous fragmentary examples) a single worked sample problem, cast in the form of the answer to a "How do I...?" question. The question in a given chapter may be fairly simple to answer (although the answer may be non-obvious!). Or it may be rather more complex, requiring a few pages of XSLT/XSL-FO code to answer really well.

The first main section of the book, on XSLT, presented me with one potential problem that the second section didn't face. As you will see, effective use of XSLT is highly dependent on effective use of the XPath standard. It was pretty safe to assume that when you came to *Just XSL*, you'd already know enough about XML; it wasn't as safe, though, to make the same assumption about your knowledge of XPath. So the first chapter of the XSLT section details use of XPath as well.

Finally, I'll also demonstrate and explain the basics of some of the more popular software tools for processing XSLT and XSL-FO.

What *Just XSL* doesn't do

In the manner of Bart Simpson (no relation) at the opening of each episode of "The Simpsons," here's a list of things that I won't do in *Just XSL*:

I will not teach you XML itself. I assume you already know it.

I will not teach you XLinks, XPointers, XML Schema, or any of the rest of the X-abbreviated standards (except, obviously, XSLT, XPath, and XSL-FO themselves). I may *refer to* those other standards at some point, and I'm not going to leave you floundering in an ocean of confusion if a particular factoid from one of them is really necessary in order to understand the reference. But I'm not going to dwell on any of them.

I will not expend a lot of time and effort showing you how to install, run, and live with the software tools I use throughout. (The surest way to make a technical book outdated as soon as possible is to season it heavily with this kind of information.) On the other hand, as you will soon see, each of these tools commonly comes with its own set of (let's be kind) idiosyncrasies; I *will* mention such quirks when they come up.

Finally, you'll find almost nothing in these pages about "how to create a Java servlet/write a CGI program/code an ASP page to process XSL." I take the word "just" in this book's title very seriously. You will find some information, with some simple examples, in one chapter on server-side XSL processing; but even this topic will cover only the use of pre-built server-side tools...not how to build such tools yourself.

A few words about me

I've been an applications developer for over 20 years, and a writer about technology for about the last 10 of those. I didn't come directly out of college and jump right into the computer world, though; I taught high school (English and journalism), and had a few odd jobs as well. Drove a cab. Worked in a publishing company warehouse. Delivered furniture. Like that.

All of which is to reassure you (and maybe—maybe even *mostly*—to reassure myself, too) that when using and thinking about technology, I tend not to be interested in the subject for its own sake. Life really is too short, you know, to be monomaniacally obsessed with the flow of electrons and how best to control and manipulate that flow.

So here's another hope I have for what you'll find in *Just XSL*: I hope not to bore either of us. Sure, I hope to show you how to make XSL work for you. But I keep thinking that we need more examples of how to *play* with serious technology than examples of how to *work* with it.

That won't come as a surprise if you've come to this book from my previous title, *Just XML*. In that book I introduced what may strike you as a bizarre application of XML: an XML vocabulary, FlixML, with which to construct reviews of generally older, low-budget B movies.* FlixML is back here in *Just XSL*, in a trivially enhanced version that lets me demonstrate more features of XSLT and XSL-FO. You'll find few if any examples of how to use XSL to (say) produce your corporate annual report; but trust me, if you can use it to produce a program brochure for a B-movie film festival—or at least, understand how *I* used it to do so —a corporate annual report should be a snap.

I'll also take a few detours from the subject at hand into exclusively B-movie territory. Each of these four so-called "B Alert!" boxes will introduce you to a different classic B flick that I think is worth taking a look at. The detours, I promise, will be brief.

If you'd like more information about FlixML (or B movies in general), drop by my Web site at www.flixml.org. You'll find sample FlixML reviews there, as well as different versions of the DTD, errata for this book (if, the gods forbid, any errata should occur), links to useful Web sites, and so on.

Don't be shy about dropping me an e-mail, either: simpson@flixml.org.

Acknowledgments

First, I owe a big debt of gratitude to the people at Prentice Hall Professional Technical Reference, who have supported and encouraged me through two editions of *Just XML* and now *Just XSL*. In particular, I'd like to thank Jeff Pepper (my first editor at PH-PTR), Paul Petralia (currently The Man), and Justin Somma.

---

*   Most readers of *Just XML* seemed to appreciate FlixML for what it was—a more or less complete demonstrator of basic principles. I was amused by the number of people who objected to FlixML's failure to be a "serious" use of XML.

Acknowledging individuals who've helped me better understand XSLT and XSL-FO is a little tricky. It's certain that I'll forget someone. Nonetheless, I can easily single out the following individuals, in no particular order, as having been particularly helpful along the way: James Clark; Michael Kay; Tony Graham and Wendell Piez, both of Mulberry Technologies; G. Ken Holman, of Crane Softwrights; Nikolai Grigoriev, of RenderX; Jonathan Marsh and Andy Kimball, of Microsoft Corporation; Kurt Cagle; David Carlisle; Dave Pawson; and Jeni Tennison. Needless to say, my gratitude to these folks doesn't imply that they are responsible for anything I've gotten wrong in this book; any mistakes and misrepresentations are mine alone.

A handful of people in no single easily classifiable category deserve my thanks in general: Neil Salkind, Craig Wiley, and the other great people at StudioB Literary Agency; Simon St. Laurent (favorite XML author and pundit to start with, and finally a great friend); and especially Captain Neil Bauman of GeekCruises.com (technology, fun, and adventure all at once—what a concept!).

Finally, of course, to my wife Toni—furious champion of whatever cause (some of them lost `<cough/>`) she takes up; caretaker to 100 percent of the neighborhood wildlife even though she's allergic to 75 percent of it; patient guide to the enigmatic ways of the Deep South; long-suffering sharer of B-grade and generally weird movies; favorite travel companion, book reviewer, and debate opponent; and in oh so many ways still a truly fiery boar (though I sometimes manage to rabbit her into a different corner of the Zodiac)—thanks, Baby.

JUST XSL

Introduction to XSL

This brief part, consisting of one short chapter, provides a bird's-eye view of the two XSL standards, XSLT and XSL-FO, including brief histories of each and their "reasons for being."

Very little actual code is presented here. For the details of coding in either of the two vocabularies, refer to the chapters in Parts 2 and 3.

Why XSL?

Shocking but true: XML (he said, whispering conspiratorially and look-ing over his shoulder) cannot do everything.

Oh, sure—without a doubt, having your data locked up in a structured-text form makes it much simpler to build applications around. But it's also true that XML is remarkably, well, *unpresentable*. No matter how beautiful its underlying logical structure might be, an XML document is pretty ugly to eyes that have grown accustomed to Web pages and sophisticated print output. (And of course, in its raw form it's completely opaque to someone who needs other than a visual display.)

Furthermore, you've probably heard (maybe even argued yourself) that XML's real strength is often not as a data-storage format but as a data-*interchange* format. Still, if you think about it, you'll realize there's nothing inherent about marked-up text that makes it especially suitable for this job, either. If you want to pass your XML into some application that doesn't know XML or into some other XML vocabulary, don't you have to write a separate translation program for every one of those occasions? What good would *that* be?

The answer to both of these dilemmas lies in recognizing that they're differ-ent expressions of the *same* dilemma, which is this: How do you easily turn your XML document into something else?

Enter XSL

The first Working Draft (WD) of a single XML vocabulary called the Extensible Stylesheet Language (or XSL) was released by the W3C in mid-1998, about six months after the publication of the XML 1.0 Recommendation itself. For anyone whose only previous exposure to the word "stylesheet" came from the Cascading Style Sheets (CSS) standard for styling HTML, XSL was a bizarre standard indeed.[1] Its bizarreness arose from two features.

First, of course, it was an XML-based stylesheet language for expressing CSS properties. Even if you were accustomed to XML markup, even if you already knew CSS, seeing them both in the same document was disconcerting.

Second, XSL's design was heavily influenced not only by CSS and XML but by a stylesheet language used for presenting SGML documents called the Document Style Semantics and Specification Language (DSSSL).

You could use something like the following DSSSL code to style a portion of a FlixML document:

```
(element (remarks)
  (make paragraph
    font-size: 12pt
    font-weight: bold
    line-spacing: 12pt
      (process-children)))
```

The first line of this code fragment declares that it applies to the element type whose name is `remarks`. Most of the subsequent lines associate the display of this element with particular font characteristics, which could also be done with CSS alone. (And note that the "terminology" is that of CSS, as well: `font-size`, `font-weight`, and `line-spacing` are also display properties known to CSS.)

But DSSSL has something CSS does not. Think of the CSS properties as adjectives in a human language (like "red," "spherical," "upside-down," "unimaginable," and so on). Their purpose is to alter the base characteristics of some underlying object: a simple noun, in the case of adjectives; or an element's content, in the case of CSS.

---

1.   XSL introduced a gratuitous bit of craziness to the language: Are these things called *stylesheets* (one word, per XSL) or *style sheets* (two words, per CSS)? Since this book is about XSL, I've opted for the former in all cases *except* when spelling out what the acronym "CSS" actually stands for.

What DSSSL added to this elementary grammar was *verbs*, such as "make paragraph" and "process-children." This sort of stylesheet language is capable not only of ornamenting content but of doing *other* things with it. In particular, make paragraph transforms the contents of a remarks element into a display unit, a paragraph; for its part, process-children tells the DSSSL-aware application to look through the stylesheet for any DSSSL code that applies to children of the remarks element, and to apply that code to any such children which happen to be in this document.[2]

Using this first WD of the XSL spec, you could create an XSL stylesheet that contained code something like the following—an XSLization, if you will, of the above DSSSL fragment:

```
<xsl:template match="remarks">
  <fo:block
    font-size="12pt"
    font-weight="bold"
    line-spacing="12pt">
    <xsl:process-children/>
  </fo:block>
</xsl:template>
```

Most of this bears a close resemblance to the DSSSL equivalent.[3] Note not only that it has been recast in XML syntax, using start and end tags for grouping instead of parentheses, but also that the element names are qualified with namespace prefixes, xsl: and fo:. (The latter, in this version of the WD, stood for "flow objects"; each flow object represented a discrete displayable unit of content.) I'll talk more about XSL's uses of namespaces later, particularly in Chapter 2.

The split: One spec becomes two

The XSL WD 1.0 standard had been floating around for just a few months when people who were using it more than casually realized it was a little overloaded and top-heavy. It was trying to do far too much in a fairly short space.

---

2. CSS doesn't do, or doesn't do well, some other things at which XSL excels. See the section "Formatting XML," later in this chapter, for further discussion of this topic.
3. This resemblance wasn't exactly coincidental. If you compare the names of the XSL standard's developers to the names of the developers of DSSSL and other such efforts, you'll find a lot of the same people.

Furthermore, one part of XSL was almost immediately recognized as being generally useful for purposes *other than* styling or displaying XML content. This was the portion of the spec represented above by the XSL elements using the `xsl:` namespace prefix—the portion that relates to transforming XML content. For example, it would be generally useful to be able to "upgrade" an XML document to conform to a newer version of the DTD on which it's based, or to translate a document from one XML vocabulary to a different one.

Finally, nailing down the flow object–related half of XSL was turning out to be an enormous job. The spec's authors wanted to reproduce CSS's capabilities, of course, enabling XML to be displayed on the Web (and presented aurally, as well); but they wanted to take XSL further—enabling XML to drive the creation of sophisticated print publications, for which CSS was mostly ill-suited.

For all these reasons, within a couple more iterations of the WD, XSL had split into two separate standards: one called XSL Transformations (XSLT) and the other, XSL Formatting Objects (XSL-FO).

E v o l u t i o n   i n   a c t i o n

Yeah: what were previously known as "flow objects" are now known as "formatting objects." Personally, I was happy with the change; "flow objects" sounds too much like jargon.

I'd probably be even happier if they replaced "objects" with something a little less like a buzzword. But I appreciate that this is a geek world, after all, and you take what you can get.

Transforming XML

A few years ago, I was treated to a demonstration of some morphing software.[4] Now, my job doesn't require that I keep up with special-purpose graphics software, and I've never done any kind of video production. So for all I know the software is way more powerful now than it was at that time.

---

4.   Morphing, in case you didn't already know, is the process of stretching and otherwise distorting the contours of one shape until it becomes another shape. This has become a special-effects commonplace in a certain sort of movie or TV program. Think of Robert Patrick, who played the bad robot in *Terminator 2*: He morphed from a literally mercurial robot into the shape of whomever he needed to resemble at the time.

In any case, what this particular software package required in order to perform its magic was that you took the starting image and the ending image and then selected points on image A that mapped onto corresponding points of image B. All the morphing software did was fill in the blanks—create intermediate images in which the image-A points moved successively closer to where they went on image B, until you ended up with image B itself.

The general idea worked something like Figure 1–1, enabling you (in this case) to turn an average everyday backyard-barbecue doofus into an ax-wielding madman posing for a B-grade horror movie poster. Just indicate a point on the top of the doofus's head that maps onto another on the top of the madman's (A to A′), a point from one left toe to another (B to B′), one from the corner of the burger spatula to a corner of the ax (C to C′), and so on. The more points you map from one image to the other, the less the software has to "guess" how to get from one image to another and the smoother the morphing transition will be.

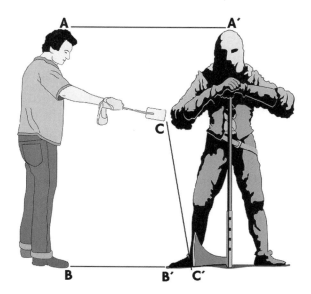

Figure 1-1 Morphing from backyard picnic-meister to lord of the chopping block. Points in the image on the left are tied to corresponding points in the image on the right. For any points for which the correspondence is not explicit, the software makes the call. Note how the chef doesn't simply change into an ax murderer in the same pose; he's actually rotated 90 degrees to face the viewer, with both hands placed atop what used to be an innocent burger-flipper held in his right hand only.

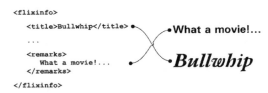

```
<flixinfo>
    <title>Bullwhip</title> •        •What a movie!...
        ...
    <remarks>
        What a movie!...           •Bullwhip
    </remarks>
</flixinfo>
```

Figure 1-2   Morphing from FlixML to...something else. As in Figure 1–1, this "morph" works because the software's user has established correspondences between the original form and the desired result. Also as in Figure 1–1, there's no particular need for the original and the final placements of a given point to be identical.

An XSLT transformation works in roughly the same fashion. Basically, the stylesheet code spells out, for each portion of some XML source document, what kind of content is to be created in a resulting document. And as with the chef-to-executioner morph, the XSLT morph does not require that the corresponding point be "in the same place"—you can shift things around. So you can wind up with something like Figure 1–2. Here, the FlixML `title` element appears in the output somewhere at the bottom, while the `remarks` element has been bumped up to the top. Notice that the two elements' contents not only are arranged differently than they were in the source document, they've also been transformed into different "kinds of things" (represented here by different font characteristics).

Of course, in a sense there's nothing remarkable about this. Programmers have been writing code for decades to transform one form of text to another. What distinguishes XSLT from these efforts are the following characteristics:

- XSLT is a *generalized* solution to the transformation problem. The same general techniques are useful regardless of the structure of the source text; you do not have to write a customized program for every different structure.
- Although you do have to write a customized *stylesheet* for every different structure, these stylesheets are generally simpler than programs developed in procedural languages such as C++ and Java.[5] Not only are they often

---

5.   This is by no means a slam at application developers who use such languages. I'm one of them, myself. What makes XSLT different here is its relative accessibility to those who haven't been trained in the black art of application development. Furthermore, for those who *have* been so trained, XSLT—once they've got the knack of it—is often more pleasant to use, because it relegates much of the tedium of housekeeping code to applications that *process* XSLT code. I'll have more to say about these *XSLT processors* (or engines) throughout this book.

simpler to develop, they're simpler for the uninitiated to read and make sense of.

- Because they're simpler to develop and to understand, XSLT stylesheets are more cost efficient over the life of a text-processing application. The staggering cost associated with developing customized programs for every single kind of document—let alone every single *document*—had always been one of the main stumbling blocks to widespread acceptance of text-processing applications. (This seemed like it would be the case even for XML itself, until XSLT came along.)

XSLT, in short, strikes an eminently reasonable balance between two conflicting goals in a text-processing application: the need for power and the need for ease of use.

Formatting XML

A few pages back, I showed you a DSSSL fragment which I compared to CSS. As I mentioned there, DSSSL—and XSL after it—added to the "styling grammar" of CSS the notion of *verbs*.

A few other things were expressed or implied in that fragment that you won't see parallels to in a CSS stylesheet.

Styling of non-element content

To repeat what I said then: The opening DSSSL instruction declares that this portion of the stylesheet applies to the *element type* whose name is `remarks`. The implication here is that DSSSL can style things other than elements—for example, attribute values. CSS, by contrast, can style element content *only*. This can be a crippling limitation of CSS for any XML application, especially one with a lot of "content" bound up in attributes. (This is the case with many empty elements, for example.)

Attributes in CSS selectors

Yes, I know: CSS selectors are perfectly capable of selecting elements on the basis of the attributes the elements have, or on the basis of those attributes' values.

> What I'm getting at here is that CSS cannot display the attributes'
> values themselves—only the values of elements that have particular
> attributes.
>
> Consider the case of a complete FlixML document. The root `flix-
> info` element has a couple of attributes: `author`, indicating who pre-
> pared that FlixML review, and `copyright`, for the year in which the
> review was prepared. So, for example, a start tag for the `flixinfo` ele-
> ment might look like this:
>
> ```
> <flixinfo author="John E. Simpson" copyright="2001">
> ```
>
> Isn't it obvious that you might want to display the author and copy-
> right date in a document? If you're using CSS alone, these attributes
> might as well not exist at all.

Reordering content

In CSS, you're stuck with the order of the original document's content. If a
FlixML `title` element appears as the first child of the root `flixinfo` element,
there's nothing your CSS stylesheet can do to make it appear somewhere else.

Hidden in this restriction is another, which is that with CSS alone you
can't use a given chunk of content more often than it appears in the source
document. For instance, you can display a movie's title in a large sans-serif font
at the head of the document, but you can't also display it in a page footer or
anywhere else in the result.[6]

Web-bound display

CSS was developed for use with HTML—for controlling the representation of
content within a scrollable browser window. And, despite minor concessions to
other media (such as CSS version 2's "paged media" properties, allowing for
insertion of page breaks), CSS is still pretty much Web-oriented.

I don't mean this as a knock on CSS at all. CSS was developed for use on the
Web, after all; arguing that it's somehow flawed because it doesn't support print
and other media equally well would be like arguing that my DVD player should
be junked because it won't feed my cats.

---

6.   Unless, of course, the title just happens to appear somewhere else, like embedded
      in the `plotsummary` element.

The point is that there are many purposes for which a Web-oriented display model is just not good enough. If it were, the Adobe Acrobat PDF format would never have attained the success it has. The XSL-FO spec attempts to redress that shortcoming in particular, by supporting not only CSS's standard property set but also new ones for such print-only elements as headers, footers, and so on.

Is CSS good for *anything* XML-related?

Oh, yes. None of these drawbacks to CSS—or even all of them, taken together—spells doom for the older stylesheet standard.

The main reason for continuing to learn and use CSS is precisely that it was built for the Web. If your chief concern about XML is how to display it on the Web, then CSS, one way or the other, is in your future.

First, CSS can style XML directly, just as it can HTML. All that's required to make this work is the use of your XML document's elements as selectors, and of course you must link the document to the CSS stylesheet. This linkage is effected with a processing instruction (PI) in the document that looks like this:

```
<?xml-stylesheet
    type="text/css" href="my_styles.css"?>
```

The `type` pseudo-attribute must have the above value if the stylesheet is to be recognized as CSS; the `href` pseudo-attribute is the name of the stylesheet in question (including the protocol, server, and path names, if necessary).

Of course, visitors to your page will need a browser capable of reading XML and applying CSS to it.

The other alternative, which we'll see lots of examples of in *Just XSL*, is to transform your XML documents to HTML, and then use CSS to style the resulting HTML document just as you usually would.[7]

Although I won't be covering CSS to any great extent in *Just XSL*, I encourage you to learn at least its basics if you're going to be doing any Web work.

---

7. Strictly speaking, the book will show you many examples of transforming XML to XHTML, the *Extensible* Hypertext Markup Language—an XML-compliant form of the more familiar HTML standard whose use the W3C now recommends. However, as you'll see, XSLT is entirely comfortable transforming to plain old HTML as well.

XML. B Movies. Together at Last.

Before diving into the technical stuff in the ensuing chapters, I want to address a couple of superficially less important questions that might be weighing on your mind:[8] Why B movies? And why FlixML?

Why B movies?

Except for special events, there are almost no traces of the following phenomenon any longer: It used to be that movies were typically released or at least shown in pairs, back in the days when the popular-entertainment norm was to spend three hours in a theater, not slumped in a recliner before a television set.

At the top of the bill would be the headline movie. This was the one with the big stars, the inflated budget, the "name" director at the top of his game.

Then there was the other one....

This other movie was usually a throwaway—a "loss leader" for the studio, one they never really expected to make a great deal of money from. The stars were up-and-comers, in some cases; in some cases, they never made another film; and in still others, they were sliding back down to anonymity after having had a hit or two. The budget was definitely not inflated, since there was no expectation of *earning* much from the film. And the director, well, maybe he (or, less often, she) was on the way to fame and fortune. More often, though, the director specialized in cranking out these inexpensive movies over the course of an entire career.

The subjects of these throwaways usually had no pretense of dealing with Life's Big Questions. They were genre pictures, almost all of them easily classified as mysteries, Westerns, science-fiction, melodrama, or horror, with little of what is now called "crossover appeal."

In short, these were mostly forgettable cinematic experiences. You might sit in the theater and watch one, but only while waiting for the main feature. And if you showed up in the middle of the warm-up picture, no great loss—you'd already seen dozens of movies like it and could easily imagine how the parts you'd missed must have gone.

Sometimes, though, one of these B movies (as they came to be known) escaped the limitations of budget and the scarcity of talent or ambition on the set. It became a *classic*, often overlooked by film historians because it wasn't easy to classify, but given new life through repeated late-night television showings and

---

8.   Probably not, though.

later by videotape and DVD release. (Even better for the connoisseur of such things, the impulse to make great B movies hasn't gone away with the demise of the double feature.)

The answer to the question of "Why B movies?" is simply that the best of them have a way of sticking in your mind, far exceeding the power of the weaker, nominally "A-list" films. I mean, sheesh, how many of Freddie Prinze, Jr.'s, half-dozen or so romantic comedies stand out from all the others? Right. Zero. Contrast that with a sleazy noir-type film like 1946's *Detour,* which—long after you've stopped laughing at the cheap lighting effects—will cast long shadows on your memory.

Why FlixML?

Well, as I mentioned in the Preface, the very last thing I wanted to do with *Just XML*—and now this book—was to bore the reader or myself.

There was also a practical side to FlixML. Finding a one-size-fits-all application that could be used throughout an entire book was not easy. I didn't want to use any heavy-duty real-world applications, like personnel, sales, and so on. (Not only have they been done to death in discussing XML, some of them require special knowledge, which I didn't want to spend time acquiring or imparting. And you know, to return to my first point, a lot of those applications *are* boring.) Everyone seems instinctively to "get" the idea of B movies, though, so the subject didn't require a lot of explanation.

Finally, a subject like B movies lent itself naturally to a full range of XML features—including not only core XML itself, but also XSL, XLink, multimedia, and so on—and all the DTD features required to support them. Furthermore, a lot of "demonstrator vocabularies" represent either a data- or a document-centric view of XML data. A FlixML document has characteristics of both, which further enhances its usefulness as a training aid.

Enough of that. Let's move into the real stuff of XSL, starting with XSLT.

XSL Transformations: XSLT

In order to make your XML "behave" as anything other than pure, content-only markup, you must transform it to something else. The hard (and hard to maintain) way to do so would be to write a separate program in some high-level language such as Java, C++, or Visual Basic.

A much simpler solution in the long run is to use a generic way of specifying what, exactly, the XML is to be transformed into. That's the role of the XSL Transformations (XSLT) specification, covered in this first big section.

Information on the XSL Formatting Objects language — one of the myriad things that you can transform your XML into with XSLT — is provided in Part 3.

CHAPTER 2

The "What" of XSLT

$\mathbf{A}$s you will soon see, XSLT—together with the related XPath standard—is a pretty enormous subject, with a lot of dependencies among different portions of the standard.

But before getting down to the nuts-and-bolts of XSLT coding, it's important that you understand some basic concepts. And that's the purpose of the first portion of this chapter.

Don't kid yourself, though; taken as a whole, this isn't a lightweight chapter. You especially cannot afford to fall asleep in the long section on XPath, which concludes (and constitutes nearly three-fourths of) the chapter. If you don't "get" XPath, then learning all the XSLT markup presented throughout the rest of the book will be an utter waste of your time!

What XSLT Is *Not*

Oddly, despite the title, Extensible Stylesheet Language Transformations has little to do with *style*. It's focused entirely on the "T" part of the abbreviation—transforming XML. It's true that some of the things you can transform XML into have certain style characteristics, but that's just coincidence as far as XSLT is concerned.

I mentioned in the preceding chapter that the grammar of XSL, and in particular XSLT, comes with "verbs" (like DSSSL) as well as "adjectives" (like CSS). It's tempting to think, therefore, that XSLT is analogous to a programming or scripting language such as C++, Perl, Java, Visual Basic, or whatever. You can probably get away with succumbing to that temptation as long as you use the word "analogous" loosely. There's quite a bit you can do with even a simple but real programming language that is utterly beyond XSLT's reach.

What XSLT *Is*

So it doesn't have much to do with style, and it's not really a programming language. What is it, then?

The formal answer

Any discussion about what XSLT is has to include, at some level, a reference to the current W3C standard. You can find it at:

www.w3.org/TR/xslt.html

> **If you're feeling adventurous...**
>
> There's also an XML-based version of the standard. You can find this at:
>
>   www.w3.org/TR/xslt.xml

This version of the standard is Version 1.0, and it became a formal W3C Recommendation in November 1999.

Version 2.0 of XSLT is already being developed, including many of the features listed in Appendix G of the Version 1.0 spec, "Features under Consideration for Future Versions of XSLT." Although as of this writing it's available only in a "Requirements" document, not as a true standard, you can find this version of the standard at:

www.w3.org/TR/xslt20req

I'll be covering the key differences between Versions 1.0 and 2.0 later in *Just XSL*, in Chapter 8. For now, you can relax, knowing that 2.0 clears up ambiguities and errors in 1.0, while adding some additional bells and whistles.

...and the less formal answer

The main thing that keeps an XSLT stylesheet from being a true "computer program" in the conventional sense is that it doesn't tell the machine how to achieve a certain result. It simply describes, in as great detail as needed, what the result is to be. It's up to an application program, called an XSLT processor or XSLT engine, to produce that result in whatever way it deems suitable.

Let's return to the morphing-software analogy from Chapter 1: All we needed to do in order to effect the morph from one image to another was provide the two images; and then iteratively, for as many points as we cared to specify, to match a point in the original image with a corresponding point in the resulting image. We didn't then have to go back and tell the morphing software how to accomplish the transition from one to the other. Indeed, it's not hard to imagine that two different software packages might take two entirely different routes—one following the straight paths suggested by the lines connecting the corresponding points in Figure 1–1, the other following an exotic blooming-fractal pattern—and arrive at the same result.

Either approach would be perfectly acceptable in terms of compliance with the XSLT standard. All that counts is that the proper result be reached.

Sneaky stuff ahead

This chapter will be grounding you in an "XSLT view of the world." The details of XSLT syntax and examples will really hit in Chapter 3.

Nonetheless, I'm going to be introducing some very basic elements of XSLT in the remainder of this chapter. If you don't get it here, don't worry...the important thing for you to take away from this chapter is an understanding of everything it covers *except* the XSLT syntax.

Basic XSLT Terminology

Although it's difficult to sort out all the terminology in advance, it will really help in the rest of this chapter (and in those that follow) if you have a handle on some elementary terms.

Source and result trees

An XSLT transformation works by specifying some *result* that is to be attained by the XSLT processor, once it has applied the transformation to specified portion(s) of a *source* document. In short, it transforms a *source tree* into a *result tree.*

The term "tree" here is intended to connote structured data of some kind, arranged in hierarchic form, but only the source tree must be XML-based. The result tree can be any type of text. You can transform XML into plain text stripped of markup, into a comma-separated-values flat file for loading into a database, into another XML vocabulary (including the XML-based form of HTML known as XHTML, as well as XSL formatting objects and so on), or into a different version of the same XML vocabulary.

Non-XML structured text

Although it does require XML in the source tree, XSLT really is result-tree agnostic. The result tree can consist of text structured using non-XML markup conventions.

For example, the Virtual Reality Modeling Language (VRML) antedated XML by a couple of years. A VRML document, which is often quite lengthy, consists of a tree of programmatic assertions about three-dimensional objects and their behavior relative to one another and to user-supplied interaction. These assertions are bracketed with curly braces, { and } characters. Comments in a VRML document are set off from the surrounding code using a leading pound (#) sign. There's no trace of the SGML-derived markup signifiers <, >, <!-- and -->—except to the extent that those characters simply need to be used in their conventional, non-markup ways.

Generating a VRML document with XSLT is an eminently reasonable goal.

Top-level elements and instructions

Both of these terms have to do with the structure of an XSLT stylesheet. The stylesheet itself is a well-formed XML document, and in order to be well-formed it must (like any well-formed XML document) have a single root element. This root element, in XSLT's case, is `xsl:stylesheet`. It takes the following form:

```
<xsl:stylesheet version="1.0"
  xmlns:xsl="http://www.w3.org/1999/XSL/Transform"
  [other namespace declaration(s)]>
```

```
   . . .
</xsl:stylesheet>
```

The version attribute (and its value, "1.0") are required for an XSLT processor to recognize this document as an XSLT stylesheet. Likewise, the namespace declaration for the xsl: prefix must have this value to satisfy the requirements both of XML itself and of XSLT.

An option you probably don't need

The XSLT spec permits you to use the element name xsl:transform for your root element, instead of xsl:stylesheet. All attributes to this alternative element type are the same as for xsl:stylesheet.

I don't know why this option was considered desirable. In a way, xsl:transform makes a bit more sense than xsl:stylesheet, since what you're doing in an XSLT document is closer to transforming than to styling.

Whatever the reason, although you do have the option—and you should feel free to use it, if you want to—be aware that few postings to XSL-related mailing lists use any root element other than xsl:stylesheet. Throughout *Just XSL*, I'll use the latter.

What appears between the xsl:stylesheet element's start and end tags is a mixture of *top-level elements* and *instructions*. These are all elements whose names are in the XSLT namespace (that is, their names all begin with the xsl: prefix[1]). The top-level elements are those elements which are permitted as immediate children of xsl:stylesheet; instructions, on the other hand, occur within the scope of certain top-level elements. (One element, xsl:variable, can appear as either a top-level element or an instruction. You'll learn about xsl:variable in Chapter 4.)

---

1.   As always when dealing with namespaces, the prefix doesn't matter. Only the namespace's Uniform Resource Identifier (URI) really counts. I'll get into this further in the section titled "XSLT and Namespaces."

Templates

I'm trying to drill this into your consciousness, in case you hadn't noticed: XSLT stylesheets do not tell a processor *how* to achieve the desired results. They tell it what the results should be, and leave the "how" up to the processor.

The specific mechanism for achieving this is the use of *templates*. A template provides the structure for some portion of the result tree which is to be created when certain conditions in the source tree are met. If you're used to object-oriented terminology, you can think of a template as a class of object; when the template actually gets created in the result tree, you have an *instance* of that class (and so people speak of "instantiating" things in the result tree).

Adding text to a template

These templates can contain literal text as well as source-tree content, by the way. With CSS, you add text to what passes for the result tree using the *generated content* feature—which is a little clunky. The way it works, when it works at all, is that the selector portion of the CSS rule uses a `:before` or `:after` "pseudo-element"; as a result, the literal text will appear before or after (respectively) the corresponding element in the source document. With XSLT, when you want to add literal text, you just plop it into the corresponding template.

Each template is contained within some top-level element—that is, a template cannot be a direct child of the root `xsl:stylesheet` element. Typically, although not always, this takes place within *template rules*. A template rule is an `xsl:template` element (which is a top-level element). This element takes a `match` attribute, whose value points the XSLT processor to some portion of the source tree; when the processor finds a matching piece of the source tree, it instantiates the template in the result tree. So a very simple XSLT stylesheet might look something like this (glossing over certain details to be covered later):

```
<xsl:stylesheet version="1.0"
  xmlns:xsl="http://www.w3.org/1999/XSL/Transform"
  [other namespace declaration(s)]>
  <xsl:template match="somethinginsourcetree">
    I found something in the source tree!
  </xsl:template>
</xsl:stylesheet>
```

This stylesheet looks for whatever *somethinginsourcetree* might represent; when and if it finds it, it places the text string "I found something in the source tree!" in the result tree at that point.

Side-effect-free processing

This is an important concept for experienced programmers to grasp, as well as for those who've never coded a single script or program. In fact, it may be even harder for experienced programmers to get used to.

XSLT takes a kind of purist approach to the notion of effecting programming-like behavior through XML. It's a purist approach in that, although there are things like verbs in XSLT (some of them even explicitly called "instructions") these things are wrapped up in XML elements.

In particular, each XSLT element in a stylesheet operates completely independently of all other XSLT elements outside its scope. Let's expand on the sample (simple) stylesheet presented a few paragraphs back, by adding some more template rules to match other pieces of the source tree:

```
<xsl:stylesheet version="1.0"
  xmlns:xsl="http://www.w3.org/1999/XSL/Transform"
  [other namespace declaration(s)]>
  <xsl:template match="somethinginsourcetree">
    I found something in the source tree!
  </xsl:template>
  <xsl:template match="somethingelse">
    I found something else!
  </xsl:template>
  <xsl:template match="stillanotherthing">
    I found still another thing!
  </xsl:template>
</xsl:stylesheet>
```

This stylesheet now contains three template rules. What takes place within the start and end tags of any given template rule's xsl:template element is utterly invisible within the start and end tags of any other's.

This "every element's behavior is self-contained" rule has two principal effects on an XSLT processor's behavior.

No predictable order of execution

Let's call the three template rules in our stylesheet A, B, and C, respectively. Because they appear in that order in the stylesheet, it might be tempting (especially if you're an experienced programmer) to think that something like the following happens:

- Look for *somethinginsourcetree,* and if you find it, instantiate "I found something in the source tree!" in the result tree; **then**...
- Look for *somethingelse,* and if you find it, instantiate "I found something else!" in the result tree; **then**...
- Look for *stillanotherthing,* and if you find it, instantiate "I found still another thing!" in the result tree.

In fact, there is no particular requirement that an XSLT processor "perform" these steps in this or in any other order. All the XSLT spec requires is that, by the time the stylesheet is fully processed—and assuming all three "somethings" appear in the source tree—all three steps will have been "performed" at some point.

As a practical matter, this means that the most likely order of execution will reflect not the structure of the stylesheet but the structure of the source tree. The stylesheet's structure—particularly, the sequence of its template rules—cannot be counted on to bear any particular relationship to the order in which things happen during a transformation.

"Variables" that do not vary

A typical block of code in a conventional programming language might look something like this (in pseudocode here, with remarks identified by a double slash at the beginning of the line):

```
//-------- step 1
//Assign value of 100 to variable x
x = 100
//-------- step 2
//Multiply variable x by 12
x = x * 12
//-------- step 3
//Display value of x
print x
```

Here, there's a location in memory, arbitrarily named x, which is accessed repeatedly at several points in the code. (Such a storage location is called a *variable.*) The x that's referred to in Step 3 is the same storage location as the x in

Steps 1 and 2. As a result, you'd naturally expect this program to display the value 1200, after running through Steps 1 through 3.

In XSLT, though, if Steps 1 through 3 are represented by three separate template rules, there's no telling *what* Step 3 will display. The first template rule indeed assigns the expected value, 100, to the variable x. But the second and third template rules cannot "see" this variable; as a result, when they operate on it they're operating on local copies of it.

Furthermore, even if these steps were somehow incorporated into a single template rule, you could assign a value to x only *once*.

The only reason that XSLT variables are called variables is that you don't know until run time what their values will be. Once set, a value remains fixed until the conclusion of the template rule (or the stylesheet as a whole, if the variable is defined in a top-level `xsl:variable` element).

XSLT and Namespaces

You probably know this already, if you've had more than casual exposure to XML. But just in case, this section provides a mini-review of namespaces in XML.

(An excellent source of information about namespaces in XML, by the way, is Ronald Bourret's "XML Namespaces FAQ," located on the Web at www.rpbourret.com/xml/NamespacesFAQ.htm.)

An XML namespace is a logical construct—a sort of abstract "cloud"—in which all the element and attribute names for a particular XML vocabulary happen to exist. So FlixML has its own namespace, the Chemical Markup Language (CML) has its own namespace, and the Scalable Vector Graphics (SVG) vocabulary has yet another. As long as a given XML document contains element and attribute names from the same namespace, there's no problem. Consider the FlixML `crew` element, for example; it's unambiguously from the FlixML namespace, and not the namespace of a hypothetical XML vocabulary describing shipboard personnel, as long as the document in which you find that element is a FlixML document.

But a problem arises when you have to mix elements from more than one vocabulary in the same document. This possibility would be kind of a stretch if all we were discussing was a hybrid FlixML and ShipFolksML document. It's not a stretch at all, though, when you're constructing a typical XSLT stylesheet.

Suppose we're in a pre-namespaces world, and we're using XSLT to transform an XML document into XHTML for display in a Web browser. When we find a particular something in the source tree, we want to create an XHTML level-1 heading in the result. We could do this with a stylesheet containing code something like this:

```
<stylesheet>
  <template match="somethinginsourcetree">
    <h1>I found something in the
      source tree!</h1>
  </template>
</stylesheet>
```

At this point, the XSLT stylesheet *as an XML document* is fairly unambiguous. The XSLT vocabulary includes elements named "stylesheet" and "template" and does not include an element named "h1." So just on the basis of the element names alone, there's no ambiguity. Even if the stylesheet processor in this pre-namespaces world knew either the XSLT or the XHTML vocabulary alone, it could—if sufficiently intelligent—still figure out what the stylesheet author wants it to do.

But suppose we're transforming our XML source to, oh, say, a vocabulary used by sign painters. Sign painters often rely on the use of templates, *physical* templates, to do their job. So we might see a stylesheet like the following:

```
<stylesheet>
  <template match="somethinginsourcetree">
    <template>Men Working Ahead</template>
  </template>
</stylesheet>
```

As human beings, you and I might be able to sort this out (sort of). But an XSLT processor uses element names *only* to figure out what is important in an XSLT sense: If an element name is an XSLT element, then the processor "pays attention to it"; otherwise, it assumes the element name goes into the result tree. In the case above, what is the innermost `template` element? Is it supposed to be an XSLT element, or an element intended to go to the result tree?

So in XSLT, namespace *disambiguation* is an extremely important concept. The way you'd probably see the above coded as a real-world XSLT stylesheet would be something like this:

```
<xsl:stylesheet version="1.0"
  xmlns:xsl="http://www.w3.org/1999/XSL/Transform"
  xmlns="http://foo.com/SignML">
  <xsl:template match="somethinginsourcetree">
    <template>Men Working Ahead</template>
```

```
  </xsl:template>
</xsl:stylesheet>
```

Here, the `xmlns:xsl` attribute is a namespace declaration, asserting that all element names (and possibly attribute names) prefixed with `xsl:` are associated with the URI "http://www.w3.org/1999/XSL/Transform" (that is, the XSLT namespace). All element names with *no* prefix, per the simple `xmlns` attribute, are associated with the URI "http://foo.com/SignML" (which is, presumably, the namespace for something like a "SignML" XML vocabulary).

What you *must* do with namespaces in a stylesheet

At a minimum, you must establish the namespace to be associated with all XSLT elements. As I mentioned before, this means you'll associate the prefix (by convention) xsl: with the URI (required) http://www.w3.org/1999/XSL/Transform.

Then, if you're transforming to XHTML or another XML vocabulary, you must provide a namespace declaration for the result tree's elements as well.

The prefix associated with the result namespace is immaterial (if you're using a prefix at all); the important part of the namespace declaration is the URI. This URI may need to be a certain value in order for a processor to recognize it. Here are some common namespace URIs that you might end up using in your own XSLT stylesheet result trees:

- For (unprefixed) elements in the **HTML 4.0** namespace: `xmlns="http://www.w3.org/TR/REC-html40"`
- For (unprefixed) elements in the **XHTML 1.0** namespace: `xmlns="http://www.w3.org/1999/xhtml"`
- For elements in the **Open eBook 1.0** namespace (for electronic books): `xmlns:eb="http://openebook.org/namespaces/oeb-document/1.0/"`
- For elements in the **Wireless Markup Language (WML)** namespace: `xmlns:wml="http://www.wapforum.org/xmlns/wml"`. (The prefix may also be `wap:`, by the way, which would be declared as: `xmlns:wap="http://www.wapforum.org/xmlns/wml"`)
- For elements in the **DocBook** (a popular SGML/XML vocabulary for technical book publishing) namespace: `xmlns:db="http://www.oasis-open.org/docbook/schema/4.1.2"`
- For elements in the **Scalable Vector Graphics (SVG)** namespace: `xmlns:svg="http://www.w3.org/2000/svg"`

> **Those crazy XSLT processors...**
>
> Note that the foregoing description of result-tree namespaces may not apply in the case of certain XSLT processors designed for transforming to only *one* particular result-tree vocabulary.
>
> The Microsoft MSXML XML/XSLT processor, in particular, has become a favorite among stylesheet and Web developers because it's useful almost exclusively for transforming XML to well-formed HTML. MSXML (at least in the context of the Internet Explorer browser) doesn't seem to care whether or not you declare your result tree as in the (X)HTML namespace.

XPath

As I've already described it, XSLT is concerned with mapping portions of the source tree to corresponding portions of the result tree. Instantiating elements, text, and so on in the result tree is fairly simple; for the most part, you simply place the things that belong in the result tree into a template rule's template.

However, I've skated over the other half of what a stylesheet needs to do, which is locating the correct bits of the source tree in the first place. The source tree can be accessed in a number of XSLT elements, always by way of a `match` or `select` attribute. For example, a template rule might look like the following:

```
<xsl:template match="stuff_from_source_tree">
  <h1><xsl:value-of select="other_stuff"/></h1>
</xsl:template>
```

The `xsl:template` element's `match` attribute tells the processor to look for *stuff_from_source_tree*; if it finds it, it should instantiate in the result tree a level-1 XHTML heading whose contents (per the value of the `xsl:value-of` element's `select` attribute) will be *other_stuff* from the source tree.

Whether for determining where to place some result-tree content (as in the `match` attribute above) or for actually *using* source-tree content somehow (as with the `select` attribute), locating source-tree content is the work of a separate standard, called XPath. The remainder of this chapter provides details on this important specification.

> **Why a separate spec?**
>
> Most of the principles eventually codified as the XPath standard were set forth in early versions of the XSL standard. As with the principles

behind XSLT itself, though, it became obvious pretty quickly that these techniques had applicability beyond stylesheet processing. Particularly, they're also useful in the XPointer spec, which locates content within a document being linked to via XLink.

The XPath standard, like XSLT, is currently a full version 1.0 W3C Recommendation. You can find it on the W3C Web site, at:

`www.w3.org/TR/xpath`

Note that the XPath-related material which follows will make for some dry reading at times. I will be providing some limited discussion and examples of the language's features, but most of this will become "interesting" only once we get into *using* XPath in XSLT... and that won't really happen until the next chapter. In the meantime, you might want to have a caffeinated beverage handy and/or be prepared to take a mental break every now and then. This is important stuff.

Expressions

For starters, XPath is not an XML-based language. Rather, it's a language for expressing things which can be made available to truly XML-based languages, such as XSLT and XPointer. The "things which can be made available" run the gamut from simple text strings and numbers on up to elaborate road maps to portions of a document's content.

No matter how simple or complex these things are, they're expressed straightforwardly in the form of *expressions*—strings of characters. For example, each of the following is potentially an XPath expression:

```
"Don't stop there!"
x + 4
//distriblink[contains(@xlink:href, "Amazon")]
```

The first is a text string; the second, some kind of numeric operation; and the third, a "road map" to an element (named `distriblink`) in a FlixML document.

For most practical purposes, when you hear or read the term "XPath expression," it's going to be a reference to the third sort only. Of course, within such an expression there may be "sub-expressions," such as the text string "Amazon" in the example just given. Probably the best way to think of expressions is this: They're like the atoms of the XPath language; in some cases you can use them in their elemental form, and in others—many others—you'll be assembling them into "compounds."

Location paths and location steps

The XPath language defines a syntax for locating or extracting nearly anything within an XML document. The "molecule" of XPath syntax is the *location path*. A simple location path is a text string—an XPath expression—which resembles a path to a file, either on a local file system or out on the Internet somewhere.

For example, consider the file system depicted in Figure 2–1.

You can easily locate one of the files in the directory tree in Figure 2–1, using a path that looks something like this:

```
/root/sub1/sub1sub2/file12.ext
```

This directs an operating system, a Web browser, or some other application to walk down the hierarchy of directories (or folders, in Microsoft Windows terms). Each succeeding slash character (/) separates a resource (directory or file) at a given level from those above or below it in the hierarchy. The leading slash tells the application to start in the root directory of the file system, Web server, or other resource; a path with this leading slash is called an *absolute* path.

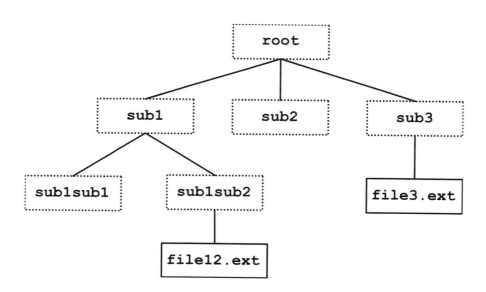

Figure 2-1 A simple file system depicted as a hierarchically arranged tree of nodes. The dotted boxes are directories or folders; the solid ones, actual file resources.

Alternatively, a *relative* path omits the leading slash. This tells the application to start "wherever it already is" and work down through the directory tree. Relative paths also may begin with certain special characters: a period (a/k/a "full stop") or a pair of periods. The single period is generally unnecessary; it simply represents "here"—the directory where you're currently located. So the following two relative paths (which assume you're starting in the root directory in Figure 2–1) are synonymous:

```
sub3/file3.ext
./sub3/file3.ext
```

They both direct the application to a file named "file3.ext," which is located in a sub-directory of the current directory (the root, in this case) whose name is "sub3."

The double period is more useful; it means "go to the parent directory"—the one immediately above the current one in the hierarchy of directories—and thus sort of re-routes the normal direction of the search, saying "go up" instead of "go down." Even better, these double periods (separated by slashes) can be combined as necessary, to take you further and further "up." Thus (assuming that "where you're currently at" is the directory named "sub1sub1" in Figure 2–1),

```
../../sub3/file3.ext
```

leads you to the parent of the current directory, then to that parent's parent, then selects the sub-directory of the parent's parent called "sub3," and finally locates the file in "sub3" named "file3.ext."

The structure of a file system is exactly analogous to the structure of an XML document. Both consist of a single root "thing" from which descend a whole family of nodes. Some of these nodes contain others, and at the very bottom of a given branch of the tree might be a simple empty container or some real content—a file, in the case of a file system, or text, in the case of an XML document. For this reason, it's not surprising that the designers of XPath used the already familiar model of file system paths as a starting point for XPath location paths.

Let's take a look at our first B movie and a FlixML document to describe it. I've selected this film not only because *Criss Cross* is a great movie, well worth hunting down if you've never seen it, but also because the corresponding FlixML review is pretty complete—lots of variations of "things to select" using XPath.

B Alert!
Criss Cross
(1949, Universal International)

Armored-car guard Steve Thompson is newly returned to his old neighborhood after two years in the service.

He's a little confused, to say the least—about his direction in life, but also about what (if anything) he wants from his ex-wife, Anna.

Part of the problem is that she's now married to the villainous gangster Slim Dundee. Thompson, in a moment of weakness, visits Anna at her and Slim's place while Slim is out. Unsurprisingly, Slim himself shows up, and in a desperate attempt to make his visit seem "innocent," Thompson claims that the reason he's there at all is that he's brought to Slim a plan to hold up the armored-car company where he (Thompson) works.

Things don't turn out the way everyone involved expects (let alone wants) them to—but then, this *is* noir, after all.

An outstanding, perverse story, well-acted and -shot. Burt Lancaster and Yvonne DeCarlo (playing Anna in *torrid* femme fatale fashion) never looked better. But the real treat in the cast is Dan Duryea's Slim, who manages to exude menace while uttering even the most innocuous phrases.

The scene in which Slim nearly catches Thompson and Anna in "the act" is wonderful. Watch as Thompson, trying to make his "plan" sound as reasonable as possible, piles on spontaneously invented detail after detail...until he's committed himself to actually going through with it!

Criss Cross's FlixML Review

```xml
<?xml version="1.0"?>
<?xml-stylesheet type="text/xsl"
  href="flixml_03.xsl"?>
<!DOCTYPE flixinfo SYSTEM
  "http://www.flixml.org/flixml/flixml_03.dtd">
<flixinfo author="John E. Simpson" copyright="2001"
  xml:lang="EN"
  xmlns:xlink="http://www.w3.org/1999/xlink/namespace/">
```

```
<title role="main">Criss Cross</title>
<genre>
  <primarygenre>&C;</primarygenre>
  <othergenre>Noir</othergenre>
</genre>
<releaseyear role="initial">1949</releaseyear>
<releaseyear role="alt">1995 (remade as "The Underneath")</
releaseyear>
<language>English</language>
<!-- Note: cross-check studio name -->
<studio>Universal International</studio>
<cast id="castID">
  <leadcast>
    <male id="BLancaster">
      <castmember>Burt Lancaster</castmember>
      <role>Steve Thompson</role>
    </male>
    <female id="YDeCarlo">
      <castmember>Yvonne DeCarlo</castmember>
      <role>Anna</role>
    </female>
    <male id="DDuryea">
      <castmember>Dan Duryea</castmember>
      <role>Slim Dundee</role>
    </male>
  </leadcast>
  <othercast>
    <male id="GBarnett">
      <castmember>Griff Barnett</castmember>
      <role>Pop</role>
    </male>
    <male id="JDoucette">
      <castmember>John Doucette</castmember>
      <role>Walt</role>
    </male>
    <male id="PHelton">
      <castmember>Percy Helton</castmember>
      <role>Frank (bartender)</role>
    </male>
    <female id="EHolland">
      <castmember>Edna Holland</castmember>
      <role>Mrs. Thompson</role>
    </female>
    <male id="MKrah">
      <castmember>Marc Krah</castmember>
      <role>Mort</role>
```

```
      </male>
      <male id="RLong">
        <castmember>Richard Long</castmember>
        <role>Slade Thompson</role>
      </male>
      <male id="SMcNally">
        <castmember>Stephen McNally</castmember>
        <role>Lt. Pete Ramirez</role>
      </male>
      <female id="JoanMiller">
        <castmember>Joan Miller</castmember>
        <role>The Lush</role>
      </female>
      <male id="JohnMiller">
        <castmember>John "Skins" Miller</castmember>
        <role>Midget</role>
      </male>
      <male id="EMorales">
        <castmember>Esy Morales</castmember>
        <role>Orchestra leader</role>
      </male>
      <male id="ANapier">
        <castmember>Alan Napier</castmember>
        <role>Finchley</role>
      </male>
      <male id="JORear">
        <castmember>James O'Rear</castmember>
        <role>Waxie</role>
      </male>
      <male id="TPedi">
        <castmember>Tom Pedi</castmember>
        <role>Vincent</role>
      </male>
      <female id="MRandall">
        <castmember>Meg Randall</castmember>
        <role>Helen</role>
      </female>
    </othercast>
  </cast>
  <crew id="crewID">
    <director>Robert Siodmak</director>
    <screenwriter>Daniel Fuchs</screenwriter>
    <screenwriter>Don Tracy</screenwriter>
    <cinematog>Frank Planer</cinematog>
    <editor>Ted J. Kent</editor>
    <score>Mikl&#243;s R&#243;zsa</score>
```

```
    <costumer>Yvonne Wood</costumer>
  </crew>
  <plotsummary id="plotID">Armored-car guard <maleref
maleid="BLancaster">Steve Thompson</maleref> is newly returned to
his old neighborhood after two years in the service.<parabreak/
>He's a little confused, to say the least -- not only about his
direction in life, but also about what (if anything) he wants from
his ex-wife <femaleref femaleid="YDeCarlo">Anna</
femaleref>.<parabreak/>Part of the problem is that she's now
married to the villainous gangster <maleref maleid="DDuryea">Slim
Dundee</maleref>. Thompson, in a moment of weakness, visits Anna at
her and Slim's place. Unsurprisingly, Slim himself shows up, and in
a desperate attempt to make his visit "innocent," Thompson claims
he's brought to Slim a plan to hold up the armored-car company
where he (Thompson) works.<parabreak/>Things don't turn out the way
everyone involved expects (let alone wants) them to, but then, this
<emph>is</emph> noir, after all.</plotsummary>
  <reviews id="revwID">
    <flixmlreview>
      <goodreview>
        <reviewtext>An outstanding, perverse story, well-acted and -
shot. Lancaster and DeCarlo (playing Anna in <emph>torrid</emph>
femme fatale fashion) never looked better. But the real treat in
the cast is Dan Duryea's Slim, who manages to exude menace with the
most innocuous phrases.<parabreak/>The scene in which Slim nearly
catches Thompson and Anna in "the act" is wonderful. Watch as
Thompson, in an attempt to make his "plan" sound as reasonable as
possible, piles on spontaneously invented detail after detail...
until he's committed himself to actually going through with it!</
reviewtext>
      </goodreview>
    </flixmlreview>
    <otherreview>
      <goodreview>
        <reviewlink
        xlink:href="http://www.moderntimes.com/palace/kc.htm">
          Michael Mills
        </reviewlink>
      </goodreview>
    </otherreview>
  </reviews>
  <distributors id="distribID">
    <distributor>
      <distribname>Reel.com</distribname>
      <distribextlink>
        <distriblink
```

```
     xlink:href="http://www.reel.com/movie.asp?MID=2273">
       </distriblink>
     </distribextlink>
   </distributor>
   <distributor>
     <distribname>Amazon.com</distribname>
     <distribextlink>
       <distriblink xlink:href="http://www.amazon.com/exec/obidos
ASIN/0783213115">
       </distriblink>
     </distribextlink>
   </distributor>
 </distributors>
 <dialog>Slim: I did you bums a favor letting you do that
   job for me. Don't forget it. You owe me.
   Understand?</dialog>
<remarks>Robert Siodmak was a European emigr&#233; who later
returned to Germany, where he continued making films well into the
'60s. But he made his reputation (and in the eyes of most critics,
never bettered himself) with about a half-dozen films made in the
dozen years he was living in the US.<parabreak/>"Criss Cross" was
to my mind easily the best of these.<parabreak/>There aren't a lot
of overt B-movie touches here; it's an exceptionally well-crafted
movie. But the lurid plot resembles something torn from the pages
of a True Confessions or similar magazine (it was actually adapted
from a novel by Don Tracy), and that alone makes it a great B film.
(The only thing reducing its B-ness rating is that apart from the
plot, it's insufficiently B-grade!)<parabreak/>I haven't seen the
1995 remake by Steven Soderbergh, but it's supposed to be pretty
decent in its own right.</remarks>
 <mpaarating id="rateID">NR</mpaarating>
 <bees b-ness="&BEE45URL;"/>
</flixinfo>
```

As with the file system depicted in Figure 2–1, this FlixML review can be depicted as a tree of containers and content, a portion of which is shown in Figure 2–2.

Just as with the earlier file-system paths, we can construct both absolute and relative location paths. For instance, to locate the title element we can use an absolute location path like this, no matter where we happen to be starting from in the tree of nodes in the document:

```
/flixinfo/title
```

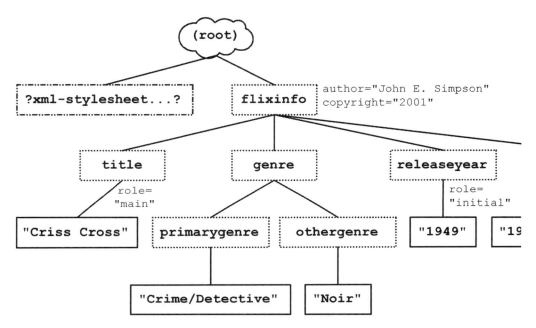

Figure 2-2 A portion of the *Criss Cross* FlixML review, depicted (like the file system of Figure 2–1) as a series of boxes containing other boxes, some of which contain text as well. Note that there are other kinds of "content" included here, though. For example, the xml-stylesheet PI, the various attributes, and indeed the document root itself are all somehow "outside" the tree of nodes established by elements and text.

And once we're down there in the title, we can locate the othergenre element using a relative location path such as this:

```
../genre/othergenre
```

This leads us one step up in the hierarchy, to the title element's parent (flix-info), and then down to the genre and finally othergenre elements.

In XPath terms, each of the expressions appearing between the slashes in a location path is called a *location step*. Except for the very last location step (which, in XPath, can never end with a slash), all the location steps in a location path are simply used to reposition you up, down, or even sideways in the document tree.

The nodes that XPath knows

As you can infer by comparing Figures 2–1 and 2–2, XPath's location steps are capable of locating much more than just simple boxes (elements) and their contents (other elements and/or text). In fact, XPath is able to locate the following kinds of *nodes* in any source document:

- root node
- elements
- text
- attributes
- processing instructions (PIs)
- comments
- namespaces

Namespace nodes?

The XPath and XSLT specs are quite smart about namespaces. As you'll see later, you can decompose the namespace information at any point in the document in pretty much any way you want to.

The one inscrutable and slightly inconsistent bit of namespace awareness, in my opinion, is the notion of a namespace *node*. The reason that it's both inscrutable and inconsistent is this: Unlike the other node types, the namespace node type has no single "thing" to put your finger on in a source document.

In general, there's a namespace node corresponding to each namespace declaration in the document. So, since our sample document has one namespace declaration (for the `xlink:` prefix), you might think the namespace node type is just a special case of the attribute node type. Not so: The namespace node is copied to all other elements within the scope of the element declaring the namespace. Therefore, since the `xlink:` prefix's declaration occurs in the root `flixinfo` element, there is *one namespace node for every element in the document*.

By the way, also note that you don't have to declare a URI for the `xml:` prefix (as used in the `xml:lang` attribute above, for example). Without such a declaration, there is *no* namespace node corresponding to the `xml:` namespace.

What's missing?

Although the nodes accessible to XPath pretty much comprise a document's entire contents, there are some things you *can't* get to with XPath. Specifically, you cannot access either the XML declaration (although it looks like a PI) or the document type declaration.

At first glance, this may seem like a somewhat arbitrary limitation. Remember though not to think of XML processing in terms of reading a physical *file* from beginning to end; think of it in terms of the information available in the logical *document*. By the time the document is made available to any XPath-aware application, it has already been parsed: The version of XML according to which the document is marked up has been noted, the document's encoding has been recognized, validation has taken place, entity substitutions have been made, any defaulted attribute values supplied by the DTD are in place just as if they'd been explicitly assigned, and so on. In effect, what the XPath-aware application sees is a complete but merely well-formed document with no XML or DOCTYPE declaration at all.

Node names

Every node in an XML document has a name. This is pretty straightforward for elements and attributes; the name of an element or attribute node is the same as the *type* of that element or attribute. So the name of the `title` element is "title," and the name of the `maleid` attribute is "maleid."

Note that element and attribute names which include a prefix actually consist of three parts: the prefix; the URI associated with the prefix; and the so-called "local name" (which is the element or attribute name *sans* prefix). In the document above, attributes associated with XLinks all include a prefix of "xlink:" in their names. Therefore, with the `xlink:href` attribute, for instance, the prefix is (of course) `xlink:`; the URI is "http://www.w3.org/1999/xlink/ namespace/"; and the local name is "href." Two names are considered functionally identical if they have the same URI and local name, *regardless* of the prefixes.

For PI nodes, the name is the same as the PI target—that is, everything between the opening `<?` and either the first space, if there is one, or the closing `?>`, if not. In the document above, there's one PI, whose name is "xml-stylesheet."

For the root node, text nodes, and comment nodes, the node name is an empty string.

Namespace nodes constitute a special case.[2] The name of a namespace node is the prefix associated with the namespace, if there is a prefix, or an empty string otherwise. Interestingly, and/or bizarrely, the name of a namespace node also includes a URI component...which is always empty!

---

2.   Are you sensing a pattern here?

String-values

Locating a node of any one of these seven types makes available a so-called *string-value*. The string-value, as the term implies, is a text string—a bit of content, in short, associated with a given node. The string-value of a node varies depending on the node type.

The string-value of a text node is, of course, whatever text it contains; the string-value of an attribute node is the attribute's value; and the string-value of a comment node is all the text within the comment's opening `<!--` and closing `-->` delimiters. So the first text node in the *Criss Cross* review—the text node contained by the `title` element—has the string-value "Criss Cross"; the `title` element's `role` attribute has the string-value "main"; and the only comment in the file has a string-value of "Note: cross-check studio name".

Beyond text, attribute, and comment nodes, though, there are some surprises in the string-values, as shown in Table 2–1.

Node-*sets*

One very interesting—and, as we will see, extremely useful—difference between a location path and its file-system counterpart is what is actually obtained (or "pointed at") by the two techniques.

Assuming no use of wildcard characters, a file-system path always locates a single resource—a single directory or file. In contrast, an XPath location path locates a *node-set*—that is, a collection of zero, one, or more nodes. Consider the

Table 2-1   XPath Node Types and Their String-Values

Node type	String-value
root node	The concatenated string-value of all text nodes in the document. *Example:* The string-value of this FlixML review's document root is "Criss CrossCrime/DetectiveNoir...decent in its own right.NR". Note that entities (such as `&C;` in the `primary-genre` element) are expanded as necessary ("Crime/Detective") before being included in the string-value.
element	The concatenated string-value of all text nodes within the element's start and end tags. *Example:* The string-value of the first `male` element is "Burt LancasterSteve Thompson".

Table 2-1   XPath Node Types and Their String-Values (continued)

Node type	String-value
PI	All the text in the PI that follows the PI's target, up to the closing ?>. *Example:* This document has one PI, the xml-stylesheet PI; because its target (the text immediately following the opening <?) is xml-stylesheet, the value of the PI is the string "type='text/xsl' href='flixml_03.xsl'".
namespace	The URI of the namespace node. *Example:* The sample review contains exactly one namespace declaration (for the xlink: prefix); because this declaration is made in the root flixinfo element, every element in the document has one namespace node, whose string-value is "http://www.w3.org/1999/xlink/namespace/".

following simple location path:

```
/flixinfo/title
```

Because the root node (/) has only one child node named flixinfo, and the flixinfo element has only one child named title, this location path locates a single node: the one element whose name is title. More precisely, it locates a node-set that just happens to consist of a single node.

On the other hand, the following location path (superficially as simple as the preceding one):

```
/flixinfo/releaseyear
```

returns a node-set consisting of *two* nodes—the two releaseyear elements.

The importance of this capability will become much greater as we get further into XPath (and eventually, into XSLT). For now, just consider how much more complicated and/or tedious processing would be, for example, if we had to locate every castmember element in the above FlixML review with a separate location path!

String-value of a node-set

A few pages back, I discussed the string-value of a node, based on the type of node.

Somewhat disconcertingly, the string-value of a node-set is *not* the

> result of concatenating the string-values of all nodes in the node-set. Rather, the string-value of a node-set is the string-value of the *first* node in it. Obviously, if there's only one node in the node-set, these are identical; less obviously, if the node-set contains more than one node, they're *not* identical. So the string-value of the following location path:
>
> ```
> /flixinfo/releaseyear
> ```
>
> (which returns a node-set containing two `releaseyear` element nodes) is simply "1949" (the string-value of the first `releaseyear`) *not* "19491995 (remade as 'The Underneath')".

Position and context

Okay, so you know that each node has a name and a value (either or both of which may be an empty string, depending on node type). You may also have guessed that any given node is a member of any number of node-sets. For example, the `title` element is a member of the following node-sets (among a *lot* of others, some more useful than others):

- all children of the `flixinfo` element,
- all elements in the document
- all elements in the document with at least one attribute
- all elements in the document that are not named "releaseyear"

Within any node-set it's a member of, a given node also has a *position*. By default, this is its position in document order, relative to all other nodes in the same node-set.

Consider the node-set consisting of all children of the `crew` element. The first node in this node-set is the `director` element; the second, the `screenwriter` element whose string-value is "Daniel Fuchs"; the third, the `screenwriter` element whose value is "Don Tracy"; and so on.

When you're using relative location paths, it's vitally important that you understand the *context* in which a given location step (and perhaps a node within the resulting node-set) is evaluated.

Now, this won't be much of an issue when you're using XPath with XPointer. In that case, you'll be accessing a single node-set (most likely consisting of only one node) and not moving around *within* that node-set. But in XSLT, this notion of context assumes enormous importance, because you basically establish an initial context and then move up, down, and perhaps sideways within it.

A simple way to think of changing context is to think of a simple location path, such as this:

```
/flixinfo/cast/leadcast/female
```

Each succeeding location step narrows the context in which all following location steps will be evaluated. As soon as the flixinfo element is named in the location path, the xml-stylesheet PI is excluded from consideration; with cast, all the other children of flixinfo are disregarded; and so on.

As you move around in a node-set, whether in a simple location path or in a more complicated fashion (as in an XSLT stylesheet), there will always be one *context node*. This is the node in whose context succeeding relative location paths (or steps in a location path) will be evaluated. In the preceding location path, at first the flixinfo element is the context node, so that when the processor hits the cast step it already "knows" which leg of the document tree is being walked; then the cast step further narrows the context, becoming the context node in which the leadcast step will be evaluated, and so on.

We'll revisit the notions of context and context node later in this chapter and again in the next, especially once we start using XPath with XSLT stylesheets.

Full location step syntax

All the location paths I've shown so far have been simple ones; their constituent location steps have each consisted of a single element name, or possibly (in the case of relative paths) the . or .. shorthand meaning "this element" or "this element's parent," respectively. If this were all there was to XPath, the spec wouldn't amount to much at all.

But XPath actually specifies a rich set of options for building any location step. These options are summed up in the full syntax for a location step, which looks something like this:

```
axis::nodetest[predicate]
```

The *axis* and *predicate* portions of this syntax are optional. If you omit the axis, you also omit the double colon; and if you omit the predicate, you also omit the square brackets surrounding it.

The general purpose of each of these components is as follows:

- The *axis* tells the XPath-aware application "which direction to look" from the context node of the moment. If you're standing in Mexico City and want to get somewhere from there, you've got at least 360 possible axes to start with (the main compass points). Not all of them will get you where you want to go, at least very quickly, but you start out by facing in *some* direction from wherever you begin. Each axis specifies some relationship to the context node, and there's a default: to consider only children of the context node.
- The *node test* directs the XPath-aware application's attention to a particular node, or class of nodes, along the indicated axis. To continue the geographic analogy, if you start out from Mexico City and face in the direction indicated by the axis, you might narrow the candidate "nodes" just to those representing other cities (as opposed to mountains, deserts, bodies of water, and so on).
- The *predicate* narrows the selection even further, by indicating some condition a node must meet in order for it to be considered a "match." So if you're in Mexico City (the context node), looking along the axis's direction, and considering going only to another city (the node test), the predicate might restrict the final list of candidates to those cities with a population greater than 100,000, or those with museums or zoos, and so on.

Let's examine each of these components in detail, starting with the one that's required in a location step: the node test.

The node test

You've got a few choices for the node test. We've already seen the most obvious one: the *name* of the desired node. So a location step of:

```
parabreak
```

locates all the nodes named "parabreak" which are children of the context node. (Remember that the default axis specification is "children of the context node.")

You have several other choices, though, each of which locates a node not by its name but by its type. These are summarized in Table 2–2.

Now let's look at some examples of these node-type tests as they might be used to find content in our sample document. (Again, remember that the default axis is children of the context node.)

Table 2-2   XPath Node-Type Tests

Value	Meaning
`processing-instruction()`	Locates a PI node, regardless of its name
`processing-instruction(`*name*`)`	Locates a PI node whose name is *name*
`comment()`	Locates a comment node
`text()`	Locates a text node
`node()`	Locates a node of *any* type

Notable exceptions

Conspicuously absent from the types of nodes you can retrieve using a node-type test alone are attribute and namespace nodes. You can locate these nodes easily enough, but you do so using special values for the axis. Hang on; you'll see examples of these in a few pages.

- If the context node is the root node, either of the following location steps will find the `xml-stylesheet` PI:

```
processing-instruction()
processing-instruction("xml-stylesheet")
```

- Assume that the context node is the `remarks` element. You can locate the document's lone comment with this location path:

```
../comment()
```

The leading `..` takes you up the hierarchy to the `remarks` element's parent, or the `flixinfo` element; the next location step in the path leads you down to *that* element's child(ren) of the comment type.

- Note that the content model for the `plotsummary` element is a mixed content model; it contains some text of its own and (optionally) some empty `parabreak` element(s) and/or `emph` elements, the latter with text-node children of their own. If the context node is the `flixinfo` element, and the location path is:

```
plotsummary/text()
```

then you locate (a) *all* of the text nodes which are children of the `plot-`

summary element, but (b) *none* of the parabreak elements, and (c) *none* of the emph elements (or their text nodes).

- If the context node is the genre element, the following location path locates a node-set whose members are the xml-stylesheet PI and the flixinfo element:

`../node()`

Wildcards in the node test

In addition to matching on a specific name or a node type, you can also use an asterisk (*) as the node test. This is a special form of the *name* node test; it says to locate a node (element or attribute only, depending on the axis) regardless of its name.

If the context node is one of the releaseyear elements in our sample document, you might use a relative location path such as this:

`../genre/*`

This locates the primarygenre and othergenre elements. The initial .. leads you up to the releaseyear's parent—that is, to the flixinfo element—and makes *it* the context node. The next location step leads you down to the context node's child named genre. And the final location step leads you to all elements which are children of the genre element, regardless of their names.

The axis

As I mentioned earlier, the optional *axis* portion of a location step directs the application to "look" up, down, or even sideways from the context node. These directions are based on a view of all the nodes in a document as something like a "family."

In a typical human family tree, from any node representing a person you can look up or down the tree to a parent or child. You can also look further up or down the hierarchy, to ancestors or descendants, and "sideways" to siblings of the same parent—or, for that matter, to cousins, second cousins, and so on. Less obviously, when you're looking up, down, or sideways, you can also see the node you're looking *from*. XPath axes are based on these "family tree" views, as well as a couple of other relationships exclusive to XPath; and although there isn't an explicit axis for every human family relationship, you can pretty much see anywhere in the tree from any given point.

There are 13 axes that may be used in a location step: child, parent, descendant, ancestor, self, descendant-or-self, ancestor-or-self, following-sibling, preceding-sibling, following, preceding, attribute, and namespace. Remember that when you use an axis, you separate its name from the node test using a double colon (::).

Looking ahead, looking back

Each axis is classified as either a forward axis or a reverse axis, depending on "which way you have to look" along that particular axis. The significance of this is that if an axis is a forward axis, the processor will see matching nodes in document order relative to the context node (i.e., the order in which they appear physically in the document); if the axis is a reverse axis, the processor sees any matching nodes in *reverse* document order relative to the context node.

The ancestor, ancestor-or-self, preceding-sibling, and preceding axes are reverse axes. All others are considered forward axes. (Well, for reasons that will be obvious when you learn about it, the direction associated with the self axis is irrelevant.)

The child axis   This is the default axis if none is specified. It points the processor "down" in the hierarchy, one level. The context node must be the root node or an element in order to look along the child axis. (That is, if the context node is an attribute, PI, or whatever, looking along the child axis will always return an empty node-set.)

The child axis also is restricted in that it enables the processor to "see" only elements, PIs, comments, and text nodes. Attribute and namespace nodes are invisible if you're looking at the context node's children. For obvious reasons,[3] the root node is never located on the child axis, no matter what the context node is. If the root node is the context node, it always has at least one child, which is the document's root *element.*

Let's take a look at a sample XSLT template rule that uses the child axis in a couple of places. (Remember that, because this is the default axis, you can omit the child:: from either of these XPath expressions.)

---

3.   I *hope* they're obvious!

```
<xsl:template match="/child::flixinfo">
  <html>
    <head>
      <title>
          FlixML Review: <xsl:value-of
          select="child::title"/>
      </title>
    </head>
  </html>
</xsl:template>
```

This template rule begins (in the `match` attribute to the `xsl:template` element) by selecting the root node's child whose name is "flixinfo". When it finds a matching portion of the source tree, it instantiates in the result tree some XHTML elements: the root `html`, a `head`, and a `title` element within the `head`. The value that's inserted in the result tree's `title` element consists of some literal text ("FlixML Review: ") and the value of the context node's child named "title". Thus, a browser viewing the result tree from this transformation will display (in this case) the string "FlixML Review: Criss Cross" in the title bar of its window.

Devil in the details

Look back a couple of sentences, and you'll find that I apparently tried to slip something by you in the explanation: "...the context node's child named 'title'." What *is* the context node at the point where the processor encounters the `xsl:value-of` element?

The answer lies in the fact that within a template rule, the context node is *changed*. At the time the above template rule as a whole is encountered, it doesn't make any difference what the context node is; the value of the `match` attribute (in this case, although not always) is an *absolute* location path. However, once that location path's condition is met and we've got a matching portion of the source tree, *that portion of the source tree becomes the new context node*. And it remains so for the life of the template rule, unless something within the template rule changes it again.

So then, at the time the `xsl:value-of` element's `select` attribute is evaluated, the context node is the root `flixinfo` element. That's why we can use a relative location step here, rather than having to repeat (with a location path such as `/child::flixinfo/child::title`) the entire context that's already been established.

The parent axis   This is the inverse of the child axis: It locates the element (or root node) immediately above the context node in the document's node tree.

The root node has no parent, obviously, but every other node in the document has exactly *one* parent. This leads to the somewhat confounding fact that, although attribute and namespace nodes can never serve as children, they *do* have parents: the elements which declare their values. Also, to repeat, note that no nodes other than elements or the root node can be located along the parent axis.

The `parent::` designation for an axis is functionally equivalent to the `..` notation in a location step. Thus, assuming that the context node is the sample document's `director` element, the following two location paths produce identical results:

```
parent::*/screenwriter
../screenwriter
```

That is, they both locate a node-set consisting of the document's two screenwriter elements.

The descendant axis   You can locate nodes further down than one level (that is, further down than what you can find using only the child axis) with the descendant axis. This extends the child axis indefinitely, to the lowest level of that particular branch of the document tree, so all the restrictions that applied to the child axis are also in place here. That is, the root node is never visible along the descendant axis, regardless of the context node, and neither attributes nor namespace nodes can be located with it.

When using the descendant axis, it's sometimes desirable to locate an entire sub-tree—that is, *all* descendants of a particular node. If you have this need, be careful when using the asterisk wildcard as the node test. For example, the following location path does not locate everything in the document:

```
/descendant::*
```

True, this will find all *elements* descended from the root node. But the asterisk wildcard will not locate the `xml-stylesheet` PI or the document's only comment. To select everything in the document (or a sub-tree of it), use the `node()` node-type test, rather than the wildcard node *name* test, e.g.:

```
/descendant::node()
```

The ancestor axis   As you might guess, this works as the inverse of the descendant axis, by extending the parent axis up through the document tree. As with the parent axis, the ancestor axis locates elements and the root node only. The root node will be located on the ancestor axis from any other node in the document, and the root node itself has no ancestors.

In a document such as the *Criss Cross* FlixML review, note that the movie's title—which might be useful almost anywhere in the document—has no descendants, and therefore cannot be located directly along the ancestor axis no matter how useful it might be. But you can use the ancestor axis in one location step and the same or a different axis in another step, within the same location path. Thus,

```
ancestor::flixinfo/child::title
```

or simply

```
ancestor::flixinfo/title
```

will locate the movie's title, no matter what the context node might be.

The paths are many

The preceding isn't the only—or even necessarily the best—way to locate the `title` element from anywhere in the document. It's just *one* way.

This will be a recurring (albeit implicit) theme throughout the remainder of this chapter and indeed the rest of the XSLT section: There is almost *never* just one way to locate a particular node or nodeset. For more on this topic, see the "How Do I...?" exercise that concludes this chapter.

The self axis   It may not be immediately obvious why you'd ever need something like the self axis, along which you can "see" only one node: the context node itself. After all, if you're already at the context node, why bother looking along an axis in the first place?

The most likely place you'll find yourself using the self axis is *within* a template rule, in the value of an `xsl:value-of` element's `select` attribute. For example, you can do something like this:

```
<xsl:template match="/descendant::comment()">
   Here's a comment for you:
     <xsl:value-of select="self::comment()"/>
</xsl:template>
```

This would instantiate in the result tree the text string, "Here's a comment for you: Note: cross-check studio name".

You'll recall that in a location step, you can always refer to the context node using a single period, or . character. This is actually a shorthand way of expressing the self axis and the `node()` node-type test together—that is,

```
self::node()
```

and simply

```
.
```

are functionally equivalent XPath expressions. In the previous example of a template rule, the context established by the `match` attribute to the `xsl:template` element was a node-set consisting of all comments in the document. Therefore, we could replace the `xsl:value-of` element in that example with one that looks simply like the following:

```
<xsl:value-of select="."/>
```

(By the way: I've never seen any statistics to this effect, but I wouldn't be surprised if this turned out to be the XSLT element most commonly used in the template portions of template rules.)

The descendant-or-self axis   This axis extends the notion of the descendant axis by adding one more node to the resulting node-set: the context node itself.

This is an important axis because, unlike the descendant axis alone, it ensures that you're getting an entire sub-tree. Consider the following location path:

```
/descendant::cast/descendant::*
```

The node-set located by this location path includes all elements that are descended from the `cast` element, but not the `cast` element itself. Therefore, instead of having a nice neat little "sub-document," if you will, with a single "root element," you've got this kind of raggedy-edged, bifurcated collection of elements—`leadcast` and all its descendants on one hand, and `othercast` and all *its* descendants on the other—with no single unifying point of descent. The following location path produces results that may be a little more logically tidy:

```
/descendant::cast/descendant-or-self::*
```

Now the "sub-document" has a true "root element" of its own: the `cast` element.

The descendant-or-self axis is so useful that there's a shortcut for it: a pair of adjacent slashes. (Strictly speaking, this is the shortcut for the descendant-or-self axis with the `node()` node-type test, or `descendant-or-self::node()`.)

Convenient, even when it doesn't make sense

You'll probably find yourself using this shortcut even when the axis in question is really the descendant axis alone (without the context node). For example,

```
/flixinfo//castmember
```

If you tease out what this location path is actually asking for, you'll get something like "locate all nodes descended from the `flixinfo` element—or the `flixinfo` element itself—which are named 'castmember'." Of course the `flixinfo` element is *never* named "castmember," so the implied "or self" doesn't make much sense. But in this case (and many other cases), we don't care whether the self node matches the test; it's just more convenient to use a pair of slashes than to key in the word "descendant" for the axis.

When you will sometimes find yourself taking advantage of this shortcut, and not caring if the self node matches, is when you're trying to locate a node of a particular type or name anywhere in the document. In the long form, for example, if you're after all PIs in the document, you might code the location path as

```
/descendant::processing-instruction()
```

To use the double-slash shortcut in a case like this, where the axis immediately follows the single slash representing the root node, you don't use *three* slashes—just two suffice:

```
//processing-instruction()
```

Finally, you can use the double slash only *within* a location path. It can't appear by itself or at the end of a location path.

The ancestor-or-self axis   Yes, this axis does what you've already guessed: It locates all nodes along the ancestor axis from the context node, *plus* the context node itself. There are no shortcuts associated with this axis (which isn't too great a difficulty, because you probably will not need to use the ancestor-or-self axis very often).

Suppose the context node is the `id` attribute in the *Criss Cross* review whose value is "BLancaster". Then the following location path:

```
ancestor-or-self::*
```

locates the id attribute itself, that attribute's parent male element, the male element's parent leadcast element, the cast element, the flixinfo element, and the root node.

The following-sibling axis   To locate all nodes that share the same parent as the context node and that come *after* the context node, in document order, use the following-sibling axis.

If the context node is the cinematog element in our sample document, you can locate the editor, score, and costumer elements in one swoop, with a location path such as this one:

```
following-sibling::*
```

The preceding-sibling axis   Like the following-sibling axis, preceding-sibling locates children of the same parent as the context node itself—but only those which come *before* the context node, in document order.

Again assuming that the context node is the cinematog element, this location path:

```
preceding-sibling::*
```

locates the director and two screenwriter elements.

The following axis   This is kind of a generalization of the following-sibling axis, in that it locates all nodes in the document—regardless of their parent—which *follow* the context node, in document order. Note that this includes all nodes you'd find on the following-sibling axis, but it explicitly excludes attribute and namespace nodes.

The definition of the word "follow" is a little tricky here. In order for a node to be visible along the following axis, it must both start and end *after the end* of the context node itself; there can't be any overlap. Thus, although the primary-genre and othergenre elements both start and end after the *start* of the genre element, they don't qualify as "following nodes" to the genre element. As a general rule, disregard any ancestors or descendants of the context node;[4] of those that remain, select only the ones which come after the context node.

---

4.   The ancestors end after the end of the context node itself, all right, but they start *before* the end of the context node; descendants aren't found on the following axis because they both start and end before the end of the context node. (You *did* follow that, didn't you?)

If the context node of the moment is the `distributors` element in our sample document, the location path `following::*` would locate the `dialog` element, the `remarks` element, the `parabreak` elements located within the `remarks` element, the `mpaarating` element, and the `bees` element.

The preceding axis   Along the preceding axis from a given context node, you'll find all nodes in the document (except attribute or namespace nodes) that both start and end *before the start* of the context node itself, including any nodes you could find along the preceding-sibling axis. As with the following axis, the easiest way to begin with the preceding axis is to disregard any ancestors or descendants of the context node; then, of all the nodes remaining, select only those that come before the context node.

If the context node is the `genre` element, using a location path of `preceding::node()` will locate the `title` element and the `xml-stylesheet` PI.

The document root, all elements, all comments, all text, and all PIs

With just a subset of what you've learned about axes so far, from any node in a document you can "see" any node in the document (except attribute and namespace nodes). The XSLT spec puts it this way: "The ancestor, descendant, following, preceding and self axes partition a document (ignoring attribute and namespace nodes): they do not overlap and together they contain all the nodes in the document."

Well, I don't know. Although this is kind of intellectually interesting, I've never been able to figure out why (or indeed *whether*) it's important *practical* knowledge. Whatever the point is, at least you can use it to reassure yourself: If what you know about those axes meets the criteria that they (a) don't overlap and (b) contain everything except the attribute and namespace nodes, then you must really *understand* those axes.

The attribute axis   This is one of two XPath axes that have no real counterpart in a family tree or bloodline. If the context node is an element, looking along the attribute axis will locate that element's attributes; if the context node is not an element, looking along the attribute axis will locate an empty node-set. As when locating elements, you can use a specific attribute name to refer to a specific attribute of the context node, or an asterisk wildcard to refer to all its attributes.

In a FlixML document, according to the DTD, all attributes that are of type ID are named "id". So we could locate all ID-type attributes in any FlixML document (perhaps in order to build a table of intra-document links) with a location path such as the following:

```
//attribute::id
```

The attribute axis has a shortcut form: the "at sign," or @ character. Thus, the following is identical to the "find all ID-type attributes" location path just introduced:

```
//@id
```

The namespace axis The final axis available for use in a location step, the namespace axis, locates all namespace nodes "visible" from a given context node. If the context node is anything other than an element, the resulting node-set is empty.

In our sample document, the `flixinfo` element declares a namespace for elements and attributes whose names begin with the `xlink:` prefix. Because the `flixinfo` element is the document's root element, the associated namespace node is visible on the namespace axis from any element in the document (including `flixinfo` itself). Therefore, the following location path always returns the same namespace node, no matter which element is the context node:

```
namespace::*
```

Shortcuts preferred

Maybe for documentation purposes—for absolute, unambiguous clarity—you'd never want to use any of the various axis-related shortcuts, such as . for `self::node()`, @ for the attribute axis, omitting the explicit `child::`, and so on. Maybe so. At the time I'm composing this paragraph, I've still got most of the book ahead of me, so maybe it's premature to say I'll never do this or that. But from where I'm sitting now, I plan to *always* use shortcuts in *Just XSL* when they're available. And it's not just me; this is the norm on XML-, XSLT-, and XPath-related Web sites, newsgroups, and mailing lists, too.

The predicate

Okay, let's see—so far, using the (optional) axis and (required) node test, you can locate a node-set from any context in the document. Some of the node-sets may contain a single node, some may contain multiple nodes, and some may contain no nodes at all. Let's ignore the empty node-set problem for now and just poke a little more into the "one or more" kind of node-set.

If a location path isolates a single node in the document, there's almost never a problem with how to treat it—in either an XSLT stylesheet or an XPointer. It is what it is, you might say. However, when there's more than one node in the node-set, you may have a dilemma: Do you want to treat all matching nodes the same way?

There are any number of cases in our sample document for which we *wouldn't* (or might not, anyhow) want to treat all matching nodes the same way. One of the most obvious is the pair of `releaseyear` elements; the initial year in which a B movie was released is always going to be the most important one. For re-releases, we might want to display the year in a smaller font, for example, or ignore the re-release year altogether. In short, what we need is the ability to *fine-tune* the set of nodes returned by a particular location step or path.

In the case of the `releaseyear` elements, this might be accomplished by answering a question which somehow dragged into the equation the value of the `role` attribute. That is, if the `role` attribute has a value of "initial," do one thing; if it has a value of "alt," do something else.

This kind of fine-tuning is handled by the location step's last component (which is optional): the *predicate*. This is tacked on at the end of a location step, as a value surrounded by square brackets and following the node test.

What goes inside the square brackets is a *logical* (or *Boolean*) test—that is, some combination of XPath expressions, strings, numbers, and operators such as = (*i.e.*, equals) and != (*i.e.*, does not equal)... basically, anything that might be used to yield a logical true or false value. The predicate's test is applied to every node that matches the attribute/node test condition. If the result of the predicate's test is true for a given node, then the node is *really* selected; if false, then the node is disregarded just as completely as if it hadn't met the attribute/node test condition.

About that name

It used to be—and maybe still is—that the word "predicate" showed up most often in elementary-school grammar lessons, where a sentence's predicate was equated more or less with its verb.

Don't think of the XPath predicate in those terms. Think of it in terms of a slightly different form of the word: predicat*ed*, as in "Whether some outcome occurs is *predicated* on something else has happened as well." The "some outcome" in XPath is determining if a node is really selected for processing; the "something else" is that the test specified by the predicate produces a true result for that node.

Here's how we could code a couple of template rules for handling the *Criss Cross* review's two `releaseyear` elements, using predicates as part of their respective location paths:

```
<xsl:template match="//releaseyear[@role='initial']">
  <h3><xsl:value-of select="."/></h3>
</xsl:template>
<xsl:template match="//releaseyear[@role = 'alt']">
  <h4><xsl:value-of select="."/></h4>
</xsl:template>
```

The `match` attribute in the first template rule says, "Instantiate the following content in the result tree only when you find a `releaseyear` element in the document *with a `role` attribute whose value is 'initial'*." When such a `releaseyear` element is located, its content is displayed as an XHTML level-3 heading. The `match` attribute in the second template rule says exactly the same thing except for the predicate, which is interpreted as "*…with a `role` attribute whose value is 'alt'.*" In this case, the value of that `releaseyear` element is copied into the result tree within a slightly smaller, level-4 heading.

Observe a few things about the predicates in these two template rules.

First, the context in which the predicate is evaluated is the node-set established by the location path at that point. Testing the `role` attribute didn't require that we repeat the `//releaseyear` within the predicate itself.

Second, what's *inside* the predicate doesn't affect the context *outside* the predicate. For example, the `xsl:value-of` elements' `select="."` attributes don't copy the values of the `role` attributes into the result tree; the `.` refers to the corresponding `releaseyear`, not to the `role` attribute.

Finally, the first template rule's predicate has no whitespace on either side of the "="; the second template rule's predicate has a space on either side of its "=". The presence or absence of whitespace in a predicate is immaterial.

Inside the predicate: Details   When coding up a predicate in your own location steps, although you may not need to worry about whitespace on either

---

Well, not quite immaterial...

Whitespace in the predicate can be *very* significant if it appears within some portion of the predicate that is *quoted*. For example,

```
<xsl:template match="//releaseyear[@role='a l t']">
```

Here, as you can see, the `role` attribute is being tested to see if its value is the letter `a`, followed by a space, followed by the letter `l`, followed by a space, followed by the letter `t`. In some FlixML document this might produce a match, but certainly not in the present one!

---

side of the operator, you *do* have to concern yourself with keeping some other punctuation exactly right.

The first such case has to do with quotation marks. An XPath location path or step most often shows up in an XSLT stylesheet enclosed in quotation marks—that is, within an attribute's value. Therefore, you must be sure that any quotation marks *within* the location path/step are properly nested within the attribute value, alternating double and single quotation marks as necessary. Thus, either of the following is correct (and both produce the same results):

```
...match="//releaseyear[@role='initial']"
...match='//releaseyear[@role="initial"]'
```

Furthermore, because quotation marks—single or double—are used within attribute values *in pairs*, to delimit internal string-values such as "initial" in the above two examples, you must watch out for *unpaired* quotation marks or apostrophes that might creep into your predicates, in order to ensure that your stylesheet remains well-formed XML.

For example, consider an XML fragment like this:

```
<dictionary>
  <phrase>
    <full>do not</full>
    <contract>don't</contract>
  </phrase>
  <phrase>
    <full>will not</full>
    <contract>won't</contract>
  </phrase>
</dictionary>
```

How would you construct a location path to find the full spelling of the contraction "won't"? A first cut might look something like this:

```
...match="//full[following-sibling::contract=won't]"
```

(Read this as, "Locate a `full` element which has a following-sibling named `contract`, assuming the latter has the value indicated to the right of the equals sign.") This doesn't parse properly, because you're looking for the string "won't," which (because it *is* a string) must be enclosed within quotation marks. So you enclose it in "properly nested" single quotation marks, as follows:

```
...match="//full[following-sibling::contract=
'won't']"
```

Now you've got a different problem, because the apostrophe is embedded in a string enclosed in single quotation marks—that is, apostrophes in their own right. You can't simply change the unbalanced apostrophe to a double quotation mark, because it will still be unpaired (and besides, will locate a string not with an embedded apostrophe, but with an embedded double quotation mark). The only way out of this dilemma is to replace apostrophes and quotation marks embedded in attribute values with their built-in XML entity references, `&apos;` and `&quot;` respectively. Thus:

```
...match="//normal[following-sibling::contract=
'won&apos;t']"
```

The same sort of consideration needs to be applied (and more commonly) when dealing with some of the logical *operators* you may use in the predicate. These operators are summarized in Table 2–3.

If you were coding the "less than" and "greater than" kinds of tests normally, in a non-markup language, you'd simply use the < and > characters, respectively. But of course these are reserved characters in an XML document, so you've got to escape them by using their corresponding entity references.

Table 2-3   Logical Operators in a Location Step's Predicate

Operator	Meaning
=	equals
!=	does not equal
&lt;	is less than
&gt;	is greater than

Table 2-3   Logical Operators in a Location Step's Predicate (continued)

Operator	Meaning
<=	is less than or equal to
>=	is greater than or equal to

(As a practical matter, processors may accept the literal > character—it's the < which *must* be escaped, because it's always assumed to begin a tag. It never hurts to be safe, though, which is why I recommend using the escaped form of both characters.)

Predicate: Special cases   I mentioned that what goes into the predicate is some kind of logical test—an expression that evaluates to a logical true or false. There are two special cases that seem to be (but aren't really) exceptions to this description of the predicate.

The first special case is based on the fact that XPath considers all possible nodes in a document tree to have a value of true or false—true if the node actually exists, false otherwise. Therefore, within a predicate you can simply include an XPath location path/step, which is interpreted as, "…if the node identified in this predicate exists."

For example, the FlixML DTD has an element, otherreview, in which to record information about outside reviews of the film in question. This element can have any number of goodreview and/or badreview children. If we wanted our stylesheet to show only the bad reviews of a film, we could construct a template rule whose xsl:template element does something like this:

```
<xsl:template match="//otherreview[badreview]">
```

In other words, "match each otherreview element for which a badreview child exists." (Note that the predicate uses a relative location path.)

The second exception to the general rule is that a predicate may have (or evaluate to) a *numeric* value. The XPath processor treats this as meaning, "…if the node is at the specified position in the node-set returned by this location step."

For instance, you can locate the first castmember element in the document with a location path such as this:

```
//castmember[1]
```

You don't have to use a literal number there, either; you can include some calculated value, or a value returned by one of the XPath functions that I'll cover in the section of that name later in this chapter.

Not really so exceptional

The use of a number in the predicate is really a shorthand for a particular form of a logical test. Specifically, it is the same as comparing the desired number to the result of the XPath `position()` function (to be covered shortly). That is, the above location path to the first `castmember` element is shorthand for

```
//castmember[position()=1]
```

Therefore, these supposedly "numeric" predicates turn out to be logical tests after all!

Compound predicates   If you need to, you can test for more than one condition in the predicate by chaining them together, separated by the keywords and and or. Thus,

```
//plotsummary[parabreak and emph]
```

selects a `plotsummary` element only if it has both a `parabreak` and an `emph` child. On the other hand,

```
//plotsummary[parabreak or emph]
```

selects a `plotsummary` element if it has a `parabreak` *or* an `emph` child.

These compound predicates can get to be quite elaborate, even unwieldy, when you're testing for more than two conditions and using both and and or. In these cases, it's generally helpful to use parentheses to group together the conditions you want to be tested together. For instance,

```
//castmember[parent::female or (ancestor::leadcast and
parent::male)]
```

locates a node-set consisting of all `castmember` elements for which either of the following conditions is true:

- The parent of the `castmember` element is a `female` element; **or**
- The `castmember` element has a `leadcast` ancestor *and* a `male` parent.

In the case of the *Criss Cross* FlixML review, the resulting node-set includes *all* the female cast members and the two males (Lancaster and Duryea) who are in the lead cast.

Changing the grouping to

```
//castmember[(parent::female or ancestor::leadcast) and
parent::male]
```

will locate all `castmember` elements for which the following two conditions are true:

- The parent of the `castmember` element is a `female` element *or* the `castmem-ber` has a `leadcast` ancestor; **and**
- The parent of the `castmember` element is a `male` element.

Sorting out what happens in this case is a little trickier; I find it easier to start with the simplest condition (here, the second condition) first. So first, look at all male cast members; of those, select only the ones who either are *female* cast members as well (hmm) or are in the lead cast. Therefore, this location path selects only the nodes representing lead male cast members—Lancaster and Duryea again—and no one else.

Compound location paths

You can select node-sets from two or more completely different location paths, allowing you to assemble a view of your source document's content that bears little if any relationship to its actual structure. You accomplish this by chaining together the separate location paths using the so-called *pipe* or vertical bar character, `|`. For example, if you want the same template rule to apply to the `plot-summary`, `goodreview`, `badreview`, and `remarks` elements in the *Criss Cross* review, you could do something like this:

```
<xsl:template
    match="//plotsummary | //goodreview | //badreview
    | //remarks">
  <p><xsl:value-of select="."/></p>
</xsl:template>
```

XPath functions

You may be surprised—I know I was—to learn that XPath isn't restricted to navigating up, down, and sideways in a document tree. It enables you to locate content in other than its "pure" form and to obtain certain kinds of information about the content other than simply where it lies within the document's structure.

Functions: Background

(If you already know in general what functions are and do, feel free to skip over this brief introduction to the basics.)

If you've had any exposure to just about any programming language—including JavaScript/ECMAScript, Visual Basic, C++, Java, whatever—you'll have encountered the notion of *functions*. It's quite common in such languages to find yourself writing the same or quite similar chunk of code over and over; a more efficient way to code such regularly repeated operations is to break out this kind of "boilerplate" code into a separate *function*. Sometimes you have to pass to the function some data it needs to perform its canned operation; some functions work on their own, without any outside data needed. The way you instruct the program to perform the function's duties is simply to use the name of the function, followed by a pair of parentheses—this is referred to as "calling the function" or "a function call"—and if you have to pass it any data, include that information within the parentheses.

One of the most important features of functions is that they *return a value*. This means you can use a function call anywhere a corresponding literal value might be used; the value calculated by the function simply stands in for the literal value.

An example of a common function that requires no outside data is one to retrieve the system's current date and time. In Microsoft's Visual Basic, this operation is performed by a function called `Now()`. Wherever you use this function, the system date/time is made available, enabling you to code things like this:

```
MsgBox "Current date/time is " + Now()
```

to display a little box containing the message (for example) "Current date/time is 6/18/01 14:20:08."

Visual Basic also includes a `Format()` function whose purpose is to display some value in a format of the programmer's choosing. You pass into the function the value you want to be formatted, and a text string that is used for specifying the desired format. For example,

```
MsgBox "The number 1 with a couple leading zeroes is " + Format(1,
"000")
```

which displays a message box containing the text, "The number 1 with a couple leading zeroes is 001."

In this example, I've passed to the `Format()` function two data values: the number 1 and the text string "000" (which tells the function that it is to return a three-digit number, even if the number passed to it takes up fewer than three digits). Each data item passed into a function is called an *argument.*

(Note, by the way, that all this terminology—"calling a function," "passing arguments," indeed the word "function" itself—isn't restricted to Visual Basic. I could have used examples from just about any programming language without changing the underlying words.)

XPath function reference

The XPath spec establishes several categories of functions that may be used in XPath location steps in various ways. Each category is named according to the kind of value returned by or passed to the functions in the category. The four categories are node-set functions, string functions, Boolean functions, and numeric functions. You can also perform a number of straight arithmetic operations which, while not functions as such, return a single value in the same way that functions do; I'll cover these at the end of the section on numeric functions.

Node-set functions   The functions in the node-set category are summarized in Table 2–4.

Table 2-4   XPath Node-Set Functions

Function call	Returns	Description
last()	number	Returns the number of nodes in the current node-set.
position()	number	Returns the position of the context node within the current node-set.
count(*nodeset*)	number	Returns the number of nodes in the *nodeset* argument.
id(*value*)	node-set	Returns the element node whose ID-type attribute has the value specified in the *value* argument.
local-name(*nodeset?*)	string	If *nodeset* argument is passed, returns a string representing the local name (that is, without a namespace prefix) of the first node in that node-set; if *nodeset* is omitted, returns the local name of the context node.

Table 2-4   XPath Node-Set Functions (continued)

Function call	Returns	Description
namespace-uri(*nodeset?*)	string	If *nodeset* argument is passed, returns a string representing the namespace URI associated with the name of the first node in that node-set; if *nodeset* is omitted, returns the namespace URI associated with the context node's name. Note that this may be an empty string, if the name isn't associated with any particular namespace URI.
name(*nodeset?*)	string	If *nodeset* argument is passed, returns a string representing the entire name (that is, including any namespace prefix) of the first node in that node-set; if *nodeset* is omitted, returns the name of the context node (including namespace prefix, if any).

All the functions in this category either operate on or return an XPath node-set. You've already seen one of these: The position() function was introduced in a box earlier, following the discussion of using numeric predicates in a location step.

In your own stylesheets, you'll probably find last(), position(), and count() to be the most frequently useful node-set functions. They're closely related, of course, because they all have to do with the number of nodes in a node-set.

A last(), but no first()?

Seems like it would make sense, doesn't it? After all, there are a lot of things you might want to do for the first node in a node-set that you wouldn't want to do for subsequent ones, right?

The reason you don't need a first() function is that you can always find the first node in a node-set using a numeric predicate with a value of 1. For example,

```
//distributor[1]
```

locates the first distributor element in a FlixML review.

As previously mentioned in passing, the `position()` function can be compared to some value in a predicate simply by using the value alone. Thus, these two predicates are identical:

```
[position()=4]
[4]
```

Note that the value of the `position()` function for a given node depends on the direction of the axis along which the node-set has been located: For forward axes, the position of a node within a node-set increments in *document order*; for reverse axes (such as the ancestor and preceding axes), it increments in *reverse document order*.

The `last()` and `count()` functions occasionally are sources of confusion for newcomers to XPath, because they both return the size of a node-set. But notice that the `count()` function takes an argument, whereas `last()` does not. This makes `last()` the function to use whenever you need to access the number of nodes in the current node-set, and `count()` whenever you need to access the number of nodes in some node-set other than the current one.

So with `last()` and `position()` together, you can do things like this:

```
Item <xsl:value-of select="position()"/>
of <xsl:value-of select="last()"/>
```

If the current node-set contains four nodes, this would result in a series of labels: "Item 1 of 4," "Item 2 of 4," and so on.

As you'll see when we get into some real XSLT processing in subsequent chapters, the `count()` function can be most useful when you're toiling away in some lower-level node-set but need to refer to the number of nodes at some higher level, or in a different branch of the tree than the one in which you're currently working. For instance, at the top of a FlixML review you might want to display a message indicating how many good and bad reviews of the film are referenced in the document. You could accomplish this with a template (within an appropriate template rule, anywhere in the stylesheet) looking something like this:

```
There are <xsl:value-of select="count(//goodreview)"/>
  good review(s) and <xsl:value-of
  select="count(//badreview)"/> bad review(s) of
  this film included in or referenced from this
  FlixML review.
```

The three functions that perform name- or namespace-related duties will not be used very often, for most purposes, but when the need arises you'll be grateful they're there.[5]

It may be tempting to use the `name()` or `local-name()` functions to test the context in which a particular node falls. For example, as I just mentioned, the `goodreview` and `badreview` elements can be children of either the `flixml-review` or `otherreview` elements, and you might want to style them differently depending on their parent. With this in mind, you might find yourself using location paths like

```
//goodreview[name(..) = "flixmlreview"]
```

and

```
//badreview[name(..) = "otherreview"]
```

This would be crazy. There's already a way to check the name of an element's parent; use the parent axis, as in

```
//goodreview[parent::flixmlreview]
```

(There is one occasionally useful purpose to which these functions can be put. XSLT gives you the option of passing a value into a stylesheet—for example, the name of a column on which to sort a table of data. I'll show you an example of this later in *Just XSL*.)

As for the `id()` function, note that it's useful only if your source document employs a DTD which declares some ID-type attribute(s). If there's no DTD, or if it doesn't declare any such attributes, then you'll never get a match on *any* value passed to the function. Of course, if there *are* some ID-type attributes, this function can be indispensable, especially since the value you pass it can be a computed value—or a value passed into an XSLT stylesheet—rather than a literal string.

---

5.   Chapter 6 discusses the Schematron XSLT-based XML document validator. Schematron runs through a document, "validates" it according to criteria impossible to express in terms of a DTD, and displays messages about portions of the document that fail such "validation." In such a case, pretty obviously, being able to display an invalid node's name can make all the difference in the world between helping a user locate the source of a problem and making the problem unfindable.

String functions   The 10 functions in this category are summarized in Table 2–5. Note that they all process string-type arguments or return string-type values.

Table 2-5   XPath String Functions

Function call	Returns	Description
`string(value?)`	string	Converts *value* argument to a string and returns the result. If *value* is a node-set, it returns the string-value of the *first* node in the node-set. If *value* is omitted, returns the string-value of the context node.
`concat(str1,str2...)`	string	Combines multiple strings into one big string, and returns the result.
`starts-with(str1,str2)`	Boolean	If the value of *str1* begins with the value of *str2*, returns the value true; otherwise returns the value false.
`contains(str1,str2)`	Boolean	If the string passed as *str1* contains the string passed as *str2*, returns true; otherwise returns false.
`substring(str,nstart, nchars?)`	string	Returns a portion of the *str* argument, starting with the character at position *nstart*; if *nchars* argument is passed, the result will contain that many characters, otherwise it will include all characters in *str* from *nstart* to the end.
`substring-before(str1,str2)`	string	Returns the portion of *str1* which appears before the string passed as *str2*.
`substring-after(str1,str2)`	string	Returns the portion of *str1* which appears *after* the string passed as *str2*.
`string-length(string?)`	number	Returns the number of characters in *string*; if *string* is omitted, returns the number of characters in the string-value of the context node.

Table 2-5   XPath String Functions (continued)

Function call	Returns	Description
`normalize-space(string?)`	string	Strips leading and trailing whitespace from *string*, and converts multiple adjacent whitespace characters within *string* to a single space, and returns the result; if *string* is omitted, returns the result of this operation on the string-value of the context node.
`translate(str1,str2, str3)`	string	Replaces individual characters appearing in both *str1* and *str2* with other characters from *str3* (see text for details).

The range of uses to which the XPath string functions can be put is enormous. In essence, they expose XML document content so that you aren't restricted to dealing just with entire nodes or their string-values.[6]

It's the simplest of the 10, but in terms of the XPath spec, the `string()` function is easily the most important—even if you never use it, you have to understand how it works. That's because the standard is littered with phrases such as "first converted to a string as if by a call to the `string()` function."

As the summary above says, `string()` always returns a string-value. The rule is simple enough: If you pass it a node-set (and the default, if no argument is passed, *is* a node-set consisting of one node—the context node), it returns the string-value of the first node in the node-set; if you pass it some other data type, it returns the string form of the argument. (So, for example, if you pass it the number 43, it returns the *string* "43". If you pass it a Boolean value or an expression that resolves to a Boolean value, it returns the string "true" or "false".)

You've already seen a couple of examples of complex code that could have been simplified if I'd already introduced you to the `concat()` function. These were examples of XSLT templates containing more than one `xsl:value-of` element. For example, you've already seen the following example.

---

6.   Depending on how excited you can get about such matters, it can feel a little like discovering that you don't have to put the whole Oreo cookie into your mouth at once: You're free to break it open to get at just the icing, if that's all you want.

```
Item <xsl:value-of select="position()"/>
of <xsl:value-of select="last()"/>
```

The same result could be achieved using the `concat()` function, as follows:

```
concat("Item ", position(), " of ", last())
```

Note that you can pass to the `concat()` function as many arguments as you want. Also, although the spec does not say so explicitly, in practice you may find that the arguments do not *have* to be strings, as with the `position()` and `last()` function calls in this example—that the processor will convert them to strings on the fly, as needed. If your particular processor objects, you can satisfy it by explicitly converting the non-string arguments. For example,

```
concat("Item ", string(position()), " of ", string(last()))
```

Because the `starts-with()` and `contains()` functions return Boolean true or false values, you'll probably find yourself using them most often in location-step predicates. For instance, you could locate all elements in the *Criss Cross* review which mention Burt Lancaster by name with a location path such as this:

```
//*[contains(., "Lancaster")]
```

The three functions that extract portions of a string—`substring()`, `substring-before()`, and `substring-after()`—are often used in concert with one another, especially when you're trying to tease apart the contents of a string that consists of discrete units of text, delimited by some character such as a space or comma.

You'll observe that each of the cast members' names in the above review appears in the form *"firstname surname."* This is suitable for producing a list of names in simply the same order as they appear in the document; however, if we wanted to make it easy to locate any one name, it would be simpler if the list appeared in alphabetical order, surname first, and perhaps separated from the first by a comma and space. For a given cast member, you could represent his or her name this way using two of these substring functions in the following fashion (assuming the context node is the given `castmember` element):

```
concat(substring-after(., " "), ", ",
substring-before(., " "))
```

Here, the `concat()` function returns a single string consisting of three parts:

- the portion of the `castmember` element's string-value that comes *after* a space;
- a comma and a blank space; and

- the portion of the `castmember` element's string-value that comes *before* a space.

The messy real world

Unfortunately, although this example works in *almost* all cases, it misses the boat on others—in any case, that is, where the cast member's name contains more than one space. That's because `string-before()` and `string-after()` search only for the *first* occurrence of the delimiter string in the target string.

Aside from the most obvious case (when a cast member's name includes a middle initial or name), there's also the problem encountered in the *Criss Cross* review: the name of one of the supporting cast members: John "Skins" Miller. His name, as processed by the above combination of the `concat()`, `substring-before()`, and `substring-after()` functions, comes out this way:

`"Skins" Miller, John`

It also breaks down if the actor or actress uses only a single name ("Madonna"), or a hyphenated one ("Ann-Margret"). There are (more or less messy) ways to get around this problem, and we'll take a look at one of them in Chapter 3.

The `string-length()` function often turns up not for display in its own right, but as a value in some context that requires a number—such as an argument passed to some other function. Think about the general question: Why would it make a difference how many characters are in a particular string?[7]

The answer to that question is often related to how to display some text. For one exotic example, if you wanted to display each character in a string in a separate cell of a table, you'd need to be able to determine how many characters there were in order to arrange the table in a reasonable fashion.

Cleaning up text before you process it can be important, especially if the text has been entered by hand. One of the most important kinds of cleaning up

---

7. Aside from special cases like the Schematron validator, mentioned a couple of footnotes ago, where you might want to confirm that some data value contains no more than a required maximum number of characters.

to do is to get rid of extraneous whitespace, and that's the realm of the `normal-ize-space()` function.

A few paragraphs back, I showed you a general algorithm for reversing the order of cast members' names, from the "*firstname surname*" form in a document to a "*surname, firstname*" form. Just to be sure that a stray double- or triple-space has not crept into a given cast member's name, or a single one at the beginning or end, it would have been a good idea to normalize its whitespace at the time we did the substringing. Something like the following would work (again assuming that `castmember` is the context node):

```
concat(substring-after(normalize-space(.), " "), ", ",
substring-before(normalize-space(.), " ")
```

Finally, there's the `translate()` function. This is something of an odd duck, probably with limited utility for most applications but, again, indispensable should the need arise. The general idea is that you want to replace individual characters in one string with individual characters in another. The most common example of an operation like this is making a string all upper- or lowercase—that is, replacing all lowercase characters with their uppercase equivalents, or vice versa.

When I'm working on a FlixML review, if I've got a favorite bit of dialogue from the movie I enter it into the `dialog` element. Although there's no formal requirement that this element's content be structured in any particular way, I always begin by using the speaker's name, followed by a colon, followed by the line of dialogue itself. I could *capitalize* the speaker's name using something like the following (assuming the `dialog` element to be the context node):

```
translate(substring-before(.), ":",
"abcdefghijklmnopqrstuvwxyz",
"ABCDEFGHIJKLMNOPQRSTUVWXYZ")
```

(Note that I've arranged the *str2* and *str3* arguments so they're immediately above and below each other. This will make it easier to see how the `translate()` function works.)

The first string passed to the function here is a substring of the `dialog` element—the portion of that element which appears before the colon. The *str2* argument is simply the lowercase alphabet, and *str3* the uppercase. The `trans-late()` function goes through the *str1* argument (the speaker's name, in this case) one character at a time, and asks the question, "Does this character appear anywhere in *str2*?" If the answer is no, the function leaves that character as is;

otherwise, it replaces the character with (hold your breath) the character from *str3* that is in the same position as the matching character in *str2*.

The `dialog` element in the *Criss Cross* review begins with the characters `Slim:`. So *str1* is "Slim". The function starts by looking at the capital "S"—is there a capital "S" in *str2*? No, so leave the capital "S" alone. Now on to the lowercase "l"—is there one of those in *str2*? Yes, at position 12. So `translate()` replaces the lowercase "l" with the character at position 12 in *str3*, that is, the uppercase "L". And so on through the entire length of *str1*, until the final value returned by the above function call is the all-uppercase `SLIM`.

Note that there's no particular requirement that you have to replace every character in *str1* with a *different* character. For example, you could "mask" all the lowercase characters in *str1* with asterisks, using code such as the following:

```
translate(substring-before(.), ":",
"abcdefghijklmnopqrstuvwxyz",
"**************************")
```

The value returned from this call to the `translate()` function would be the string `S***`.

This function, by the way, can also be used to *remove* specific characters from *str1*. To do so, just make *str2* longer than *str3*; any of the excess characters in *str2* will be stripped from *str1*. Thus,

```
translate('1005006',
"1234567890",
"123456789")
```

strips out all zeroes from the *str1* value, returning the string `156`.

And now you're wondering...

...what happens when *str3* is longer than *str2*?

Nothing exotic happens (unfortunately for those of you who were hoping that the answer would expose something really interesting about the XPath spec). The excess characters at the end of *str3* are ignored, just as if they hadn't been entered at all.

Boolean functions   Table 2–6 summarizes the five Boolean XPath functions. All five functions return a Boolean true or false value, making them particularly well suited for use in the predicate portion of a location step.

Table 2-6   XPath Boolean Functions

Function call	Description
boolean(*value*)	Converts *value* to true or false (see text for details)
not(*boolean*)	If *boolean* is true, returns false, and vice versa
true()	Returns the value true
false()	Returns the value false
lang(*string*)	If the language in which the context node is presented (as determined by any xml:lang attributes in scope for the context node) is the same as the language represented by *string*, returns true; otherwise returns false

The boolean() function is useful in ways that might not be immediately obvious. Its usefulness stems from the fact that basically anything which might be passed in as *value* will have a true or false value based on whether *value* is, respectively, actually useful or not.

For instance, if a node exists, it has a *Boolean* value of true (aside from its *string*-value, which might be used in most contexts). When discussing predicates, I mentioned that you can test for the existence of a particular node simply by putting a reference to the node in a predicate; the reason this works is that an XPath expression such as

//flixmlreview[goodreview]

("locate a flixmlreview element only if it's got a goodreview child") is a kind of shorthand for

//flixmlreview[boolean(goodreview)]

Likewise, a string has a value of true only if it's non-empty—if it contains at least one character. This means you can test (say) for a useful goodreview element in a subtler way:

//flixmlreview[boolean(string(goodreview))]

The previous example simply tested whether goodreview existed at all; this one confirms both that it exists *and* that it is not empty.

Finally, if *value* is supposedly numeric, boolean(value) will return true only if the number is a legitimate number. This makes the boolean() function useful for confirming that a calculation can be safely performed, before actually performing it.

The `not()` function can engender some consternation in newcomers to XML, particularly when it shows up in a predicate. Look at the following two template rules; can you tell what happens if the source tree contains a single `releaseyear` element, with *no* `role` attribute at all? (Note that the FlixML DTD does not require a `role` attribute on this element, and provides no default if none is explicitly provided.)

```
<xsl:template match="//releaseyear[@role!='alt']">
  Template 1: Found no releaseyear whose role is "alt"
</xsl:template>
<xsl:template match="//releaseyear[not(@role='alt')]">
  Template 2: Found no releaseyear whose role is "alt"
</xsl:template>
```

If the `role` attribute is completely missing, the location path in the first template rule's `match` attribute will locate nothing at all; as a result, this template rule will not instantiate its template in the result tree. The second template rule, on the other hand, locates the `releaseyear` element, determines that it doesn't have a `role` attribute of "alt," and places in the result tree the string "Template 2: Found no releaseyear whose role is 'alt'". The difference between the two predicates is that the first one requires *both* that a `role` attribute be present *and* that its value be "alt" (otherwise, the template will not be instantiated); the second, on the other hand, allows *either* of the two conditions—"the attribute is not present" *or* "the attribute is present, but has the wrong value"— to be true in order to instantiate its template.

The two functions `true()` and `false()` will not see much use in your stylesheets, with one (remotely possible) exception which I will cover in the discussion of named templates in Chapter 4.

As for the `lang()` function, concern yourself with using it only if (a) your source document makes use of explicit `xml:lang` attributes and (b) you really need to keep multiple languages sorted out. The general idea is that, for example, I could build an index of all French-language B movies, with a location step such as this:

```
title[lang("FR")]
```

The XPath-aware processor is supposed to be reasonably intelligent about matching these language codes. For instance, according to an example provided in the spec, the expression `lang("EN")` will return a value of true if the actual value of the xml:lang in scope at the point of the context node is EN, en, or en-us.

Glossing over some details

The above location step would not be useful for most FlixML work, because each FlixML document provides information on only a single B film with (typically) just a single title. However, as you will learn in Chapter 5, it's entirely possible to process *multiple* documents with a single stylesheet. In that context, a location step something like the one above would be eminently practical.

Numeric functions   This XPath function category includes five functions that (as the name implies) perform various numeric operations. The values returned from all five are numeric. These functions are summarized in Table 2–7.

Table 2-7   XPath Numeric Functions

Function call	Description
number(*value?*)	Converts *value* to numeric form, for use in calculations, numeric sorting, and so on. Boolean true converts to the value 1; false, to 0. If *value* is a node-set, it is first converted to its string-value and then converted to a number if possible. If *value* is omitted, returns the result of converting the context node's string-value to a number. If *value* cannot be converted to a number, returns the special value NaN (for "not a number").
sum(*nodeset*)	Returns the sum of all nodes in the passed *nodeset* argument, after converting each to a number.
floor(*number*)	Returns the largest integer which is less than or equal to *number*.
ceiling(*number*)	Returns the smallest integer which is greater than or equal to *number*.
round(*number*)	Returns the integer whose value is closest to *number*. If there are two such numbers (i.e., *number* contains a decimal portion of .5), returns the higher of the two numbers.

The number() function is useful in the same respect that the string() function is—there are implicit numeric conversions elsewhere in the spec, and you can understand these only if you understand how the explicit conversion provided by number() works. However, I find it also useful in its own right.

The main reason this is so, of course, is that you want to ensure that a calculation meant to produce a number isn't going to go belly-up simply because a particular node is empty (in which case, say, you might prefer to substitute a value of 0 for the missing value). Handling numbers with XPath is trickier than handling strings; after all, each node doesn't have a number-value, only a string-value!

Although FlixML isn't a particularly number-driven application, it won't be uncommon when processing many XML source trees to need something like the sum() function. For example, an application might record region-by-region sales of some product, something like the following:

```
<sales>
  <region name="East">12347</region>
  <region name="West">88832</region>
  <region name="South">34588</region>
  <region name="North">78206</region>
</sales>
```

You could display the total sales across all regions with an XSLT xsl:value-of element, like this:

```
Total, all regions:
  <xsl:value-of select="sum(//sales/region)"/>
```

This would place into the result tree the string, "Total, all regions: 213973".

Number formatting

If you're concerned about how to format numbers—for example, inserting a comma into the value of the above sum() function's result—you'll need to look into certain XSLT features, particularly the format-number() XSLT function. (XSLT functions are covered in Chapter 4.) XPath itself is concerned with the number only as a number, and in this sense a comma would simply, well, get in the way. The only punctuation XPath recognizes as legitimately part of a number are the decimal point and minus sign; if the so-called "number" contains anything else, such as plus signs or commas, the value is not recognized by XPath as a numeric value.

Finally, let's look at the floor(), ceiling(), and round() functions: These are related to one another, in the sense that each returns an integer (whole number) as a result of examining an argument with a possibly fractional component. The effects of the first two are best understood with a simple demonstration template such as this,

```
<xsl:value-of select="The number 1.25 is between "/>
<xsl:value-of select="floor(1.25)"/> and
<xsl:value-of select="ceiling(1.25)"/>
```

which displays, "The number 1.25 is between 1 and 2."

The round() function does pretty much what you'd expect, as summarized in Table 2–7. The XPath spec kind of wanders off into some strange territory when discussing round(), more or less muttering to itself about "negative infinity," "positive infinity," and "negative zero." In the event that you encounter these values in the real world of your XML applications, just understand that all three values, when rounded, equal themselves (just as if they were integers).

Numeric/Arithmetic operators: +, -, *, div, mod   As I said at the beginning of this section, the XPath numeric or arithmetic operators (summarized in Table 2–8) are not really functions. However, in the sense that you "pass data to" and "get data back from" these operators, they do *behave* rather like functions.

Table 2-8   XPath Numeric/Arithmetic Operators

Operator (example)	Description
num1 + num2	Adds *num1* to *num2*, returning the sum
num1 - num2	Subtracts *num2* from *num1*, returning the difference
num1 * num2	Multiplies *num1* and *num2*, returning the product
num1 div num2	Divides *num1* by *num2*, returning the quotient
num1 mod num2	Returns the remainder of dividing *num1* by *num2*

In short, you have available in XPath the same basic arithmetic operations you do in most other applications. The only two possible surprises are the div and mod operators.

In most programming languages, division is represented by a slash character, /. Of course, this character has special meaning in an XPath expression—it's used to separate location steps—so the XPath language's authors came up with a reasonable substitute in div.

As for mod (which is short for *modulus*), you may be familiar with it (or an operator like it) already. (Some programming languages use a percent sign, %, to represent the modulus.) It is particularly useful in XSLT when you need to do something different every N times. For example, you might want to color every even row in a listing green and leave every odd row uncolored. In pseudo-code, so as not to torture you with the XSLT details for now, this operation would look something like this:

```
If position() mod 2 = 0
  Color this row green
Else
  Leave this row uncolored
```

Whatever N is desired, substitute it for the 2 in the above: for every third row, use 3; every fourth, 4; and so on.

One minor thing to be concerned about when using the minus (-) operator is that you should leave whitespace on either side of it—or at least, before it. This is because a hyphen is a legitimate character in an XML name. Consider the following two XSLT fragments:

```
<xsl:value-of select="releaseyear - 1"/>
<xsl:value-of select="releaseyear-1"/>
```

The first will display the value of the releaseyear element, minus 1; the second, the value of the element whose name is releaseyear-1 (which will display absolutely nothing, at least if this is a FlixML source tree you're processing!).

How Do I ...
Find anything in an XML document, anywhere, using XPath?

Okay, that's a virtually impossible question to answer. Not because it's impossible to answer for a particular document, but because it's impossible to answer in a way that's going to be correct for *any* document. Each document, and certainly each XML vocabulary, has its own unique element and attribute names, text content, general structure, and so on.

I can give you a few general guidelines, though. And after I've done that, I can take you on a kind of whirlwind tour of how you might locate a particular something in our *Criss Cross* review, in a number of ways from simple to ridiculously complex.

General guidelines

#1: Avoid the leading // in XSLT stylesheets

This is arguably the best single guideline you can carry with you into the next chapter. The reason for it is hard to explain at this point, but it has to do with processing efficiency. As you will see, in an XSLT stylesheet, most template rules establish their own contexts *within a context* established by other template rules. Using a leading double slash—that is, an absolute location path requesting a particular node type on the descendant-or-self axis from the document root—is horribly inefficient. Even if your documents are fairly small and efficiency is not a major concern, the leading double slash often does not get you what you want in XSLT. (We'll see an example of why not in Chapter 3.)

Note that I've consciously used the leading double slash in many examples in this chapter; doing so has allowed me to avoid constantly having to identify the context node. Furthermore, the leading // is very important in XPointer applications. But that, as the saying goes, is a whole 'nother book.

#2: Simple is generally better...

Although it's possible (as you'll soon see) to construct working XPath expressions of almost infinite complexity, it's hard to imagine why you'd want to, except as an intellectual or academic exercise.

XPath's flexibility—its infinite variety, if you will—doesn't originate from anything but a desire to *make it impossible* not *to find something*. There are likely to be a thousand routes to any given data item, but the shortest, most direct route (in XPath, as in most problem domains) is likely to be the most efficient and practically workable one.

Also remember that sometimes you may be called upon to explain what it is that a particular chunk of XSLT code does. If it makes use of a particularly hairy and long-winded XPath location path which could have been handled more simply, you may find it hard to explain just what you were getting at...or why you were getting there *that* way!

#3: ...But don't fear the complex

Again the mantra: XPath's major role is to *make it impossible* not *to find something* in an XML document. Most things will be easily findable; some few things may require an XPath expression that jumps through hoops before returning the right content. The ability to jump through hoops is one of XPath's strengths—don't be afraid to use it!

As a personal aside, when I was first learning this stuff I was terrified of location paths with a predicate in any but the last step, such as this one:

```
//castmember[ancestor::leadcast]/following-sibling::role
```

They just *looked* inscrutable, almost completely impenetrable, you know? But it turns out that such location paths are marvelously straightforward ways of getting exactly the right thing as efficiently as possible.

Whatever makes you nervous about XPath—if anything does—play around with it until you get it. It's there for some reason, after all.

#4: Locate by *structure, not by content*

When I was explaining how to use the XPath `translate()` function earlier in this chapter, I mentioned that when I code a FlixML document's `dialog` element, I code the name of the speaker first, followed by a colon, followed by the line of dialogue.

Now, it's theoretically possible that knowing about this coding foible of mine, I could locate the `dialog` element in a FlixML document using something like the following:

```
//*[contains(substring-before(., " "), ":")]
```

That is, "Locate the first element of any name which contains a colon in the portion of the element's content before the first space."

Aside from the fact that this is a dreadful violation of Guideline #2 above,[8] it's also dreadfully prone to breaking—easily returning no result at all, even if there is in fact a `dialog` element in the document.

In some cases you won't be able to avoid looking for specific string-values, portions of string-values, exact numbers, and so on. If you find yourself doing so

---

8.   And Guideline #1, if you try it inside an XSLT stylesheet.

often in your location paths, at least in an XSLT stylesheet, you're probably coding for *this* document in this vocabulary, not for *any* document in it.

Exception to the rule

Many attributes in many vocabularies have a fairly limited range of allowable values. In such cases, don't hesitate to use your knowledge of the vocabulary in question to query on attribute values. It's elements (and unconstrained CDATA-type attributes, with no defaults) whose values you've got to avoid misusing.

Flights of fancy: Winging around the *Criss Cross review*

In what follows in this section, understand that I'm being only half-serious. The point is not to recommend one approach over another, to show off my cleverness, or any such thing. The point is simply to demonstrate (I hope) the range of options available when getting from one point in an XML document to another using XPath.

As the starting point—the context node—in the *Criss Cross* review, I've arbitrarily selected a point buried pretty far down in the document: the second `distriblink` element, which points to the page on Amazon.com where you can buy a copy of the videotape. The target node—the one I'm trying to get to—is, oh, say, the `id` attribute on Edna Holland's `female` element.

As a testing device, to be sure all of these eight location paths produce exactly the same result, I used an XSLT stylesheet containing the following template rule:

```
<xsl:template
  match="distriblink[contains(@xlink:href,'amazon')]">
  <h3>Current distriblink points to:
    <xsl:value-of select="@xlink:href"/></h3>
  <h3>Value of Edna Holland's id attribute is:</h3>
  <h4><xsl:value-of select="testpath"/></h4>
</xsl:template>
```

The `xsl:template` element's `match` attribute sets the desired context node for evaluating a given location path. (Just to be sure I've got the right one, I've included a level-3 heading which displays this `distriblink` element's `xlink:href` attribute.) I'll replace *testpath* with whichever location path is being tested at the time. If a given *testpath* works, the template rule will display "Value of Edna Holland's id attribute is:" as an XHTML level-3 heading, and "EHolland" as an XHTML level-4 heading.

- **Path #1:** `select="id('EHolland')/@id"`
  Translation: Locate the attribute named "id" of the element whose ID-type attribute's value is "EHolland".
  Discussion: This is probably the single most efficient way to get to our desired target. It leverages the knowledge that the attribute whose name is "id" is indeed an ID-type attribute, and that therefore there is only one attribute with the indicated value. Note that the `id()` function locates the element node with that `id` attribute, *not* the `id` attribute itself; obtaining the value of the `id` attribute itself requires the second location step. Interestingly, also note that using the `id()` function works just fine if you use a relative location path.
- **Path #2:** `select="//@id[.='EHolland']"`
  Translation: Locate an attribute named "id" anywhere in the document, as long as its value is "EHolland".
  Discussion: This is a rough equivalent of Path #1, to be used either if you didn't know that the `id` attribute was an ID-type attribute or if you knew that it wasn't. The leading `//` violates Guideline #1, but it is probably forgivable in a fairly short document such as this. Also note that if the attribute in question is *not* an ID-type attribute, this risks returning a node-set consisting of more than one attribute with that name and value.
- **Path #3:** `select="//othercast/female[1]/@id"`
  Translation: Locate the attribute named "id" of the first `female` child of an `othercast` element.
  Discussion: Simple and direct, this one produces the correct results only as long as we don't shuffle the position of the desired `female` element (for example, by adding another `female` element ahead of it in the `othercast`).
- **Path #4:** `select = "ancestor::flixinfo/cast/othercast/female/@id[. = 'EHolland']"`
  Translation: Go up the document tree to the context node's `flixinfo` ancestor, then walk down the tree through the `cast` and `othercast` levels to the `female` element whose attribute named "id" has the value "EHolland".
  Discussion: Marginally more efficient (at least in this case) than beginning the location path with `//cast`, this one goes back up the current tree of

nodes until it finds one named `flixinfo`, then works its way back down a specific leg of the tree to the desired attribute.

• **Path #5:** `select="preceding::*/@id[.='EHolland']"`

Translation: Look for an element along the preceding axis from the context node, regardless of its name, whose attribute named "id" has the value "EHolland".

Discussion: The `distriblink` element is pretty far down in the document tree, close to the end, so looking along the preceding axis is likely to limit the initial node-set very little, if at all. Basically, every node along that axis must be visited to see if it's got an `id` attribute with the desired value.

• **Path #6:** `select="preceding::*[text()='Edna Holland']/../@id"`

Translation: Look for an element along the preceding axis from the context node, regardless of its name, which has a text node whose value is "Edna Holland"; when you find it, go up to its parent and get the value of the parent's attribute whose name is "id".

Discussion: Disregards the `id` attribute value, instead seeking on the string-value of what turns out to be a `castmember` element; then it goes up to the `castmember`'s parent (`female`) element and gets its `id` attribute.

• **Path #7:** `select="preceding::*/@*[starts-with(., 'EHo')]"`

Translation: Look for an element of any name along the preceding axis from the context node, and locate any attribute of that element which begins with the three-letter string "EHo".

Discussion: Very similar to Path #5, this one says it doesn't care what the attribute's name is, as long as its value starts with the letters indicated.

• **Path #8:** `select="//*[substring-before(., 'land')='EHol'] | //@*[substring-before(., 'land')='EHol']"`

Translation: Starting at the document root, locate any element *or* any attribute whose string-value has the four-letter string "EHol" before the first occurrence in that string-value of the four-letter string "land".

Discussion: This path will grab any elements or attributes whose string-values are structured as the two predicates require.

CHAPTER 3

XSLT Stylesheet Basics

With XPath and some basic concepts nailed down, you're ready to move into the real world of XSLT stylesheet construction.

(About that word "basics" in this chapter's title: This chapter covers enough XSLT for you to accomplish, I don't know, perhaps 50% of what you'll need to do with XSLT. So there's quite a bit in here on what might be considered "intermediate" XSLT, too; much more of that will be covered in Chapter 4, "Journeyman XSLT.")

Laying the Foundation

In this brief section, I'll provide some general information to get you started using your own XSLT stylesheets, for processing FlixML or any other XML vocabulary.

Linking a stylesheet to an XML document

Officially, the way to connect a stylesheet to an XML document is with a PI in the document's prolog. (By "the document," I mean the document that you want styled/transformed, of course—not the stylesheet.) This PI, with all its pseudo-attributes, takes the following form:

```
<?xml-stylesheet type="text/xsl" href="uri"
    title="title" charset="charset"
media="media" alternate="yesorno"?>
```

For most purposes, the only pseudo-attributes you'll need to concern yourself with are `type` and `href`; the others are optional. The pseudo-attributes may appear in any order and are specified in a separate W3C standard, "Associating Style Sheets with XML Documents" (www.w3.org/TR/xml-stylesheet/).

A wrinkle in time

The "Associating Style Sheets with XML Documents" specification pre-dates the final version of the XSLT specification by several months. Probably for this reason, all the examples in the former use references to CSS, not XSLT, stylesheets. Nonetheless, rest assured that the description applies to XSLT as well.

This W3C standard says that the semantics of the PI's pseudo-attributes are the same as their counterparts in HTML 4.0. (In HTML 4.0, linking to a stylesheet is accomplished with a `link` element whose `rel` attribute has a value of either "stylesheet" or "alternate stylesheet.") By "semantics," the standard means that these pseudo-attributes *mean* the same thing as their counterparts in HTML 4.0, and can probably be expected to have the same or similar values as well. Here's a description of each.

- `type`: If the stylesheet is an XSLT stylesheet, this pseudo-attribute *must* have the value `text/xsl`. (Currently your only other choice for styling XML is CSS. If that's what you're using, the value of this pseudo-attribute must be `text/css`.[1])
- `href`: This is the URI of the stylesheet. It can be absolute (i.e., including the `http://` protocol, and so on) or relative to the location of the document itself. It also can consist entirely of a fragment identifier—that is, a pointer to a location *within* the document itself, allowing you to embed an XSLT stylesheet within your XML document. I'll cover embedding stylesheets later in this chapter;[2] for now, realize that very few, if any, applications support this feature—most, or all, handle external stylesheets only.
- `title`: The value of this pseudo-attribute is simply a descriptive name or other identifier for the stylesheet. Together with the `alternate` pseudo-

---

1.   And also, of course, you need another book!
2.   See "The id attribute" below, under the discussion of the `xsl:stylesheet` element.

attribute and possibly some others, this would (in theory) allow a user of your document to choose which of several stylesheets she'd like to use. See the short section following this one for information on alternate stylesheets.

- `charset`: A character set is a combination of two things: an abstract set of characters which can be represented, and a set of specific bit or byte patterns which can be used to represent those characters. Common values include, for example, "ascii", "us-ascii", "Shift_JIS", and so on. Other than making this pseudo-attribute available, the XSLT spec doesn't go into any detail about it, and it's not immediately obvious what use a processor might make of the information.
- `media`: Default value (according to HTML 4.0) is "screen"; other options are "tty", "tv", "projection", "handheld", "print", "braille", "aural", and "all". Multiple values can be specified in a comma-separated list, such as

  `media="handheld, print, aural"`

  The idea here is that you can specify what output devices this stylesheet is supposed to address. It doesn't automatically make your stylesheet suitable for the indicated device(s), but simply alerts software of your *claim* that it's suitable.
- `alternate`: Allowable values are "yes" or "no" (the default). This is used when you're specifying more than one stylesheet with a given document. See the "Alternate stylesheets" section below for more details.

The "Associating Style Sheets with XML Documents" spec was something of a rush job. As the "Rationale" section tacked on at the end says,

> There was an urgent requirement for a specification for style sheet linking that could be completed in time for the next release from major browser vendors. Only by choosing a simple mechanism closely based on a proven existing mechanism could the specification be completed in time to meet this requirement.

As a result of this haste, you may come to feel (as I evidently do!) that this standard turned out a bit more ragged than is customary for W3C Recommendations. My advice is to include the `type` and `href` pseudo-attributes in every `xml-stylesheet` PI; use `title`, `media`, and `alternate` if you must; and avoid `charset` altogether.

Enhancing/Mangling the media pseudo-attribute

The Apache Project's open-source "Web publishing" package, called Cocoon (including the Xalan XSLT processor), introduced some alternatives to the media pseudo-attribute values discussed above. Cocoon is preconfigured to accept values for media of "explorer," "opera," "java," "lynx," "wap," and "netscape," depending on the browser you want to target. (The "java" value, says the Cocoon User Guide, targets "any Java code using standard URL classes.")

This is either a good or a bad thing, depending on your point of view. It certainly represents, to my mind, a continuation of the "best viewed with Browser X" silliness of the old HTML Web.

I'll have more to say about Cocoon later in the book (especially in Chapter 7).

Alternate stylesheets

There's no requirement that your XML document be styled (or transformed) in just one way, using one stylesheet. You can direct a "user agent" (or UA—a software program, such as a browser, which is responsible for applying the stylesheet) to consider several stylesheets at once, and pick the one it wants, using multiple xml-stylesheet PIs.

As an example, suppose you've developed one XSLT stylesheet for transforming FlixML reviews to HTML, a second for transforming them to a form suitable for display on a portable device such as a PDA, and a third for print formatting. In any FlixML review for which you wanted to provide these alternatives, you'd include in the prologue these three PIs:

```
<?xml-stylesheet type="text/xsl" alternate="yes"
  media="handheld" title="PDA format"
  href="handheld.xsl"?>
<?xml-stylesheet type="text/xsl" alternate="yes"
  media="print" title="Formatted for print"
  href="print.xsl"?>
<?xml-stylesheet type="text/xsl" alternate="no"
  media="screen" title="Normal formatting for Web"
  href="default.xsl"?>
```

Note that only one of the three has an alternate pseudo-attribute of "no". The title pseudo-attributes, in theory, might be used to present a user with a menu-like set of choices, something like the following:

```
Select your preferred stylesheet:
  PDA format
  Formatted for print
  Normal formatting for Web
```

As I said, that's in theory. Unfortunately, I don't know of any UAs that actually give users that sort of option. At best, the UA will probably select only the one PI whose media pseudo-attribute the UA is prepared to deal with; a Palm OS-based device, for example, might recognize only a stylesheet associated with the handheld media.

If you need to offer multiple stylesheets to your users, a better cross-platform solution, at least for now, is probably to present the menu yourself, using server-side prompting or some kind of client-side Dynamic HTML/JavaScript mechanism to apply the selected stylesheet in a form *other* than through a PI. A simple example of some of the things you need to consider when doing this is given in the "How Do I...?" exercise that appears at the end of Chapter 4.

Role of the processor

I discussed the XSLT processor (sometimes called the XSLT engine) briefly in Chapter 2. Here are some more details about what the processor does and how it does it.

An XSLT processor is an application program that reads an XML source tree and an XSLT stylesheet to be applied to that source tree, producing a result tree according to the templates instantiated by the stylesheet.

The general flow of the work a processor performs might be described as follows:

- Parse the stylesheet for well-formedness. If any unrecoverable errors, report them and stop processing.
- Parse the source document into an in-memory tree-like structure—the source tree. If any unrecoverable errors, report them and stop processing.
- If no unrecoverable errors, for every node in the source tree:
  Check the stylesheet to see if there are any matching template rules for this node.
  If more than one template rule matches the node, resolve the conflict as described later in this chapter.
  If only one template rule matches the node, instantiate the corresponding template in the result tree.

If no template rule matches the node, use whichever built-in template rule applies. (I'll cover the built-in template rules shortly.)

Note that an XSLT processor is not the same thing as a "parser" (i.e., an XML processor). However, it does need to *include* or *use* a parser; before the transformation itself happens, the first thing the processor needs to do is confirm that both the source tree and the stylesheet itself are at least well-formed—which is indeed within the scope of things that a parser does.

No "valid" stylesheets

Occasionally this question comes up on mailing lists: "How do I validate my XSLT stylesheet?"

The answer is that you can't (or almost never can); the best you can do is establish that it's well-formed. The reason you can't readily validate most XSLT stylesheets is that they usually mix elements from more than one XML namespace, which effectively makes validation impossible. For example, an XSLT template rule might look something like this:

```
<xsl:template match="something">
  <h1>A Level-1 Heading</h1>
</xsl:template>
```

This template rule contains an element from the XSLT namespace (`xsl:template`) and one from the (X)HTML namespace (`h1`). Under neither of those two namespaces' sets of rules could an `h1` element be considered a *valid* child of an `xsl:template` element. Furthermore, there's no conceivable DTD (which, after all, would be required for validation) that could be used for validating *all possible* result-tree elements that might show up in an XSLT stylesheet. All we can say with certainty is that this template rule and others like it are well-formed.

The XML Schema standard, recently finalized as a W3C Recommendation (in May 2001), may make it possible to validate an XML document comprising mixed vocabularies—including, of course, an XSLT stylesheet. (Naturally, this depends on the availability of XML processors to do this kind of validation, which are a little sparse on the ground at the moment.) And of course, "smart" XSLT editors and other authoring tools may (when and if they appear in force) forbid the construction of "invalid" XSLT stylesheets in practice.

Chapter 7 takes a look at some specific XSLT processors. For now, all I want to describe is how various XSLT processors in widespread use might be considered to fall into one or more of the quadrants depicted in Figure 3–1.

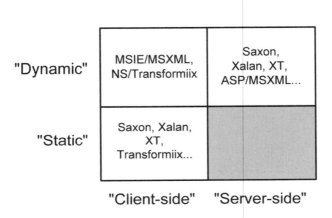

Figure 3-1   Some common XSLT processors, by category. The "Static/Server-side" category is grayed out because Web applications that do their work on a server don't do so in a "static" fashion (at least in the sense described in the text).

First, to dispense right away with a central misconception about XSLT: It is *not* meant solely—or even mostly—for use in transforming to (X)HTML on the Web. So the client-side-to-server-side dimension needs to be understood in terms of general client-server terminology, not necessarily as it's employed on the Web. That is, *client-side* means that the processing is performed by the consumer or receiver of the data, which might be a browser or some entirely different application. *Server-side*, on the other hand, means that the processing is performed by the producer or transmitter of the data—which, again, might be a Web server or something like a database application.

All of that said, the Web *does* afford a commonly understood practical application of the client-server dimension, and Figure 3–1 is geared primarily to representing XSLT processors in use on the Web.

The terms "static" and "dynamic," as I'm using them here, don't have any official standing, so take this with a grain of salt. They just seem like the best words to describe the different approaches taken by different processors.

By *static*, I mean something similar to the old-fashioned term *batch* to describe a certain kind of, well, "dumb" processing. Schematically, this might be represented by something like Figure 3–2.

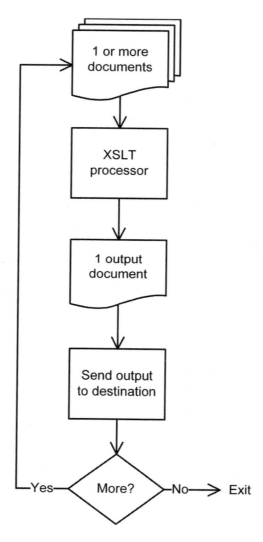

Figure 3-2 General approach taken by a static XSLT processor. Note that the first step generally involves only a single document for a given pass through the process, although it could be (as shown here) a "stack" of documents.

The general idea of a processor using the static model is that you feed the processor a document (or two documents, or three, etc.), often using a command-line interface rather than some kind of graphical user interface (GUI).

The processor takes the inputs, parses them, reads the stylesheet, and applies the latter's rules to transform the inputs into a single output. This single output is sent to some destination, such as a file on the host operating system. If there's another transformation still to be performed, the process begins again and repeats until all transformations are completed.

What you end up with as the result of this kind of static processing is a "stack" of one or more outputs (one per transformation). These outputs might be HTML documents that can be read by any Web browser and can—just like HTML documents created from scratch—include all kinds of DHTML and Java-Script effects, animated images, forms, and so on. What makes them static is that the outputs are in a "frozen" form. Open one of them today at 4:00 p.m. and they'll look the same way they will tomorrow at 7:00 a.m.[3]

Dynamic XSLT processing, on the other hand, generates an output on the fly when requested by some application (such as a Web browser). Schematically, this resembles Figure 3–3.

The flow depicted in Figure 3–3 seems simpler than that of Figure 3–2, because it's shorter and doesn't require the iterative "process until no more transformations required" loop. Actually, however, a dynamic processor will probably be a little more complex program than a static one. That's because a dynamic processor typically needs to both perform its transformations on the fly *and* present the results to the user in some meaningful way. A static processor, by contrast, needs only to perform the transformations (with the exception that it still needs to report any errors encountered and recover from them, ignore them, or stop processing, depending on the tool and how it's configured).

Referring back to Figure 3–1—the "processors by quadrant" figure—note that most processors could appear in more than one quadrant. These tend to be Java-based applications which can run from the command line, across various platforms, and/or within a server-based environment (e.g., as servlets). The one called Saxon, for instance, can be run as a static/client-side program or as a dynamic/server-side one.

Also note that there were only two processors listed in the dynamic client-side quadrant. Both of the processors in question—MSXML and Transformiix—are dependent on the presence of a browser (Microsoft Internet Explorer [MSIE] and Netscape 6 [NS], respectively) to provide their client-side behavior,

---

3.   Unless, as probably should go without saying, another transformation is done in the meantime.

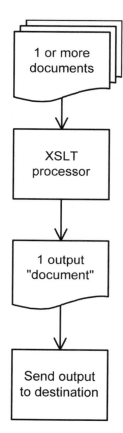

Figure 3-3   General approach taken by a dynamic XSLT processor. This is a truncated form of the processing flow represented by Figure 3–2's static processor; what's missing, basically, is the loop back to process more inputs. A number of things are gained, too—see the text for a description of these.

showing the result of a transformation within a browser's window. (As an aside, also note that the MSXML processor shows up in *only* the two dynamic quadrants.) These tools, therefore, are limited by a requirement that a particular browser be present on a user's machine. On the other hand, because both processors are fully compliant with the XSLT spec (with minor exceptions), they provide excellent development and testing facilities...as long as you're transforming to (X)HTML!

> ### MSXML as a general-purpose XSLT processor
>
> The Microsoft MSXML processor is encapsulated in a DLL which performs multiple XML-related functions—XML parsing, XSLT processing, and (in the newest version 4.0) XML Schema processing. Like any DLL, its features may be invoked by any Windows-based program which needs access to them.
>
> Thus, while MSXML is "built into" MSIE, it can also be "built into" programs written in Visual Basic, Visual FoxPro, Visual C++, and so on, whenever there's a need for those features. This makes a broad range of XML services (such as XML importing and exporting) available to such programs.

Processors and the `xml-stylesheet` PI

I opened the previous section of this chapter with the sentence, "Officially, the way to connect a stylesheet to an XML document is with a PI in the document's prolog."

All these processors provide you with some ability to ignore that PI, though, in favor of transforming the source document according to some other stylesheet's rules. For those which can be run in "static mode," this is generally accomplished with command-line switches. For instance, the XT processor uses a command line structured like this:

```
xt sourcedoc stylesheet resultdoc
```

while Saxon's is as follows:

```
saxon -o resultdoc sourcedoc stylesheet
```

For the dynamic and server-side XSLT processors, the association with a stylesheet can be accomplished through script or programming language means. We'll see examples of this later in *Just XSL*.

So, which should you use?

This is a tough question to answer without kind of bobbing and weaving, because the answer must be hedged all around with the phrase, "It depends…." Nonetheless, here are some guidelines to selecting an XSLT processor.

Pick by quadrant   Server-side, static, dynamic…? You need to consider your ultimate processing environment.

Platform-bound vs. platform-independent   This will determine—to some extent—whether you'll be choosing a Java-based processor (which can run in many different environments) or a strictly Microsoft solution.

Standards compliance and stability   The processors whose names appeared in Figure 3–1 are all, to a greater or lesser extent, standards-compliant. There are some exceptions, though. For instance, XT was developed by the editor of the XPath and XSLT specifications, which would seem to make it a likely candidate for compliance; however, XT's final version was released a few weeks before the final version of the spec itself, with the result that it lacks a couple of last-minute features.

Stability is a little trickier to judge. Generally you can equate it with longevity: The longer a product has been around, the more likely it is either to be stable or at least to have a user community familiar with its charming (or otherwise) quirks. Of the processors mentioned in Figure 3–1, Transformiix is probably (as of this writing, in early 2001) the least mature product; XT, Saxon, and Xalan have been around (and standards-compliant) the longest.

Why pick just one?   Finally, you know, it's really not inappropriate to pick one processor for one purpose and another for a completely different one. For instance, if you're transforming from XML to (X)HTML, it's hard to beat the MSIE/MSXML combination as a development platform...even if the ultimate processing is not going to occur in a Microsoft environment. Given the knowledge that XT is quite fast, maybe you'd rather be running that as a production system (as long as you don't need those fallen-through-the-last-minute-cracks features). And so on.

The no-choice choice

Of course, you may not really have a choice of XSLT processor at all. Your employer or customer may have made the choice for you. Or you may have chosen some general-purpose XML authoring/document-management tool that includes a particular processor. Note that this argues in favor of learning XSLT in its own right, rather than simply as "something the processor does."

What I'll be using

This chapter and the next are devoted almost entirely to general principles of transforming an XML source tree into a result tree using XSLT. *What kind of result tree* really doesn't matter much for learning these general principles. I'll be transforming from XML to XHTML for most (but not all) of the examples here and will therefore be using the MSIE/MSXML combination. Aside from its ease as a development tool for such transformations, it's also easier for me to do screen shots demonstrating one effect or another.

However, on occasion I'll need to show you a result tree (or a portion thereof). MSIE/MSXML isn't a good tool for that purpose, because the result tree, such as it is, is sent directly to the browser—there's no result tree to grab.[4]

For these occasions, I'll be using the popular Saxon, developed by Michael Kay.

XSLT Stylesheet Structure

An XSLT stylesheet is basically a single "wrapper" element, xsl:stylesheet, containing one, two, a dozen, several hundred, or however many other elements are necessary to perform all required transformations from source to result tree. The elements appearing as children of the xsl:stylesheet element are called *top-level elements,* all of which—like xsl:stylesheet itself—come from the XSLT namespace. Many of them contain other elements from the XSLT namespace as well (these are called *instructions*), and they may also contain elements and other markup in the result tree's namespace.

In this section, I'll give you an overview of the kinds of work performed by the basic top-level elements and instructions. (Details will follow, in subsequent sections of this chapter and in subsequent chapters.)

First, though, I'm going to revisit the xsl:stylesheet element itself. I first introduced this in Chapter 2, but at that time provided you only with elementary information about it.

---

4. Microsoft does make available at their Web site a number of utilities providing such features as displaying the transformation's result tree, validating an XML document, and so on. Even if not really suitable for heavy-duty production use in saving result trees to separate documents, these utilities demonstrate that MSXML, as it runs in MSIE, is just a fraction of the MSXML features it's *possible* to use.

The `xsl:stylesheet` element (revisited)

When I covered `xsl:stylesheet` before, I concentrated on helping you get the namespace declarations right. Of course, namespace declarations can be included in any XML (or XSLT) element; knowing how to code them isn't by any means an XSLT-specific skill. But the `xsl:stylesheet` element takes several attributes all its own, according to the following general syntax:

```
<xsl:stylesheet version="number"
  id="id"
  extension-element-prefixes="tokens"
  exclude-result-prefixes="tokens" >
```

The `version` attribute

The `version` attribute (which must be present) declares which version of the XSLT specification this stylesheet conforms to. As of mid-2001, the only widely supported value for this attribute is "1.0". However, work has begun on Version 2.0 of the XSLT spec, so you may find a few processors accepting "2.0" as a value, too. (The work on Version 2.0 is still in very rough form; don't get too far ahead of yourself!)

What might be the significance to a processor of knowing which version of the XSLT spec a given stylesheet conforms to? Right: It tells the processor what level of features and functionality it might need to handle. A Version 2.0–aware processor, for example, might be able to accept anything compatible with Version 1.0 or 2.0, whereas a Version 1.0–aware processor would be able to process just that one feature set.

(XSLT comes with a set of built-in mechanisms for determining within a stylesheet if a particular feature is known to the current processor and, if not, "falling back" to some alternative processing. I'll discuss this fallback feature, as well as the related "forwards-compatible processing" feature, in Chapter 6, Advanced XSLT.)

The `id` attribute

The `id` attribute (which is optional) assigns an identifier to the `xsl:stylesheet` element. This identifier serves one purpose only: It allows you to *embed* a stylesheet within the document it is meant to transform.

Consider a FlixML document within which we wanted to embed a stylesheet, rather than linking to an external one. To do so, we'd make the `href` pseudo-attribute of the `xml-stylesheet` PI a relative one, whose value is preceded by the "pound sign" (# character) commonly used in URIs to denote a fragment identifier. What follows the # is the value of the `xsl:stylesheet` element's `id` attribute. So we'd have something like this:

```
<?xml-stylesheet type="text/xsl" href="#innerstyle" ?>
<flixinfo>
  <xsl:stylesheet version="1.0" id="innerstyle">
  ...
  </xsl:stylesheet>
</flixinfo>
```

See the way the PI's `href` pseudo-attribute maps to the `xsl:stylesheet` element's `id` attribute?

Now, don't leap from this brief description of "embedded stylesheets" to conclude that this is a particularly rewarding arena to romp around in. In fact, software supporting this feature is pretty thin on the ground, as the saying goes. And what software does support it, does so inconsistently.

Even when it's supported, it's not *used*

Interestingly, the current version of Saxon dropped support for embedded stylesheets, even though earlier versions supported it. The program's author, Michael Kay, has reported that it's quite difficult to implement properly, so he dropped it as an experiment to see how many complaints he got.

Answer: none.

If Saxon was little-used, this wouldn't be a definitive bit of data; under the circumstances, though—Saxon is *very* popular—I think it says a lot.

So what's the point of using embedded stylesheets?

Mostly, this is just a throwback to a similar (but much more widely supported) mechanism in HTML documents, allowing the embedding of CSS style rules in a `style` element. There are some nominal advantages to them; for example, if the stylesheet and document are served in a single bundle, there may be a performance advantage.

The biggest drawback to embedding stylesheets (aside from the spotty software support) is that it overturns the chief advantages of using stylesheets in the first place: separation of content from presentation, and "shareability" of style

and other presentation characteristics (which can be accomplished only by putting stylesheets into separate documents).

So here's the bottom line: Know about the embedded-stylesheet feature.
Heck, experiment with it if you'd like. Just don't *count* on it.

A non-ID-type attribute named "id"

By the way, although the attribute described here is *named* "id," the
odds of its actually being an ID-type attribute are slim to none. That's
because—as I mentioned both in Chapter 2 and earlier in this chapter—a document mixing elements from the XSLT namespace with
those from another will almost certainly not be validatable according
to a DTD's rules, and a DTD is the only resource that can declare an
ID-type attribute.

The `extension-element-prefixes` attribute

Prefixes. What associations does that word summon forth in your head?

Right: *namespace* prefixes. The optional `extension-element-prefixes`
attribute designates the prefixes to be used for *extension elements* which may
appear somewhere within the scope of the XSLT element to which this attribute
applies.

Extension elements are an XSLT feature that enables vendors to *legally* add
to the list of legitimate elements in a stylesheet. This practice has been controversial in the past, both with earlier versions of XSLT and with other W3C standards. For instance, browser vendors have been notorious for inventing quote-
unquote "HTML" elements supported only by their own browser. For a vendor
to do so with XSLT, they must provide to users of those elements a namespace
URI to be associated (via a prefix) with the elements' names.

The XT processor, for instance, allows use of a special `xt:document` element in a stylesheet. (This element is used for producing multiple result trees
from a single transformation.) If you are using the XT processor and use this or
any other XT-provided extension element in a stylesheet, you could add the following attributes to your `xsl:stylesheet` element:

```
extension-element-prefixes="xt"
xmlns:xt="http://www.jclark.com/xt"
```

(Don't forget to include the namespace declaration as well. Otherwise, your XSLT processor will squawk—and rightfully so—that you're using an unknown namespace prefix.)

If you're using more than one extension element prefix in a stylesheet, the attribute's value is a whitespace-delimited list of those prefixes. For instance (namespace declarations omitted here),

```
extension-element-prefixes="xt saxon"
```

By the way, this latter case may seem a bit... well, *odd* in at least one respect: When[5] would you ever use more than one XSLT processor for your stylesheet? You wouldn't—not at the same time. But you or your users might use more than one processor over the course of a stylesheet's lifetime, and you may want to make the stylesheet flexible enough to work in a number of these environments. So, buried within the stylesheet would be a conditional statement: If XT is in use, use the `xt:document` element; if Saxon is in use, use the `saxon:document` element; and so on.

(Conditional processing is covered in Chapter 4. Testing for the features available at the time of the transformation is covered in Chapter 6, Advanced XSLT.)

You might be wondering why you need a special attribute for this purpose at all. Doesn't simply declaring the non-XSLT namespace solve the problem?

It solves one problem, of course, which is to make the specified prefix available for use in the stylesheet. The specific problem addressed by this attribute is the default behavior of *any* compliant XSLT processor:

- For all elements whose names are prefixed with "xsl:" (or whatever prefix is associated with the XSLT namespace), process those elements according to the rules of the appropriate version of the XSLT spec.
- Put all other elements into the result tree.

The `extension-elements-prefix` attribute adds a third (and optional) kind of processor behavior: Treat any elements whose names are prefixed as follows in a way which *this specific processor* knows about. That is, such elements extend the functionality of XSLT itself (hence the name).

---

5.   To say nothing of *how*.

Using with other elements

You can use this attribute with (a) the xsl:stylesheet element (as discussed in this section), (b) result-tree elements, or (c) extension elements themselves. In cases (b) and (c), though, you must prefix the attribute name itself with xsl:, as in

```
<p xsl:extension-element-prefixes="abc">
  <abc:fancynewelement/>...</p>
```

The exclude-result-prefixes attribute

Prefixes again. This time, though—obviously—we're talking about excluding them from the result tree. More precisely, we're going to exclude not the prefixes themselves, but the namespaces associated with them.

The situation in which the optional exclude-result-prefixes attribute addresses is not one you'll need to be overly concerned with for simple, straightforward transformations, such as XML-to-HTML. It *can* be a critical situation if you're transforming from one XML vocabulary to another, depending on how smart the downstream application is about namespaces and what, exactly, is in your result tree. For example, when transforming a schema to a different version of the same or an equivalent schema, two companies may need to use different element names, or add more attributes, in their two variants of what is, in effect, the same document type.

Once again, the problem occasionally arises because of XSLT processors' default behavior. In this case, the sometimes-problematic behavior is to copy to the result-tree elements all namespace nodes in effect for those elements in the stylesheet. (An exception to this general rule is any namespace node that has something to do with processing the stylesheet itself—for example, those associated with the xsl: prefix and any prefixes listed in the value of the extension-element-prefixes attribute.)

To illustrate, consider a hypothetical stylesheet. The details of this stylesheet don't matter;[6] the important thing about it is its xsl:stylesheet element, whose start tag looks like this:

```
<xsl:stylesheet version="1.0"
  xmlns:xsl="http://www.w3.org/1999/XSL/Transform"
```

---

6.   And at this point, they most likely wouldn't make much sense to you anyway.

```
xmlns:abc="http://www.foo.com"
xmlns:flixml="http://www.flixml.org/flixml">
```

An XSLT processor will know that the namespace node associated with the xsl: prefix is not to be copied to the result tree. But the processor doesn't know what to do with the namespace nodes for elements (and possibly attributes) whose names begin with the abc: and flixml: prefixes. Will they be meaningful, *useful* in any way, to a downstream application? The processor doesn't know. So, to be on the safe side, it will copy those namespace nodes—the declarations—to the result tree.

Now, chances are this won't be a practical problem. But it may confuse you later, and it may confuse some other reader of your result tree, to find unnecessary namespace declarations in the transformed results. If you want to prevent certain namespace declarations in the stylesheet from being copied to the result tree, use the exclude-result-prefixes attribute. For example,

```
<xsl:stylesheet version="1.0"
  xmlns:xsl="http://www.w3.org/1999/XSL/Transform"
  xmlns:abc="http://www.foo.com"
  xmlns:flixml:"http://www.flixml.org/flixml"
  exclude-namespace-prefixes="abc flixml">
```

excludes both the abc: and flixml: namespace declarations from the result tree.

Don't confuse the downstream application, either!

This is all well and good for cleaning up your result tree so that it includes *only* the namespaces necessary for later processing.

However, it'd generally be a mistake to make a habit of excluding *all* namespace declarations from the result. In the above case, if your result tree actually includes elements (or attributes) whose names are prefixed abc: or flixml:, and if the downstream application is namespace-aware, it will probably complain about the undeclared prefixes. Moral: Don't be too obsessive about cleaning up "unwanted" namespaces.

By the way, as with the extension-element-prefixes attribute, you can put the exclude-result-prefixes attribute on any element in your stylesheet, not just xsl:stylesheet. If you do so, remember to prefix the attribute name with whatever prefix is associated with the XSLT namespace, for example, xsl:exclude-result-prefixes.

Note that you can exclude from the result tree the *default* namespace, as well as any tied to a particular prefix. For instance, assume that the above `xsl:stylesheet` element looked like the following, instead:

```
<xsl:stylesheet version="1.0"
  xmlns:xsl="http://www.w3.org/1999/XSL/Transform"
  xmlns="http://www.foo.com"
  xmlns:flixml:"http://www.flixml.org/flixml"
  exclude-namespace-prefixes="flixml">
```

Here, the simple `xmlns` attribute asserts that *unprefixed* element names in the result tree are to be associated with the "http://www.foo.com" namespace. To keep this namespace from being copied to the result tree, use the keyword `#default` in the list of excluded prefixes; for example,

```
exclude-namespace-prefixes="#default flixml"
```

Categories of top-level elements

An `xsl:stylesheet` element can have as children any number of the 12 top-level elements which might be grouped into the 7 categories outlined in Table 3–1. These aren't "official" categories, just ones I've created for purposes of discussing them in some kind of organized fashion.

(Note that the `xsl:variable` and `xsl:param` elements may be used either as top-level elements or as instructions, with different effects and for different purposes. Also, although the XSLT standard doesn't classify the `xsl:import` as a top-level element, it's hard to imagine why not—this element can indeed appear only as a child of `xsl:stylesheet`.)

The remainder of this chapter will consider the first category only (as well as much of what can appear *within* the one element in that category); the remaining six categories will be discussed in later chapters.

Table 3-1   Top-level XSLT elements, by category

Description	Top-level element(s)
instantiating result-tree content	`xsl:template`
declaring content for (re)use within a stylesheet (see Chapter 4)	`xsl:variable`, `xsl:param`, `xsl:attribute-set`
controlling the form or type of the result tree (see Chapter 4)	`xsl:output`, `xsl:strip-space`, `xsl:preserve-space`

Table 3-1 Top-level XSLT elements, by category (continued)

Description	Top-level element(s)
mapping a namespace in the stylesheet to a different one in the result (see Chapter 4)	`xsl:namespace-alias`
declaring number formats for use with `format-number()` function (see Chapter 5)	`xsl:decimal-format`
keying content for easy retrieval and grouping (see Chapter 5)	`xsl:key`
modularizing stylesheets for reuse (see Chapter 6)	`xsl:import, xsl:include`

Instructions

As the name implies, XSLT elements classified as *instructions* provide some kind of specific direction to the XSLT processor; these elements appear as children of specific top-level elements or other instructions.

Table 3–2 lists the elements that can appear as instructions in a stylesheet. See the bulleted list following the table for comments and caveats that apply to understanding and using it.

Table 3-2 XSLT Instruction Elements

Name	Allowable children	Used in template and…
INSTANTIATING RESULT-TREE CONTENT: TEMPLATES 101		
`xsl:value-of`	(empty)	
"LOOPING"		
`xsl:apply-templates`	`xsl:sort, xsl:with-param`	
`xsl:for-each`	`xsl:sort, template`	
`xsl:apply-imports`	(empty)	

Table 3-2   XSLT Instruction Elements (continued)

Name	Allowable children	Used in template and...
CONDITIONAL PROCESSING		
`xsl:if`	template	
`xsl:choose`	`xsl:when`, `xsl:otherwise`	
`xsl:when`	template	`xsl:choose`
`xsl:otherwise`	template	`xsl:choose`
INSTANTIATING EXPLICIT NODE TYPES		
`xsl:element`	template	
`xsl:attribute`	template	`xsl:attribute-set`
`xsl:comment`	template	
`xsl:processing-instruction`	template	
`xsl:text`	(text)	
REUSING STYLESHEET CONTENT		
`xsl:variable`	template	
`xsl:param`	template	
`xsl:call-template`	`xsl:with-param`	
`xsl:with-param`	template	`xsl:call-template`
`xsl:attribute-set`	`xsl:attribute`	
SORTING CONTENT		
`xsl:sort`	(empty)	`xsl:apply-templates`, `xsl:for-each`

Table 3-2   XSLT Instruction Elements (continued)

Name	Allowable children	Used in template and...
COPYING CONTENT		
xsl:copy	template	
xsl:copy-of	(empty)	
(COVERED IN LATER CHAPTERS)		
xsl:number	(empty)	
xsl:fallback	template	
xsl:message	template	

Here's what to make of Table 3–2:

- The first column is a simple list of the instruction-type element names.
- Column 2 shows what the element may contain. In general, this may be other instructions' names, the label "(empty)," or the label "template." I'm using "template" in this table in the same way the XSLT spec does when describing an element's contents: "any mixture of text nodes, [result-tree] elements, extension elements, and XSLT elements from the instruction category." It's important to recognize, in this clot of verbiage, the significance of the phrase "any mixture": In some cases, only certain combinations are allowed; and for most elements whose contents are listed as "template" the contents may also be empty. One instruction, xsl:text, may contain only text.
- The third column lists which specific instruction-type element(s) may or must contain the element listed in this row. Note that all instruction-type elements can also show up, at one level or another, within a template (as defined under the preceding bullet).
- Rows in the table are grouped according to the section in this chapter, or later ones, in which those instructions are covered.

The instruction-type elements will be covered throughout this chapter, Chapter 4 (Journeyman XSLT), Chapter 5 (XSLT Functions), and Chapter 6 (Advanced XSLT), in the context of appropriate top-level elements or in sections of their own.

Instantiating Result-Tree Content: Templates 101

Just about the simplest and most common activity you'll have a given XSLT stylesheet engaged in is the creation of a result tree. Depending on your needs, this can also turn out to be the most complex and bizarrely unique task at hand. At whichever extreme you happen to be working, or anywhere in between, creating a result tree occurs when you fill in a *template*, especially within the scope of an `xsl:template` element.

This section of the chapter is devoted entirely to discussing the `xsl:template` element and its contents. Before diving into that important discussion, however, it'll be helpful to have another sample FlixML document to discuss.

B Alert!

Caged Heat (1974, New World Pictures

Take an Oscar-winning director of movies like *Philadelphia* and *Silence of the Lambs;* a cinematographer on such diverse projects as *Something Wild* and *The Sixth Sense;* a member of the seminal late '60s to early '70s rock band the Velvet Underground and producer of Siouxsie and the Banshees; and a handful of B-movie queens— take them all back 25 or 30 years and put them at legendary B-film producer Roger Corman's New World studio. Tell them to come up with a women-in-prison scenario that fits the studio's limited budget of $165,000.

What they—Jonathan Demme, Tak Fujimoto, and John Cale (plus all those B queens)—come up with is *Caged Heat.*

I won't try to kid you. *Caged Heat* is a cheaply made movie, with plenty of what were (even in the 1970s) standard-issue "jailhouse ladies" touches. But it's also graced with some moments of— for lack of a better term—art, and the story line sidesteps some of the genre's more outrageous anti-feminist trappings.

It's the story, mostly, of one Jacqueline "Jackie" Wilson (played by Erica Gavin), who's been arrested and jailed on trumped-up charges (although she wasn't completely innocent, either) in a women's prison of uncertain location. This prison has been the-center of a number of experiments in such progressive rehabilita-tive treatments as electroshock therapy, directed by the bizarre (and, needless to add, male) prison doctor. The wheelchair-bound woman warden is not an evil person, but she is greatly misguided, with the result that the inmates are subjected to various indignities and outright dangers.

Jackie and a couple of friends manage to escape. After one of the weirdest bank heists in film history (involving the women bank robbers' robbing not the bank per se, but a gang of *male* bank robbers who showed up at the same time), the women return to the prison to help the women still behind bars escape. In the ensuing gun battle, both the misguided warden and the wicked doctor are shot and killed.

Caged Heat was apparently the last film made by Erica Gavin (who'd appeared earlier in the justifiably much-reviled *Beyond the Valley of the Dolls*). The warden was played by Barbara Steele, in a role which Demme wrote just for her; Steele had appeared in quite a number of Italian schlock-horror films in the 1960s, but also was a featured player in Fellini's (justifiably revered) "$8\frac{1}{2}$."

Caged Heat's FlixML review

```
<?xml version="1.0"?>
<?xml-stylesheet type="text/xsl"
  href="flixml.xsl"?>
<!DOCTYPE flixinfo SYSTEM
  "http://www.flixml.org/flixml/flixml_03.dtd">
<flixinfo author="John E. Simpson" copyright="2001"
  xml:lang="EN"
  xmlns:xlink="http://www.w3.org/1999/xlink/namespace/">
  <title role="main">Caged Heat</title>
  <title role="alt">Caged Females</title>
  <title role="alt">Renegade Girls</title>
  <genre>
    <primarygenre>Action</primarygenre>
    <othergenre>Prison</othergenre>
    <othergenre>Woman in Jeopardy</othergenre>
  </genre>
  <releaseyear role="initial">1974</releaseyear>
  <language>English</language>
```

```
<studio>New World Pictures</studio>
<cast id="castID">
<leadcast>
    <female id="EGavin">
      <castmember>Erica Gavin</castmember>
      <role>Jacqueline Wilson</role>
    </female>
    <female id="JBrown">
      <castmember>Juanita Brown</castmember>
      <role>Maggie</role>
    </female>
    <female id="BSteele">
      <castmember>Barbara Steele</castmember>
      <role>Superintendent (Warden) McQueen</role>
    </female>
    <female id="RCollins">
      <castmember>Roberta Collins</castmember>
      <role>Belle Tyson</role>
    </female>
    <female id="EReid">
      <castmember>Ella Reid</castmember>
      <role>Pandora</role>
    </female>
    <female id="CSmith">
      <castmember>Cheryl "Rainbeaux" Smith (inspiration for
      "Boopsie"?)</castmember>
      <role>Lavelle</role>
    </female>
  </leadcast>
  <othercast>
    <male id="">
      <castmember></castmember>
      <role></role>
    </male>
    <female id="">
      <castmember></castmember>
      <role></role>
    </female>
  </othercast>
</cast>
<crew id="crewID">
  <director>Jonathan Demme</director>
  <screenwriter>Jonathan Demme</screenwriter>
  <cinematog>Tak Fujimoto</cinematog>
  <sound>Alex Vanderkar</sound>
  <editor>Johanna Demetrakas</editor>
```

```
    <editor>Michal Goldman</editor>
    <editor>Carolyn Hicks</editor>
    <score>John Cale</score>
    <speceffects>Charles Spurgeon</speceffects>
    <proddesigner>Eric Thiermann</proddesigner>
    <makeup>Rhavon</makeup>
    <costumer>Deborah Paul ("Wardrobe Assistant")</costumer>
  </crew>
  <plotsummary id="plotID">It's the story, mostly, of one
Jacqueline (Jackie) Wilson, arrested and jailed on trumped-up
charges (although she wasn't completely innocent, either) in a
women's prison of uncertain location. This prison has been the
center of a number of experiments in such progressive
rehabilitative treatments as electroshock therapy, directed by the
bizarre (and, needless to add, male) prison doctor. The wheelchair-
bound woman warden is not an evil person, but greatly misguided,
with the result that the inmates are subjected to various
indignities and outright dangers.<parabreak/>Jackie and a couple of
friends manage to escape. After one of the weirdest bank heists in
film history (involving the women bank robbers' robbing not the
bank per se, but a gang of male bank robbers who showed up at the
same time), the women return to the prison to help the women still
behind bars escape. In the ensuing gun battle, both the misguided
warden and the wicked doctor are shot and killed.
  </plotsummary>
    <reviews id="revwID">
      <flixmlreview>
        <goodreview>
          <reviewtext>Caged Heat is a cheaply-made movie, with plenty
of what were (even in the 1970s) standard-issue "jailhouse ladies"
touches. But it's also graced with some moments of -- for lack of a
better term -- art, and the story line sidesteps some of the
genre's more outrageous anti-feminist trappings.</reviewtext>
        </goodreview>
      </flixmlreview>
      <otherreview>
        <goodreview>
          <reviewlink
xlink:href="http://www.prisonflicks.com/Cagedh.htm">Prison Flicks</
reviewlink>
        </goodreview>
        <goodreview>
          <reviewlink
xlink:href="http://www.awcm.com/caps2/cap00120.htm">Amazing World
of Cult Movies (AWCM)</reviewlink>
        </goodreview>
```

```
    <badreview>
      <reviewlink
xlink:href="http://www.filmcritic.com/misc/emporium.nsf/
2a460f93626cd4678625624c007f2b46/
70d37148256673c4882567c600195dd0?OpenDocument">filmcritic.com
(Christopher Null)</reviewlink>
      </badreview>
    </otherreview>
  </reviews>
  <distributors id="distribID">
    <distributor>
      <distribname>Reel.com</distribname>
      <distribextlink>
        <distriblink
        xlink:href="http://www.reel.com/movie.asp?MID=3693"/>
      </distribextlink>
    </distributor>
    <distributor>
      <distribname>Amazon.com</distribname>
      <distribextlink>
        <distriblink
xlink:href="http://www.amazon.com/exec/obidos/ASIN/6304564414"/>
      </distribextlink>
    </distributor>
    <distributor>
      <distribname>Yahoo! Video Shopping</distribname>
      <distribextlink>
        <distriblink
xlink:href="http://shopping.yahoo.com shop?d=v&amp;cf=product&amp;
hf2k=1&amp;clink=&amp;id=1800202978"/>
      </distribextlink>
    </distributor>
  </distributors>
  <dialog></dialog>
  <remarks>Caged Heat was apparently the last film made by Erica
Gavin (who'd appeared earlier in the justifiably much-reviled
Beyond the Valley of the Dolls). The warden was played by Barbara
Steele, in a role which Demme wrote just for her; Steele appeared
in quite a number of Italian schlock-horror films in the 1960s, but
also was a featured player in Fellini's (justifiably revered) 8-1/
2.</remarks>
  <mpaarating id="rateID">R</mpaarating>
  <bees b-ness="&BEE4URL;"/>
</flixinfo>
```

> ### "Pretty-printed" XML source documents
>
> The foregoing FlixML *Caged Heat* review, like nearly all the XML source in this book, uses whitespace—particularly newlines and tab characters—to make the document structure more obvious and easily understood. However, this can introduce some surprises into the results of your XSLT transformations (such as newlines or tabs showing up in the result when you don't really want them there). For the most part, the XSLT code in *Just XSL* assumes that extraneous whitespace has already been stripped from the source document, so I don't have to constantly include verbiage like "After removing all white space...."
>
> More detailed coverage of XSLT's whitespace issues appears in Chapter 4.

Locating source-tree "triggers" with `xsl:template`

The purpose of the `xsl:template` top-level element is mainly to locate portions of the source tree that will trigger some effect in the result tree. Its general syntax is

```
<xsl:template match="pattern"
  name="templatename" priority="number"
  mode="mode">
  ...template...
</xsl:template>
```

Here are descriptions of the four attributes:

- `match`: This is required, unless there's a `name` attribute. Its value is an XPath location path to content in the source tree. This may not be a variable. (Variables are discussed in Chapter 4, in the section titled "Reusing Stylesheet Content.")
- `name`: This is optional. If present, no `match` attribute may be present as well. Its value is an XML *name* (i.e., a string of letters, digits, underscores, and/or periods, no embedded whitespace or other special characters, starting with a letter or underscore). The purpose of this attribute is to give the template a name, which enables it to be reused in various places throughout the stylesheet. (See "Reusing Stylesheet Content" in Chapter 4.)

- priority: This is optional. Its value is a number that designates a priority (higher numbers are higher priorities), used in resolving conflicts if a given chunk of content is located by more than one xsl:template element's match attribute. The value can be a positive or negative number. See "Conflict resolution," below, for more information.
- mode: optional. Its value is an XML name, whose purpose is to allow a given match pattern to be applied for explicitly different occasions. See the section titled "Template modes" for more information.

By far the most common form of the xsl:template element is one with just a match attribute. If there is a match attribute (regardless of the presence of other attributes), the xsl:template and its contents are referred to collectively as a *template rule*; if there is a name attribute instead, the xsl:template and its contents are referred to collectively as a *named template*.

Whether it's a template rule or a named template, the actual content of the xsl:template element is known simply as a *template*. The template provides a blueprint of sorts for what the result tree is supposed to look like at that point. When something in the source tree is located by the match pattern (or when the named template is invoked, if this isn't a template rule), the template is instantiated in the result. (Note that xsl:template can be an *empty* element. Translated into plain English, this might be read as something like, "When you find this portion of the source tree, *do nothing*.")

Consider the following simple template rule:

```
<xsl:template match="/flixinfo">
  Caged Heat
</xsl:template>
```

This instructs the XSLT processor to locate a flixinfo child of the root node; if it finds such a node-set in the source tree, it adds the text "Caged Heat" to the result tree at that point.

Conflict resolution

Here's the problem any well-meaning XSLT processor sometimes faces: Given a stylesheet containing dozens of template rules, what should the processor do if a given portion of the source tree is located by more than one template rule? For example, here are three template rules which all locate the main title element in the *Caged Heat* FlixML review:

```
<xsl:template match="/flixinfo/*">
  Found a child of the flixinfo element!
</xsl:template>
<xsl:template match="/flixinfo/title">
  Found a title element!
</xsl:template>
<xsl:template match="/flixinfo/title[.='Caged Heat']">
  Found the "Caged Heat" title element!
</xsl:template>
```

The authors of the XSLT spec had several choices for how the processor should be required to behave in this kind of case, including these:

- Accept the first—or the last—matching template rule and ignore the others for this particular bit of content.
- Report this as an error condition and stop processing.
- Use some kind of tie-breaking mechanism to figure out what to do.

The first choice would be kind of arbitrary; it would also violate the "side-effect-free" processing model I described earlier, under whose rules the order of the template rules in a stylesheet is completely insignificant.

Choice #2 would be acceptable, except that (a) there are many cases where you *do* want one kind of processing for a general case (as with the `/flixinfo/*` location path) and a different one for a specific (as with either of the other two location paths), and (b) it would annoy the heck out of XSLT stylesheet developers with its constant nagging.

This left the third option. The tie-breaking or *conflict resolution* rules of XSLT basically say to look at the conflicting template rules and select the one that most specifically matches the source tree at that point; if there are still two or more conflicting template rules, the processor is free to either report it as an error or accept the last one in the stylesheet (where "last" means in the stylesheet's document order—closest to the `xsl:stylesheet` element's end tag).

The spec goes even further, to define how the processor should arrive mathematically at a determination of "how specific" a given match pattern is. This specificity is a function of calculating a *priority* for each conflicting template rule which lacks an explicit one (in the `priority` attribute); highest priority wins. Here's the series of logical steps:

1. Check the *import precedence* of all matching template rules; eliminate from consideration all those with lower import precedence than the matching

template rule or rules with the highest import precedence. (Import precedence is an issue when you're importing other stylesheets to this one, as discussed in Chapter 6.) If none of the conflicting patterns have been imported from other stylesheets, all have the same import precedence; in this case—or if any of the remaining template rules still have the same precedence—go on to step 2.

2. Look at the template rules, if any, with a `priority` attribute. Compare them to one another and to all other remaining template rules in conflict. For the latter, compute a default priority as follows:

   a. Is the location path in the `match` attribute a *compound* location path, containing multiple alternatives separated by a pipe (`|`) character? If so, treat it like a set of separate template rules, one for each alternative location path, and continue.

   b. Does the pattern consist of just an XML name on the child or attribute axis, or does it take the form `processing-instruction(target)` on the child axis? If so, then the priority is 0. (Remember that the child axis is the default.)

   c. Does the pattern use the wildcard `*` on the child or attribute axis? If so, assign a priority of –0.25.

   d. Otherwise, does the pattern consist of just a node test on the child or attribute axis? If so, assign a priority of –0.5. Note that the only kind of node test still remaining after the preceding steps will be a node-*type* test.

   e. Otherwise, use a priority of 0.5.

3. If there's still a conflict, this is an error. The XSLT processor can flag it as such, or simply choose to use the last conflicting template rule.

Since most match patterns, by far, take the form of an explicit element or attribute name on the child or attribute axis, most match patterns therefore end up with a default priority of 0.

Assume the source-tree node being evaluated is the `title` element corresponding to the main title, *Caged Heat.* Note that all three template rules potentially match this node. Applying the above algorithm to the three conflicting template rules set up at the start of this section, we come up with default priorities as follows:

- `match="/flixinfo/*"`: default priority is –0.25 (uses a wildcard on the child axis).

- `match="/flixinfo/title"`: default priority is 0 (uses a named node on the child axis).
- `match="/flixinfo/title[.='Caged Heat']"`: default priority is 0.5 (the "otherwise" case).

Therefore, the pattern that will be selected for processing the "Caged Heat" `title` element in our sample document is the third—the most specific—one.

(For the other two `title` elements, whose values do not equal "Caged Heat," only the first two patterns are in conflict. For them, the second template rule will apply, since its default priority of 0 is higher than that for the first, –0.25.)

If there are still ties...

As a rule, you can count on most (if not all) XSLT processors to apply the "last conflicting pattern wins" rule, rather than to simply throw in the towel and report an error. Although the latter behavior is, strictly speaking, compliant with the spec, it's probably not what most *users* of XSLT want.

If you've been paying attention, you'll have realized that this processor behavior violates the side-effect-free rule. Be that as it may, this provides developers of XSLT processors with an escape hatch, letting them choose the approach they want to take. They can report the error—technically, the "more correct" approach—or they can opt for "more practical" and simply use the last conflicting template rule.

Transferring source to result tree with `xsl:value-of`

If all you could do was put literal text strings in the result tree whenever you found a match, XSLT would be a pretty stupid spec. Unsurprisingly, therefore, it also gives you the option of transferring content from the source to the result tree.

The mechanism for doing this is the empty `xsl:value-of` element, whose general syntax is:

```
<xsl:value-of select="pattern"
  disable-output-escaping="yesorno" />
```

The `select` attribute is required. Its value can be any of a number of things:

- An XPath location path: If this is a relative location path, it is relative to the context established by the `xsl:template` element's `match` attribute.
- Some other XPath expression, including strings (distinguished from location paths using nested quotation marks), numeric expressions, calculated values, function calls, and so on.
- A variable or parameter reference: Variables and parameters are covered in Chapter 4, in the section titled "Reusing Stylesheet Content."

The `disable-output-escaping` attribute is optional. For details on its use, see the section in Chapter 4 titled "Controlling the Result Tree's Form/Type."

The `xsl:value-of` element is the formal XSLT equivalent of the CSS "generated content" feature, although the XSLT form is (to my way of thinking, anyhow) both simpler and more flexible.[7]

You can mix up literal text and text from the source tree in a single template, and there's no restraint on how many `xsl:value-of` elements a given template may contain.

Here are a handful of template rules using various forms of the `xsl:value-of` element's `select` attribute; see the notes which follow for an explanation of each:

```
<!-- Template rule #1 -->
<xsl:template match="//director">
  Director: <xsl:value-of select="."/>
</xsl:template>

<!-- Template rule #2 -->
<xsl:template match="//director">
  <xsl:value-of select="concat('Director: ', .)"/>
</xsl:template>

<!-- Template rule #3 -->
<xsl:template match="/">
  A FlixML Review by
  <xsl:value-of select="flixinfo/@author"/>
</xsl:template>

<!-- Template rule #4 -->
<xsl:template match="//dialog[.=''] |
```

---

7.   It's certainly one heck of a lot less *tortured*. When I first saw CSS's `:before` and `:after` selectors, which are used to effect generated content, I thought for sure someone had set out to *discourage* the use of generated content.

```
/flixinfo[not(dialog)]">
<xsl:value-of select="'This review has no dialog
element!'"/>
</xsl:template>
```

- Template rule #1 instantiates in the result tree the literal text "Director: " followed by the value of the `director` element, when it locates such an element in the source tree.
- Template rule #2 does the same thing as template rule #1, but it instantiates the result-tree content using the XPath `concat()` function for combining multiple strings into a single one.
- Template rule #3 instantiates in the result tree the words "A FlixML Review by ", followed by the value of the `flixinfo` element's `author` attribute, when it locates the source tree's root node.
- Template rule #4 matches either an empty `dialog` element or a `flixinfo` element with *no* `dialog` child; if it finds either of those two kinds of node, it places into the result tree the string "'This review has no dialog element!" Note that the entire string as it appears in the `select` attribute must be enclosed in embedded quotation marks or apostrophes; otherwise, the processor would try to read the string as a location path.

Transferring source-tree content using `xsl:value-of` is different from *copying* source-tree nodes. The former always yields a node-set's string-value; the latter results in creating a complete copy, including the markup associated with the node-set in question. (For information about copying source-tree nodes to the result tree, see the section titled "Copying content" in Chapter 6, Advanced XSLT.)

Literal result elements

I've mentioned a few times that any element whose name is not in the XSLT namespace and is not otherwise involved in stylesheet processing (per the `extension-elements-prefix` attribute on the `xsl:stylesheet` element) is copied straight into the result tree, including its attributes, text nodes, and so on. These elements are referred to in the spec as *literal result elements*.

For example, if you're transforming a FlixML document to XHTML, you'd typically have a stylesheet that looks in part something like the following:

```
<xml:stylesheet version="1.0"
  xmlns:xsl="http://www.w3.org/1999/XSL/Transform"
  xmlns="http://www.w3.org/1999/xhtml">

  <xsl:template match="/">
    <html>
      <head>
        <title>FlixML Review:
          <xsl:value-of select=".//title[role='main']"/>
        </title>
      </head>
      <body>
        ...etc. ...
      </body>
    </html>
  </xsl:template>

</xsl:stylesheet>
```

The `xsl:stylesheet` element declares the XSLT version as required, and also declares two namespaces: Elements (and attributes, if any) whose names are prefixed `xsl:` are from the XSLT namespace; elements whose names have *no* prefix are from the XHTML namespace. The one template rule shown here matches on the source tree's root node; when it finds that root node, the template rule instantiates in the result tree a mix of literal result elements from the XHTML namespace (`html`, `head`, `title`, and `body`), literal text, *and* some content transferred from the source tree.

Instantiating element nodes vs. "writing tags"

If you want to provoke instant impatience, if not animosity, on XML- and XSLT-related mailing lists, just ask a question that includes phrases like "I want to put a tag…" and "How do I write a tag which…?"

The problem isn't that the people on those lists aren't helpful; they are quite helpful, in my experience, even to the point of helping to debug complex stylesheets over the course of many messages.

The problem is the form of the question. You must never think in terms of "writing tags"—for example, in terms of putting the characters <, h, t, m, l, and > in the result tree whenever you need to create an `html` element. Even though that's what it looks like you're doing when you include a literal `html` result element in your template—even though you have to key in those characters in that order if you're hand-coding the stylesheet—you're *not* using XSLT to write tags. XSLT can't write tags. It can, however, instantiate element nodes (among other kinds).

The real problem with the "writing tags" phrase is that it can fool you into creating (or rather, trying to create) non-well-formed stylesheets. You cannot "write a start tag" in one template rule and "write the corresponding end tag" in another, for example. When I'm hand-coding an XSLT stylesheet, as soon as I code the start tag of any element I immediately code its end tag, and only then do I go back to insert stuff between the two of them. This pretty much guarantees that I don't think of the start and end tag as two distinct "things" to be written out independently of each other. If you're cursed with a similarly lazy turn of mind, you have my sympathy, and you might want to adopt the same (or a similar) practice.

Invoking template rules with `xsl:apply-templates`

I've made a certain amount of noise about how what goes on in one template rule is independent of what goes on in another, in support of XSLT's side-effect-free processing model. Now the truth comes out: That wasn't entirely accurate.

The fact is, most XSLT stylesheets use a kind of "trickle-down" model wherein template rules corresponding to upper nodes of the source tree *invoke* template rules corresponding to children of those nodes; those children's template rules invoke template rules for *their* children and so on, down the tree, until each node has been either processed or skipped.

The device used to invoke a child's template rule from within its parent's is the `xsl:apply-templates` element, structured as follows:

```
<xsl:apply-templates select="pattern"
  mode="mode">
  [optional xsl:sort and/or xsl:with-param elements]
</xsl:apply-templates>
```

Both the `select` and the `mode` attributes are optional, and if there are no `xsl:sort` or `xsl:with-param` elements to be used (which is the most common case), the `xsl:apply-templates` element will be empty. Thus, the simplest form of this element is this:

```
<xsl:apply-templates/>
```

When used this way, the element's purpose might be translated into plain English as, "Look for and apply templates relating to *any* children of this node which might be present in the source tree."

Looking ahead

I'll cover using the `xsl:sort` element in Chapter 4, in the "Sorting Content" section. The `xsl:with-param` element is documented in the "Reusing Stylesheet Content" section of that chapter. For now, let's keep things simple and concentrate on the most common kind of `xsl:apply-templates` element: the *empty* kind.

All right now, wake up, what follows is very important: The `xsl:apply-templates` element *implicitly changes the context node* used for evaluating match patterns of template rules. In other words, if you use this trickle-down model religiously, only one match pattern in any of the stylesheet's template rules (the one for the root node) need be an absolute location path; the others can simply be relative paths, which will be evaluated in the context of higher-level template rules.

Let's consider a simple XML document (not, for once, a FlixML document):

```
<elem_A>
  <elem_B>...</elem_B>
  <elem_B><elem_C/></elem_B>
  <elem_D/>
</elem_A>
```

A stylesheet to process this document would consist, of course, of the root `xsl:stylesheet` element, within which might be five template rules (one for the root node, and one for each of the element types—A, B, C, and D—in the source tree). The corresponding `xsl:template` elements would look something like the following:

```
<!-- Template rule #1: for root node -->
<xsl:template match="/">
  ...
  <xsl:apply-templates/>
  ...
</xsl:template>

<!-- Template rule #2: for root (A) element -->
<xsl:template match="elem_A">
```

```
  . . .
  <xsl:apply-templates/>
  . . .
</xsl:template>

<!-- Template rule #3: for B elements -->
<xsl:template match="elem_B">
  . . .
  <xsl:apply-templates/>
  . . .
</xsl:template>

<!-- Template rule #4: for C elements -->
<xsl:template match="elem_C">
  . . .
</xsl:template>

<!-- Template rule #5: for D elements -->
<xsl:template match="elem_D">
  . . .
</xsl:template>
```

Template rule 1 matches the root node. If it exists (which, of course, it always does), some optional content (the "...") is placed into the result tree. Then it invokes the template rule(s) for all of the root node's children, via the `xsl:apply-templates` element.

Each of template rules 2 through 5 matches a specific element type, optionally creating some result-tree content but also invoking template rules for source-tree content that stands in a child relationship to the current node type. Template rules 4 and 5 match C and D elements, which have no children, so there's no need to invoke a child template rule within those two template rules.

The overall processing flow looks something like Figure 3–4.

It remains true that the template rules in the stylesheet can *appear* in the stylesheet in any order at all. However, they will be *processed* in a specific order, based on the structure of the source tree. That is, as Figure 3–4 illustrates: Process the root node. Process any children of the root node (just the A element, in this case). Within the A element, process any children; if the child of A is a B, process its children as well.

The structure of the result tree will be basically the structure of the template rules as depicted in Figure 3–4, assuming you worked from top to bottom and left to right. We can demonstrate this easily by adding some additional text

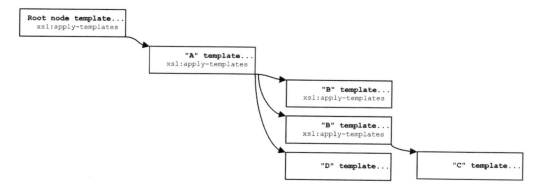

Figure 3-4   An XSLT stylesheet "trickling down" from higher-level template rules to lower. Because the sample source document's first B element has no children, the xsl:apply-templates element in that template rule has no effect for that instance of the B element; however, the *second* instance of B *does* have a C child to be processed.

and literal result elements to the stylesheet, to transform the source tree into an XHTML result tree:[8]

```
<!-- Template rule #1: for root node -->
<xsl:template match="/">
  <html>
    <head><title>ABCD Test</title></head>
    <body>
      <h1>Found the root node!</h1>
      <xsl:apply-templates/>
    </body>
  </html>
</xsl:template>

<!-- Template rule #2: for root (A) element -->
<xsl:template match="elem_A">
  <h2>Found an A node!</h2>
  <xsl:apply-templates/>
</xsl:template>

<!-- Template rule #3: for B elements -->
<xsl:template match="elem_B">
```

---

8.   Note that the stylesheet's xsl:stylesheet element also must reflect the correct XHTML namespace for this transformation to work correctly.

```
  <h3>Found a B node!
    (position #<xsl:value-of select="position()"/>)</h3>
  <xsl:apply-templates/>
</xsl:template>
<!-- Template rule #4: for C elements -->
<xsl:template match="elem_C">
  <h4>Found a C node!
    (position #<xsl:value-of select="position()"/>)</h4>
  <xsl:apply-templates/>
</xsl:template>
<!-- Template rule #5: for D elements -->
<xsl:template match="elem_D">
  <h3>Found a D node!
    (position #<xsl:value-of select="position()"/>)</h3>
</xsl:template>
```

Running this stylesheet against the above XML source document produces a result tree that looks as follows (courtesy of Saxon):

```
<html xmlns="http://www.w3.org/1999/xhtml">
  <head><title>ABCD Test</title></head>
  <body>
    <h1>Found the root node!</h1>
    <h2>Found an A node!</h2>
    <h3>Found a B node! (position #1)</h3>...
    <h3>Found a B node! (position #2)</h3>
    <h4>Found a C node! (position #1)</h4>
    <h3>Found a D node! (position #3)</h3>
  </body>
</html>
```

Watching out for whitespace

As I mentioned earlier, the various XML fragments covered here are displayed in "pretty-printed" form. If you actually process the document *as displayed* with the above spreadsheet, you'll see some surprising results as values of the position() function. I'll explain these surprising results in Chapter 4, in the discussion of the xsl:strip-space and xsl:preserve-space elements.

When viewed in the Microsoft Internet Explorer browser, this transformation looks like Figure 3–5.

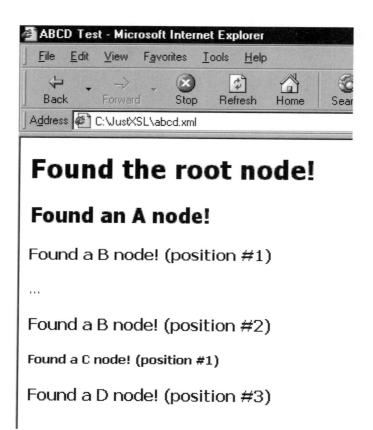

Figure 3-5   The result tree from the transformation diagrammed in Figure 3–4 (with headings added), as viewed in the MSIE browser. Text is displayed in a heading size corresponding to the level in the source tree (root node as a level-1 heading, `elem_A` node as a level-2, and so on). Also notice the interesting position numbers; see the text for an explanation.

As you can see, the nodes being processed are numbered according to their position to aid in identification. Why do the positions go 1, 2, 1, and 3 rather than (say) 1, 2, 3, and 4?

The answer is that each template rule is processed in the context of the node-set established by the invoking `xsl:apply-templates` element. That is, when the processor hits the `xsl:apply-templates` element in template rule #2—the template rule for the `elem_A` element—that `xsl:apply-templates` implicitly establishes a node-set consisting of *all* children of `elem_A`. So the first child is an `elem_B` node; the second child is an `elem_B` node; the third (and final) child is an `elem_D` node. The `elem_C` node, for its part, exists within a node-set established by the second `elem_B` element's `xsl:apply-templates`; because it's the only child of this element, its position is 1. The nodes' positions are their positions within the node-set established by the parent template's `xsl:apply-templates` element, not within the node-set consisting of all elements (or nodes) in the document.

One other potential mystery crops up in this output: the "..." in the portion of the result tree corresponding to the first `elem_B` element in the source tree. Clearly, it's got something to do with the "..." in the source tree, but we haven't used an `xsl:value-of` in the stylesheet. So where did it come from? I'll get to this in a moment, in the section titled "Built-in template rules."

My favorite shortcut

I'm *soooo* happy to get this business out of the way—this business about being able to use relative location paths in match patterns, I mean. Whenever I've shown you a match pattern or complete sample template rule to this point, I've always had to use an absolute path, even though I knew it wasn't the norm.

From here on, unless for some reason it's absolutely necessary, I'll use the more common relative location paths in example code. Just understand that this probably means the example is a fragment of a larger stylesheet, which includes a higher-level template rule establishing the limited context within which this match pattern will be evaluated.

The `select` attribute

The `xsl:apply-templates` element takes an optional `select` attribute. The value of this attribute is a relative location path, indicating which *specific* child(ren) of the context node should be processed at that point.

Given the above brief example XML document, coding template rule #2's `xsl:apply-templates` element with *no* `select` attribute is the same thing as coding it in the following form:

```
<xsl:apply-templates select="elem_B | elem_D"/>
```

That is, "Process the children of the context node whose names are either `elem_B` or `elem_D`." If for some reason we wanted to suppress the `elem_D` template rule, we could do so using the following:

```
<xsl:apply-templates select="elem_B"/>
```

The template rule for `elem_D` is still in the stylesheet, but it's never invoked.

(To suppress the processing of *all* of `elem_A`'s children, completely remove the `xsl:apply-templates` element from `elem_A`'s template rule.)

The mode attribute

The value of this attribute is meant to match the value of some `xsl:template` element's `mode` attribute. See the section titled "Template modes" for details.

Attribute value templates

One of the syntactic briars the XSLT standard's authors had to deal with was the issue of getting source tree or other "generated" content into attribute values. Consider the common case, for example, of grabbing from the source tree a URI that is to be used as the value of an `href` or `src` attribute to a result-tree `a` or `img` element. A newcomer to XSLT generally starts out trying to do something like this:

```
<a href="<xsl:value-of select='@my_uri'/>">Link</a>
```

This *looks* pretty ghastly, and it will be rejected outright by a processor's XML parser even before it gets to the XSLT stage. (The `<` and—to be safe—the `>` characters would have to be escaped with `&lt;` and `&gt;` entity references, which as it happens wouldn't work anyway.)

Return of an old nemesis

Trying to do something like the above—embedding the `xsl:value-of` element in the `href` attribute—is a particularly refined form of the "writing tags" mindset I ranted about a few pages back. In theory, yes, it would be possible to "write an attribute value" in this way…but there's no way at all to embed an element node within an attribute node.

The solution to this problem is to take the value of such a hypothetical `xsl:value-of` element's `select` attribute and use it literally, enclosed within "curly braces"—the { and } characters—in an attribute where you need it. Thus, the above incorrect code fragment can be coded correctly (and much more simply) this way:

```
<a href="{@my_uri}">Link</a>
```

The curly braces, with their attribute-value contents, are called an *attribute value template* (frequently abbreviated AVT).

Note that the word *attribute* in the term *attribute value template* refers to the fact that the string-value in question will *go into* an attribute value, not that it necessarily *comes from* an attribute value. Any legitimate XPath expression may go into an AVT, including location paths (relative or full), function calls, literal text, and so on. For instance,

```
<meta name="keywords"
  content="{flixinfo/title[role='main']}"/>
```

creates an XHTML meta tag in the result tree, whose content attribute (at least for the *Caged Heat* FlixML review) will have the value "Caged Heat."

You can use an AVT to assign a value to any attribute of any literal result element (such as the a and meta elements in the preceding examples). You can also use one in a number of attributes for a number of elements in the XSLT namespace, as summarized in Table 3–3.

Table 3-3   XSLT Elements/Attributes Which Can Use AVTs

Element	Attribute(s) which can use AVTs	Covered in section/chapter
xsl:attribute	name, namespace	"Instantiating explicit node types," below
xsl:element	name, namespace	"Instantiating explicit node types," below
xsl:number	format, lang, letter-value, grouping-separator, grouping-size	Chapter 5
xsl:processing-instruction	name	"Instantiating explicit node types," below
xsl:sort	lang, data-type, order, case-order	"Sorting content," below

An AVT alternative

Anything you can do with an AVT in a literal result element you can also do with the `xsl:attribute` element (whose purpose is to add a computed attribute to some result-tree element). Using `xsl:attribute` gives you a couple other features, though: It lets you calculate (using an AVT in the `name` attribute) the *name* of the created attribute as well as its value, and it can be stored in a named attribute set.

The `xsl:attribute` element is covered in the "Instantiating Explicit Node Types" section in Chapter 4. I discuss named attribute sets in "Reusing Stylesheet Content" in that chapter, as well.

Template modes

Driven as it is by XPath, the XSLT match pattern offers an incredible range of options for transforming even subtly different content in subtly different ways. For example, you can process a film's main `title` in one way, the first of its alternate `titles` in another, and all other alternate `titles` in still another, using a series of `xsl:template` elements whose start tags look something like the following three fragments:

```
<xsl:template match="title[role='main']">
<xsl:template match="title[role!='main' and
  position()=1]">
<xsl:template match="title[role!='main' and
  position()!=1]">
```

However, there are some occasions for which you need to process the *same* piece of the source tree more than once, for entirely different purposes. This is accomplished using template *modes*—that is, special forms of the `xsl:apply-templates` and `xsl:template` elements working together.

In the case of a FlixML review, say, we might want to include the film's main `title` element in a browser's window title bar, in a large heading at the top of a Web page, and in a footing showing the title and copyright date of the review. If we have only a single template rule whose `match` attribute has a value of `title[role="main"]`, we're stuck; that template rule will be processed exactly once. So here's what we do instead:

- Include (in the template rule for the `flixinfo` element) three different `xsl:apply-templates` elements for processing the `title` element. These three `xsl:apply-templates` elements will each have a unique value for its `mode` attribute.

- Create three different `xsl:template` elements—one for each of the `xsl:apply-templates` elements' `mode` attributes.

An (abbreviated) stylesheet to do this would look like the following:

```
<xsl:stylesheet version="1.0"
  xmlns:xsl="http://www.w3.org/1999/XSL/Transform"
  xmlns="http://www.w3.org/1999/xhtml">

  <xsl:template match="flixinfo">
    <html>
    <head>
     <title>
       <!-- Process title element for browser title -->
       <xsl:apply-templates
         select="title[@role='main']" mode="titlebar"/>
     </title>
    </head>
    <body>
     <!-- Process title element for page heading -->
     <xsl:apply-templates
       select="title[@role='main']" mode="heading"/>
     <p><i>[body of review goes here]</i></p>
     <!-- Process title element for page footing -->
     <xsl:apply-templates
       select="title[@role='main']" mode="footing"/>
    </body>
    </html>
  </xsl:template>

  <-- Template rule for browser-window title -->
  <xsl:template match="title[@role='main']"
    mode="titlebar">
    FlixML Review: <xsl:value-of select="."/>
  </xsl:template>

  <-- Template rule for page-heading title -->
  <xsl:template match="title[@role='main']"
    mode="heading">
    <h1><xsl:value-of select="."/></h1>
  </xsl:template>

  <-- Template rule for page-footing title -->
  <xsl:template match="title[@role='main']"
```

```
   mode="footing">
   <div align="center">
     <p><i>This FlixML review of
     "<xsl:value-of select="."/>"
     copyright <xsl:value-of select="../@copyright"/>
     by <xsl:value-of select="../@author"/></i></p>
   </div>
 </xsl:template>

</xsl:stylesheet>
```

After applying this transformation to the *Caged Heat* review, the result tree looks like this:

```
<html xmlns="http://www.w3.org/1999/xhtml">
  <head>
    <title>FlixML Review: Caged Heat</title>
  </head>
  <body>
    <h1>Caged Heat</h1>
    <p><i>[body of review goes here]</i></p>
    <div align="center">
      <p><i>This FlixML review of "Caged Heat"
      copyright 2001 by
      John E. Simpson</i></p>
    </div>
  </body>
</html>
```

If linked to the above stylesheet, the FlixML document appears in the MSIE browser as shown in Figure 3–6.

Built-in template rules

Depending on how you look at it, your work with XSLT will be made easier or more complex thanks to the presence of built-in template rules laid out by the XSLT specification. Since the spec's authors could not, of course, anticipate every single source-tree element or other node *name*, they had to build these around node *types*.

Not counting the xsl:stylesheet wrapper element, a complete stylesheet which spelled out these template rules explicitly would look like the following (see the bulleted list which follows for a description of each):

Figure 3-6 The *Caged Heat* FlixML review's main `title` element, processed three different ways using three different template rules and the `mode` attribute.

```
<!-- Elements and root node -->
<xsl:template match="*|/">
  <xsl:apply-templates/>
</xsl:template>

<!-- Text and attribute nodes -->
<xsl:template match="text()|@*">
  <xsl:value-of select="."/>
</xsl:template>

<!-- PI and comment nodes -->
<xsl:template
  match="processing-instruction()|comment()"/>
```

- Elements and root node: The built-in template rule for elements and the root node is simply to process all templates for all children of the context node.

- Text and attribute nodes: The string-value of each text and attribute node is transferred to the result tree by this built-in template rule's `xsl:value-of` element.
- PI and comment nodes: Because this `xsl:template` is an empty element, the built-in treatment of PIs and comments is to do nothing.

Note that the only things being placed in the result tree by these template rules are the string-values of text and attribute nodes—no XHTML markup or other literal result elements. If you actually use this as the stylesheet for the *Caged Heat* review, therefore, this displays as shown in Figure 3–7.

Figure 3-7   A portion of the *Caged Heat* FlixML review, using only the built-in templates to transfer the source tree's text and attribute nodes to the result tree. But where *are* the attribute nodes? See text for the answer.

One of the seemingly odd things about these built-in template rules has to do with their treatment of attribute nodes. The built-in template rule for attributes, after all, says to transfer their values (with text nodes) to the result tree. In Figure 3–7's screen capture, shouldn't we see something like "mainEN-Caged HeataltENCaged FemalesaltENRenegade Girls," and so on—that is, showing the values of all attributes as well as text nodes?

To help puzzle out this mystery, think of what I said earlier about lower-level template rules and the context in which they operate: They operate in the context of `xsl:apply-templates` elements in *higher-level* template rules. So then, which built-in template rule invokes the one for processing text and attribute nodes? Right, the one that processes elements and the root node and includes the following:

```
<xsl:apply-templates/>
```

Because this `xsl:apply-templates` has no `select` attribute, it tells the processor to process all template rules for all nodes that are children of the context node. Now think back to the discussion of the XPath child axis. Remember this strange little bit of XPath genealogy: Elements are considered parents of their attributes (and their text nodes, and so on), but attributes (unlike text nodes) are *not* considered children of their elements. And that's why the attribute values do not show up in the result tree constructed by the built-in template rules.

Weasel wording

I don't know about you, but when I first figured out this little bit of verbal legerdemain in the spec my jaw must have dropped three inches. I mean, it makes sense once you get it. It still seemed kind of sneaky, though.

As long as you consider an attribute to be an aspect of some other thing (an element or its content), rather than a thing in itself, there's a certain logic to this. I wouldn't get too hung up on the apparent paradox if I were you. Just take it at face value.

If you'd really like to see all the content from your source tree, including not only text nodes and attribute values but also PIs and comments, you need to tweak the built-in templates a bit. At a minimum, here's what they'd need to look like:

```
<!-- Elements and root node (tweaked) -->
<xsl:template match="*|/">
  <xsl:apply-templates
    select="* | text() | @* | comment() |
    processing-instruction()"/>
</xsl:template>

<!-- Text and attribute nodes (untweaked) -->
<xsl:template match="text()|@*">
  <xsl:value-of select="."/>
</xsl:template>

<!-- PI and comment nodes (tweaked) -->
<xsl:template
  match="processing-instruction()|comment()">
  <xsl:value-of select="."/>
</xsl:template>
```

The main change is to the built-in template rule for elements and the root node. Now there's a `select` attribute, whose value is a compound location path locating all child elements, child text nodes, attributes, child comments, and child PIs, respectively, of the context node. Also, the built-in template rule for PIs and comments is no longer empty; it contains an `xsl:value-of` element to transfer each PI's or comment's content to the result tree.

The result, as viewed in MSIE, looks like Figure 3–8.

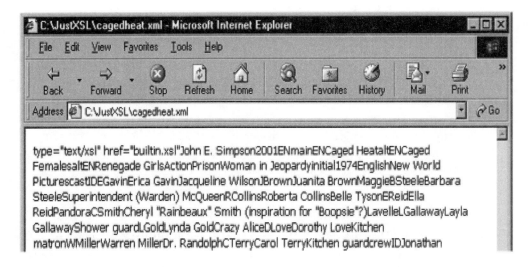

Figure 3-8 *Caged Heat* review, using "tweaked" built-in templates to display attribute values, PIs, and comments, as well as text nodes.

Straightening it up

Well, now you've got all the content from your source tree into the result. It's still not especially readable, though. So what you might want to do at this point is create a true XHTML result tree. In the body of the transformed document, you'd have a table two columns wide; in the first column would appear the name of the node if it has one, or the words "PI" (plus the PI target) or "COMMENT" if not; and in the second, the node's string-value.

A complete stylesheet to do this would look as follows:

```
<xsl:stylesheet version="1.0"
  xmlns:xsl="http://www.w3.org/1999/XSL/Transform"
  xmlns="http://www.w3.org/1999/xhtml">
```

```
<!-- Root node: Create root XHTML elements and table,
  then apply templates for all children of root node. -->
<xsl:template match="/">
  <html>
  <head><title>Complete Dump of XML Document</title></head>
    <body>
      <table border="1">
        <tr>
          <th>Name or Type</th>
          <th>String-value</th>
        </tr>
        <xsl:apply-templates
          select="* | text() | @* | comment()
          | processing-instruction()"/>
      </table>
    </body>
  </html>
</xsl:template>

<!-- Element nodes: Create a table row with boldface
  element name in column 1, and value of text node
  (if any) in column 2. Then process all children
  of this element. -->
<xsl:template match="*">
  <tr>
    <td valign="top"><b><xsl:value-of
      select="name()"/></b></td>
    <td valign="top"><xsl:value-of select="text()"/></td>
  </tr>
  <xsl:apply-templates
    select="* | text() | @* | comment()
    | processing-instruction()"/>
</xsl:template>

<!-- Attribute nodes: Create a table row with attribute
  name (prefixed with "@") in column 1, and value of
  attribute in column 2. -->
<xsl:template match="@*">
  <tr>
    <td valign="top">@<xsl:value-of select="name()"/></td>
    <td valign="top"><xsl:value-of select="."/></td>
  </tr>
</xsl:template>

<!-- Text nodes: Suppress unless explicitly displayed
```

```
  elsewhere. -->
<xsl:template match="text()"/>

<!-- PIs: Create a table row with "(PI)" and the PI
  target in column 1, and the PI's value in column 2. -->
<xsl:template
  match="processing-instruction()">
  <tr>
    <td valign="top">(PI)<xsl:value-of select="name()"/></td>
    <td valign="top"><xsl:value-of select="."/></td>
  </tr>
</xsl:template>

<!-- Comments: Create a table row with "(COMMENT)" in
  column 1, and value of comment in column 2. -->
<xsl:template
  match="comment()">
  <tr>
    <td valign="top">(COMMENT)></td>
    <td valign="top"><xsl:value-of select="."/></td>
  </tr>
</xsl:template>

</xsl:stylesheet>
```

The beginning of the *Caged Heat* review as processed by this stylesheet now appears in MSIE as shown in Figure 3–9.

Loose ends

There's a strange little bit of code in the "XML document dump" stylesheet I just showed you, and that's the template rule for handling text nodes:

```
<!-- Text nodes: Suppress unless explicitly displayed
  elsewhere. -->
<xsl:template match="text()"/>
```

Why, you might wonder, should text nodes be suppressed?

This is a personal foible with which you may or may not be comfortable. But as a matter of course, I *always* include this template rule in my stylesheets. The reason is that the built-in template rule for text nodes assumes you want to transfer them all to the result tree, and I find this an unwarranted assumption in many—maybe most—cases. What you often end up with, thanks to this built-in rule, is stray text scattered throughout your document at one point or another.

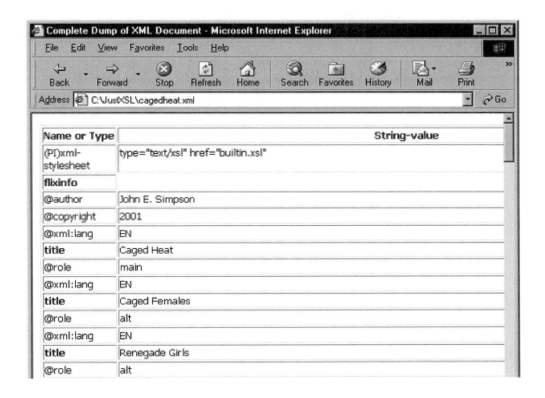

Figure 3-9 A "dump" of the contents of the *Caged Heat* FlixML review, in a more legible format (and with much more complete contents) than that provided by the built-in template rules.

Flip back to the text following Figure 3–5. In that figure, a stray "..." showed up in the result tree, even though we hadn't asked for it. The reason it did so was the built-in rule for text nodes; without that rule, you'd have seen only what you really needed to see for purposes of the explanation at that point.

My preference is to start out by suppressing all text nodes and then "reveal" them using templates that transfer the text content to the result tree, one containing element at a time. This seems to me to provide a much finer level of control over what goes into the result tree than the default, which is to assume that everything should be dumped there.

If you return the built-in template rule for text nodes to the previously introduced stylesheet, as shown in Figure 3–10, you see all text nodes in the document *before* the table, which (in theory) is all you really want to see.

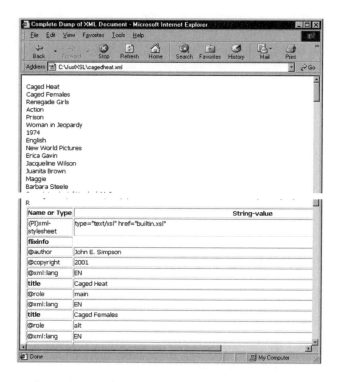

Figure 3-10   Same document and stylesheet as shown in Figure 3–9, except that text nodes are no longer suppressed. All text nodes in the document are listed before the table.

I don't know. Like I said, this is a matter of personal taste, and you may prefer the built-in template rule's behavior. (My wife imagines me to be a control freak,[9] and maybe this is just another manifestation of that imagined tendency: that it drives me crazy not to have control over my documents' text nodes.)

Missing in action

Notably absent from the built-in template rules and the discussion above is any mention of namespace nodes.

I'll leave to you the job of incorporating their names and values into the stylesheet, if you're really interested. Be prepared for some sur-

> prises, though. For starters, remember that the only axis along which namespace nodes are visible is the namespace axis. Also remember that if a namespace is declared in a document's root element, there will be a corresponding namespace node for every element in the document.

How Do I...
Generate entity references and other markup in the result tree?

If you're asking this question, you *may* not be paying attention. See, the word "generate" is just a fancy way of saying "write"—and (as you know by now, right?) *you can't "write" tags (or any other markup) to the result tree with XSLT.* All you can do is create—instantiate—*nodes*. I'm going to be covering this at greater length at various points through the remainder of the chapter, so don't worry if it still hasn't sunk in. It will.[10]

There's one question it doesn't quite put to rest in newcomers' minds, however. That's the question of how to get "named entity references" which (X)HTML knows about into the result tree. These are the useful short and easily remembered names for various special characters, such as © for the copyright symbol (©) and ü for "lowercase u with an umlaut" (ü).

Unfortunately, there's no 100% easy way to do this. The standard answer is to look up the numeric value for the entity and then use *it*, rather than the name. So, to insert a copyright symbol in the result tree, you'd do something like this:

```
<p>Copyright &#169; 2001</p>
```

You can also include an internal DTD subset in your stylesheet's prolog. For example,

```
<!DOCTYPE xsl:stylesheet [
<!ENTITY copy "&#169;" >
]>
```

---

9. She's wrong, of course.
10. It better.

This would let you use the `&copy;` entity in your stylesheet, recoding the above p element, for example, this way:

```
<p>Copyright &copy; 2001</p>
```

None of this helps you get a `&copy;` entity reference *into the result tree*, however. These procedures simply get the correct character—what the `&copy;` entity reference stands for—into the result tree. The main problem, really, is that an XSLT processor can put whatever it wants into the result tree when generating such special characters, as long as whatever it puts there "works."

If you really, really, *really* need to end up with something like `&copy;` in your output, you might want to take a look at the `xsl:output` element, using a `method` attribute with a value of `html`. I'll cover this element near the end of Chapter 4, in the section titled "Controlling the Result Tree's Form/Type."

"Looping"

The programmers among you are probably familiar with the concept of a "do-while" or "for-each" construct. This is a bit of code which runs repeatedly, for some specified number of times or while some condition is true. For instance, you might have a code fragment such as the following (in pseudo-code):

```
x = 1
do while x < 5:
  print x
  x = x + 1
end do
```

Some storage location (a variable) named "x" is initialized to the numeric value 1. Then the do-while block of code begins, running for as long as the value of x is less than 5—iteratively displaying the value of x and incrementing that value by 1. So this loop runs four times; on the fifth pass, the value of x is no longer less than 5, so the loop stops running.

There's a construct available in XSLT, an element temptingly named `xsl:for-each`, that may appear to function in the same way. I'll show you how to use it first. Immediately thereafter, I'll show you some reasons why *not* to confuse it with a real programming-style for-each loop…and maybe why not to use it at all.

Instantiating occurring content with `xsl:for-each`

The `xsl:for-each` element takes only a single attribute, `select`, which is required. Like other attributes by that name elsewhere in XSLT, this `select` attribute's value is an XPath expression selecting nodes for some operation or another.

Where you use an `xsl:for-each` element is within the template portion of some `xsl:template` element. A relative location path in the `select` attribute is evaluated in the context of whatever node-set is established by the `xsl:template` element's `match` attribute.

The occasion in which you'd typically use an `xsl:for-each` is when there's some regularly repeating data structure in the source tree and a corresponding regularly repeating structure (tables are a favorite structure) to be built in the result tree. For instance, a FlixML review often provides links to more than one external review of the movie in question. For each of these external reviews there are two pieces of information: the URI of the external link and the name of or other descriptive phrase for the review.

Refer back to the *Caged Heat* FlixML document. Note the structure of the external reviews: They're contained in `reviewlink` elements within `goodreview` and `badreview` elements (which, in turn, are within an `otherreview` element, within the `reviews` element, within the root `flixinfo` element). What I'd like to do is create a two-column table representing these "other reviews"; in the first column will be some indication that it's a good or bad review; in the second, a standard hypertext link to the review.

To accomplish this, I'll use a couple of simple images (one called "goodreview.jpg" and one called "badreview.jpg"—those names are significant!) and the following two template rules:

```
<xsl:template match="flixinfo">
  <html>
  <head><title>FlixML Review</title></head>
    <body>
      <h2>External Reviews of <i><xsl:value-of
        select="title[@role='main']"/></i>:</h2>
      <xsl:apply-templates select="reviews"/>
    </body>
  </html>
</xsl:template>

<xsl:template match="reviews">
  <table border="0">
    <xsl:for-each select="otherreview/*">
      <tr>
        <td><img src="{name()}.jpg" /></td>
        <td>
```

```
    <a href="{reviewlink/@xlink:href}"><xsl:value-of
      select="."/></a>
    </td>
    </tr>
  </xsl:for-each>
  </table>
</xsl:template>
```

The first template rule, for the root `flixinfo` element, creates the basic XHTML document framework. Note that its `xsl:apply-templates` element invokes the template rule for only one child of `flixinfo`–the `reviews` element.

The second template rule handles the `reviews` element, setting up a table. As you can see, the rows and table cells are instantiated in this template *within* an `xsl:for-each` element, which selects all children of the `otherreview` element. The first column of the table contains the image whose name corresponds to the name (see the XPath `name()` function?) of the child of the `otherreview` element currently being processed; it uses an AVT to build the name of this image. Column 2 contains the actual hyperlink; again, an AVT is used to assign content from the source tree to an attribute value (the `href` attribute, in this case).

Note, in particular, that within the `xsl:for-each` "loop" the context has shifted. That template rule's `match` pattern sets the context initially to the `reviews` element; the `xsl:for-each` element's `select` attribute narrows the context further, so that relative URIs in XPath location paths within that element's scope will be relative to *any children of the* `otherreview` *child of the* `reviews` *element.* Thus,

- the XPath `name()` function call will return either the string "goodreview" or the string "badreview";
- the AVT that assigns a value to the a element's `href` attribute refers to the `reviewlink` child of the context node (that is, the `reviewlink` child of a `goodreview` or `badreview` element); and
- the `.` in the `xsl:value-of` element's `select` attribute refers to the context node's string-value (the context node being a `goodreview` or `badreview`).

When you apply this stylesheet to the *Caged Heat* FlixML document, you get the following result tree:

```
<html>
  <head><title>FlixML Review</title></head>
  <body>
    <h2>External Reviews of <i>Caged Heat</i>:</h2>
```

```
    <table border="0">
      <tr>
        <td><img src="goodreview.jpg"/></td>
        <td><a
href="http://www.prisonflicks.com/Cagedh.htm">Prison Flicks</a></
td>
      </tr>
      <tr>
        <td><img src="goodreview.jpg"/></td>
        <td><a href="http://www.awcm.com/caps2/cap00120.htm">
        Amazing World of Cult Movies (AWCM)</a></td>
      </tr>
      <tr>
        <td><img src="badreview.jpg"/></td>
        <td><a
href="http://www.filmcritic.com/misc/emporium.nsf/
2a460f93626cd4678625624c007f2b46/
70d37148256673c4882567c600195dd0?OpenDocument">
        filmcritic.com (Christopher Null)</a>
        </td>
      </tr>
    </table>
  </body>
</html>
```

If viewed in MSIE, the document appears as in Figure 3–11.

Pros and cons of using `xsl:for-each`

The `xsl:for-each` element is something of a...well, a "hot button" would be overstating the case...let's just call it an occasional focus for debate.

The main problem with it, really, is the name, and in particular the associations of that name for people coming to XSLT from traditional programming languages. See, you can't really *do* anything inside this "loop," because XSLT is not a traditional programming language. The only thing that happens inside an `xsl:for-each` element is that *some portion of some template rule is instantiated for each node in the selected node-set.* You can't increment variables, as in the sample pseudo-code at the beginning of this section; you can't work your way through a string of text, a word at a time; you can't do anything else you might be used to doing in a programming language's loop structure. The `xsl:for-each` is simply like an automated cookie-making machine—get node, *stamp!*; get node, *stamp!*; get node, *stamp!*—cranking out a series of cookie-cutter shapes filled in with dough from one node after another, until the node-set is exhausted. That's it.

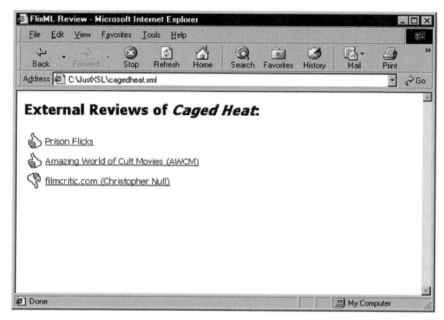

Figure 3-11   Results of transforming FlixML otherreview element to XHTML table, using `xsl:for-each`.

So, if you've got the programming background, don't let yourself be seduced by the element's name.

The other thing that's a (lesser) problem with `xsl:for-each` is that for most repetitive operations its purpose is redundant. This is because most such operations are performed on children of some current node, and there's a perfectly useful way to do that already: the `xsl:apply-templates` element, with a corresponding template rule.

So what's the `xsl:for-each` good for? What it's good for is processing some repeated structure either (a) deeper than children of the current node, or (b) along a different axis from it than the child axis.

The XSLT code whose results appear in Figure 3–11 is an example of the first use of `xsl:for-each`, because its `select` attribute burrowed down *two* levels (to the "grandchild" level) from the current node, the `reviews` element, rather than just one. This could have been accomplished with a couple of separate trickle-down template rules—one for `otherreview`, and one for its `goodreview/badreview` children—but the `xsl:for-each` is both more convenient and concise to code and somewhat easier to follow.

Checking some axis other than the child axis is *really* fertile ground for
`xsl:for-each`, because the child axis is, after all, only one of many possible axes.
For instance, we could build two lists from information about a film's cast: one
showing all the *characters*, in alphabetical or some other order, and one showing
all the *cast members* who played those roles. Note that according to the FlixML
DTD, each `castmember` element always precedes the `role` element for that person. Each item in each list could link to its counterpart in the other list, with the
hyperlinks built inside an `xsl:for-each` "loop" examining the following-sibling
axis for the `castmember` list (which would locate the corresponding `role`) and
the preceding-sibling axis for the `role` list (pointing to the corresponding castmember).

My bottom line advice: Continue to use the trickle-down arrangement of
`xsl:apply-templates` and `xsl:template` elements for processing children of
the current node; use `xsl:for-each` for processing nodes in any relationship to
the current node *other than* children.

Journeyman XSLT

Well, you've come pretty far. What you learned about XPath and XSLT in Chapters 2 and 3 have put you well on the way to constructing bare-bones stylesheets.

But *mastering* XSLT, ah, that's what you're after, isn't it? The stylesheet language features covered in this chapter will round out your toolkit, ensuring that you'll be able not merely to "make do" with XSLT, but to do whatever you want with it (almost). Just about every one of these techniques is one that you'll need sometime soon in the "real XSLT" world—maybe not later today, maybe not tomorrow or next week. But the week after that, yes.

Conditional Processing

As with `xsl:for-each`, the ability to do "conditional processing" in XSLT seems related to a particular feature common among traditional programming languages. In this case, though, the analogy is more exact.

Here's the general idea, expressed in pseudo-code:

```
if SomeCondition = True
  do something
otherwise
  do something else
end if
```

Although—just as with `xsl:for-each`—you still can't "do" anything like real programming languages allow inside the if/otherwise branches in an XSLT stylesheet, you *can* instantiate alternative portions of a template based on conditions inherent in the source tree.

One condition: `xsl:if`

The first form of XSLT conditional processing uses an `xsl:if` element as a wrapper for the template to be instantiated if the condition is true. The condition itself is spelled out in the `xsl:if` element's required `test` attribute, which is structured in the same way as an XPath location step's predicate (without the enclosing `[` and `]` brackets) and likewise yields a value of true or false. Any relative location paths in the test attribute's value are evaluated in terms of the context node in effect at the point of the `xsl:if`.

One common use of `xsl:if` is in constructing *delimited lists*—that is, strings of text made up of discrete substrings, separated from one another by commas, a comma-space combination, tabs, or whatever. When building such lists, the particular problem is that every substring other than the first is preceded by the delimiter.[1]

Look at *Caged Heat*'s lead cast list. We could build a table from it, using various techniques covered so far, with (say) the cast member's name in column 1 and the role he or she played in column 2. However, it would take up much less space in the display if we could turn these lists of names/roles into a simple, single text string. The following template rule, which uses the `xsl:if` element, accomplishes this:

```
<xsl:template match="cast">
  <p>
    <xsl:for-each select="leadcast/*">
      <xsl:if test="position() != 1">, </xsl:if>
      <xsl:value-of select="castmember"/> as
      <xsl:value-of select="role"/>
    </xsl:for-each>
  </p>
</xsl:template>
```

Here, the `xsl:if` element's `test` attribute says, "Only instantiate the template herein if the current node is not the first one in the node-set currently

---

1.   Or, alternatively, that every substring but the *last* is *followed by* the delimiter.

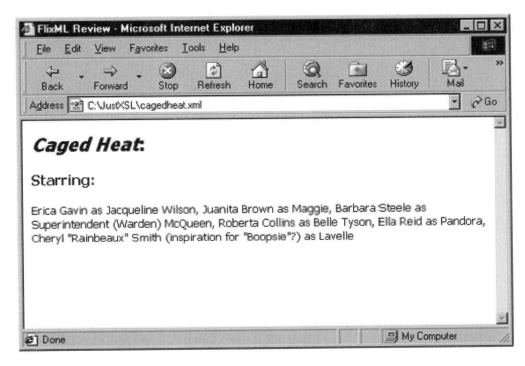

Figure 4-1 Lead cast of *Caged Heat*, represented as a single text string in which the name of every cast member but the first is preceded by a comma and space. Note the parenthetical aside about Cheryl "Rainbeaux" Smith, who (according to at least one un-confirmed source) was supposedly the inspiration for the character Boopsie, in Garry Trudeau's "Doonesbury" comic strip.

being processed." (That node-set is established by the `xsl:for-each`, which grabs each child, `male` or `female`, of the `leadcast` element.) The template in question is a comma followed by a blank space.

After adding a suitable heading to the result tree, you can see the results of this template rule in Figure 4–1.

If you wanted, you could extend this template rule further with another `xsl:if` element, testing to see if the current was the *last* cast member and, if so, adding the word "and" and a space after the ", " delimiter:

```
<xsl:template match="cast">
  <p>
    <xsl:for-each select="leadcast/*">
```

```
    <xsl:if test="position() != 1">, </xsl:if>
    <xsl:if test="position() = last()"> and </xsl:if>
    <xsl:value-of select="castmember"/> as
    <xsl:value-of select="role"/>
  </xsl:for-each>
 </p>
</xsl:template>
```

The relevant portion of the result tree would now display as shown in Figure 4–2.

Starring:

Erica Gavin as Jacqueline Wilson, Juanita Brown as Maggie, Barbara Steele as Superintendent (Warden) McQueen, Roberta Collins as Belle Tyson, Ella Reid as Pandora, and Cheryl "Rainbeaux" Smith (inspiration for "Boopsie"?) as Lavelle

Figure 4-2   A somewhat finer-turned version of the lead cast than that in Figure 4–1. Note the insertion of the "and " before Cheryl "Rainbeaux" Smith's name.

Still not perfect

I'm not going to belabor this point further, but the code we've got to this point still has some easily broken assumptions built into it.

In particular, the display will "break" if there's only one lead cast member, or if there are only two. If only one, the cast member's name will be preceded by the word "and" (because a single cast member is, indeed, the *last* cast member in the list); if two, the word "and" will be preceded by the comma-space combination (which is aberrant punctuation in English—a two-member list would normally be separated by the word "and" *only*).

Remember in your own coding to consider and provide "escape hatches" for all possibilities. In a case such as this, providing such an escape hatch will probably be better accomplished not with a series of `xsl:if` elements but with the `xsl:choose` block, discussed next.

Multiple conditions: `xsl:choose`

When you've got more than one alternative to test for, you can use a separate `xsl:if` element for each. This can grow unwieldy pretty quickly as the number of conditions grows; furthermore, it can be pretty inefficient, especially for long lists. (Every condition will always be tested, even if they're mutually exclusive.)

In XSLT, testing for multiple conditions is best done with an `xsl:choose` element. This element has no attributes; its only purpose is to provide a "wrapper" for the list of conditions. Each explicit condition is coded in an `xsl:when` element which, like `xsl:if`, has a `test` attribute setting forth a logical test which will result in a true or false value. An optional `xsl:otherwise` element may appear after the list of `xsl:when` elements, and its template will be instantiated in the event that none of the conditions is true.

The reason the `xsl:choose` block is potentially more efficient than a series of `xsl:if` elements is that each `xsl:when` is tested in order; when the first one is found that returns a true value from the test, its template is instantiated and *none* of the succeeding `xsl:when` elements is even tested. This means you can structure your `xsl:choose` block for maximum efficiency by placing the test most likely to be true as the first `xsl:when`, the next most likely to be true as the second `xsl:when`, and so on.

One common use for the `xsl:choose` block is as an answer to a question such as, "How do I color every other [node, row, whatever] differently?" This is an especially handy technique for long rows of tabular data, in which it's easy for the eye to inadvertently skip down or up to the next or preceding row. (Office-supply vendors sell special paper whose rows are alternately colored in this way, using terms like "ledger paper," "blue/green bar," and so on.)

Yeah, it's *common*, but...

...this probably isn't much more efficient than using a pair of `xsl:if` blocks, if indeed it's more efficient at all. (With only two alternatives, the pair of `xsl:if` elements potentially "wastes" only one test.) It does enable me to give you an answer to this frequently asked question; whether that's a good thing depends on whether you'd ever have asked it in the first place!

To use this technique, we'll take advantage of the fact that "every other row" is just an idiomatic way of saying "every two rows"—with something to happen on the even rows, and something else on the odd ones. I mentioned in Chapter 2 that this kind of problem was naturally handled using the XPath mod operator.

So then, let's apply the every-other-row coloration to the film's crew members and their titles:

```
<xsl:template match="cmw">
  <table>
    <tr>
      <th align="left">Position</th>
      <th align="left">Name</th>
    </tr>
    <xsl:for-each select="*">
      <xsl:choose>
        <xsl:when test="position() mod 2 != 0">
          <!-- Give odd rows silver background -->
          <tr style="background-color: silver">
            <td><xsl:value-of select="name()"/></td>
            <td><xsl:value-of select="."/></td>
          </tr>
        </xsl:when>
        <xsl:otherwise>
          <!-- Give even rows white background -->
          <tr style="background-color: white">
            <td><xsl:value-of select="name()"/></td>
            <td><xsl:value-of select="."/></td>
          </tr>
        </xsl:otherwise>
      </xsl:choose>
    </xsl:for-each>
  </table>
</xsl:template>
```

Applying this template rule to the *Caged Heat* FlixML document results in a display like the one in Figure 4–3.

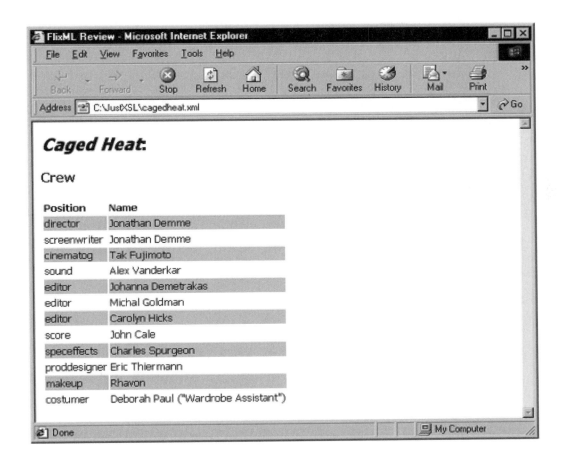

Figure 4-3 Using an `xsl:choose` block to display alternate rows of a node-set in different colors. In the "Position" column, I've simply inserted the name of the element; this really works in only about 50% of cases. "Cinematog"? "Speceffects"? If this really bothers you, you could use a named template to create the position, passing it the element name as a parameter and using the name or not, depending on which name it was. Named templates are covered later in the chapter.

Instantiating Explicit Node Types

So far, you know how to instantiate two things in a transformation's result tree: literal *text* and literal *result elements*. Although these may represent three-fourths or (probably) even more of a given result tree, the fact remains there are some things you just can't do, or do really well, with literal content. In such cases, you need to fall back on XSLT's facilities for instantiating explicit node types, whose contents—even whose very names—can be calculated based on something in the source tree.

Using `xsl:element`

The purpose of the `xsl:element` is to instantiate in the result tree an element node and its content, if any. Anything you can do with literal result elements you can do with `xsl:element` (perhaps in concert with `xsl:attribute`, discussed next), but the reverse is not necessarily true.

Here's the general syntax of `xsl:element`:

```
<xsl:element
  name="name"
  namespace="uri"
  use-attribute-sets="names">
  [Content, if any]
</xsl:element>
```

Of the attributes, only name is required. The values for the attributes are as follows:

- name: the name of the element to be placed in the result tree. This can be an AVT or a straightforward text string.
- namespace: the URI of the namespace to be associated with the created element's name. Like name, this can be an AVT.
- use-attribute-sets: a space-delimited list of the names of named attribute sets. (For information about named attribute sets, see the section in this chapter titled "Reusing Stylesheet Content.")

As a simple example of how to use `xsl:element`, the following two templates do exactly the same thing: instantiate an XHTML p (paragraph) element whose contents consist of one of *Caged Heat*'s alternate titles:

```
<!-- Template #1: literal result element -->
<p><xsl:value-of select="//title[@role='alt']"/></p>
```

```
<!-- Template #2: xsl:element -->
<xsl:element name="p">
  <xsl:value-of select="//title[@role='alt']"/>
</xsl:element>
```

While this example may be educational, it's hardly *interesting*. Why would you want to code something in such a relatively complex form, when you could use the much simpler literal-result-element form?

The most common answer is hidden in the fact that the element name may be an AVT. This situation will not arise often when transforming to XHTML, but it can be pretty much unsolvable if you encounter it when transforming to a different XML vocabulary—or to a different version of the same one.

Suppose I want to transform a FlixML document, such as the one on *Caged Heat*, into a different movie-review vocabulary in which there's not just a single title element, with a role attribute whose value is either "main" or "alt," but two distinct elements: main_title and alt_title, respectively. I could do this with a template rule that looked something like this pseudo-code:

```
for each title element
  if the role attribute is "main"
    instantiate a literal main_title element
  else
    instantiate a literal alt_title element
  end if
end for
```

This would work, true. It's a little clumsy, though, especially when you consider that we really need to handle the case in which the role attribute is missing altogether or equals something besides "main" or "alt." Using xsl:element will be more elegant and simpler, when you consider the extra "what-if" conditions:

```
for each title element
  if the role attribute is "main" or "alt"
    instantiate a calculated {@role}_title element
  else
    instantiate a literal main_title element
  endif
end for
```

In actual XSLT code, the above would be represented by a template rule such as the following:

```
<xsl:template match="title">
  <xsl:choose>
```

```
    <xsl:when test="@role='main' or @role='alt'">
      <xsl:element name="{@role}_title"><xsl:value-of
select="."/></xsl:element>
    </xsl:when>
    <xsl:otherwise>
      <main_title><xsl:value-of select="."/></main_title>
    </xsl:otherwise>
  </xsl:choose>
</xsl:template>
```

Running this template rule through Saxon (and also changing the root `flixinfo` element's name, just to keep from confusing this with a real FlixML document!) results in the following:

```
<flixinfo_new>
  <main_title>Caged Heat</main_title>
  <alt_title>Caged Females</alt_title>
  <alt_title>Renegade Girls</alt_title>
  ...
</flixinfo_new>
```

Another reason for `xsl:element`

Aside from the ability to create calculated element names, `xsl:element` also gives you finer control over the namespace declarations copied to a given element, by way of the `xsl:element` element's `namespace` attribute. Of course, you can copy a namespace to *all* elements in a given portion of the result tree by including its declaration in the `xsl:stylesheet` element; but if you want to copy it just to a particular element, use `xsl:element` with the `namespace` attribute.

Doing this for the foregoing example creates the following result tree:

```
<flixinfo_new>
  <main_title xmlns="http://www.flixml.org/flixml">Caged
Heat</main_title>
  <alt_title xmlns="http://www.flixml.org/flixml">Caged
Females</alt_title>
  <alt_title xmlns="http://www.flixml.org/flixml">Renegade
Girls</alt_title>
</flixinfo_new>
```

If I'd simply included that `xmlns` namespace declaration on the `xsl:stylesheet` element, it would have been copied to the result `flixinfo_new` element instead of all the `main_title` and `alt_title` elements.

Whether this feature will matter in a given case, of course, depends on the extent to which namespaces themselves matter in that case.

(X)HTML to XML transformations?

Occasionally—not often, but sometimes—a seemingly straightforward but actually pretty complicated question comes up on XML-related mailing lists or newsgroups. The exact wording varies, but roughly it goes like this: "I've got a bunch of HTML documents I'd like to transform to XML. How do I do that?" The answer comes in two parts.

The first part of the answer doesn't really have anything to do with XSLT as such. It says that your HTML must have two characteristics:

1. It must be at least well-formed HTML, if not (strictly speaking) XHTML. This allows the original document to function as an XSLT source tree in the first place.
2. All the elements in the HTML document that you want to transform to their XML counterparts must have `class` attributes providing the names of the elements to which you want to transform them. (If "all" is not practical, then shoot for "as many as possible.") This makes *much* easier the task of mapping source to result tree.

Assume I've got an HTML document lying around, describing *Caged Heat*. Assuming also that it's well-formed HTML, it might look, in part, something like the following, in order to meet condition #2:

```
<html>
  <head><title>FlixML Review: Caged Heat</title></head>
  <body class="flixinfo">
    <h1 class="title"><span class="role_main">Caged Heat</span></h1>
    <h2 class="title"><span class="role_alt">Caged Females</span>
</h2>
    <h2 class="title"><span class="role_alt">Renegade Girls</span></
h2>
    [etc.]
  </body>
</html>
```

Transforming this kind of "fully meaningful" HTML to XML is fairly straightforward, using `xsl:element` to construct (in this case) FlixML elements whose names map onto the values of the HTML elements' `class` attributes—or, in the case of the `span` elements above, adding attribute-value pairs to the newly created elements based on the value of the `span` elements' `class` attributes. The transformation might look, in part, something like the following:

```
<xsl:template match="*[@class]">
  <xsl:element name="{@class}">
    <xsl:value-of select="."/>
  </xsl:element>
  <xsl:apply-templates/>
</xsl:template>
```

Unfortunately, very few HTML documents are marked up in a form even remotely "semantically meaningful." This means the process of converting normal HTML documents to XML data stores is probably going to be extremely tedious, requiring quite a bit of hand-tweaking, use of the Unix sed and grep commands, and so on. (If the HTML documents were generated from a database or other automated procedure, the transition to XML is likely to be much less painful.)

Using xsl:attribute

The xsl:attribute element does for result-tree *attributes* what xsl:element does for result-tree *elements*: It provides a way to instantiate an attribute whose name (and possibly value) is not known until the time the transformation takes place.

The general syntax of this element is

```
<xsl:attribute
  name="name"
  namespace="uri">
  [template]
</xsl:attribute>
```

where

- *name* is the name of the attribute to be created, represented either as a plain text string or as an AVT;
- *uri* is the namespace URI to be associated with this attribute's name; and
- *template* is the value to be assigned to the attribute.

Placement of the xsl:attribute in its enclosing template rule is very important: It *must* immediately follow the start tag of the literal result element or xsl:element element to which the attribute is to be applied. If you're using more than one xsl:attribute for a given parent element, obviously only one xsl:attribute will immediately follow the parent; in this case, all `xsl:attribute` elements for the same parent element must appear one after another.

Note that it's perfectly legal, if you're using a literal result element, to mix literal attributes *in* the element's start tag and `xsl:attribute` elements *following* the start tag. Thus, the following is acceptable:

```
<xsl:template match="plotsummary">
  <p style="background-color: silver">
    <xsl:attribute name="class">
     <xsl:value-of select="name()"/>
    </xsl:attribute>
    <xsl:value-of select="."/>
  </p>
</xsl:template>
```

This creates the following in the result tree, at the point where the `plotsummary` element is located in the source tree:

```
<p style="background-color: silver"
  class="plotsummary">
  [contents of plotsummary element appear here]
</p>
```

When transforming a regular XML vocabulary (such as FlixML) to XHTML, using `xml:element` (as I mentioned above) probably doesn't serve much purpose. The XHTML tagset is too limited; the need to "calculate an element name" just doesn't square with the relatively simple result trees possible with XHTML. The situation isn't much different with the `xsl:attribute` element; the names of XHTML's attributes are straightforward, and their values can be as easily assigned with an AVT as with `xsl:attribute` (if not more easily).

Again, though, if you're translating to a different "real XML" vocabulary, `xml:attribute` can be irreplaceable.

In the discussion of `xsl:element`, I used as an example the FlixML `title`/`role` element/attribute combination, showing how you could create new element names based on this combination. There's also a FlixML "pure element" that could easily be turned into an element/attribute combination using either `xsl:element` or a literal result element, in concert with `xsl:attribute`. This is the set of sub-elements that are children of the `genre` element.

As you can see from either the FlixML DTD or the *Caged Heat* review, the `genre` element takes two possible children: `primarygenre` and `othergenre`. A template rule to convert a single `genre` element block into a succession of `genre` elements, each with its distinguishing (say) `genretype` attribute, might look something like the following:

```
<xsl:template match="genre">
  <genres>
    <xsl:for-each select="*">
      <genre>
        <xsl:attribute name="genretype"><xsl:value-of
          select="substring-before(name(), 'genre')"/>
        </xsl:attribute>
        <xsl:value-of select="."/>
      </genre>
    </xsl:for-each>
  </genres>
</xsl:template>
```

Note that the `xsl:attribute` element appears immediately following the `genre` literal result element's start tag, but before that element's actual template (content). The value of the `genretype` attribute is calculated, based on our knowledge that the name of the element being converted to an attribute can be either "othergenre" or "primarygenre."

If this template rule is the only one (other than the root-element template rule) in a stylesheet similar to the one used as an example above, for the `xsl:element` element, the result tree from it is as follows:

```
<flixinfo_new>
  <genres>
    <genre genretype="primary">Action</genre>
    <genre genretype="other">Prison</genre>
    <genre genretype="other">Woman in Jeopardy</genre>
  </genres>
</flixinfo_new>
```

We're not saying good-bye to `xsl:attribute`

Not yet, anyway.

It turns out that `xsl:attribute` has one important capability with no real analogy in `xsl:element`—the capability to group together attribute definitions for use like "boilerplate attributes," in what are called *named attribute sets*. I'll cover this feature shortly, in the section titled "Reusing Stylesheet Content."

Using `xsl:comment`

To put a comment into the result tree, use a simple `xsl:comment` element. This element has no attributes; the element's content will be placed between the comment's `<!--` and `-->` delimiters.

For example, we know there are `copyright` and `author` attributes to the `flixinfo` element in a FlixML review. Of course, we could *display* this information on a Web page easily enough, by extracting these attributes' values and placing them in (say) p or `div` elements in the XHTML result tree. It might also be useful, however, to include this information in a comment at the top of the generated result tree, directed to the attention of someone who is viewing the XHTML source code.

This could be accomplished with a template rule such as the following:

```
<xsl:template match="/">
  <html>
    <xsl:comment>
      This auto-generated XHTML was created by an XSLT
      stylesheet, applied to a FlixML review by its
      author, <xsl:value-of select="flixinfo/@author"/>.
      Contents copyright &#169;
      <xsl:value-of select="flixinfo/@copyright"/> by
      <xsl:value-of select="flixinfo/@author"/>. All
      Rights Reserved.
    </xsl:comment>
    <head><title>FlixML Review</title></head>
    <body>
      <i>[body of review goes here]</i>
    </body>
  </html>
</xsl:template>
```

This template rule generates the following result tree:

```
<html xmlns="http://www.w3.org/1999/xhtml">
  <!-- This auto-generated XHTML was created by an XSLT
  stylesheet, applied to a FlixML review by its
  author, John E. Simpson.
  Contents copyright © 2001 by
  John E. Simpson. All Rights Reserved. -->
  <head><title>FlixML Review</title></head>
  <body>
    <i>[body of review goes here]</i>
```

```
  </body>
</html>
```

It probably goes without saying, but I'll say it anyway, just in case: The reason you need an `xsl:comment` element, instead of just a "literal result comment" mechanism for placing comments into the result tree, is that such "literal result comments" would be assumed to be comments which applied to the stylesheet—not to the result tree. With elements, there's the convenient XML namespace convention to sort out which elements are in the stylesheet itself and which are intended for the result tree; but comments, being comments, can't be "namespaced."

Adding scripts to XHTML result trees

A favorite device of Web-page authors and developers is enclosing JavaScript code within comments. This causes the script to be hidden from older browsers, which didn't know about JavaScript and tended to simply display the code as if it were text. A simple example might look something like this:

```
<html>
<head>
<title>Scripted Comments</title>
<script language="javascript">
<!--
// Begin script hiding
function showBox() {
alert("{Some message or another}");
}
// End script hiding
-->
</script>
</head>
  <body onLoad="showBox()">See the box?</body>
</html>
```

The comment delimiters, `<!--` and `-->`, hide the body of the script from the older browsers, while the double slash, `//`, functions to comment out a line *within* the script itself. (The double slash at the start of a line is the JavaScript comment delimiter.)

It's easy enough to instantiate such a "comment/script" in an XHTML result tree, using the `xsl:comment` element to wrap the script. However, you've got to be extra careful if the script contains any characters—particularly ampersands or "less-than" (<) characters—that might cause the stylesheet itself, *as an XML document,* to fail to be well-formed.

For a simple example, let's create a result tree that includes a JavaScript function to pop up an alert-box if the number 1 is less than the number 2.[2] Here's some XSLT to do this—you can run it against a FlixML review or any other XML document, since its only match pattern is against the root node.

```
<xsl:stylesheet version="1.0"
  xmlns:xsl="http://www.w3.org/1999/XSL/Transform"
  xmlns="http://www.w3.org/1999/xhtml">

<xsl:template match="/">
<html>
<head>
<title>Scripted Comments</title>
<script language="javascript">
<xsl:comment>
// Begin script hiding
function showBox() {
if (1 &lt; 2) {
  alert("{Some message or another}");
  }
}
// End script hiding </xsl:comment>
</script>
</head>
  <body onLoad="showBox()">See the box?</body>
</html>
</xsl:template>

</xsl:stylesheet>
```

Note that the JavaScript if statement escapes the "<" using an entity reference. If you replace the entity reference < with a literal <, the stylesheet won't even parse as legitimate XML.

Using entity references has a couple of drawbacks, though:

• It makes the code harder to read, especially for someone who might not be

---

2. Of course, the number 1 is *always* less than the number 2, so the alert-box should always be displayed. The point here is to demonstrate how to get a "<" into the result tree, not to demonstrate some kind of exotic JavaScript technique.

familiar with markup-based entities.

- It becomes even harder to read if there are a *lot* of markup-reserved characters to be escaped.

The standard, "pure XML" way to get around these problems would be to enclose the script not only in XHTML comment delimiters (to hide the script from older browsers) but also in a CDATA section (to shield its contents from parsing). The trick here is to be sure that the CDATA section delimiters, `<![CDATA[` and `]]>`, are *also* hidden from browsers, as normal browsers hiccup quite loudly when handed such code. The best solution for that is to put the CDATA delimiters on the JavaScript-comment lines, like this:

```
<script language="javascript">
<xsl:comment>
// Begin script hiding <![CDATA[
function showBox() {
if (1 < 2) {
  alert("{Some message or another}");
  }
}
// ]]> End script hiding </xsl:comment>
</script>
```

This serves two purposes: It lets the stylesheet use the literal "<", and it hides the script in a way that's become common on Web pages.[3]

And a final complication

The one remaining possible problem with the above solution comes from XML's requirement that a CDATA section *not* include the character sequence "]]>", because that would cause the section to end prematurely.

In this context, you need to be sure that the *JavaScript code itself*

---

3.   I'm grateful to Simon St. Laurent (highly visible founder and administrator of the XHTML-L mailing list and participant on many others) for this excellent "CDATA in a comment" tip.

> doesn't contain the "right bracket-right bracket-greater than"
> sequence. I don't know what JavaScript circumstances would require
> you to use it, but if you do, you'll need to fall back on some alternative
> solution. One (if you just need the sequence for cosmetic reasons)
> might be to insert a space between the two right brackets. Or you can
> explicitly end the CDATA section just before the >, escape the > using
> >, then start a new CDATA section. Just be aware that you may need
> to do *something* extra (and perhaps something extra-bizarre) in this
> case.
>
>   The best solution of all is *not* to incorporate the JavaScript code
> directly in the body of the result tree. Rather, put it into a separate
> file—a JavaScript library—that your XHTML invokes via the src
> attribute of the script element, e.g.:
>
> ```
>    <script language="JavaScript" src="myScript.js" />
> ```

(I'll have more to say about dealing with special characters in your XSLT
stylesheets in a little bit, in the section of this chapter titled "Controlling the
Result Tree's Form/Type.")

Using xsl:processing-instruction

The xsl:processing-instruction element instantiates a PI in the result tree.
Its general syntax is this:

```
<xsl:processing-instruction
  name="target">
  [PI content]
</xsl:processing-instruction>
```

Using it is pretty straightforward. The name attribute assigns the PI's target,
and the content between the element's start and end tags becomes the content
of the PI—the string of text appearing in the PI between the target and the closing ?> delimiter.

By now, the most familiar sort of PI to you should be the xml-stylesheet
PI, used to link an XML document to a stylesheet. Earlier, I showed you a template rule that used the xsl:attribute element for converting a couple of
FlixML's elements into element/attribute combinations; I could add an xml-
stylesheet PI to the result tree by adding an xsl:processing-instruction
element to the root node's template rule as follows:

```
<xsl:template match="flixinfo">
  <xsl:processing-instruction name="xml-stylesheet">
    type="text/xsl" href="flixinfo_new.xsl"
  </xsl:processing-instruction>
  <flixinfo_new>
    <xsl:apply-templates select="genre"/>
  </flixinfo_new>
</xsl:template>
```

The result tree from the revised xsl:attribute demonstrator stylesheet will now be this:

```
<?xml-stylesheet type="text/xsl"
  href="flixinfo_new.xsl" ?>
<flixinfo_new>
  <genres>
    <genre genretype="primary">Action</genre>
    <genre genretype="other">Prison</genre>
    <genre genretype="other">Woman in Jeopardy</genre>
  </genres>
</flixinfo_new>
```

(By the way, note the placement of the xsl:processing-instruction element within the root element's template rule. It was placed *before* the start of the result tree's root flixinfo_new element, to ensure that the xml-stylesheet PI would go in the prolog, where it belongs.)

Using xsl:text

As with literal result elements and attributes, placing literal text into the result tree would seem to be—and is—pretty much a matter of determining the right template rule into which to insert it, and then just, well, *putting* it there.

You may run into a couple of problems in special cases, though, and in such cases you'll need to fall back on the xsl:text element. Its general syntax is this:

```
<xsl:text disable-output-escaping="yesorno">
  [text to be instantiated]
</xsl:text>
```

The two following lines of code produce identical results if used in a template:

```
FlixML Review
<xsl:text>FlixML Review</xsl:text>
```

Now let's look at the special circumstances in which the literal text will *not* be sufficient, and we'll need to resort to xsl:text.

Markup-significant characters

First, there's an occasional problem having to do with characters that have special meaning when used in markup contexts.

If the XSLT processor thinks your result tree is a markup-based document, such as XML or (X)HTML, it will take certain actions to "protect" the result tree—to ensure that it's at least well-formed. For example, it will represent special characters (those troublesome < and & characters, especially) in some escaped form.

You already know that you can't put a literal "<" in an XML document, including an XSLT stylesheet, so you already know you've got to escape it somehow. When your literal text includes an escaped special character like <, the XSLT processor is *not* going to put an *unescaped* < into the result tree. The processor, too, will escape it.[4] Remember, *this is the behavior you want in almost all cases.* You *want* your result tree to include escaped forms of any markup-significant characters.

> ## Really! No kidding!
>
> I can't tell you how many times a newcomer to XSLT pops up with this notion—the notion that, dang it, he or she *wants* the literal "<" or "&" in the result tree.
>
> No, he or she does *not* want that—not if the output format is (X)HTML or some other markup-based vocabulary. If a raw, hand-created HTML document doesn't accept a literal "<" character, then don't expect a machine-generated HTML result tree to be somehow treated specially by a downstream Web browser.

Anyway, just accept it as a matter of *fact*—not of taste, preference, the universe's perverse sense of humor, or whatever—that you do indeed want the XSLT processor to escape special characters when you're instantiating a markup-based result tree.

---

4. It's not required to use the same escaping mechanism that you used. For instance, it might put that one character in a CDATA section of its own, or it might use a numeric rather than a named entity reference. The one thing it will not do on its own is put the < there.

However, you definitely do not want this behavior if you're creating something *other* than markup. Consider a source tree that includes the following fragment in a hypothetical markup language for capturing mathematical and logical operations:

```
<if>
  <term>X</term>
  <operator>lteq</operator>
  <term>Y</term>
  <then>
    <term>X</term>
    <operator>increm</operator>
  </then>
</if>
```

You already know enough about XSLT to transform this source tree into the following result:

```
if (X &lt;= Y {X++;})
```

What you don't know how to do yet is how to create *this* result:

```
if (X <= Y {X++;})
```

Here's the solution; pay particular attention to the template rule for handling operator elements in the source tree:

```
<xsl:template match="if">
  if (<xsl:apply-templates/>)
</xsl:template>

<xsl:template match="term">
  <xsl:value-of select="."/>
</xsl:template>

<xsl:template match="then">
  {<xsl:apply-templates/>;}
</xsl:template>

<xsl:template match="operator">
  <xsl:choose>
    <xsl:when test=".='lteq'">
      <xsl:text
        disable-output-escaping="yes">&lt;=</xsl:text>
    </xsl:when>
    <xsl:when test=".='increm'">++</xsl:when>
```

```
  </xsl:choose>
</xsl:template>
```

This solution sets the `disable-output-escaping` attribute to "yes," overriding its default value of "no." (That is, it tells the XSLT processor, "*Disable* the escaping of special characters on output.") Since the characters used to replace the "increm" value of the operator element have no special significance in markup, there's no need to use the `xsl:text` element here.

Ampersands in URLs

Aside from JavaScript, which I covered in discussing `xsl:comment`, another common context in which people think their result tree quote-unquote "*must*" include an unescaped special character is in URIs, especially those that trigger some CGI-based query. For example,

```
http://www.foo.com/cgi-bin/qry?name=me&addr=MyCity
```

They quickly learn, of course, that in order to represent this URI in their document or stylesheet, they've got to escape the ampersand, as in the following:

```
http://www.foo.com/cgi-
  bin/qry?name=me&amp;addr=MyCity
```

From that point, however, they mistakenly assume they must somehow turn the escaped form back into the unescaped one. If your (or someone else's) server doesn't accept the `&amp;` form as-is in the URI, without requiring a literal `&`, then rest assured that the problem is not with your markup—the server in question needs upgrading. The escaped form of the bare ampersand is an acceptable character in a URI, and has been for some time.

Special whitespace handling

Here's a pop quiz for you. Take a look at the following two template rules; what do you think the output will look like?

```
<xsl:template match="flixinfo">
  <html>
    <head><title>FlixML Review</title></head>
    <body>
      <h2>Characters (space) Actors</h2>
      <xsl:apply-templates select="cast"/>
```

```
  </body>
 </html>
</xsl:template>

<xsl:template match="cast">
 <xsl:for-each select="*/*">
   <xsl:value-of select="role"/> <xsl:value-of
select="castmember"/><br />
 </xsl:for-each>
</xsl:template>
```

The first template rule's pretty easy, right? It builds the basic framework of an XHTML document. In the `body` element of that result will be a somewhat enigmatic level-2 heading, plus whatever is instantiated in the template rule for the `cast` element.

Then we go down to the second template rule—the one invoked by the first, within the result tree's `body` element. It looks like what we'll get is…hmm, the name of a character in the film, a space, and the name of the actor who played that part. (Aha. So that's what the level-2 heading meant.)

Unfortunately, that's not exactly what we *do* see, as shown in Figure 4–4.

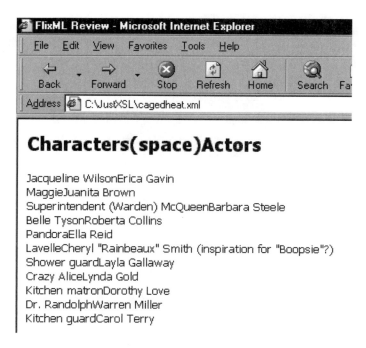

Figure 4-4   The mystery of the disappearing space.

The reason the blank space disappeared from between the values of the two adjacent elements, `role` and `castmember`, is once again the default behavior of an XSLT processor. In this case, what's going on is that XSLT processors *ignore any whitespace-only text nodes in the result tree.*

Why is that a useful default to have? The main reason is that, by far, most such text nodes aren't really meant to be passed downstream; they're there for legibility of the stylesheet only. (Remember that the general category of "whitespace characters" includes newlines, tabs, and so on, as well as garden-variety blank characters.) So when—as in this case—you need to force the processor to recognize this whitespace as significant, you need an override mechanism. That's the `xsl:text` element.

To use it in the above stylesheet, replace the blank space between the two `xsl:value-of` elements with the following:

```
<xsl:text> </xsl:text>
```

Now, as shown in Figure 4–5, the page displays as desired.

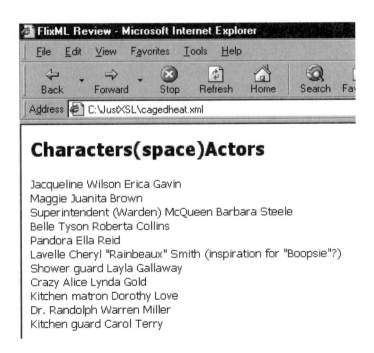

Figure 4-5 Return of the missing space between the names of characters and cast members' names, using `xsl:text`.

As with special markup characters, this kind of special treatment of whitespace can be most significant when creating result trees in some form besides XHTML or other markup. For instance, if you're transforming your source tree to a tab-delimited flat file for loading into a database or spreadsheet, you need to wrap each tab character *and* newline (which marks the end of a "record") in an xsl:text.

Here's an example. The following stylesheet transforms the character/cast member names to a flat file whose "fields" are separated by tab (	 entity reference) characters, with a newline (
) at the end of each "record."

```
<xsl:stylesheet version="1.0"
  xmlns:xsl="http://www.w3.org/1999/XSL/Transform">

<xsl:template match="flixinfo">
rolecastmember
<xsl:apply-templates select="cast"/>
</xsl:template>

<xsl:template match="cast">
<xsl:for-each select="*/*"><xsl:for-each select="*/*"><xsl:value-of
select="role"/><xsl:text>&#9;</xsl:text><xsl:value-of
select="castmember"/><xsl:text>&#10;</xsl:text></xsl:for-each></
xsl:for-each>
</xsl:template>

</xsl:stylesheet>
```

Showing the unshowable
In the stylesheet above, I used entity references to represent the tab and newline so you'd be able to see where those characters go. I could have more easily just keyed them in from the keyboard (in fact, initially I did so); but then the locations of the tab and newline wouldn't be as obvious.

The result tree from this transformation is shown below (I've replaced tabs in the output with → characters for readability here):

```
role→castmember
Jacqueline Wilson→Erica Gavin
Maggie→Juanita Brown
Superintendent (Warden) McQueen→Barbara Steele
Belle Tyson→Roberta Collins
```

Pandora→Ella Reid
Lavelle→Cheryl "Rainbeaux" Smith (inspiration for "Boopsie"?)
Shower guard→Layla Gallaway
Crazy Alice→Lynda Gold
Kitchen matron→Dorothy Love
Dr. Randolph→Warren Miller
Kitchen guard→Carol Terry

Reusing Stylesheet Content

Those of you who've had more than middling experience with real programming languages will be familiar with the virtues of reusable code. Why write some chunk of program code five or ten times in the identical way, or just by changing one or two little pieces of it?

This concept has carried over into XSLT in ways ranging from the tiny to the very large.

At the small end, it's easy to create, for example, some boilerplate template that can be reused in as many separate template rules as we want. At the high end of the scale, we can create entire stylesheets for embedding in other stylesheets. The high end I'll cover in Chapter 6, "Advanced XSLT," but in this section you'll learn about all the rest of it.

Variables

One of the low-end sorts of code reuse that programmers employ is referred to under the umbrella term "constants." Although its exact form varies with the syntax of the programming language in question, the programmer declares the value of a constant in code that might look something like the following at the top of a program or module:

```
Const MY_CONSTANT = "Here is some boilerplate text"
```

Then, whenever she wants to use the string, "Here is some boilerplate text," she just needs to use MY_CONSTANT instead. This makes program code more concise and much more easily maintainable; in order to change all occurrences of that string, she just has to change the declaration of MY_CONSTANT, and the change is instantly propagated out to all occurrences of it in the program.

You can declare such constants in your stylesheets, too, using a simple form of the xsl:variable element, declared as a top-level element. For instance,

```
<xsl:stylesheet version="1.0"
  xmlns:xsl="http://www.w3.org/1999/XSL/Transform">
```

```
<xsl:variable name="MY_CONSTANT" select="'Here is some
boilerplate text'"/>
```

[rest of stylesheet]

```
</xsl:stylesheet>
```

Now you can include the string "Here is some boilerplate text" in many locations throughout your stylesheet—typically in a template. The way you refer to this variable, once it's been declared, is to prefix its name with a dollar sign ($ character).

For instance,

```
<xsl:template match="something_in_source_tree">
  <p><xsl:value-of select="$MY_CONSTANT"/></p>
</xsl:template>
```

When the XSLT processor locates *something_in_source_tree*, whatever it is, it instantiates in the result tree an XHTML p element whose contents will be the string "Here is some boilerplate text."

Notice in the xsl:variable element which declared MY_CONSTANT that the select attribute's value was enclosed in embedded quotation marks. You saw something like this early in Chapter 3, in the discussion of templates (particularly, in the sub-section titled "Transferring source to result tree with xsl:value-of"). Just as in that earlier discussion, the reason for the embedded quotation marks is to prevent the processor from interpreting the value as an XPath location path.

Implied in that statement is a nugget of extra strength in variables, and also a nugget of potential confusion, and I'll cover both the strength and the confusion in a moment. First, though, let's look at the complete general syntax of xsl:variable:

```
<xsl:variable
  name="name"
  select="expression">
  [template]
</xsl:variable>
```

The *name*, of course, is the name by which the variable will be known. (In the xsl:variable element's name attribute, the $ sign is not used; that's required only when the variable is referred to elsewhere.)

Most importantly, a variable has a value, and the value is assigned either with the `select` attribute or with the optional *[template]*. That is, if you use the `select` attribute, the `xsl:variable` element must be empty; if you do not use the `select` attribute, there must be a *[template]*. So what's the difference between the two ways of assigning a value?

If you use the `select` attribute, the variable's value will always be a text string. It might be a literal text string, as above, or (if there's an XPath location path in the `select` attribute's value) it might be a node-set with a string-value, or it might be a Boolean true or false, or a number; but in any case, the value which the variable has will always be a string.

Now take a look at the following top-level variable declaration:

```
<xsl:variable name="auth_copy"
  select="concat(/flixinfo/@author, '/',
  /flixinfo/@copyright)"/>
```

In the case of the *Caged Heat* review, this declares a variable, `auth_copy`, which will be replaced with the string "John E. Simpson/2001" whenever it's referred to in the stylesheet where the variable is declared.

What's important about this example is that it shows why XSLT variables are *called* "variables" and not "constants": In most cases by far, their values are unknown until run time—they *vary* depending on some condition in the source tree.

Also, note that variables can be used in places other than the `select` attribute of an `xsl:value-of` element. For instance,

```
<xsl:if test="contains($auth_copy, 'Simpson')">
  John (or someone in his family) wrote this review!
</xsl:if>
```

As the value of the `select` attribute in a variable declaration, you can use a regular XPath expression like the following:

```
<xsl:variable name="title" select="//title"/>
```

Because this location path returns a node-set, the variable's value will be set to the string-value of the first node in the node-set, or "Caged Heat" in this case.

Now let's take a look at using a template to assign a variable's value, rather than the `select` attribute.

Templates as variable values

Here's a variable declaration using a template, instead of a `select` attribute to the `xsl:variable` element:

```
<xsl:variable name="temp_demo">
  <p>Some <i>italicized</i> text</p>
</xsl:variable>
```

What is the "value" of the variable `temp_demo`? As it happens, it's not simply a string-value, it's a collection of nodes:

- a text node consisting of a newline and tab (between the `>` in the `xsl:variable` element's start tag and the `<` in the p element's start tag);
- a p element node, containing two text nodes ("Some " and " text"), and an i element node, containing a text node ("italicized"); and
- a text node consisting strictly of a newline (between the `>` which closes the p element's end tag and the `<` at the start of the `xsl:variable` element's end tag).

> **Invisible whitespace-only nodes**
>
> As I discuss at the end of this chapter, the Microsoft XSLT processor—although compliant with the XSLT standard in almost every other respect—by default disregards any whitespace-only text nodes, such as those described in the first and third bullets above.

In short, you end up with something like a node-set or, indeed, a complete sub-tree. It's depicted schematically in Figure 4–6.

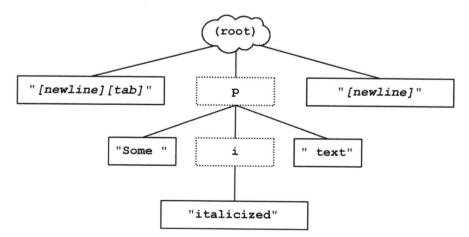

Figure 4-6   The "something like a node-set" contained in a typical `xsl:variable` element's template. In fact, it's *exactly* like a node-set, except for one thing…

As you can see, it may not be the kind of node-set you're used to encountering. Typically, you'll be dealing with node-sets consisting of elements only, or attributes only, or text nodes only, and so on. But it's *possible* to construct an XPath expression to extract a node-set that looks like this.

But what makes this truly—almost radically—different from the node-sets you're used to so far is that *its content does not come from the source tree*. In fact, its content, having been constructed in a template, can be considered part of the *result* tree.

And that's why this represents a new data type (neither string, nor Boolean, nor numeric, nor node-set), called a *result tree fragment*.

Result tree fragments

Result tree fragments (or RTFs, as they're generally known) are like node-sets, indeed like entire XML documents, in a number of respects.

- First, a given RTF (and each of the nodes it contains) has a string-value.
- Second, each RTF has a root "thing" in which the whole collection of nodes resides.
- Third, there's no limit on the *types* of nodes an RTF may contain. The example laid out above contained only text and element nodes (as well as a kind of "root node"); it could just as easily have contained attributes, PIs, and so on.

An RTF is also like any other template: It may contain a mixture of elements from both the XSLT and result-tree namespaces. Its content is well-balanced. (That is, it's not necessarily well-formed, because it doesn't require a root element, but all the elements within it are either empty or properly balanced with start-/end-tag pairs.)

Under Version 1.0 of XSLT, though, for all these wonderful things an RTF is like and *is*, there are only two things you can do with one:

- You can copy an RTF to the result tree. Simply declaring the containing variable, with the RTF contents, does not instantiate the RTF. What instantiates the RTF—puts it in the result tree for real—is *referencing* the variable with an `xsl:copy-of` element. Using the `xsl:copy-of` element is covered in Chapter 6.
- You can treat the RTF like a string. That is, you can do things such as concatenating its value with other strings, or substringing it, and so on, with

XPath string functions; and you can put its string-value (as opposed to its tree of nodes) into the result tree with

```
<xsl:value-of select="$variable_name"/>
```

The string-value of a variable is derived exactly like the string-value of an element: It's the concatenation of all text nodes contained by the variable. Consider the effect of using the following in a template elsewhere in the same stylesheet in which the variable `temp_demo` has been declared as above:

```
<xsl:value-of select="$temp_demo"/>
```

This instantiates in the result tree the text string "Some italicized text" (with those whitespace-only text nodes fore and aft). Similarly,

```
<xsl:value-of
    select="substring-before($temp_demo, ' ')"/>
```

instantiates the string "Some." And so on.

Treating RTFs as node-sets

It'd be wonderful if you could get at an RTF's contents and perform node-set operations on them. This would allow you to do "multi-pass" kinds of processing on the source tree before putting it into the result, by transforming a portion of the source tree into an RTF (one pass) and then applying sorting, grouping, selection, or other further transformations on the RTF itself (subsequent passes).

As I said, under Version 1.0 of XSLT, that's simply not possible. Copy an RTF, or "string" it: That's all you can do.

However, the possibility of treating RTFs like node-sets is potentially so powerful that all major XSLT 1.0 processors provide an *extension function*, the `node-set()` function, which converts a templated variable into a true node-set. If using an extension function offends your standards-compliant sense of ethics, consider that the ability to treat a templated variable like a node-set is almost certain to be included in a later version of the XSLT spec.

Although you can't use a variable whose value is an RTF as the value of an `xsl:template`'s `match` attribute, you *can* use it as the value of an `xsl:for-each`'s `select` attribute (as well as in certain other limited contexts). This lets you loop through an RTF's "tree" just as if it existed in the source tree. For instance,

```
<xsl:for-each select="$temp_demo/p">
```

> This says to process each p element which is a child of the
> `$temp_demo` variable's "root node."
> I'll cover the `node-set()` function (as well as XSLT's standard and
> other extension functions) in Chapter 5. A look at what's coming in
> future versions of XSLT is provided in Chapter 8.

Variable scope

Whether you're assigning a variable's value with the `select` attribute or with a
template, you must understand that a variable is "known" only within its parent
element. If the `xsl:variable` element is a top-level element, then its value can
be used anywhere in the stylesheet. If, however, the `xsl:variable` element is
used as an instruction, within some `xsl:template` or other element, then it's
invisible outside the scope of that element.

"Scope"? Huh?

You probably know, or can figure out, what I mean by "scope" here.
Just in case, though, by "scope" I'm referring to "the area between the
start and end tags of some element in an XSLT stylesheet."

Thus, if the `xsl:variable` element is a top-level element, its value is
known to (and can be used in) every element between the
`xsl:stylesheet` element's start and end tags, including lower-level as
well as other top-level elements. If the `xsl:variable` element is being
used as an instruction within some lower-level element, its value is
known only in the range between its parent element's start and end
tags.

Also, remember that although the order of top-level elements (particularly `xsl:template` elements) is not important in general to how a
stylesheet is processed, the order of instructions *within* top-level elements is very important. Unless there's some reason to do otherwise,
put your lower-level `xsl:variable` elements *before* any references to
them.

A variable's scope has a number of implications for how you use it:

• First and most obviously, you can't refer to the variable outside of its parent
  element's scope. If you try to do so, the XSLT processor will complain that
  you're referencing an unknown variable.

- Second, you can declare a variable in a top-level `xsl:variable`, and a variable of the same name in an `xsl:variable` contained in some lower-level element, but the two variables are not the *same* variable. For instance, changing the value in one of those two locations will not affect its value in the other.
- Third, you can declare a variable in an `xsl:variable` within a lower-level element, and a variable of the same name in some other lower-level element, but these two variables also do not refer to the same value.
- Fourth, within a given template containing an `xsl:variable` element, you can't have a second `xsl:variable` element declaring a variable of the same name. This is an error.
- Finally, and perhaps most subtly, a variable assumes the context of its containing element.

Let's take a closer look at this last implication.

Variables and context   Assume you've got a top-level variable that needs to refer to something in the source tree. What is the context at the point at which an XPath expression in the variable declaration is encountered?

To put it concretely, assume the following is a top-level variable declaration in a stylesheet processing the *Caged Heat* review:

```
<xsl:variable name="all_of_it" select="*"/>
```

What is the value of the variable at any point in the stylesheet which subsequently refers to $all_of_it?

We can test this easily enough, using the above declaration and a single template rule, as in the following:

```
<xsl:template match="/">
  <html>
  <head><title>FlixML Review</title></head>
    <body>
      <h2>Value of $all_of_it:</h2>
      <div><xsl:value-of select="$all_of_it"/></div>
    </body>
  </html>
</xsl:template>
```

Figure 4–7 shows the *Caged Heat* review transformed by the above stylesheet.

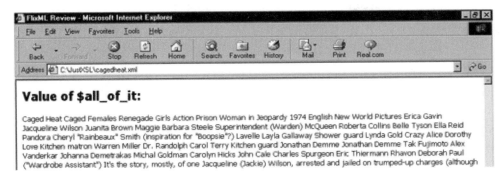

Figure 4-7 The value of a top-level variable that contains all of the *Caged Heat* FlixML review's elements. Looks like the value of the root element (`flixinfo`), doesn't it?

As you can see, the relative XPath expression `*` (which appears as the value of the `xsl:variable` element's `select` attribute) is evaluated in the context at that point: "Get all children of the context node." Since the context node here is the source tree's root node, the string-value you get is the same as if you'd requested the contents of the root `flixinfo` element.

Now let's take the `xsl:variable` declaration and push it down, into a lower-level template rule:

```
<xsl:template match="flixinfo">
  <html>
  <head><title>FlixML Review</title></head>
    <body>
      <xsl:apply-templates select="genre"/>
    </body>
  </html>
</xsl:template>

<xsl:template match="genre">
  <xsl:variable name="all_of_it" select="*"/>
  <h2>Value of $all_of_it:</h2>
  <div><xsl:value-of select="$all_of_it"/></div>
</xsl:template>
```

Now the `xsl:variable` element is "known" only within the scope of its parent `xsl:template` element, which narrows the context for all relative XPath location paths therein to just a portion of the source tree—the portion contained by the `genre` element. Thus, the `*` that's used as the value of the `xsl:variable`'s `select` attribute now looks at all children of the new context node and returns a node-set consisting of the primarygenre and two other-genre elements. Because the string-value of a node-set is simply the string-value of its first node, the results now look like the screen shot in Figure 4–8.

Figure 4-8 The value of a variable declared exactly like the one in Figure 4–7, but pushed down to a lower-level parent element (genre, in this example). Like all other relative XPath location paths, those used in variable declarations are sensitive to the context in which they're used.

Parameters

An XSLT parameter is similar to an XSLT variable—so similar, in fact, that you refer to a parameter the same way you do to a variable, by prefixing its name with a dollar sign.

> **No difference at all?**
>
> According to one portion of the XSLT 1.0 Recommendation, there are only variables, which may be declared in one of two ways: using xsl:variable or xsl:param (to be covered momentarily). This seems to me like hair-splitting. Common usage—indeed, the standard itself, elsewhere—considers variables and parameters as related but separate kinds of beasts.

Parameters are declared with an xsl:param element, which like xsl:variable can be a top-level element or an instruction. The syntax and restrictions are the same, too:

```
<xsl:param
  name="name"
  select="expression">
```

```
[template]
</xsl:param>
```

where the parameter's value is defined by either the `select` attribute (in which case the element must be empty) or the optional template (in which case there may not be a `select` attribute).

What distinguishes parameters from variables is this: The value of a parameter, as established by the `xsl:param` element, is merely its *initial* value—a default, if you will, which can be overridden at the time the parameter is invoked. Thus, whereas a variable's value is assigned once and remains fixed for the life of the transformation, parameter values can be reassigned as many times as necessary.

The most common use of parameters is with named templates, which I'll cover shortly. Also very useful, though, are *global parameters*—those defined in top-level `xsl:param` elements—and we'll look briefly at them first.

Global parameters

When you define a parameter in a top-level `xsl:param`, its value (like that of a top-level `xsl:variable`) is accessible anywhere within the stylesheet. Its initial value, as assigned by the `xsl:param`, can also be overridden if the parameter is invoked from a higher level.

That ought to be setting off alarm bells in your head. What's at a higher level, after all, than a top-level element—given that the `xsl:stylesheet` element must contain everything else in the stylesheet?

The answer is that the `xsl:stylesheet` (the stylesheet itself) can be "contained" in two ways:

- It can be imported into another stylesheet, so that its content is then logically contained by *that* stylesheet's `xsl:stylesheet` element. I'll cover importing stylesheets in Chapter 6, "Advanced XSLT."
- The stylesheet is "contained" by the operating system/environment that invokes the XSLT processor.

This second view of a stylesheet is *always* in effect, so you don't have to do anything special to "make it happen." And it has one lovely practical implication: You can override a global parameter by telling the XSLT processor what the override value should be.

Naturally, how you "tell the XSLT processor" anything depends entirely on which XSLT processor you're trying to communicate with. If the processor is being used in a static way, from the command line, you generally pass the overriding parameter values using command-line switches; dynamic processors receive overriding parameter values from scripts.

For now, just as an example, let's look at overriding a parameter using Saxon in its command-line (static) mode.

Consider the following extracts from an XSLT stylesheet:

```
<xsl:param name="bgcolor" select="'white'"/>
<xsl:param name="fgcolor" select="'black'"/>

<xsl:template match="flixinfo">
  <html>
    <head>
      <title>FlixML Review</title>
      <style>
        .title {background-color: <xsl:value-of select="$bgcolor"/>;
          color: <xsl:value-of select="$fgcolor"/>}
      </style>
    </head>
    <body>
      <div class="title">
        <xsl:apply-templates select="title"/>
      </div>
    </body>
  </html>
</xsl:template>

<xsl:template match="title[@role='main']">
  <h1><xsl:value-of select="."/></h1>
</xsl:template>

<xsl:template match="title[@role='alt']">
  <h2><xsl:value-of select="."/></h2>
</xsl:template>
```

Two global parameters are defined here: bgcolor (whose default value is the text string "white") and fgcolor ("black"). Each of these parameters is referenced once, in a style element that sets CSS properties for a class called title; any result-tree element with a class attribute of "title" will have its background color set to white, and its foreground color to black.

Simply running this stylesheet against the *Caged Heat* review with Saxon, not overriding the global parameters, produces the following result tree:

```html
<html>
  <head><title>FlixML Review</title></head>
  <style>
    .title {background-color: white;
     color: black}
  </style>
  <body>
    <div class="title">
      <h1>Caged Heat</h1>
      <h2>Caged Females</h2>
      <h2>Renegade Girls</h2>
    </div>
  </body>
</html>
```

When you view this output in a browser (or at least, a browser that understands CSS), you see something like what's shown in Figure 4–9.

Figure 4-9   Saxon's output using default values for the `bgcolor` and `fgcolor` global parameters. That's MSIE on the left, obviously, and Netscape 6 on the right.

With Saxon at the command line, you provide parameter overrides using simple `name=value` pairs. Thus, we can override the `bgcolor` parameter using this command line:

```
saxon -a cagedheat.xml bgcolor=silver
```

(In this example, the `-a` command-line switch tells Saxon to use the `xml-stylesheet` PI to determine which stylesheet to use. The processor's default behavior is to accept the name of the stylesheet on the command line, following the name of the XML document to be transformed.)

This produces the following result tree, which differs from the previous one only in the CSS `background-color` property setting:

```
<html>
  <head>
    <title>FlixML Review</title>
    <style>
      .title {background-color: silver;
        color: black}
    </style>
  </head>
  <body>
    <div class="title">
      <h1>Caged Heat</h1>
      <h2>Caged Females</h2>
      <h2>Renegade Girls</h2>
    </div>
  </body>
</html>
```

In a browser, this displays as shown in Figure 4–10.

Figure 4-10 Saxon's result tree, with the `bgcolor` global parameter's default value ("white") overridden on the command line (to "silver"). Again, MSIE on the left, Netscape 6 on the right.

Finally, of course, you can override *both* the `bgcolor` and `fgcolor` global parameters with something like this command line:

```
saxon -a cagedheat.xml bgcolor=black fgcolor=white
```

This reverses the original settings of the corresponding CSS properties, with results as shown in Figure 4–11.

Figure 4-11 Saxon's result tree, viewed in MSIE, as a result of overriding both the `bg-color` and `fgcolor` global attributes.

Skimming the surface

The example above is kind of interesting or cute, but it only hints at the capabilities of global parameters and how they can be used in your stylesheets—especially how overriding them can customize a stylesheet's operation.

There are some things you *can't* do with global parameters (or with regular ones, or with plain old variables, for that matter). On the whole, though, I encourage you to experiment with the parameterizing features of whatever XSLT processor you decide to use.

Named templates

A *named template* is to a stylesheet what a function is to a programming language: a way to encapsulate commonly used code and perhaps to customize or otherwise affect its behavior by passing data to it.

As the term implies, a named template is like any other template, except that it has a name. That is, the corresponding `xsl:template` element has no `match` attribute, but it *does* have a (required) `name` attribute. The value of the `name` attribute is a text string by which the template will be "known" elsewhere in the stylesheet. In order to put the contents of a named template into a real template, you simply include an `xsl:call-template` element at that point.

The general syntax of this element is this:

```
<xsl:call-template
  name="name">
  [optional xsl:with-param]
</xsl:call-template>
```

The optional `xsl:with-param` element passes a parameter to the template. If you're not passing a parameter, the `xsl:call-template` element will be empty.

For instance,

```
<xsl:template name="backtotop">
  <p>
    [ <a href="#top">Return to Top</a> ]
  </p>
</xsl:template>

<xsl:template match="flixinfo">
  <html>
    <head>
      <title>FlixML Review</title>
    </head>
    <body>
      <a name="top" />
      <xsl:for-each select="*">
        <h2>"<xsl:value-of select="name()"/>" element</h2>
        <xsl:if test="@*">
          <h4>
          <xsl:for-each select="@*">
            @<xsl:value-of select="name()"/>: <xsl:value-
of select="."/>
          </xsl:for-each>
          </h4>
        </xsl:if>
        <xsl:value-of select="."/>
        <xsl:call-template name="backtotop"/>
      </xsl:for-each>
    </body>
  </html>
</xsl:template>
```

The named template at the top of this extract sets up a simple, conventional "Back to Top" link, with an XHTML `a` element enclosed in a `p` element. The `a` element's `href` attribute points to a location in the result tree that will be named "top".

In the template rule, which processes the `flixinfo` element, a number of things are going on. First, there's the usual code to set up an `html` root element (and `head`, `title`, and `body` descendants) in the result tree. Then there's an empty `a` element, which uses the `name` attribute to associate this point in the result tree with the name "top." The body of the template rule comprises a pair of nested `xsl:for-each` elements, one for all children of the `flixinfo` element and one for all attributes (if any) of those children. Following a dump of each child's data to the result tree, an `xsl:call-template` element invokes the template whose name is "backtotop"—that is, the named template previously defined.

When viewed in MSIE, this result tree appears as in Figure 4–12.

Figure 4-12   Using a named template to instantiate the same result-tree content (here, a "Return to Top" hyperlink) repeatedly. Note the status bar's value, while the cursor hovers over the generated hyperlink.

Passing parameters to named templates

A simple named template can be a useful tool in its own right, for those occasions when you need to duplicate entire blocks of result-tree content. Far more useful and powerful, though, is the ability to pass data into a named template, in the same manner that arguments are passed to a programming language function; this passed data can then affect the nature of what is actually instantiated in the result tree at that point.

To make this work, you declare the parameter within and at the start of the named template itself. Then, at any point where you invoke the template, using `xsl:call-template` as in the preceding example, immediately (within the `xsl:call-template`) supply the override value using an `xsl:with-param` element. This is a simple element that assigns a value to the parameter using either a `select` attribute or a template, just as a variable or parameter definition does. That is, the general structure looks something like this:

```
<xsl:template name="some_temp">
  <xsl:param name="some_param" select="'some_value'"/>
  [do something with $some_param]
</xsl:template>

<xsl:template match="something_in_source">
  <xsl:call-template name="some_temp">
    <xsl:with-param name="some_param"
     select="'other_value'"/>
  </xsl:call-template>
</xsl:template>
```

See the way this all fits together? The some_temp named template does something with a parameter, some_param, which it declares; this parameter has a default value of "some_value". The template rule that matches something_in_source invokes the named template, and—using the xsl:with-param element—*overrides* the value of the some_param parameter. Thus, when some_temp does its "something," it will no longer be using "some_value" but the override value, the string "other_value".

Let's look at a simple demonstration case. This is based on a recognition that a FlixML review contains a couple (often long) lists of things which can be represented in two-column XHTML tables: the cast members (for which the columns might be the actor's or actress's name followed by the name of the character played—the role) and crew (crew member's name, crew member's position or "title"). We're going to define a simple named template to instantiate a kind of generic table-header row and two parameters (which can be overridden) to fill in the column headings:

```
<xsl:template name="tbl_head">
  <xsl:param name="col_1" select="'Col 1'"/>
  <xsl:param name="col_2" select="'Col 2'"/>
  <tr>
    <th><xsl:value-of select="$col_1"/></th>
    <th><xsl:value-of select="$col_2"/></th>
  </tr>
</xsl:template>

<xsl:template match="leadcast">
  <h2>Lead Cast</h2>
  <table border="1">
    <xsl:call-template name="tbl_head">
      <xsl:with-param name="col_1" select="'Name'"/>
      <xsl:with-param name="col_2" select="'Role'"/>
    </xsl:call-template>
    <xsl:for-each select="*">
      <tr>
        <td><xsl:value-of select="castmember"/></td>
        <td><xsl:value-of select="role"/></td>
      </tr>
    </xsl:for-each>
  </table>
</xsl:template>

<xsl:template match="crew">
  <h2>Crew</h2>
  <table border="1">
    <xsl:call-template name="tbl_head">
      <xsl:with-param name="col_2" select="'Title'"/>
    </xsl:call-template>
    <xsl:for-each select="*">
      <tr>
        <td><xsl:value-of select="."/></td>
        <td><xsl:value-of select="name()"/></td>
      </tr>
    </xsl:for-each>
  </table>
</xsl:template>
```

The template rule for processing the leadcast element invokes the named template, tbl_head, and overrides both parameters' values; the one for processing the `crew` element overrides the `col_2` parameter only.[5] MSIE displays the review, transformed via this stylesheet, as shown in Figure 4–13.

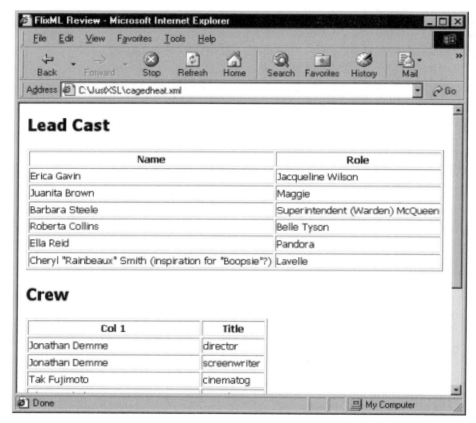

Figure 4-13   Overriding both the `col_1` and `col_2` table headers in a named template (for the Lead Cast table), and the `col_2` table header only (for the Crew table).

Recursion with named templates and parameters

I've mentioned before that XSLT's loop-like features, `xsl:for-each` and `xsl:apply-templates`, don't provide you with true equivalents of looping

---

5.   Not that the default value of `col_1` is particularly attractive; I just want to show you what happens when you *don't* override a parameter's initial value.

features available in programming languages. In particular, all that `xsl:for-each` and `xsl:apply-templates` permit is repeatedly stamping out a template, given some repetitive structure (such as a list of nodes) in the source tree. You can't use them to reassign values to variables, process successive pieces of a text string, or do any of the other kinds of iterative processing familiar to programmers.

However, you *do* have the ability to achieve some of the same effects of traditional programming loops, using named templates, parameters, and a principle called *recursion.*

To understand recursion, start by thinking of a hypothetical function, similar to the XPath functions you already know about. The purpose of this function is to compare several strings and return the longest one. Let's name this function `string-biggest()`, and assume that it takes one argument—a node-set.

To make `string-biggest()` work using recursion, it would need to do something like the following (in pseudo-code):

```
function string-biggest(nodeset):
  if nodeset is not empty
    assign first string to a variable X
    assign variable Y's value by:
      calling string-biggest()
        (passing as nodeset all nodes BUT the first)
    if length of X is > length of Y
      return X
    else
      return Y
    end if
  otherwise
    return ""
  end if
```

What makes this recursive is the portion of the function's code where `string-biggest()` invokes itself. A recursive function is one that "calls itself" repeatedly. (In order for this to work, there must be some "shut-off" condition that occurs; otherwise the loop repeats forever.)

In XSLT, we might do the following:

```
<xsl:template match="flixinfo">
  <html>
  <head><title>Recursion Demo</title></head>
    <body>
      <h2>Longest Crew Member's Name:</h2>
      <xsl:apply-templates select="crew"/>
```

```
      </body>
    </html>
</xsl:template>

<!-- This template behaves like the string-biggest()
   function which was pseudo-coded in the text -->
<xsl:template name="string-biggest">
  <!-- The "nodeset" parameter is like the argument
     passed into the function -->
  <xsl:param name="nodeset"/>
  <xsl:choose>
    <!-- Is the nodeset to be processed empty? -->
    <xsl:when test="$nodeset">
      <!-- Parameter isn't empty... -->
      <!-- Declares a variable, "first-node," whose
        value equals the string-value of the first node
        in the passed parameter -->
      <xsl:variable name="first-node"
        select="$nodeset[1]"/>
      <!-- Declares another variable,
        "biggest-other-node," by calling this named
        template... and passing it the *rest* of the
        nodeset being processed -->
      <xsl:variable name="biggest-other-node">
        <xsl:call-template name="string-biggest">
          <xsl:with-param name="nodeset"
            select="$nodeset[position()!=1]"/>
        </xsl:call-template>
      </xsl:variable>
      <xsl:choose>
        <!-- Is the (current) first node longer than
          the (current) remaining node? -->
        <xsl:when test="string-length($first-node) &gt; string-
length($biggest-other-node)">
          <!-- First node is longer -->
          <xsl:value-of select="$first-node"/>
        </xsl:when>
        <xsl:otherwise>
          <!-- Remaining node is longer -->
          <xsl:value-of select="$biggest-other-node"/>
        </xsl:otherwise>
      </xsl:choose>
    </xsl:when>
    <xsl:otherwise>
      <!-- Parameter is empty; just return an
        empty string -->
```

```
     <xsl:value-of select="''"/>
    </xsl:otherwise>
  </xsl:choose>
</xsl:template>

<xsl:template match="crew">
  <p>
    <xsl:call-template name="string-biggest">
      <xsl:with-param name="nodeset" select="*"/>
    </xsl:call-template>
  </p>
</xsl:template>
```

What's going on inside the named template can be a little mind-bending when you first see it. In general, its purpose is to *delay returning a value* to the template rule processing the crew element *until it has repeatedly compared each value in the list to the currently longest value.*

We can start to trace the activity in this named template by considering the value of the nodeset parameter originally passed to it by the crew element's template rule. There are 12 nodes originally, whose string-values are listed in Table 4–1.

Table 4-1   String-values of Children of the crew Element

Original position	String-value	Length
1	Jonathan Demme	14
2	Jonathan Demme	14
3	Tak Fujimoto	12
4	Alex Vanderkar	14
5	Johanna Demetrakas	18
6	Michal Goldman	14
7	Carolyn Hicks	13
8	John Cale	9
9	Charles Spurgeon	16
10	Eric Thiermann	14

Table 4-1   String-values of Children of the `crew` Element (continued)

Original position	String-value	Length
11	Rhavon	6
12	Deborah Paul ("Wardrobe Assistant")	35

Given that 12 nodes are passed to the named template, 11 comparisons must be made: comparing the first to the second, the longest of those two to the third, the longest of *those* two to the fourth, and so on. (Note that when the current "first-node" is compared to the rest of the nodes, the comparison takes advantage of the fact that the string-value of a node-set is the string-value of the first node in it.) The details are these:

- On the first pass through, "Jonathan Demme" is compared to "Jonathan Demme". Because the former is not longer than the latter, the template's value at the time this first comparison is complete is the value of the latter.
- The template calls itself, trimming off the first node in the `nodeset` parameter before passing it.
- "Jonathan Demme" is compared to "Tak Fujimoto". The first string is longer than the second, so the template's current value remains "Jonathan Demme".
- The template calls itself again, again removing the first node in `nodeset` before passing it.
- "Jonathan Demme" is compared to "Alex Vanderkar". The first string is not longer than the second; therefore the template's current value is reset to "Alex Vanderkar."
- Processing continues through the remaining nodes in `nodeset`; the template's final value will be whichever of the 12 nodes had the longest value, and that node's string value is the one which will be instantiated as the content of the `crew` template rule's p element.

An imperfect example

Actually, it's not necessarily true that this named template finds *the* longest string-value; that's because a given node-set may include more than one node with the longest string-value. What this named template finds is the *last* node with the longest string-value. If there were

> another node, further along in the `crew` element, whose string-value's length was also 35 characters, the `string-biggest` named template would return *that* node's value, not the one for "Deborah Paul ('Wardrobe Assistant')."
>
> Note, by the way, that a recursive named template seems to violate the rule that variables can't be updated. This one, for example, resets the value of the `first-node` variable for each pass through the loop. In a larger sense, though, it still fits the criterion: Each variable is set (declared) at only a single point in the template.

Recursion is an extremely valuable skill to have when constructing XSLT stylesheets, particularly complex ones. You can use it not only for iteratively processing strings but also for tasks such as finding the sum of some calculated number (like unit price times quantity). If you find yourself in a bind, unable to do some repeated operation with the tools XSLT gives you "natively," consider doing it inside a recursive template, instead.

Named attribute sets

The final kind of "reusable code" you can include in your XSLT stylesheets, named attribute sets, allows you to easily assign the same attributes to more than one element.

There are two possible advantages to this. First, it may make your stylesheet more concise; second, even in cases where using a named attribute set is more verbose than explicitly assigning the duplicate attributes several times, it will make your stylesheet more easily maintainable. (Change the attributes' values in one spot, instead of in many.)

Creating a named attribute set is easy; just use the top-level `xsl:attribute-set` element, whose general syntax is as follows:

```
<xsl:attribute-set name="name"
  use-attribute-sets="attrib_sets_to_include">
  [content: xsl:attribute element(s)]
</xsl:attribute>
```

where:

- the `name` attribute (required) is the name by which this attribute set will be known;

- the `use-attribute-sets` attribute (optional) is a whitespace-delimited list of the names of *other* attribute sets you'd like to include in this one; and
- *[content: xsl:attribute element(s)]* is a set of one or more `xsl:attribute` elements, establishing names and values for all the attributes you'd like to include in this named attribute set (other than those defined in the attribute sets, if any, named in the `use-attribute-sets` attribute).

To actually apply the attributes identified in one or more named attribute sets to some element, include with that element a `use-attribute-sets` attribute whose value (as described in the second bullet above) is a whitespace-delimited list of attribute-set names. (Note that if the element in question is coded as a literal result element, rather than using an `xsl:element` element, you'll have to include the `xsl:` namespace prefix on its name: `xsl:use-attribute-sets`.)

One simple instance in which I often find myself using this element is setting up XHTML tables. The default behavior of a browser is to "auto-fit" columns—to make them as wide as needed for the widest table cell, and no wider or narrower. This leads to results like the ones you see in Figure 4–13, a few pages ago. It doesn't look, well, *professional*, because the eye (at least my eye) prefers things aligned as much as possible.

So in my XSLT stylesheets, I typically have something like the following declared as attribute sets:

```
<xsl:attribute-set name="table-2col">
  <xsl:attribute name="width">90%</xsl:attribute>
  <xsl:attribute name="cellspacing">3</xsl:attribute>
  <xsl:attribute name="cellpadding">3</xsl:attribute>
  <xsl:attribute name="border">0</xsl:attribute>
</xsl:attribute-set>

<xsl:attribute-set name="td-col1">
  <xsl:attribute name="width">33%</xsl:attribute>
  <xsl:attribute name="valign">top</xsl:attribute>
</xsl:attribute-set>

<xsl:attribute-set name="td-col2">
  <xsl:attribute name="width">67%</xsl:attribute>
  <xsl:attribute name="valign">top</xsl:attribute>
</xsl:attribute-set>
```

Then I'll use those attribute sets in template rules like these slightly modified versions of the template rules behind Figure 4–13:

```
<xsl:template name="tbl_head">
  <xsl:param name="col_1" select="'Col 1'"/>
  <xsl:param name="col_2" select="'Col 2'"/>
  <tr>
    <th xsl:use-attribute-sets="td-col1">
      <xsl:value-of select="$col_1"/>
    </th>
    <th xsl:use-attribute-sets="td-col2">
      <xsl:value-of select="$col_2"/>
    </th>
  </tr>
</xsl:template>

<xsl:template match="leadcast">
  <h2>Lead Cast</h2>
  <table xsl:use-attribute-sets="table-2col">
    <xsl:call-template name="tbl_head">
      <xsl:with-param name="col_1" select="'Name'"/>
      <xsl:with-param name="col_2" select="'Role'"/>
    </xsl:call-template>
    <xsl:for-each select="*">
      <tr>
        <td xsl:use-attribute-sets="td-col1">
          <xsl:value-of select="castmember"/>
        </td>
        <td xsl:use-attribute-sets="td-col2">
          <xsl:value-of select="role"/>
        </td>
      </tr>
    </xsl:for-each>
  </table>
</xsl:template>

<xsl:template match="crew">
  <h2>Crew</h2>
  <table xsl:use-attribute-sets="table-2col">
    <xsl:call-template name="tbl_head">
      <xsl:with-param name="col_2" select="'Title'"/>
    </xsl:call-template>
    <xsl:for-each select="*">
      <tr>
        <td xsl:use-attribute-sets="td-col1">
          <xsl:value-of select="."/>
        </td>
        <td xsl:use-attribute-sets="td-col2">
          <xsl:value-of select="name()"/>
```

```
          </td>
        </tr>
      </xsl:for-each>
    </table>
  </xsl:template>
```

With a CSS style to alter the background color of table headers, the data from Figure 4–13 now displays as shown in Figure 4–14, thanks to the fact that both tables—and their headers and table cells—now share common attributes:

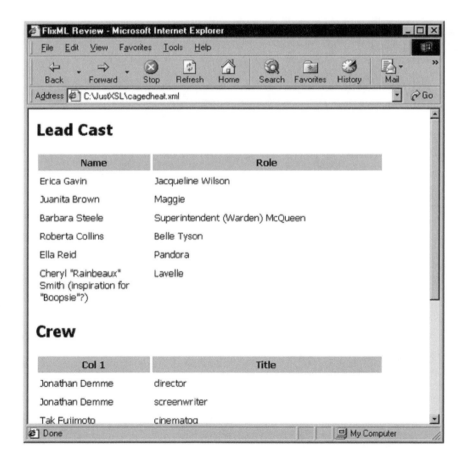

Figure 4-14   Same data and template rules (viewed with MSIE) as in Figure 4–13, except that the tables' layouts are controlled using common named attribute sets.

Sorting Content

Often, the order in which you want your content to appear in the result tree is different from the order in which it appears in the source. Controlling this is fairly easy, using the `xsl:sort` element. The general syntax of this element (which looks more complex than it really is) is this:

```
<xsl:sort
 select="expression"
 lang="langcode"
 data-type="text_number_name"
 order="ascending_descending"
 case-order="upper_lower-first" />
```

Note that `xsl:sort` is always empty and can appear only as a child of the `xsl:apply-templates` or `xsl:for-each` elements.[6] If you use it with `xsl:for-each`, it must be the *first* child of that element.

Now let's take a look at those five attributes. (Except for `select`, by the way, any or all of them can be assigned values using AVTs.)

The `select` attribute

The value of the `select` attribute is most often an XPath location path, relative to the context currently established by either the `xsl:apply-templates` or `xsl:for-each` element. The attribute's value will be used as the *key* for the sorting operation—that is, the value on which you want to sort the data. (The default value is `.`, meaning "sort on the string-value of the current node.")

For instance, take a look at the external reviews of *Caged Heat*. Such reviews are linked to from a FlixML document using a `reviewlink` element, whose `xlink:href` attribute provides the URI of the review and whose `#PCDATA` content is the name or a brief description of the site/page being linked to.

We could produce a sorted table of these external reviews—sorted on the name/description—using a template rule something like the following:

---

6. Why just these two? Because they're the ones which stamp out multiple identically-structured chunks of a result tree. (If a structure occurs only once, there's no need to sort it.) The `xsl:sort` defines for its parent element the order in which to do the stamping-out.

```
<xsl:template match="reviews">
  <table>
    <xsl:for-each select="otherreview/*">
     <xsl:sort select="reviewlink"/>
     <tr>
       <td><a href="{reviewlink/@xlink:href}"><xsl:value-of
select="reviewlink"/></a></td>
     </tr>
    </xsl:for-each>
  </table>
</xsl:template>
```

In MSIE, this template rule (as well as a descriptive level-2 heading set up in the template rule for the root `flixinfo` element) displays as shown in Figure 4–15.

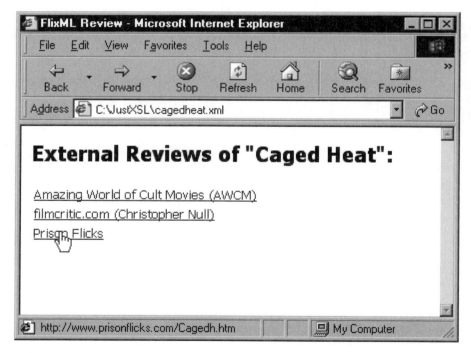

Figure 4-15   A sorted list of the names/descriptions of links to external reviews. Note that the XHTML links' `href` attributes are constructed from the corresponding `reviewlink` elements' `href` attributes, with an AVT.

Knowing your limits

One thing you may be tempted to try—for all of about five minutes—is building a variable from information in the source tree, and using that as a sort key. This is a lot harder than it looks, because of the limitation on placement of the `xsl:sort` element and variable-scope constraints. (You can't put an `xsl:variable` element in an `xsl:apply-templates` at all, which means you've got to use `xsl:for-each` to do the sort... but then you can't declare the variable to be used as a sort key before the `xsl:sort` element, because that element has to be the *first* child of the `xsl:for-each`.)

I've solved this problem once, but trust me, it wasn't pretty. Basically, the idea was to sort not the source tree itself but a result-tree fragment (RTF) holding the contents of the node-set I wanted to sort, including a "dummy field" that functioned as the artificial sort key. It worked, but when I showed it to other XSLT users, they agreed with me that it was like the dog that danced the rumba on its hind legs in the old vaude-ville act: What was surprising wasn't how well it functioned, but that it functioned at all.

The `lang` attribute

The value of this attribute is constrained in the same way as the value of XML's built-in `xml:lang` attribute: It must be a legitimate "language code." (This is usu-ally a two-character code such as EN, NO, ru, jp, and so on.) The purpose of the `lang` attribute is to identify the language in which the sort key (identified by the `select` attribute) is represented.

Why would it be important to tell the processor what the sort key's language is? Because different languages have different sorting rules. For example, Span-ish commonly considers the "Ch" letter combination as though it were a sepa-rate, single letter altogether, between C and D. If you sort a Spanish-language dictionary as if it were English, the Spanish words *cable, chorro,* and *color* (for *cable, jet* or *spurt,* and *color,* respectively) sort in that order; if you sort them in tradi-tional Spanish order, they'll sort as *cable, color, chorro.*

The default value for `lang` depends on the environment in which the pro-cessor is running.

The `data-type` attribute

This attribute instructs the processor to treat the sort key (specified by the `select` attribute) as text or numeric, using the values `text` (the default) or `number`, respectively.

The difference in how sorting works with the attribute's two values will be obvious if you consider the following excerpt from an XSLT stylesheet to process the *Caged Heat* review; pay particular attention to the `xsl:sort` element in the first template rule:

```
<xsl:template match="flixinfo">
  <html>
    <head>
      <title>Datatype Demo</title>
    </head>
    <body>
      <table border="1">
        <tr>
          <th>Elem Name</th>
          <th>Children/Attribs</th>
        </tr>
        <xsl:apply-templates
          select="*[count(*|@*) &gt; 0]">
          <xsl:sort select="count(*|@*)"/>
        </xsl:apply-templates>
      </table>
    </body>
  </html>
</xsl:template>

<xsl:template match="*">
  <tr>
    <td><xsl:value-of select="name()"/></td>
    <td align="right"><xsl:value-of
      select="count(*|@*)"/></td>
  </tr>
</xsl:template>
```

Basically, all this stylesheet does is process the `flixinfo` element and all its children—but of the latter, it selects only those for which the number of child elements and attributes together is greater than 0. (That is, children of `flixinfo` with no child elements and no attributes will not be considered. This eliminates the `language`, `studio`, `dialog`, and `remarks` elements.)

For the `flixinfo` element itself, the stylesheet simply instantiates the basic XHTML result tree including a two-column table. The `xsl:apply-templates` element contains an `xsl:sort` element which sorts the child elements on the basis of the number of their child elements and attributes. Note that there is no `data-type` attribute for this `xsl:sort`, and therefore the default is `text`.

Results of the sort are as shown in Figure 4–16.

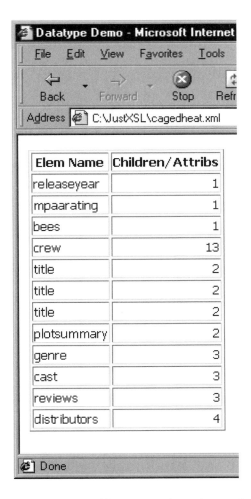

Elem Name	Children/Attribs
releaseyear	1
mpaarating	1
bees	1
crew	13
title	2
title	2
title	2
plotsummary	2
genre	3
cast	3
reviews	3
distributors	4

Figure 4-16 Sorting a numeric value (the count of an element's child elements and attributes) as if it were text. This would be (or rather, *look*) pretty much dead-on if it weren't for the `crew` element's count.

To correct the problem, we'd just add the `data-type` attribute to the `xsl:sort` element, and set its value to `number` so it looks as follows:

```
<xsl:sort select="count(*|@*)" data-type="number"/>
```

Now the sorted results look (or rather, *are*) much more reasonable, as seen in Figure 4–17.

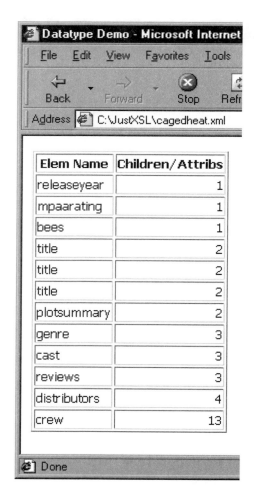

Figure 4-17   Sorting a numeric value *as* a number. Note the big (only) difference from the listing in Figure 4–16—the positioning of the `crew` element at the *end* of the list.

More than two `data-type` values

Actually, the XSLT spec allows a third value for the `data-type` attribute—or, rather, a third *type* of value. This is a "QName"—that is, an XML name qualified if necessary with a namespace prefix. The intention here is to leave the door open for using data types possibly to be defined by the XML Schema standard.

For example, if XML Schema defines a data type called "date," this might be useful for sorting dates in something other than the convenient yyyy-mm-dd format, such as 1-3-1996. Presumably, the `xsl:sort` element's `data-type` attribute in this case would take a value such as "xsd:date". (The conventional namespace prefix for elements and attributes in the XML Schema namespace is `xsd:`.)

The `order` attribute

The `order` attribute takes one of two values, `ascending` (the default) or `descending`. As you can probably guess, this causes the list of items to be sorted in "natural" lowest-to-highest order, or in highest-to-lowest if desired.

In the previous example, I could have sorted the list of elements in descending numeric order (putting the `crew` element at the top) with this `xsl:sort` element:

```
<xsl:sort select="count(*|@*)" data-type="number"
  order="descending"/>
```

The `case-order` attribute

This final attribute to the `xsl:sort` element is, like the `lang` attribute, included primarily in support of internationalization. It can take one of two possible values, `upper-first` or `lower-first`, which indicate that uppercase letters are to sort before their lowercase equivalents or vice-versa, respectively. There is no specific default; the default depends on the language in use.

The importance of the `case-order` attribute likewise depends on the language. For example, logographic (such as Chinese) and syllabic (such as Japanese and Korean) writing systems do not provide the concept of "case" at all; all of their characters may be said to be in the same case. For such languages, specifying a `case-order` attribute would be pretty silly.

Even within languages and writing systems you might think would share a lot in common, there can be differences. For instance, if the language in question is Danish or German, `upper-first` is the norm; if it's Swedish, `lower-first` is used.

The moral of the story about using the `case-order` attribute is twofold: (a) know your data and (b) know what you're doing.

And then the third fold: Know your software

With the `case-order` attribute, as with `lang`, it quite possibly makes a *huge* difference which processor you're using.

For instance, building an XSLT processor in certain languages such as Java may simplify making them "international-aware," assuming the developer knows how to leverage the languages' built-in facilities. With other languages (or, let us admit, with other developers) the support for multinational writing systems may be slim to nonexistent.

Controlling the Result Tree's Form/Type

Throughout this (and the preceding) chapter, I've been demonstrating XSLT using XHTML, for the most part, as the target vocabulary (i.e., the result tree). As I said early on, for purposes of learning most XSLT features, the nature of the result tree doesn't make any difference—you just have to know enough about the result tree's "language" to know what ways of instantiating it make sense.

But some kinds of results demand special treatment. A "result tree" is, after all, just a conceptual construct: an in-memory representation of the structure of the output document. When it *becomes* a document and gets written out as a file, to standard output or a Web browser, and so on—whenever the result tree is *serialized* to its final form—the processor may have to deal with several issues that have nothing to do with its representation as a tree.

The `disable-output-escaping` attribute

You've already seen one useful form of controlling the result tree. This was the `disable-output-escaping` attribute on the `xsl:value-of` and `xsl:text` elements.

As explained under the discussion of `xsl:text`, this attribute instructs the processor *not* to escape special characters like <, >, and & when it builds the result tree.

What's interesting about this attribute is that you can put it on any literal result element as well as `xsl:value-of` and `xsl:text`. To do so, just add the `xsl:` namespace prefix to the attribute's name. For example,

```
<p xsl:disable-output-escaping="yes">...</p>
```

`xsl:output`

XSLT is generally an XML-to-XML tool. The source tree, of course, must always be XML (otherwise, the use of XPath location paths would fail). If the result tree is also XML, the processor will take care of certain loose ends for you (such as properly escaped representation of special characters like the < and &).

But often you may not want to be "helped" like this; and even when you are transforming to XML, you may need to be able to put things into the result tree (like a document type declaration) that you otherwise can't. Welcome to the (top-level) `xsl:output` element.

Its general syntax is as follows:

```
<xsl:output
  method="html_text_name_xml"
  version="version"
  encoding="encoding"
  omit-xml-declaration="yesorno"
  standalone="yesorno"
  doctype-public="publicid"
  doctype-system="systemuri"
  cdata-section-elements="names"
  indent="yesorno"
  media-type="mediatype" />
```

We'll take a look at the `method` attribute in some detail first.

The `method` attribute

Probably the single most important attribute of the lot is `method`, because it determines if you also need to (or even can) use any of the others. Its value is either one of the fixed strings `html`, `text`, or `xml`, or a namespace-prefixed *name* (e.g., `oeb:openebook` or some such). Note that the latter case is completely outside the scope of the XSLT spec—what the processor will do with such an output method is undefined. (I won't cover this option further.)

You might think, given XSLT's naturally XML-to-XML character, that `xml` is the default value of the `method` attribute. (I know I did, originally.) That's not the case, however. The first thing the processor will do, in the absence of an explicit `method` attribute, is determine if the output is supposed to be *HTML* (and there's no "X" before that, either), using a series of tests. If

- the root node of the result tree has an element child (i.e., a root element), and
- the local name of the root element (i.e., sans any prefix) is "html," and

- the root "html" element has no namespace URI associated with it, and
- the only text nodes in the result tree *before* the root element consist of whitespace,

then the value of the method attribute is assumed to be html. If any of these conditions is false, the output method is assumed to be xml.

The main idea behind the method attribute is to provide some way of telling the processor how to treat certain special conditions that might come up in the course of serializing the result tree. For example, if the method attribute's value is html, empty elements (such as br, hr, and img) will be output by the processor in "HTML form"—as start tags without end tags—rather than in true XML form.

In brief, here's what the spec says about each of the three output methods.[7]

When method="xml"   The output does not necessarily have to be a well-formed XML *document*; it can be something the spec calls "a well-formed XML external general parsed entity."

The difference between a document and an "external general parsed entity" is determined by examining what the root node contains. If the root node has no text children, and a single root element child, then this is a well-formed XML *document*—otherwise it's just an external general parsed entity (which I'll call by the abbreviation EGPE[8] for the remainder of this discussion).

What's an EGPE good for? Of course, you can't (despite the "parsed" in the term) actually submit such a thing to an XML parser on its own. However, you can *include* such a thing in a well-formed document. If your EGPE is saved in a file called my_egpe.xml, for instance, you might have a document such as this:

```
<!DOCTYPE my_root [
<!ENTITY ext_data SYSTEM "my_egpe.xml">
]>
<my_root>
  [various contents]
  &ext_data;
</my_root>
```

---

7.   Not counting the *"name"*-type value, which no one seems to know quite what to make of…except, probably inevitably at some point, vendors. It's hard to imagine a loophole through which *no* vendor would ever want to steer their product.

8.   You won't find this abbreviation anywhere else, as far as I know. The unabbreviated form is darned tedious to keep retyping, though.

This makes the concept of an EGPE enormously appealing as a way of aggregating or including fragments of auto-generated XML and text content which can be plugged into standard "wrappers."

When `method="html"` When the `method` attribute has a value of `html` (either derived as explained above or explicitly assigned), the result tree is serialized using HTML (the default version is 4.0) rather than XML conventions.

One of the most obvious differences is that, because HTML does not recognize the special XML empty-element form (*<elementname/>*), certain elements must be serialized in a form that HTML *does* recognize—that is, as plain old start tags without matching end tags. The elements in question are `area`, `base`, `basefont`, `br`, `col`, `frame`, `hr`, `img`, `input`, `isindex`, `link`, `meta`, and `param`.

Don't get confused!

Remember that this is a description of how the XSLT processor "writes out" the result tree. Your XSLT stylesheet is still an XML document, no matter what the output looks like; therefore you're obliged to include *well-formed* elements in your result tree, such as `<hr/>` or `<br></br>`.

While I'm on the subject, you may have noticed in many sample XHTML result trees which I've shown so far that empty elements, such as `<br/>`, are shown as `<br />`, with a space before the terminal "/>". Some unsung hero, possibly the author of a browser's HTML parser, noticed a while back that representing an empty element this way doesn't break older browsers which don't know anything at all about XML. (If you omit the space, some older browsers ignore the element altogether. If you use the empty start tag/end tag pair syntax, some older browsers treat it as two succeeding occurrences of the start tag only.)

Whoever discovered this older-browser quirk deserves a big thanks from the rest of us. For the most part, it enables us to generate XHTML which can be read by both XML-aware and older browsers.

The `html` output method also enables the XSLT processor to skirt some of the thornier problems of handling content in an XML context. The principal ones are these:

- The processor is required to disregard case differences in element names (e.g., to recognize that a `td` element is the same as a `TD` element).[9]
- Markup-related special characters (`<`, `>`, and `&`) are not to be escaped when they appear in `script` and `style` elements.
- The `<` character won't be escaped when it appears in an attribute value.
- PIs in the result tree will terminate with a simple `>`, rather than the `?>` combination.
- Some attributes of some HTML elements are used to indicate a Boolean "true" condition, simply by using the attribute name alone without assigning it a value. For instance, an option button in a form, specified using the HTML `option` element, can be initialized to its "pushed-in" value as follows:

```
<option selected>
```

  The XMLized form of this (adopted by XHTML) would be to assign a value to the attribute which equals the name of the attribute, that is, `selected="selected"`. The `html` output method ensures that these attributes will be output in the "short form" understandable to older browsers.

- If there's a named character-entity reference known per whatever version of HTML the result is being serialized to, the processor is free to replace numeric entity references with their named form. For example, the UK pound symbol (£) can be represented as a numeric entity, `&#163;`—indeed, this form *must* be used in an XSLT stylesheet, unless some named entity reference is declared in a DOCTYPE declaration in the stylesheet's prolog. The processor is permitted to change this to the HTML entity reference `&pound;`.

When `method="text"`   The `text` output method isn't much different from the `xml` output method, in that text nodes in the result tree are written out literally. However, it's also different from the `xml` output method in that *markup* in the text *is simply written out as in its literal form*. Thus, using `method="text"` in the

---

9.   Like the box above says on a related matter, this doesn't eliminate the requirement that your stylesheet itself be well-formed. You can't balance a `<td>` start tag with a `</TD>` end tag. (I'm not even sure that "balance" is the word I want there, but you get the idea.)

`xsl:output` element is like putting an `xsl:disable-output-escaping="yes"` attribute on every result-tree element. Although the stylesheet itself must still be well-formed XML, the serialized form of the result tree can contain any text content, none of which will be helpfully "translated" to its markup-safe form.

Here's a sample stylesheet that can be applied to the *Caged Heat* FlixML review. It doesn't look all that different from many of the stylesheets in this chapter or the one before it, except for the `xsl:output` method:

```
<xsl:output method="text"/>

<xsl:template match="flixinfo">
  <html>
    <head>
      <title>Text Output Demo</title>
    </head>
    <body>
      <table border="1">
        <tr>
          <th>Elem Name</th>
          <th>Delimiter</th>
        </tr>
        <xsl:for-each select="*">
          <tr>
            <td><xsl:value-of select="name()"/></td>
            <td>&lt;</td>
          </tr>
        </xsl:for-each>
      </table>
    </body>
  </html>
</xsl:template>
```

At first glance, this seems to be producing a basic XHTML page, containing a two-column table. In column 1 will appear the names of all children of the root `flixinfo` element; in column 2 of every row of this table will be a < character (in its unescaped form, of course, as I've already told you will happen with the `text` output method).

Running this against the *Caged Heat* review with Saxon produces the following, perhaps surprising result tree:

```
Text Output DemoElem
NameDelimitertitle<title<title<genre<releaseyear<language<studio<ca
st<crew<plotsummary<reviews<distributors<dialog<remarks<mpaarating<
bees<
```

In short, the `text` output method emits *no* markup.

The other `xsl:output` attributes

As you read through the descriptions of the remaining attributes of the `xsl:output` element, Table 4–2 may be a useful reference. Not all of those other attributes apply to all output methods, and Table 4–2 summarizes the differences.

Table 4-2   Valid `xsl:output` Attributes for Given Output Methods

Output method	Valid `xsl:output` attributes (other than `method`)
`xml`	`version, encoding, omit-xml-declaration, standalone, doctype-public, doctype-system, cdata-section-elements, indent, media-type`
`html`	`version, encoding, doctype-public, doctype-system, indent, media-type`
`text`	`encoding, media-type`

The `version` attribute   This identifies the version of the markup standard with which the serialized result is to comply. Default for the `xml` output method is "1.0"; for the `html` output method, "4.0".

The `omit-xml-declaration` attribute   If the output method is `xml`, by default the XSLT processor sticks an XML declaration at the beginning of the output stream. This default XML declaration will declare the version (currently `1.0`) and encoding (the processor may use either `UTF-8` or `UTF-16`).

You can override this default behavior by specifying a value of "yes" for the `omit-xml-declaration` attribute. If you suppress the XML declaration this way, using the `encoding` or `standalone` attribute (described next) doesn't make a lot of sense—since those two attributes customize the form of the XML declaration.

The `encoding` attribute   This attribute serves the same purpose as the encoding declaration in the XML declaration—to inform a processor of the document being output by this transformation what encoding is being used. The default may be (at the XSLT processor's discretion) either `UTF-8` or `UTF-16`; if any other value is specified that the XSLT processor doesn't recognize, it's free either to replace that value with `UTF-8` or `UTF-16`, or to issue an error message.

The `standalone` attribute   As in the standalone declaration in an XML declaration, this can have a value of "yes" or "no". There's no default value for this attribute, meaning that if the attribute is completely absent, the processor is supposed to *not* assign one.

The `doctype-public` attribute   When you're transforming to XML or HTML, you can have the XSLT processor place a document-type (DOCTYPE) declaration in the output using this and/or the `doctype-system` attribute. The DOCTYPE declaration will be placed in the document prolog, just before the root element's start tag. If there's no `doctype-system` attribute, this attribute is ignored even if specified. (This is consistent with XML's requirement that a public ID alone isn't good enough—a system URI is also required.)

The value of the `doctype-public` attribute should be a legitimate public identifier, such as `-//W3C//DTD HTML 4.01//EN` for outputting HTML 4.01. However, the XSLT spec is silent on what happens if the value is something meaningless.[10]

The `doctype-system` attribute   To output a DOCTYPE declaration which points to a DTD which can be used to validate the output document, enter the URI of that DTD as the value of the `doctype-system` attribute.

Consistent with the XML standard's requirements for a DOCTYPE declaration, if you specify both a public and a system ID, the former will be prefaced by the XSLT processor with the keyword PUBLIC; if a system ID only, it will be prefaced with the keyword SYSTEM. As with the `doctype-public` attribute, the XSLT processor should not be counted on to verify that you've entered a legitimate value for this attribute—at most, it may check that the URI follows allowable URI syntax.

The `cdata-section-elements` attribute   If you're outputting to XML and the result tree contains one or more elements whose contents you'd like to enclose in CDATA sections, enter their names in a whitespace-delimited list as the value of this attribute. In addition to bracketing the content with the `<![CDATA[` and `]]>` delimiters, the XSLT processor will write out special characters in their unescaped form (e.g., < rather than `&lt;`).

At various points in this chapter, I've discussed the XSLT processor's handling of these special characters and generally discouraged you from trying to

---

10.   We can probably safely assume that in this case, whatever happens is not what one *needs* to happen.

circumvent this behavior. The `xml:output` element's `cdata-section-elements` attribute is no exception. Again, all it controls is how the result tree gets written out; it doesn't get you off the hook for producing a well-formed result tree in the first place.

The `indent` attribute   The default value for this attribute is "no"; in this case, the XSLT processor is free to write out the result tree as if it were one big string. Often, though, you want the output to be in "pretty-printed" form, with elements at successively deeper levels of the tree separated from one another with newlines and indented with tabs or blank spaces. In such cases, set the indent attribute to "yes".

This can be a little complicated, and some processors may be better at it than others. The trick is not to introduce "pretty-printing" whitespace into any elements that already contain text—including whitespace—as a result of the transformation.

In general, it's probably a good idea to avoid using the `indent` attribute for all but the most casual purposes. Because it's not a required attribute, the XSLT processor is free to ignore it. And if you're using MSXML within the MSIE browser, it certainly makes sense for the processor to ignore it—the pretty-printing effect is lost in a browser window that normalizes whitespace. If you really need to pretty-print a transformation's result tree, a better, more rigorous solution is to develop a stylesheet that creates a pretty-printed result tree explicitly, using non-breaking spaces, tabs, even an XHTML table. The source tree for this stylesheet would be the result tree from some previous transformation.

The `media-type` attribute   The default value for this attribute depends on the output method. For `xml`, the default is "text/xml"; for `html`, "text/html"; and for `text`, "text/plain".

The "media type" of an Internet resource is sometimes referred to as its MIME type, where MIME is an acronym for Multipurpose Internet Mail Extensions. This lies way outside the scope of XML itself, let alone XSLT; it has to do with how a resource is transmitted and what happens at the receiving end. The XSLT standard, therefore, doesn't really say what the XSLT processor is supposed to do with this information. As an experiment, I just tried setting the attribute's value in a stylesheet which I then ran against the *Caged Heat* FlixML document, using the normally comprehensive Saxon as the XSLT processor. Absolutely nothing happened, which is probably pretty much what you should expect with any general-purpose XSLT processor.

Controlling Whitespace in the Source Tree

That section heading is a bit misleading; you can't really control whitespace (or anything else) *in the source tree* from within a stylesheet. However, you can control how the stylesheet "sees" text nodes consisting only of whitespace.

`xsl:strip-space` and `xsl:preserve-space`

These two top-level (and empty) elements work in tandem to control how the processor handles whitespace-only text nodes.

Each of the two elements has a single required attribute, `elements`, whose value is a whitespace-delimited list of element names.

By default, all whitespace-only text nodes are preserved exactly as they appear in the document in question. This means, in effect, that the following is implicit in any XSLT stylesheet:

```
<xsl:preserve-space elements="*"/>
```

Therefore, if you must strip whitespace-only text nodes from just a handful of elements, you only need to use `xsl:strip-space` to identify those elements—no need to include an `xsl:preserve` space for all the others.

By the way, to "strip" whitespace-only text nodes means to completely remove them from the source tree. This doesn't remove the containing *element* node from the source tree; nor, of course, does it *really* affect the source document in any way. It simply makes the containing element appear empty as it is represented in the source tree.

Why would you want to do this—to strip out extraneous whitespace? It can't hurt anything, right? The main reason you'd want to do it is that the XSLT processor can't be expected to use a validating parser—that is, in this case, a parser which "knows" that a particular element may or may not contain #PCDATA content. This can play havoc with your use of the `position()` function, in particular. Consider the following source document:

```
<alphabet>
<a>
</a>
<b>
</b>
<c>some text<d> </d></c>
</alphabet>
```

Pretty straightforward, right? The root element, alphabet, contains three other elements—a, b, and c—and the c element contains a mixture of text and element d. Now see if you can anticipate what the following stylesheet will produce:

```
<xsl:template match="alphabet">
  <html>
    <head><title>Whitespace</title></head>
    <body>
      <table border="1">
        <xsl:apply-templates/>
      </table>
    </body>
  </html>
</xsl:template>

<xsl:template match="*">
  <tr>
    <td><xsl:value-of select="name()"/></td>
    <td>pos #<xsl:value-of select="position()"/></td>
  </tr>
  <xsl:apply-templates/>
</xsl:template>
```

This also looks pretty straightforward. It looks like the alphabet element in the source tree triggers the construction of an XHTML table; each row in the table consists of an element's name and its position among all its siblings. (The second template rule's xsl:apply-templates element ensures that the whole document tree will be processed, not just the children of the alphabet element.)

So, since the a element is the first child of alphabet, its position will be 1, b's will be 2, and c's will be 3. Right?

Surprisingly, the answer is no. What you actually see from this stylesheet is a result tree that looks like the following:

```
<html>
  <head><title>Whitespace</title></head>
  <body>
    <table border="1">
      <tr><td>a</td><td>pos #2</td></tr>
      <tr><td>b</td><td>pos #4</td></tr>
      <tr><td>c</td><td>pos #6</td></tr>
      <tr><td>d</td><td>pos #2</td></tr>
    </table>
```

```
   </body>
</html>
```

When viewed in the browser, this result tree looks like what's shown in Figure 4–18.

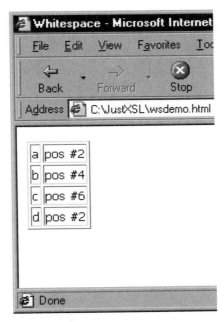

Figure 4-18   Counting nodes in a source tree that includes whitespace-only text nodes (result tree created by Saxon). A little surprising; shouldn't the positions be 1, 2, and 3 for a, b, and c, respectively? And why is d the second child of its parent, c...?

To understand why this output is being generated, take a look at element d in the source tree, which (according to the table above) is child #2 of its parent, the c element. What's the first child? The first child is a text node, the string "some text". And that's the reason for the seemingly goofy numbering of the positions of the a, b, and c elements: Each is preceded by a text node—each text node consisting of whitespace only (a newline).

To correct the problem, you simply override the default behavior of the XSLT processor with a catch-all xsl:strip-space:

```
<xsl:strip-space elements="*"/>
```

The result tree that comes out of Saxon now looks much more reasonable:

```
<html>
  <head><title>Whitespace</title></head>
  <body>
    <table border="1">
      <tr><td>a</td><td>pos #1</td></tr>
      <tr><td>b</td><td>pos #2</td></tr>
      <tr><td>c</td><td>pos #3</td></tr>
      <tr><td>d</td><td>pos #2</td></tr>
    </table>
  </body>
</html>
```

Note that element d's position hasn't changed; its preceding sibling (the words "some text") is a *non-whitespace-only* text node, which will never be stripped from the source tree.

Processor differences

This is one of the few areas in which the Microsoft XSLT processor fails to yield results identical to those from processors such as Saxon, and that's why the screen shot in Figure 4–18 shows you an HTML document (output from Saxon) rather than an XML document viewed natively in MSIE.

Microsoft's explanation of this behavior has always struck me as weasel-worded: The idea, they say, is that the browser is not the XSLT processor; the browser is a "shell" application which simply invokes the XSLT processor as needed. Microsoft has built this controlling application in such a way that, by default, the XSLT processor is instructed to *ignore* whitespace-only text nodes. You can tell it to pay attention to such text nodes by setting a property in a script, but there's no way to tell the browser itself to do so.

Of course, if you accept the argument that the browser is under no obligation to honor XSLT spec-mandated behavior in this respect, then it's not obligated to do so in any other respect, either. This deviation from the spec's straight-and-narrow is all the more egregious because Microsoft, for once, seems to have hewed to its straight-and-narrow nearly everywhere else.

How Do I...
Link to more than one stylesheet for multiple output devices?

Early in Chapter 3 I covered using multiple `xml-stylesheet` PIs with different `media` pseudo-attributes, all but one of which had an `alternate` pseudo-attribute with a value of `yes`. For instance (to repeat, in somewhat simpler form, the example I used there):

```
<?xml-stylesheet type="text/xsl" alternate="yes"
  media="handheld" href="handheld.xsl"?>
<?xml-stylesheet type="text/xsl" alternate="yes"
  media="print"href="print.xsl"?>
<?xml-stylesheet type="text/xsl" alternate="no"
  media="screen" href="default.xsl"?>
```

A document containing these three PIs in its prolog could therefore, in theory, be used in three separate environments; the application running in each environment would recognize the `media` pseudo-attribute value intended for it, and load the corresponding stylesheet.

We're still at an early stage in all of this, though, and I wouldn't count on the theory to match the reality.

One thing I've seen a few people experimenting with to achieve the same effect (sort of) is a smarter version of the "browser detection" schemes common on Web sites. This requires the use of script, such as JavaScript or VBScript; you test the environment variable named HTTP_USER_AGENT (which tells you what "browser" or other application is running on the client side) and take action depending on what that variable tells you. Instead of testing just for the strings that identify the Microsoft or Netscape browser, though, now you've got to test for specific PDAs or WAP[11]-enabled cell phones.

For instance, a script for processing different vendors' WAP-enabled devices might look something like this (in pseudo-code):

---

11.   WAP = "Wireless Application Protocol." This is the equivalent of HTTP for sending "Web pages" to wireless devices. The XML dialect used for such devices is not XHTML, but something called WML (for "Wireless Markup Language").

```
if HTTP_USER_AGENT contains "Ericsson"
  use Ericsson-specific stylesheet
else
  if HTTP_USER_AGENT contains "Nokia"
    use Nokia-specific stylesheet
else
    use generic WAP stylesheet
  endif
endif
```

For maximum portability—and performance—in cases like this, you probably want to do the processing not in the client itself, but on the server.

CHAPTER 5

XSLT Functions

As you already know, the XPath standard defines numerous *functions*—add-ons to the spec's core functionality that give you access to sundry kinds of information about node-sets, strings, Boolean values, and numbers.

XSLT, too, comes with a set of built-in functions. XSLT's function library enhances your ability to examine and manipulate source-tree data in ways the true XML-based XSLT syntax does not permit. All of these functions return a value (just as XPath functions do), and that value can be used in various ways (such as in an `xsl:value-of` element's `select` attribute).

Many of the functions built into XSLT can be used on their own. A few are used strictly—or nearly always—with particular XSLT elements, and I've deferred covering such elements until this chapter, so they can be seen in the context in which you're most likely to find and use them. This chapter includes sections which follow the four general categories of functions established by the spec:

- Processing multiple source documents
- Using keys
- Numbering
- Miscellaneous built-in functions

There's also a fifth function category, *extension functions*, with its own section in this chapter. Extension functions provide features that a given XSLT processor's vendor or developer imagines[1] will be useful to XSLT stylesheet authors. These extension functions are (with one important exception) processor-specific; therefore, I'll show you how to use them in general, but I'll provide details on only a couple of them (including that important exception).

Processing Multiple Source Documents

Powerful though an XSLT stylesheet's elements and attributes may be, they're hamstrung by a bizarre limitation: A given stylesheet using just elements and attributes can process only *one* source document at a time.

Why more than one source document?

Why do I call this a "bizarre" limitation? Why would you ever need to process more than one document at a time?

Let's look at two common situations in which having access to more than one source document can be critical. (There are others; but these are, I think, the most obvious.)

"Anthologies"

If you've ever developed your own XML vocabulary, you may have experienced the anguish of one decision in particular. That decision may be described as, "Will each of my XML documents represent *a collection of many things* or *a single instance of something?*"

In FlixML's case, for instance, I had to decide if each FlixML document should represent several movies (probably grouped together by genre, language, studio, or what-have-you) or a single movie.

Each approach offered its own advantages and disadvantages. If each document represented several movies, it'd be a lot easier to provide all the information on many different movies at one time. But a given movie's information would probably have to be "cloned"—copied to more than one master document—if the movie represented more than one genre, language, and so on; this would introduce a lot of complexity in terms of keeping all the clones in sync with one another as I made updates.

---

1.   Even justifiably, in some cases!

On the other hand, I could require that each FlixML document include information about no more than one movie. The downside to this approach would be that I'd need some way of aggregating multiple films' data when the need arose. The upside was that I wouldn't need to keep multiple copies of the data in sync across multiple master documents. That was the convincer, in my mind. (It's enormously appealing as a convincer to anyone who works with relational databases.)

Other options

Not to belabor a subject only marginally related to XSLT, but there are other ways around this "one thing vs. collection of many things" dilemma.

For instance, if I'd opted for the "collection" approach, the root element might have been called, say, b-movies. Its content model would have looked something like this:

```
<!ELEMENT b-movies (flixinfo+) >
```

That is, each b-movies element would contain one or more of the flixinfo elements which (in the actual version of FlixML) contain all the real data about the movie in question.

However, XML 1.0 doesn't require that a valid document have as its root the one element which contains all possible elements defined by a given DTD. A perfectly valid FlixML document in this hypothetical case could have as its root element either b-movies, or flixinfo, or crew, or distriblink, or.... I rejected this approach because I wanted to *forbid* the creation of "master documents" containing information about more than one film.

It's also possible to create a completely separate vocabulary whose DTD includes an external parameter entity pointing to the FlixML DTD, permitting the construction of "master documents" outside FlixML's pale. For instance, this master DTD might include declarations such as the following:

```
<!ENTITY % flixml SYSTEM
  "http://www.flixml.org/flixml/flixml_03.dtd">
%flixml;
<!ELEMENT b-movies (flixinfo+) >
```

Obviously, there's nothing I can do to stop anyone from creating such a master document. The best I can say is, it won't be FlixML!

So, given that I chose the "one movie per document" approach, I still need some way of resolving the occasional, "Yeah, but what about handling more than one movie at a time?" question. Basically, what's needed is the ability to create an *anthology* of separate XML documents of a particular type—or, rather, the ability to view some arbitrary collection of XML documents *as if* they were such an anthology.

Lookup/Driver documents

In discussing the "anthology" problem above, I mentioned its appeal to a database developer: Keeping all the data about *one kind of thing* in *one* place obviates the need to keep multiple copies in sync with one another.

The flip side is that you often need to refer to *more than one kind of thing* at a time. This need is often addressed in a database using what are sometimes called *lookup tables*; outside of a database, you may see it being handled by a technique called a *driver file*.[2]

Examples of this abound. For instance, all the information about employees might be in one database table, and all payroll and other accounting data in a completely different table (or database, even). The payroll system occasionally needs to use non-payroll information about an employee (such as his address, for printing on a paycheck)—but that doesn't mean that the payroll system needs to *contain* that information itself. It simply needs some way to *obtain* that information from the employee table or database.

Likewise, it would be tempting to include within FlixML some elements and attributes in which to record biographical information about a film's cast and crew members. Tempting, maybe, but also crazy. First, this would be re-creating the problem of storing things redundantly, on a smaller scale. (A biographical note would have to be cloned to every FlixML document for a movie with that cast/crew member.) Second, well, just as an abstract objection, that'd be kind of diluting the purpose of FlixML, wouldn't it?

Much better would be to have a completely different vocabulary—BiogML or whatever—in whose document(s) my stylesheets could simply *look*

---

2.   I'm not using "driver" here in the sense of "device driver." What I'm getting at is the use of some external file to *drive* the behavior of an application (an XSLT stylesheet's processing, in this case).

up the desired information, incorporating it as needed with the data in FlixML documents.

Driver documents, as I'm calling them here, are special-purpose documents, often small and/or one-off, whose sole purpose is to "steer" an XSLT transformation. You'll see an example of one of these later in the chapter, in the "How Do I ...?" section.

The XSLT `document()` function

The `document()` function returns a node-set, consisting of the entire tree of nodes in some external document (external, that is, to both the source tree and the stylesheet itself). Portions of this tree of nodes can be referenced using XPath expressions in combination with a call to `document()`.

The general syntax of a call to the `document()` function is

```
document(object, nodeset)
```

where

- *object* is either a string or a node-set that can be resolved to one or more strings, providing the URI(s) of the document(s) to be referenced; and
- *nodeset* is an optional argument used for "adjusting" the base URI used to resolve relative URIs in *object*. (By default, the base URI for resolving such URIs is the URI of the stylesheet itself.) You'll almost never see a call to the `document()` function that actually uses this second argument,[3] and none of the examples I provide will do so.

Need a FlixML fix?

In this chapter, I'll simply be referring to the two FlixML documents introduced in earlier chapters—reviews of *Criss Cross* and *Caged Heat*. These are, respectively, crisscross.xml and cagedheat.xml.

In the next chapter I'll introduce a new movie, with a new document (a review of *When Dinosaurs Ruled the Earth*).

---

3. Why not? Because if you need to refer to a document in some location other than the stylesheet itself, it's generally just as easy—and frequently *clearer*—to use absolute URI(s) as the first argument.

As an example of using document(), assume that in the same directory as our stylesheet we've got an XML document called genres.xml. Its content looks like the following (which is trimmed—you should be able to get the idea with just a portion of the file):

```
<genres>
  <genre>
    <name>Action</name>
    <desc>Plot moves forward as a result of decisive, often violent
action (as the name implies). Generally short on character
development. Seldom seen by itself, rather in concert with some
other genre.</desc>
    <avatar>Any of Schwarzenneger's blockbusters, e.g. "Terminator"
series</avatar>
  </genre>
  <genre>
    <name>Camp</name>
    <desc>"So bad it's funny" -- that is, funny BECAUSE it's bad.
This is not the same as Comedy, because in a Comedy the humor is
intentional. The humor in a Camp film often wears thin after the
first 30 minutes or so.</desc>
    <avatar>"Plan 9 from Outer Space"</avatar>
  </genre>
  <genre>
    <name>Comedy</name>
    <desc>Audience laughs (ideally). This is distinguished from Camp
(q.v.) in that the humor in a Comedy is intentional. Some people
would classify over-the-top comedies like "Killer Tomatoes" as
camp; I don't.</desc>
    <avatar>"Young Frankenstein"</avatar>
  </genre>
  <genre>
    <name>Crime/Detective</name>
    <desc>Protagonists/Antagonists on opposite sides of the law.</
desc>
    <avatar>"He Walked by Night"</avatar>
  </genre>
</genres>
```

Each genre has a name element, a description (in the desc element), and the title of an archetypal example of the genre in question (in the avatar element).

What we'd like to do in this example is link the contents of a FlixML review's `primarygenre` element to the corresponding description from genres.xml. A stylesheet to do so might include a template rule such as the following, which uses the `document()` function:

```
<xsl:template match="primarygenre">
  <h3>Primary Genre:</h3>
  <table width="60%" cellpadding="3" cellspacing="3"
   border="1">
    <tr>
      <th>Name</th>
      <th>Description</th>
    </tr>
    <tr>
      <td valign="top">
        <xsl:value-of select="."/>
      </td>
      <td valign="top">
        <xsl:value-of select="document('genres.xml')//desc[preceding-
sibling::name=current()]"/>
      </td>
    </tr>
  </table>
</xsl:template>
```

Here, the call to the `document()` function (with the subsequent location path) is used to navigate down to the `desc` element with a preceding-sibling `name` element that matches the value of the `primarygenre` element.

Looking ahead

Note the use of the `current()` function in the location path's predicate. I'll detail the purpose of this function later in this chapter, in the "Miscellaneous Functions" section. For now, just understand that it's returning the value of the FlixML document's `primarygenre` element.

Results of applying this template rule to the FlixML review of *Caged Heat* appear as shown in Figure 5–1.

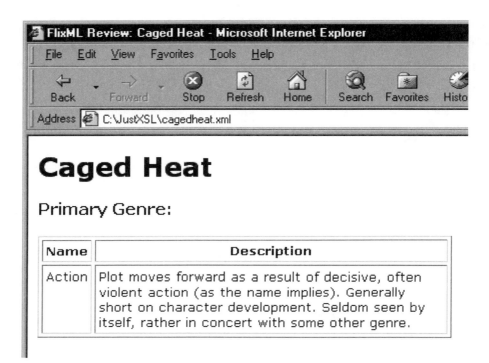

Figure 5-1   Information from the source tree is shown in the main page heading (the film's main title) and the first column of the table (the value of the primarygenre element). Information from an external file, corresponding to the primarygenre element, appears in the table's second column. I didn't want to delve into JavaScript coding here, but it wouldn't be hard to have this table pop up in a secondary browser window when the user clicks on the primarygenre element, rather than showing the full description in the same page as the film's main information.

Assigning the external document tree to a variable

It's possible (depending on how the given XSLT processor is built) that making repeated calls to the document() function for the same external document would be quite inefficient.

For example, the processor may assume that, on average, most calls to document() will be "one-time" calls—used to retrieve a single data item, after which that document doesn't need to be referred to again. With this assumption in mind, the processor's developer would logically assume that (for efficiency's sake) the external document's tree should *not* be retained in memory.

To the extent that this hypothetical scenario is true (and it seems reasonable), for those occasions when you *do* need to refer to the same document several times, you'd probably want the external tree available on demand, without having to do a re-read of the document—working something like a browser cache. A good tactic to use in this case is to assign the external document to a global variable, which can then be navigated around as needed elsewhere in the document.

B movies—actually, most movies—don't fall neatly into one genre or another. In fact, even two genres often aren't enough. So we could display the names and descriptions of *all* a film's genres with a single call to the document() function, with code like the following:

```
<xsl:variable name="genres"
  select="document('genres.xml')"/>

<xsl:template match="genre">
  <h3>Genres:</h3>
  <table width="60%" cellpadding="3" cellspacing="3" border="1">
    <tr>
      <th>Name</th>
      <th>Description</th>
    </tr>
    <xsl:for-each select="*">
      <tr>
        <td valign="top">
          <xsl:value-of select="."/>
        </td>
        <td valign="top">
          <xsl:value-of select="$genres//desc[preceding-
sibling::name=current()]"/>
          (Archetype: <xsl:value-of select="$genres//
avatar[preceding-sibling::name=current()]"/>)
        </td>
      </tr>
    </xsl:for-each>
  </table>
</xsl:template>
```

Here, the genres.xml document tree is loaded into a global variable called genres. This variable is referenced not just once but twice for every primary-genre *and* othergenre element, within the xsl:for-each embedded in the template rule. Again looking at the *Caged Heat* review, results are as shown in Figure 5–2.

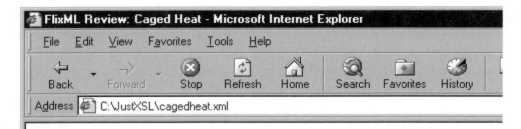

Figure 5-2 Information on multiple genres retrieved with a single call to the `document()` function, storing the external document's tree in a variable. Note that this example retrieves from the external file not only the genre's description but also the title of an archetypal example of the genre. If each data item had been retrieved with its own call to `document()`, producing the second column of this table would have required *six* calls to `document()` altogether.

Using Keys

As you know, an XML vocabulary can define a kind of intra-document linking mechanism using ID- and IDREF-type attributes. FlixML has quite a few ID-type attributes (which from here on I'll simply call IDs—you get the idea) and also a couple of IDREFs.

There's no requirement that an XSLT processor do so, but it's reasonable to expect that it would use ID-type attributes to construct an *index*. Because each element with an ID is thus uniquely identified, using the XPath `id()` function will immediately locate that element; but the "immediately" works best—most quickly—when there's already a road map of sorts into the document: "ID value 'xyz' is located here; 'abc,' there" and so on.

Drawbacks to using ID-type attributes

Handy though they are, IDs suffer a number of drawbacks as an indexing mechanism.

- To use IDs at all requires that the document in question be *valid*. If there's no DTD, there's no way to determine that a given attribute is of the ID type. Therefore, if your documents are simply well-formed—or if the XSLT processor uses a parser that doesn't check the DTD for ID-type attributes—you can't use the `id()` function to locate content.
- There's only one "class" of IDs in a given document. For instance, FlixML has IDs of two kinds: those used to index elements (for use in building a table of contents) and those used to build cross-references between information about cast members and *references to* those cast members. But I can't use `id()` to grab an element with an ID of just one of those two *kinds* of ID, ignoring the others.
- Any element can have no more than one ID, and no more than one element can have a given ID. Maybe this seems like a strange kind of "drawback" to you; after all, the uniqueness of IDs is what enables them to be used so efficiently. Why throw away that advantage? The answer is that a non-unique index would be a great way to immediately locate all elements that share some common characteristic.
- IDs, by definition, provide indexing only on attribute values. Furthermore, their values are constrained in that they must be valid XML names: Each value must start with a letter or underscore, can include no whitespace, and

so on. Much more flexible as an indexing scheme would be one that could be constructed around, say, element content instead of attribute values; eliminating the "XML names only" requirement would enable the index to be used in a more natural way on values such as employee IDs, book ISBNs, and so on—unique identifiers that begin with (or consist entirely of) *digits*.

All of these drawbacks are addressed in XSLT by the use of *keys*. Keys are created on nodes in a source document using the `xsl:key` element; the XSLT `key()` function retrieves the source-document node(s) matching a particular key value.

Assigning a key with `xsl:key`

A *key*, in XSLT terms, is something like an attribute: It has a name and a value. There's a third dimension to understanding a key, however, which is that one or more nodes in a given document will have a key by that name, of that value. (This dimension exists for IDs, too, of course—there's a node-set of exactly one element with a given ID's value.) You establish a key by identifying these three components with the `xsl:key` element, which takes the following general form:

```
<xsl:key
  name="keyname"
  match="pattern"
  use="expression" />
```

All three attributes are required, and they correspond to the name, node-set, and value dimensions of the key's definition, respectively.

The `xsl:key` element is a top-level element. Given that the `match` attribute locates the node-set which will be assigned the key, then, you might think it must be relative to the context visible at that point—that is, the source tree's root node. This isn't the case, though. For example, an `xsl:key` element could index a FlixML document using keys assigned to the various cast members' name in something like this fashion:

```
<xsl:key name="cast_key"
  match="castmember"
  use="expression"/>
```

That is, the value of the `match` attribute need not take the full `flixinfo//cast-member` form.

The value of the `use` attribute, however, *is* relative—to the context established by the value of the `match` attribute. For instance, we could build a key on the `distriblink` elements in a FlixML document, using their `xlink:href` attributes to provide the key's values, as follows:

```
<xsl:key name="distrib_key"
  match="distriblink"
  use="@xlink:href"/>
```

The `use` attribute here says to "look along the attribute axis from the context node"—the `distriblink` element—to obtain the `distrib_key` key's values.

Note that this `distrib_key` key is likely to function much like an ID, because its value for any matching node (the URI where a film can be purchased or rented, or of the distributor itself if no film-specific page is available) is likely to be unique. (Put another way, no two distributors' pages will have the same URI.) This needn't be the case, though. For instance, take a look at this `xsl:key` element:

```
<xsl:key
  name="personnel_key"
  match="castmember | crew/* "
  use="substring-after(., ' ')"/>
```

This key's value (identified by the `use` attribute) is the text string which appears *after* the first space in the cast or crew member's name—that is, his or her surname. In most cases, of course, this will still yield a unique key. But in some cases it may not. When you apply this key definition to the *Caged Heat* review, for example, if you retrieve all nodes with a `personnel_key` value of "Demme," you'll get two nodes: one for the director, one for the screenwriter.

"Use case" for non-unique keys

Still not convinced of the usefulness of non-unique keys? A common use for them is *grouping*—displaying, say, a heading giving the value that several nodes have in common, followed by (usually) a sorted list of details about the nodes that share that value. You'll see an example of this in Chapter 6, "Advanced XSLT."

Retrieving nodes with a given key: The `key()` function

The flip side of the `xsl:key` element is the XSLT `key()` function, which retrieves the source-tree node(s) which match the given key name and value.

This is roughly what the XPath `id()` function does, in that it returns a node-set matching the specified values. With that function, though, you only had to pass it one value—the value of the desired ID-type attribute. To retrieve node(s) matching a key, on the other hand, you've got to pass `key()` not only the value, but also the *name* of the key in question. (With `id()`, the attribute's name didn't matter, because no matter what the attribute's name, all IDs are considered "the same": They're all attributes whose values are of the ID type.) Thus, the general syntax for a call to the `key()` function is this:

```
key(keyname, object)
```

The *keyname* argument is a string giving the name of the key whose corresponding node(s) you're interested in retrieving, and *object* is either a single string (if you're searching for a specific value) or a node-set. In the latter case, the value of each node in *object* is used to match against the nodes using this key, and the function returns the union of *all* matching nodes.

As an initial example, let's start with a look at this key definition:

```
<xsl:key
  name="pers_key"
  match="castmember | role | crew/*"
  use="."/>
```

This establishes a key which is the union of (a) all `castmember` elements, (b) all `role` elements, and (c) all children of the `crew` element. The value of each key in the node-set will be the string-value of each element in the node-set. Therefore, once this key has been defined, we can use it to retrieve one or more nodes corresponding to the name of any person in either the cast or the crew, in something like the following fashion:

```
<xsl:for-each
  select="key('pers_key', 'Jonathan Demme')">
  <xsl:choose>
    <xsl:when test="name() = 'castmember'">
      ...played <xsl:value-of select="//role[preceding-
sibling::castmember = 'Jonathan Demme']"/><br />
    </xsl:when>
    <xsl:when test="name() = 'role'">
      ...was played by <xsl:value-of
  select="//castmember[following-sibling::role = 'Jonathan
Demme']"/><br />
```

```
  </xsl:when>
  <xsl:otherwise>
    ...was in the crew -- his/her position was "<xsl:value-of
select="name()"/>"<br />
  </xsl:otherwise>
  </xsl:choose>
</xsl:for-each>
```

This `xsl:for-each` block grabs every node in the `pers_key` key's node-set whose key value is the string "Jonathan Demme." Then it tests the name of the matching node to see if its name indicates that the person in question is an actor/actress, a character in the film, and/or a crew member, respectively, and displays a text string that varies accordingly.

In this particular case, the ability to search on a person's name would have limited utility, *except* that the value of the `key()` function's second argument can be a variable or parameter. This allows us to change the above as follows (assuming an `xsl:variable` or `xsl:param` element to declare the variable or parameter as desired):

```
<xsl:for-each select="key('pers_key', $pers_name)">
  <xsl:choose>
    <xsl:when test="name()='castmember'">
    ...played <xsl:value-of select="//role[preceding-
sibling::castmember = '$pers_name']"/><br />
    </xsl:when>
    <xsl:when test="name()='role'">
    ...was played by <xsl:value-of select="//castmember[following-
sibling::role = '$pers_name']"/><br />
    </xsl:when>
    <xsl:otherwise>
    ...was in the crew -- his/her position was "<xsl:value-of
select="name()"/>"<br />
    </xsl:otherwise>
  </xsl:choose>
</xsl:for-each>
```

Now this is a truly useful bit of code, because it's general-purpose—driven by (say) a global parameter whose value is passed into the stylesheet from the outside environment. For instance, if we pass in "Jonathan Demme" as the value of the `pers_name` parameter, the above code produces results as shown in Figure 5–3 when run against the *Caged Heat* FlixML review.

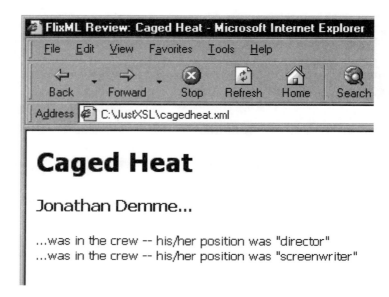

Figure 5-3   Result of passing "Jonathan Demme" as the value of the `pers_name` para-meter used to select from a keyed node-set (in this case, one consisting of the names of everyone in the cast or crew of *Caged Heat*). Note that using a key here lets us retrieve *two* nodes; if we'd used an ID-type attribute instead, we could get at most a single node.

The second example of using the `key()` function I'll show you demon-strates a trick I like to use with keys.

Let's suppose that, for some reason, we wanted to establish a key such that it identified all elements whose text nodes contain the letter "J." (This is a com-pletely arbitrary and highly unlikely scenario; choose another if you'd like.) An `xsl:key` element for this condition might look as follows:

```
<xsl:key
  name="letter_key"
  match="*[text()]"
  use="contains(text(), 'J')"/>
```

Notice in particular about this the value of the `use` attribute. The value is a call to the `contains()` function, which returns a true or false value depending on whether the element has a text node whose value, respectively, contains or does not contain the letter "J." (If the element has no text node at all, it won't be considered for the resulting node-set—it'll fail the test in the `match` attribute's predicate.)

Next, we'll want a global parameter which can both have a default value and be overridden, if necessary, by the outside environment:

```
<xsl:param name="true_false" select="'true'"/>
```

Hamstrung by the spec

Boy, it'd be great if we could also have used an "overrideable" parameter for the *letter* in question. Something like this:

```
<xsl:param name="key_letter" select="'J'"/>
```

Then the idea would be to use this parameter in the `xsl:key` element's use attribute, in this fashion:

```
<xsl:key
  name="letter_key"
  match="*[text()]"
  use="contains(text(), $key_letter)"/>
```

Unfortunately, the XSLT processor chokes when it hits the `$key_letter` reference in the above; you can't use a variable reference there. I'm not sure whether the limitation is in XPath or in XSLT, but it doesn't really make any difference—you can't use it.

And yes, I've also tried `string($key_letter)`, an AVT like `{$key_letter}`, and so on. It just won't work. We're stuck with looking for a literal value, apparently.

Now we can set up code such as the following:

```
<xsl:variable name="contain_or_lack">
  <xsl:choose>
    <xsl:when test="$true_false = 'true'">containing</xsl:when>
    <xsl:otherwise>lacking</xsl:otherwise>
  </xsl:choose>
</xsl:variable>
<h3>Elements w/text nodes <xsl:value-of select="$contain_or_lack"/>
"J"</h3>
<table border="1">
  <tr>
    <th>Elem</th>
    <th>Pos</th>
    <th>Value</th>
  </tr>
  <xsl:for-each select="key('letter_key', $true_false)">
    <tr>
      <td valign="top"><xsl:value-of select="name()"/></td>
```

```
      <td valign="top"><xsl:value-of select="position()"/></td>
      <td><xsl:value-of select="text()"/></td>
    </tr>
  </xsl:for-each>
</table>
```

The first thing the above accomplishes is to establish a local variable, contain_or_lack, whose value will be the string "containing" or the string "lacking," depending on whether the value of the true_false parameter is true or not. This variable's value is then used in a level-3 heading, indicating whether the table that follows shows text nodes *containing* or *lacking* the letter J.

Finally, the code creates a three-column table. Column 1 holds the name of the element containing or lacking the letter "J"; column 2, that element's position within the keyed node-set; and column 3, the value itself. Applied to the *Caged Heat* review, and allowing true_false to default to true, this block of code displays as shown in Figure 5–4.

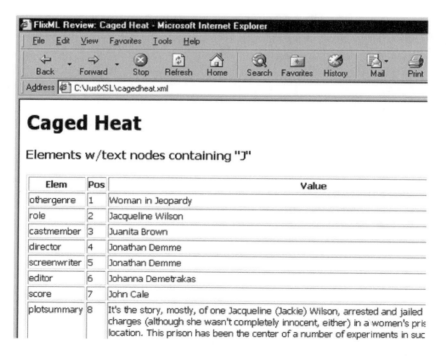

Figure 5-4   Using xsl:key and the key() function to produce a two-valued keyed node-set: Every node in the node-set will have the key value true or false, depending on (in this case) whether the text node contains or lacks a capital "J." Aside from the general two-valued business, the other interesting thing about this example is the second column of the table. The position displayed is the position within the keyed node-set, not within the document.

Note that the above keyed node-set technique produces results identical to using a global variable with the `select` attribute. For example,

```
<xsl:variable name="letter_var"
  select="//*[contains(text(), $letter_key)]"/>
```

and then changing the `xsl:for-each` element's `select` attribute so it points to the variable rather than the keyed node-set:

```
<xsl:for-each select="$letter_var">
```

The downside to using a variable is that you can't easily test for the "false" condition with the same variable; you need to set up a second one, such as this:

```
<xsl:variable name="letter_var_false"
  select="//*[not(contains(text(), $letter_key))]"/>
```

For what it's worth, when you override `true_false` with the string "false," the block of code above produces the results shown in Figure 5–5.

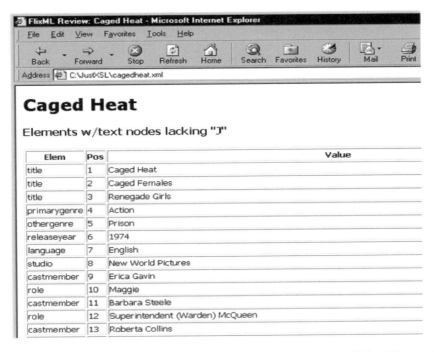

Figure 5-5 Overriding the `true_false` global parameter (using "false" instead of the default "true") in the code that produced Figure 5–4. This partial screen shot doesn't show all text nodes lacking a capital "J"; in the *Caged Heat* review there are 45 such text nodes altogether.

Keying an external document

When I covered the document() function earlier, I mentioned that storing an external document's tree of nodes in memory—in a variable—made sense for efficiency's sake, if you're going to be repeatedly revisiting the external document's contents. It would be wonderful if you could build a keyed node-set from an external document, for even greater efficiency. Unfortunately, the document() function can't be used in a match pattern (such as the one appearing as the value of the xsl:key element's match attribute).

However, somewhat oddly, you *can* build and use a key from an external document indirectly.

Let's return to the example we last used in the discussion of the document() function. To refresh your memory, we had an external "lookup table" of film genres consisting of elements and text nodes in the following sort of structure:

```
<genres>
   <genre>
     <name>[genre name]</name>
     <desc>[description]</desc>
     <avatar>[title of typical movie]</avatar>
   </genre>
   <genre>
     <name>[genre name]</name>
     <desc>[description]</desc>
     <avatar>[title of typical movie]</avatar>
   </genre>
   [etc.]
</genres>
```

We'll start out by adding an xsl:key element to the stylesheet:

```
<xsl:key name="genre_key" match="genre" use="name"/>
```

As before, remember that the value of the match attribute isn't relative to anything in particular at this point. *Only when we use the key() function will the key's context be established.* Therefore, we can replace the earlier xsl:value-of element (whose select attribute used a rather tortured predicate to get the proper desc and avatar elements) with one that calls the key() function.

There's one more trick we've got to use, though. First, here are the original contents of the "Description" table cell from the earlier stylesheet:

```
<xsl:value-of select = "$genres//desc[preceding-sibling::name =
current()]"/>
```

```
(Archetype: <xsl:value-of select =
"$genres//avatar[preceding-sibling::name =
current()]"/>)
```

We can't simply replace the values of the two select attributes above with calls to the key() function, like this:

```
<xsl:value-of select="key('genre_key', .)/desc"/>
(Archetype: <xsl:value-of select="key('genre_key', .)/avatar"/>)
```

This works except for one thing: The context in which the key's match attribute is evaluated is all wrong. It points to the source tree, not to the external document genres.xml (where our desc and avatar elements are).

Recall from the previous chapter that the xsl:for-each element was good not just for instantiating a particular template over and over but also for momentarily changing the context node. Armed with that memory,[4] what we're going to do first is save the key value we want to retrieve in a variable, and then use xsl:for-each to change the context in which the above xsl:value-of elements will be evaluated. Here's how the code for the contents of the table cell (td element) now looks:

```
<xsl:variable name="genre" select="."/>
<xsl:for-each select="document('genres.xml')">
  <xsl:value-of select="key('genre_key', $genre)/desc"/>
  (Archetype: <xsl:value-of select="key('genre_key', $genre)/
avatar"/>)
```

Note that

- the xsl:for-each is used here *only* to shift the context to the external document; and
- the key value passed to the key() function is not a simple ., but the value of the genre variable that was assigned before entering the xsl:for-each block.

Applying this modified stylesheet to the *Criss Cross* review displays results as in Figure 5–6.

---

4.   You *did* remember that, didn't you?

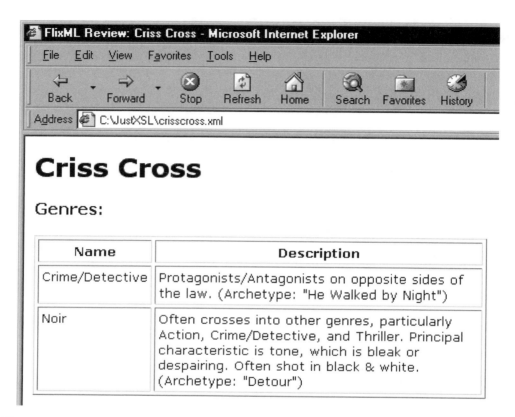

Figure 5-6   Using a key to retrieve data from an external file. Remember two things about keys: (a) Their performance advantages go up the more nodes there are in the keyed data and the more often those nodes are accessed; and (b) each keyed node-set will require some up-front "build time" to construct the corresponding index. Whether to use keys is a decision to make based on *both* of those issues.

Numbering

This section deals with two issues that could have been treated separately but are not infrequently needed together. Those are the issues of *formatting numbers* and *numbering lists of things.*

Departing from the norm

In the initial formatting-numbers section of *Just XSL*, I'm not going to try force-fitting FlixML to demonstrate something it's not really well-suited to demonstrate. (There aren't many numbers in a FlixML document, except implicit ones—node-set counts, for instance.)

Instead, I'm going to use as a demonstrator application the following simple document:

```
<theater_take>
  <day name="Friday">
    <screen number="1" capacity="1804">
      <showing rate="Twilight">
       <adults>
         <count>125</count>
         <take>375</take>
       </adults>
       <children>
         <count>111</count>
         <take>249.75</take>
       </children>
      </showing>
      <showing rate="Regular">
       <adults>
         <count>383</count>
         <take>2776.75</take>
       </adults>
       <children>
         <count>267</count>
         <take>1201.5</take>
       </children>
      </showing>
    </screen>
    <screen number="2" capacity="1724">
      <showing rate="Twilight">
       <adults>
         <count>74</count>
         <take>222</take>
       </adults>
       <children>
         <count>107</count>
         <take>240.75</take>
       </children>
      </showing>
      <showing rate="Regular">
       <adults>
         <count>126</count>
         <take>913.5</take>
       </adults>
```

```
    <children>
      <count>165</count>
      <take>742.5</take>
    </children>
    </showing>
  </screen>
</day>
<day name="Saturday">
  <screen number="1" capacity="1804">
    <showing rate="Twilight">
    <adults>
      <count>643</count>
      <take>1929</take>
    </adults>
    <children>
      <count>724</count>
      <take>1629</take>
    </children>
    </showing>
    <showing rate="Regular">
    <adults>
      <count>821</count>
      <take>5952.25</take>
    </adults>
    <children>
      <count>898</count>
      <take>4041</take>
    </children>
    </showing>
  </screen>
  <screen number="2" capacity="1724">
    <showing rate="Twilight">
    <adults>
      <count>507</count>
      <take>1521</take>
    </adults>
    <children>
      <count>472</count>
      <take>1062</take>
    </children>
    </showing>
    <showing rate="Regular">
    <adults>
      <count>697</count>
      <take>5053.25</take>
    </adults>
```

```
     <children>
       <count>701</count>
       <take>3154.5</take>
     </children>
   </showing>
  </screen>
 </day>
</theater_take>
```

As you can see, this represents a movie theater's ticket sales for a couple of days. The theater in question has two screens, one with a seating capacity of 1804 and one with 1724. For each screen there are two daily showings, a "Twilight" and a "Regular" showing, and at each showing adult and children tickets are tabulated separately. (Although the information isn't in this XML document—perhaps it's in a lookup document!—it's possible to determine that tickets for adults cost 7.25 for the regular showing and 3.00 for the twilight; and tickets for children 4.50 for the regular, 2.25 for the twilight. We don't know what the unit of currency is.)

First-cut stylesheet

The initial stylesheet for converting this data into an XHTML table contains four "trickle-down" template rules, as I've been calling them. One processes the root `theater_take` element, setting up the general structure of an XHTML document:

```
<xsl:template match="theater_take">
  <html>
  <head><title>Weekend Ticket Sales</title></head>
  <body>
    <xsl:apply-templates/>
  </body>
  </html>
</xsl:template>
```

The second template rule (invoked by the `xsl:apply-templates` above) processes each `day` element in the source tree. It constructs a table for the current `day` element, including column headings, and then invokes the template rule(s) for processing the `day` element's children:

```
<xsl:template match="day">
  <h2><xsl:value-of select="@name"/> Ticket Sales</h2>
  <table>
    <tr style="background-color: silver">
      <th>Screen</th>
      <th>Showing</th>
```

```
         <th>Audience</th>
         <th>Count</th>
         <th>Capacity</th>
         <th>Amount</th>
      </tr>
      <xsl:apply-templates/>
   </table>
</xsl:template>
```

Third, invoked by the `xsl:apply-templates` element in the preceding fragment is a template rule for processing data for the two screens at the theater. This is easily the simplest template rule of the four:

```
<xsl:template match="screen">
   <xsl:apply-templates/>
</xsl:template>
```

Finally, easily the *biggest* (and most important) template rule in the stylesheet is the one for processing each showing at each screen. This is the template rule we're really going to be concerned with here. It looks like this:

```
<xsl:template match="showing">
   <!-- Process each child (adults/children) of showing
      element -->
   <xsl:for-each select="*">
      <!-- Sort by "rate" ("Regular"/"Twilight" in
         descending order), then by name of this child
         ("adults"/"children") -->
      <xsl:sort select="../@rate" order="descending"/>
      <xsl:sort select="name()"/>
      <tr>
         <!-- Set up 6-column table row. If this is the
            first child ("adults"), make the first two
            columns (screen number and "rate") span two
            rows. -->
         <xsl:if test="position()=1">
            <td align="center" rowspan="2" style="background-color:
silver"><xsl:value-of select="../../@number"/></td>
            <td align="center" rowspan="2" style="background-color:
silver"><xsl:value-of select="../@rate"/></td>
         </xsl:if>
         <!-- Add columns representing adults/children,
            number of tickets sold, percent of the given
            screen's capacity, and "take" (revenue) from all
            ticket sales. -->
         <td><xsl:value-of select="name()"/></td>
         <td><xsl:value-of select="count"/></td>
```

```
    <td><xsl:value-of select="count div ../../@capacity"/></td>
    <td><xsl:value-of select="take"/></td>
  </tr>
</xsl:for-each>
<!-- Add a row for showing the totals (tickets sold,
  percent capacity, and "take") for this screen and
  showing. -->
<tr style="background-color: silver">
  <td colspan="3">Screen <xsl:value-of select="../@number"/>/
<xsl:value-of select="@rate"/> Totals</td>
    <td><xsl:value-of select="sum(.//count)"/></td>
    <td><xsl:value-of select="sum(.//count) div ../@capacity"/></td>
    <td><xsl:value-of select="sum(.//take)"/></td>
  </tr>
</xsl:template>
```

Partial results of this first-cut transformation appear in MSIE as shown in Figure 5–7.

Friday Ticket Sales

Screen	Showing	Audience	Count	Capacity	Amount
1	Twilight	adults	125	0.06929046563192904	375
		children	111	0.061529933481152994	249.75
Screen 1/Twilight Totals			236	0.13082039911308205	624.75
1	Regular	adults	383	0.2123059866962306	2776.75
		children	267	0.14800443458980045	1201.5
Screen 1/Regular Totals			650	0.360310421286031	3978.25
2	Twilight	adults	74	0.042923433874709975	222
		children	107	0.06206496519721578	240.75
Screen 2/Twilight Totals			181	0.10498839907192575	462.75
2	Regular	adults	126	0.07308584686774942	913.5
		children	165	0.095707656612529	742.5
Screen 2/Regular Totals			291	0.1687935034802784	1656

Saturday Ticket Sales

Screen	Showing	Audience	Count	Capacity	Amount
1	Twilight	adults	643	0.35643015521064303	1929
		children	724	0.401330376940133	1629
Screen 1/Twilight Totals			1367	0.7577605321507761	3558

Figure 5-7 Initial transformation of theater ticket sales data to an XHTML table. This is rather ugly.

Some of the cleanup of these results doesn't require knowledge of XSLT at all; we'll want all the numeric data (except for the screen numbers) aligned right, for instance, which we can accomplish simply with `align` attributes to the various `td` elements. But to *really* clean up these numbers, we'll need to leverage an XSLT function and—optionally—an XSLT element as well.

Formatting numbers with (surprise!) `format-number()`

XSLT's `format-number()` function is used to convert numeric values to string form, formatted in a way that is appropriate for some particular presentation purpose. Examples of occasions on which you'd want to do something like this include displaying integers with a fixed number of places, including leading zeroes if needed, and displaying monetary figures using currency and decimal characters.

The general syntax for a call to the `format-number()` function is

```
format-number(number, formatpattern, dec_format?)
```

where

- *number* is the number whose value is to be formatted;
- *formatpattern* is a specially formatted string which is used as a model for formatting *number*; and
- *dec_format?* is an optional argument, a string providing the name of some "decimal format" declared elsewhere in the stylesheet.

I'll cover the third argument in detail in a moment. For now, let's look at that second argument, *formatpattern*.

Format patterns

XSLT has borrowed from Java[5] the idea of a *format pattern*. This is a simple text string, structured in a way that acts as a kind of mold into which you can pour a raw numeric value. The numeric value then adopts the "shape" of the format pattern.

---

5.   And from some other languages, but Java is the only one mentioned by name in the XSLT spec. In other languages, this is sometimes called something like a "picture string."

Each pattern consists of a sub-pattern for positive values of the number and an optional sub-pattern for negative values. (If the latter isn't supplied, a negative number by default will display exactly as the corresponding positive value, with a minus sign appended to the start of the resulting string.) Each sub-pattern takes the following form:

```
{prefix}number{.fraction}{suffix}
```

The curly braces aren't literally included in the sub-pattern; they're just there to show you which pieces of the sub-pattern are optional.

The four components of the sub-pattern are these:

- `prefix`: Basically, this includes any Unicode character(s). What you enter as the prefix will be tacked on, as literal text, to the beginning of the resulting string. You might use the prefix to represent a euro sign (€), for example.
- `number`: This, the "whole number" portion of the format pattern, is represented by various combinations of special characters, which I'll cover in a moment.
- `.fraction`: This is used for patterning the fractional portion of a number. It's represented using the same characters as `number`, as we'll see in a moment.
- `suffix`: This is like the prefix, except that the character(s) here will be tacked on as literal text to the *end* of the resulting string. For instance, you might use "USD" (for "US dollars").

Obviously, the most important parts of the format pattern are the number and fraction, which provide the "shapes" into which a given number's value is poured. These "shapes" are specified using a series of special characters adopted from the Java Development Kit (JDK) version 1.1. The characters and their purposes are listed in Table 5–1. Next, we'll get into some specific examples.

Table 5-1 Format Pattern Characters

Character	Description
0	Digit placeholder; will always display as either a 0 or the corresponding digit from the number (used to ensure leading zeroes)
#	Digit placeholder; if the corresponding digit from the number is missing, displays nothing (suppresses leading zeroes)
.	Decimal point placeholder

Table 5-1   Format Pattern Characters (continued)

Character	Description
,	Grouping separator; used mostly for separating every three digits ("thousands separator") but in some locales for separating every four ("ten thousands separator")
;	Separator between sub-patterns (sub-pattern to left shows format for positive numbers; to right, negative numbers)
-	Default prefix for negative numbers
%	Causes number to be multiplied by 100 and followed by a percent sign (%)
?	Causes number to be multiplied by 1,000 and followed by a per-mille sign (‰)
any	Any other character can be used in the pattern; will display as a literal value at that position
'	Used for quoting (escaping) the above special characters so they'll be interpreted as literal characters rather than placeholders

As a simple example of how to use these format pattern characters, consider the XML document and stylesheet introduced above for recording and displaying theater ticket-sales information. This particular theater has only two screens, but in order to make the stylesheet useful for any theater using the same document structure, including 20-screen multiplex monstrosities, assume we always want the screen number to display as two digits—with a leading zero, if needed. Referring back to the stylesheet and Figure 5–7, you can see that the screen number is displayed in a couple of spots (in column 1 of the result-tree table, and again in its totals row). To force a leading zero to display, replace each of those occurrences with a call to `format-number()`. For example,

```
format-number(../../@number, '00')
```

for displaying the screen number in column 1 of the table, and

```
format-number(../@number, '00')
```

for displaying the screen number in the totals row.

> ## Or use a variable!
>
> This is an easy use case for a variable, by the way. Rather than calling `format-number()` twice, with a slightly different location path, you can set up a variable declaration. Put it immediately after the last `xsl:template` element's start tag, just before the `xsl:for-each`. (That placement will ensure that the variable is in scope for both of the places where you need to use it.) Something like this:
>
> ```
> <xsl:variable name="scr_num" select="format-
>   number(../@number, '00')"/>
> ```
>
> Then you can replace both original references to the raw screen number with `$scr_num` references instead. For example,
>
> ```
> <xsl:value-of select="$scr_num"/>
> ```

As you can see, the second argument to `format-number()` is here simply two 0s. This doesn't mean "display two zeroes here"; it means that the 0s are placeholders: Each 0 (per Table 5–1) stands in for a number in the corresponding position in the number to be formatted, whatever it is. For screen number 1, the 1 corresponds to the second 0 (digit immediately to the left of the decimal point, if there were one). There is no other digit in the screen number, so the placeholder is displayed there instead.

Now look at the column headed "Count" in Figure 5–7. Most of those numbers are smaller than 1,000; but when they're larger than that, we want them to display with commas as "grouping" separators. The format pattern to use for this is `#,###` (or rather `#,##0`—this will always display something, even if it's just a single 0).

Note that there are again two references to the `count` figure. However, we won't be able to use a variable in this case. Why not? Because the first reference to `count` uses `count` alone, to represent the raw number of tickets sold on that day, that screen, at that showing, at that rate (adults/children); the second reference is to the *sum* of ticket sales for that day, screen, and showing. These two references would therefore have to be replaced by the following two separate uses of `format-number()`, respectively:

```
<xsl:value-of select="format-number(count,
  '#,##0')"/>
<xsl:value-of select="format-number(sum(.//count),
  '#,##0')"/>
```

Next, let's jump over the column headed "Capacity" for a moment and look at the "Amount" column. Some of the numbers here have a fractional portion, some are integers; we could do with a thousands separator here, too, and maybe a currency symbol. Assuming the currency symbol in this case is the euro, we'll need to use an entity reference (€) in the format pattern, and maybe separate it from the amount itself using a single space. For instance,

```
<xsl:value-of select="format-number(take,
  '&#8364; #,##0.00')"/>
<xsl:value-of select="format-number(sum(.//take),
  '&#8364; #,##0.00')"/>
```

Note a couple of things about this format pattern, by the way. First, the entity reference to the euro character and the space that follows it both make up the *prefix* portion of the sub-pattern. Second, the sub-pattern includes two trailing 0s after the decimal point; this is interpreted as "always show two digits here, even if the number being formatted has a fractional part of fewer than two digits."

Okay, now let's back up to the "Capacity" column. The figure that goes here is the result of dividing the actual number of tickets sold by the given screen's capacity—that is, it represents a *percentage* of the screen's capacity. So we want to be sure to use the percent sign in the two format patterns, respectively:

```
<xsl:value-of select="format-number(count
  div ../../@capacity, '0.00%')"/>
<xsl:value-of select="format-number(sum(.//count)
  div ../@capacity, '0.00%')"/>
```

The modified stylesheet is now complete; the all-important template rule for the showing element now looks like this:

```
<xsl:template match="showing">
  <!-- Set up a variable for displaying screen number
    as two digits (leading 0 if needed) -->
  <xsl:variable name="scr_num"
    select="format-number(../@number, '00')"/>
  <!-- Process each child (adults/children) of showing
    element -->
  <xsl:for-each select="*">
    <!-- Sort by "rate" ("Regular"/"Twilight" in
      descending order), then by name of this child
      ("adults"/"children") -->
    <xsl:sort select="../@rate" order="descending"/>
    <xsl:sort select="name()"/>
    <tr>
```

```
        <!-- Set up 6-column table row. If this is the
          first child ("adults"), make the first two
          columns (screen number and "rate") span two
          rows. -->
        <xsl:if test="position()=1">
          <td align="center" rowspan="2" style="background-color:
silver"><xsl:value-of select="$scr_num"/></td>
          <td align="center" rowspan="2" style="background-color:
silver"><xsl:value-of select="../@rate"/></td>
        </xsl:if>
        <!-- Add columns representing adults/children,
          number of tickets sold, percent of the given
          screen's capacity, and "take" (revenue) from all
          ticket sales. Numeric values to be formatted
          depending on type of numeric data. -->
        <td align="right"><xsl:value-of select="name()"/></td>
        <td align="right"><xsl:value-of
          select="format-number(count, '#,##0')"/></td>
        <td align="right"><xsl:value-of
          select="format-number(count
          div ../../@capacity, '0.00%')"/></td>
        <td align="right"><xsl:value-of
          select="format-number(take,
          '&#8364; #,##0.00')"/></td>
      </tr>
    </xsl:for-each>
    <!-- Add a row for showing the totals (tickets sold,
      percent capacity, and "take") for this screen and
      showing. Format numbers as appropriate. -->
    <tr style="background-color: silver">
      <td colspan="3">Screen <xsl:value-of
      select="$scr_num"/>/<xsl:value-of
      select="@rate"/> Totals</td>
      <td align="right"><xsl:value-of
        select="format-number(sum(.//count),
        '#,##0')"/></td>
      <td align="right"><xsl:value-of
        select="format-number(sum(.//count)
        div ../@capacity, '0.00%')"/></td>
      <td align="right"><xsl:value-of
        select="format-number(sum(.//take),
        '&#8364; #,##0.00')"/></td>
    </tr>
  </xsl:template>
```

The completely formatted table now displays as shown in Figure 5–8.

Friday Ticket Sales

Screen	Showing	Audience	Count	Capacity	Amount
01	Twilight	adults	125	6.93%	€ 375.00
		children	111	6.15%	€ 249.75
Screen 01/Twilight Totals			236	13.08%	€ 624.75
01	Regular	adults	383	21.23%	€ 2,776.75
		children	267	14.80%	€ 1,201.50
Screen 01/Regular Totals			650	36.03%	€ 3,978.25
02	Twilight	adults	74	4.29%	€ 222.00
		children	107	6.21%	€ 240.75
Screen 02/Twilight Totals			181	10.50%	€ 462.75
02	Regular	adults	126	7.31%	€ 913.50
		children	165	9.57%	€ 742.50
Screen 02/Regular Totals			291	16.88%	€ 1,656.00

Saturday Ticket Sales

Screen	Showing	Audience	Count	Capacity	Amount
01	Twilight	adults	643	35.64%	€ 1,929.00
		children	724	40.13%	€ 1,629.00
Screen 01/Twilight Totals			1,367	75.78%	€ 3,558.00

Figure 5-8 Same data as in Figure 5–7, but with the numeric formatting considerably cleaned up. Looks to me like this theater owner needs to take a hard look at whatever he was showing on Friday.

Negative numbers

As indicated in the description of patterns and sub-patterns, a pattern can include a sub-pattern just for negative numbers. This wouldn't really apply to the ticket-sales example, but you could format some number with this optional pattern in the following manner:

```
format-number(number, '0;(0)')
```

> Translated, this means: "Format *number* as at least one digit if it's positive; if it's negative, enclose it within parentheses." So the number 12 would simply display that way; the number –12 ("negative twelve") would display as (12).

Using customized formats: `xsl:decimal-format`

The `format-number()` function is useful in most cases with just the first two arguments: the number to be converted and the format pattern for its "shaping." However, there's a third optional argument which can be passed to it. This is a string, the name of a decimal format.

You create a decimal format to be used in this way using the top-level `xsl:decimal-format` element, whose general syntax is this:

```
<xsl:decimal-format
  name="formatname"
  decimal-separator="dec_char"
  grouping-separator="group_char"
  infinity="inf_string"
  minus-sign="minus_char"
  NaN="NaN_string"
  percent="pct_char"
  per-mille="pml_char"
  zero-digit="zero_char"
  digit="digit_char"
  pattern-separator="sep_char" />
```

Only `name` is specifically required, although to make any actual use of a given decimal format, you'll also need to include at least one other attribute.

If you're really observant, you'll have noticed something interesting about this list of attributes: With only a couple of exceptions, they've got counterparts in the list of format pattern characters in Table 5–1. That's no coincidence; the values of the `xsl:decimal-format` element's attributes are used to override the defaults for (a) *characters displayed* in place of placeholder characters and/or (b) *the placeholder characters themselves*, as used in a format pattern. Table 5–2 summarizes.

Table 5-2   `xsl:decimal-format` Attributes and Their Effects

Attribute	Affects display	Overrides placeholder
decimal-separator	Y	Y
grouping-separator	Y	Y

Table 5-2 `xsl:decimal-format` Attributes and Their Effects

Attribute	Affects display	Overrides placeholder
infinity	Y	
minus-sign	Y	
NaN	Y	
percent	Y	Y
per-mille	Y	Y
zero-digit	Y	Y
digit		Y
pattern-separator		Y

The idea of the `xsl:decimal-format` element is that special circumstances may require the following special effects:

- You need to change the default format-pattern placeholder characters, and/or
- You need to change the display of specific characters or strings *returned* from `format-number()`.

If the attribute's value is used to override the corresponding placeholder in a format pattern, you use the overriding value in the format pattern rather than the one specified in Table 5–1. If the attribute's value is used to affect the display—the value returned from `format-number()`—you may or may not need to use a different placeholder (depending on whether the "Overrides placeholder" column in Table 5–2 is Y or blank, respectively).

Note also, by the way, that declaring an `xsl:decimal-format` element does not necessarily automatically affect *all* calls to `format-number()`. It affects only those calls to `format-number()` which include the third optional argument, and then only when the `name` attribute of the `xsl:decimal-format` element matches the value of that third argument.

As an example, consider that some countries switch the purposes of the default decimal and grouping separators. In such countries, this number (using default separators)

```
1,000.25
```

would be represented as

```
1.000,25
```

To ensure that numbers were displayed in the latter format, we could set up a named decimal format as follows:

```
<xsl:decimal-format
  name="reverse_sep"
  grouping-separator="."
  decimal-separator=","/>
```

To format some number using this decimal format, we'd call format-number() with the third argument as well as the first two:

```
format-number(number, '#.##0,00', 'reverse_sep')
```

Note that (per Table 5–2) the overriding grouping-separator and decimal-separator placeholder characters are used in the format pattern and also show up in the displayed number.

NaN and infinity attributes   These are the two oddballs in the lot—the xsl:decimal-format attributes with no real counterparts in Table 5–1. Their purposes are to provide string values to be returned when what is supposedly a number actually either is not numeric at all ("Not a number," as I mentioned in discussing the XPath num() function in Chapter 2) or equates to infinity, respectively. The default values for these are the strings "NaN" and "Infinity," and that's where the attributes' names come from.

You may want to override these string values more often than the specific format-pattern characters—particularly "NaN," which can probably be figured out if a reader tries hard enough but will almost certainly result in initial confusion. An xsl:decimal-format element to override them might look like this:

```
<xsl:decimal-format name="bad_num"
  NaN="#ERROR/NON-NUM#"
  infinity="#ERROR/INFINITY#"/>
```

This might be particularly useful in displaying the results of calculations, as here:

```
format-number(count div capacity, '0.00%', 'bad_num')
```

Numbering lists

Just about any text-content presentation system worth its salt includes some facility for numbering items in lists. Certainly XHTML does, with the `ol` (for "ordered list") element and its `li` ("list item") children. You may not always be transforming to such a convenient result tree, though. And even when you are, facilities such as those provided by XHTML's ordered list may simply not be sufficient.

The march of time

As if those objections weren't enough, various specialized forms of the XHTML ordered list are on their way out, to be replaced by special CSS display properties. So even if you can *today* create all the numbered lists you want, don't count on being able to do so in the not-so-distant future.

To cite one obvious example, just look through the pages of *Just XSL*. Notice the table and figure numbers: Table 5–1; Table 5–2; Figures 5–1, 5–2, 5–3, and so on. This is a common kind of "numbered list" in publishing applications.

Less common in general, but also quite common in some contexts, is the use of page numbering to reflect (say) chapter number, section number within that chapter, topic number within that section, and page number within that topic. For example, page numbers in a chapter might be numbered 1.1.1.1, 1.1.1.2, 1.1.2.1, and so on.

And then there's the granddaddy of all numbered lists: the outline—not only in its basic form (I, A, 1, a, (1), (a), etc.) but also in various exotic forms (I, I.1, I.1.a, and so on).

To create an ordered list with XSLT, use the `xsl:number` element. Watch out, though. For a feature with such an easy-to-grasp purpose, `xsl:number` can be kind of dizzying to use in practice. Its general syntax is this:

```
<xsl:number
  level="single_multiple_any"
  count="count_pattern"
  from="from_pattern"
  value="number-expression"
  format="fmt_string"
  lang="lang"
  letter-value="alphabetic_traditional"
  grouping-separator="sepchar"
  grouping-size="grpsize" />
```

Before getting into these attributes, think about what you want an ordered list to do: You want it to assign some kind of value to one item in a list, the next highest value to the next item in the list, and so on. The word *list* is loosely defined here, by the way; it needn't be, you know, like a list of brief phrases. Each item in this kind of list can go on for pages, if necessary. The sequencing is the important thing.

Given that, what do you think xsl:number by itself might do *when no attributes at all are included?* Answer: It does exactly the same thing the position() function does. That is, the following two template rules

```
<xsl:template match="distributor">
  <xsl:number/>. <xsl:value-of
    select="distribname"/><br />
</xsl:template>

<xsl:template match="distributor">
  <xsl:value-of select="position()"/>. <xsl:value-of
    select="distribname"/><br />
</xsl:template>
```

both produce the result shown in Figure 5–9 when run against the *Caged Heat* FlixML review.

Figure 5-9 The simplest kind of ordered list imaginable. Using xsl:number or position()? Only the stylesheet's author knows for sure!

Okay, now that we've got the no-attributes case out of the way, let's dive into what goes on with all of those attributes.

The first thing an XSLT processor does for each item in the list is construct an "item number" using the specified (or defaulted) values of the `level`, `count`, and `from` attributes together, so I'll cover them first—singly, then taking all three together.

level

Valid values are `single` (the default), `multiple`, and `any`.

- `level="single"`: This is typically used when the things in your list are all considered the same sort of things. There's no hierarchical relationship among them; they're all at the same level of the hierarchy (in fact or conceptually). For example, book chapters and page numbers are numbered consecutively in most cases.
- `level="multiple"`: This value asserts that items in the list share some kind of hierarchical relationship(s), such as chapters within a book, sections within a chapter, and so on. This is the one to use when you want to construct a complex kind of numbering, such as the pages within sections/sections within chapters/chapters within a book kind of numbering hierarchy.
- `level="any"`: This value forces the XSLT processor to number the items sequentially, *regardless of any hierarchical relationship(s)* they may have with one another. The classic example of this kind of numbering is footnotes in a book or chapter; the footnote reference can occur anywhere in the document in question—in a regular paragraph, in a figure caption, in a note or sidebar, and so on—and the numbers are incremented irrespective of the level at which the references appear.

count

The value of this attribute is a match pattern indicating what nodes are to be counted, at however many levels are indicated by the `level` attribute.

The default, says the spec in a characteristically dreadful burst of self-referential jargon, is this:

the pattern that matches any node with the same node type as the current node and, if the current node has an expanded-name, with the same expanded-name as the current node.

Translated, what this says is that the default is whatever type of node is currently being processed in the level of the template where the `xsl:number` appears. If the current node has a name—which would be true of elements, attributes, and PIs—the default value of the `count` attribute will be that name.

Thus, in the basic code preceding Figure 5–9, the `xsl:number` element appeared in a template rule matching the `distributor` element. Since no count attribute was explicitly provided, what the `xsl:number` element was counting there was—surprise!—the `distributor` elements.

from

This attribute's value is also a match pattern, indicating at which node counting actually (re)starts. The default behavior is to (re)start the numbering at a node that doesn't actually exist, and hence the numbering simply goes up indefinitely.

level, count, and from considered together

These three attributes are somewhat interdependent in their effects. To see how, let's number the cast members' names in a FlixML document and vary the values of these three attributes one at a time.

The basic template rule we'll start with looks like this:

```
<xsl:template match="cast">
  <xsl:for-each select="leadcast|othercast">
    <h3><xsl:number level="single"/>. <xsl:value-of
select="name()"/></h3>
    <xsl:for-each select=".//castmember">
      <xsl:number level="single"/>. <xsl:value-of select="."/><br />
    </xsl:for-each>
  </xsl:for-each>
</xsl:template>
```

As you can see, there are two `xsl:number` elements—one for each of the `leadcast` and `othercast` elements, one for each of the descendant `castmember` elements—and each `xsl:number` element currently has only a single attribute, `level`, which is set to the default value of `single`. The result tree from this transformation, applied to the *Criss Cross* review, appears as in Figure 5–10.

1. leadcast

1. Burt Lancaster
1. Yvonne DeCarlo
1. Dan Duryea

1. othercast

1. Griff Barnett
1. John Doucette
1. Percy Helton
1. Edna Holland
1. Marc Krah
1. Richard Long
1. Stephen McNally
1. Joan Miller
1. John "Skins" Miller
1. Esy Morales
1. Alan Napier
1. James O'Rear
1. Tom Pedi
1. Meg Randall

Figure 5-10   First-cut version of our numbered cast list. Not exactly useful numbering, is it? See the text for an explanation.

What's going on here is that items are being numbered "sequentially" only to the extent that they're at the same level of the hierarchy—that is, they must *share the same parent* and *share the same node type and name* in order for any of these numbers really to go up. Clearly, although leadcast and othercast share the same parent and node type, they don't have the same name; so each of them constitutes a separate "list" consisting of a single item. On the other hand, all the castmember elements numbered by the innermost xsl:number have the same node type and name...but they *don't* share the same parent. (Each is the child of a different male or female element.) So each castmember is in its own list, as well.

We'll start by varying the level attribute which applies to the leadcast/othercast elements, changing its value to multiple. A portion of the results is shown in Figure 5–11.

1. leadcast

1. Burt Lancaster
1. Yvonne DeCarlo
1. Dan Duryea

1. othercast

1. Griff Barnett
1. John Doucette
1. Percy Helton

Figure 5-11 Same data as in Figure 5–10, changing the `leadcast`/`othercast` numbering level to "multiple." Don't see any difference, do you? Neither do I.

The reason this doesn't elicit any different result at this point is that we've set the numbering level to `multiple`, but we've still let the `count` and `from` attributes assume their default values. Let's try adding a `count` attribute. What we'll tell the XSLT processor with this attribute is to number nodes in this list sequentially with every new `cast`, `leadcast`, or `othercast` element; that is, the `xsl:number` element now looks like this:

```
<xsl:number level="multiple"
  count="cast | leadcast | othercast"/>
```

Figure 5–12 shows partial results.

1.1. leadcast

1. Burt Lancaster
1. Yvonne DeCarlo
1. Dan Duryea

1.2. othercast

1. Griff Barnett
1. John Doucette
1. Percy Helton

Figure 5-12 We've changed the count attribute so it counts changes in any of three elements: `cast`, `leadcast`, or `othercast`. However, note that these elements occupy only *two* levels (`leadcast` and `othercast` are siblings, both being children of `cast`), and hence the resulting multi-level numbering shows only two numbered levels. The `cast` element never changes—there's only one `cast` element being considered in the source tree, so the number at its level stays at 1. The `leadcast` element is the first item at the next level (number 1.1, in other words), and `othercast` is the second (1.2).

Next change: I'll leave the `count` attribute set as above, and simply change the `level` attribute's value to any:

```
<xsl:number level="any"
  count="cast | leadcast | othercast"/>
```

What this tells the processor is to consider the `cast`, `leadcast`, and `othercast` elements to be members of the same numbered list. However, here the placement (context) of the `xsl:number` element assumes significance: It's inside an `xsl:for-each` that selects *only* the `leadcast` and `othercast` elements. (That is, although the cast element is "numbered," it's not selected and hence its number value is not instantiated here.) The relevant portion of the result tree displays as in Figure 5–13.

2. leadcast

1. Burt Lancaster
1. Yvonne DeCarlo
1. Dan Duryea

3. othercast

1. Griff Barnett
1. John Doucette
1. Percy Helton

Figure 5-13 Counting the `cast`, `leadcast`, and `othercast` elements as part of the same list, irrespective of their levels in the hierarchy...but *showing* only the `leadcast` and `othercast`. Probably a technique of limited usefulness!

This isn't a reasonable way to number these two items, so I'll leave the `level` attribute's value at `any` and change the `count` attribute's value, indicating that I want to count only the `leadcast` and `othercast` elements:

```
<xsl:number level="any" count="leadcast | othercast"/>
```

Now, let's turn our attention to the numbering of the `castmember` elements. We already know that simply changing the value of the `level` attribute from `single` to `multiple`, without also specifying the other two attributes, will have no effect on the output. So I'll leave the other two attributes as they are (that is, allow them to default), and change the level directly from `single` to any:

```
<xsl:number level="any"/>
```

A portion of the results is shown in Figure 5–14.

1. leadcast

1. Burt Lancaster
2. Yvonne DeCarlo
3. Dan Duryea

2. othercast

4. Griff Barnett
5. John Doucette
6. Percy Helton

Figure 5-14 Changing the numbering of `castmember` elements from `single` to `any`. Note that this is similar to how you might number footnotes in a document, especially if they're to be gathered as endnotes at the document's end: They don't restart numbering at each "parent" (`leadcast` and `othercast`, here), but are all members of one big "master list" of items.

To restart numbering of the `castmember` elements so that each cast list is considered a separate list, I'll add a `from` attribute:

```
<xsl:number level="any" from="leadcast | othercast"/>
```

Now the lists are truly separate, as you can see from Figure 5–15.

1. leadcast

1. Burt Lancaster
2. Yvonne DeCarlo
3. Dan Duryea

2. othercast

1. Griff Barnett
2. John Doucette
3. Percy Helton

Figure 5-15 Leaving `level` set to "any," but supplying a value for the `from` attribute. When a node matching the `from` attribute's pattern is found, numbering starts over again.

Playing games with axes

One thing you may have noticed in the values for the `count` and `from` attributes is that, although they're XPath-based relative location paths, they don't follow the rule in effect elsewhere in XSLT: that the default axis for relative location paths is the child axis.

For instance, in the example shown in Figure 5–15, the context node at the point of the `xsl:number` element is a `castmember` element. The `xsl:number` element's `from` attribute here has a value of "`leadcast | othercast`"—neither of those elements clearly being a child of `castmember` in any FlixML document.

Basically, imagine what you're doing with `xsl:number` is assigning a sequence number to something at the bottom level of a hierarchy. In these terms, the "breakpoints"—the points where the number value changes—will always be at some level *higher than or equal to* the level of the node being numbered. Put another way, the default axis for the `count` and `from` attributes' patterns is the ancestor-or-self axis.

I've never seen it described exactly this way, but that's what it boils down to.

What we've got so far may well be sufficient for our needs. I'm going to take it one step further, though. I'm going to set up the numbering of the `castmember` elements so that it's a two-level number, with the first position representing the number of the "main category" (1 or 2, for `leadcast` or `othercast`, respectively) and the second position representing the number of the `castmember` within that category. The innermost `xsl:number` element will therefore look like this somewhat surprising variation on what we've already got for it:

```
<xsl:number level="multiple"
  count="leadcast | othercast | male | female" />
```

What's surprising is the sudden appearance of the `male` and `female` elements in the equation. If we're supposed to be counting `castmembers`, why count their parent elements?

The answer is, precisely, that each `castmember` element exists *within* a `male` or `female` element. If you replace the "`male | female`" in the above pattern with a simple "`castmember`," the numbers generated will always be 1—the `castmember` is always its parent's first child, even though we don't (in theory) care about the parent element at this point. On the other hand, counting the `male` and `female` children of the `leadcast`/`othercast` "main categories" ensures that we get nicely sequential multi-level numbering, as you can see in Figure 5–16.

1. leadcast

1.1. Burt Lancaster
1.2. Yvonne DeCarlo
1.3. Dan Duryea

2. othercast

2.1. Griff Barnett
2.2. John Doucette
2.3. Percy Helton

Figure 5-16 "Cast categories" numbered from beginning to end, using a `level` of "any," and cast members numbered sequentially, in hierarchical form, within each category—using a `level` of "multiple" and a (cough) carefully controlled value for the `count` attribute.

This doesn't really exhaust the variety of combinations of the `level`, `count`, and `from` attributes of `xsl:number`. But it should help you get started in conducting your own experiments with that element.

Now, let's move on to the remaining attributes.

value

This attribute lets you override the default *value* of the `xsl:number` element, which is the position of a node within a list, by specifying some literal numeric value.

"Talk about *useless*," you might be thinking. "Why would you want to assign the same numeric value to every item in a list?"

The answer is that the value of this attribute is not, technically, a simple number, but a *numeric expression*. Thus, it can be the result of some kind of calculation. For instance, I could change the `xsl:template` element I've got so far to include the following modified version of the outermost `xsl:number` element:

```
<xsl:number level="any" count="leadcast | othercast"
  value="position() * 100"/>
```

Results of this change are shown in Figure 5–17.

100. leadcast

1.1. Burt Lancaster
1.2. Yvonne DeCarlo
1.3. Dan Duryea

200. othercast

2.1. Griff Barnett
2.2. John Doucette
2.3. Percy Helton

Figure 5-17   Calculating the value of `leadcast` and `othercast`'s numbering. This is something like the numbering of courses in a college catalog—indeed, if you had course descriptions and their associated "levels" you could produce the catalog without pre-assigning any course numbers at all.

Some experiments aren't worth it...

…and such is the case with using a calculated `value` attribute for multi-level numbering. If the `level` attribute's value is `multiple`, *assigning* a `value` attribute makes the list behave as though the `level` attribute's value were `any`. Thus, if you wanted the cast members' names in Figure 5–17 to be numbered (say) `100.100`, `100.200`, and so on, you'd need to use some other method than simply assigning a `value` attribute to a single `xsl:number` element. (Hint: Use *two* `xsl:number` elements, separated by a literal ".")

`format`

As with the format patterns used with the format-number() function's second argument, this attribute consists of a kind of mold into which a number's value will be poured. The attribute's value consists of a set of alphanumeric *format tokens*, separated by non-alphanumeric characters which will be used as literal characters when making up the number as a whole. You can use this attribute with the remaining ones to format some quite exotic number-formatting variations.

Table 5–3 summarizes the effects of various format tokens.

Table 5-3   Format Tokens Used in `xsl:number`'s `format` Attribute

Format token	Description
1	Number will be represented with no leading 0s.
01	Number will be represented in two-digit form, including a leading zero. (Numbers greater than 99 will be represented with no leading 0s.)
001	Number will be represented in three-digit form, including one or two leading 0s, as needed, for values less than 100. (Note that this kind of format token can be expanded as needed—e.g. 0001 for four-digit numbers, and so on.)
A	"Numbering" will begin with a capital A, followed by capital B, and so on. "Numbers" greater than 26 will go AA, AB, AC, and so on.
a	"Numbering" will begin with a lowercase a, followed by lowercase b, and so on. "Numbers" greater than 26 will go aa, ab, ac, and so on.
I	Number will be represented using Roman numerals, starting with I, then II, III, IV, and so on.
i	Number will be represented using lowercase Roman numerals, starting with i, then ii, iii, iv, and so on.
anything else	"Numbering" will start with the indicated value and go up. This depends on the ability of the XSLT processor to recognize the indicated value *as* a number; it's intended to provide support for numbering systems other than Arabic, alphabetic, and Roman. If the processor doesn't recognize the format token as a number, it's supposed to treat it as if it were 1.

Here are some examples of the `format` attribute with various arrangements of format tokens:

- `format="1"`: Numbering will be a simple sequence (1...9, 10, 11, etc.).
- `format="0001"`: Numbering will be a simple sequence represented as four (or more) digits (0001...0009, 0010...9999, 10000, etc.).

- `format="01.001"`: Multi-level numbering, with the first level represented as a two- (or more-) digit number and the second as a three- (or more-) digit number, separated by a period (01.001, 01.002...02.001, 02.002, etc.).
- `format="I. A. 1. a (1) (a)"`: Traditional "outline-style" numbering, for a six-level multiple numbering scheme.

In connection with that last example, by the way, note that if there are more levels in the actual multi-level hierarchy of data than you provide formatting for, the last format token in the `format` attribute's value continues to apply to further levels. For instance, if your `format` attribute looks like

`format="01.001"`

and there's a third level in the hierarchy being counted, items at that third level will be numbered as if the `format` were

`format="01.001.001"`

and so on.

lang

As it does pretty much everywhere else in XML land, an attribute named `lang` in the context of numbering indicates which human language's conventions will be observed—in this case, when generating numbered lists. The value is one of the standard language codes: for example, `EN`, `de`, `tw`, `IT`, and so on.

letter-value

The `letter-value` attribute is used to get around a thorny problem not only in the "built-in" format tokens but also in those possible in many other languages. To see the problem, think of a `format` attribute such as the following:

`format="(I)"`

Based on what you already know, you can pretty much figure out that the generated number(s) will be enclosed in parentheses, and that their values will start at I, then II, then III, IV, and so on. Right?

Not so fast. You can't jump to that conclusion because of the "anything else" format token option. The default behavior of the processor is, indeed, to assume that the numbering is Roman-style, starting with Roman numeral I; but the stylesheet author's intention may be that this format means *alphabetic*-style, starting with a capital "I."

The `letter-value` attribute takes two possible values: `traditional` (the default, which means that these letters-used-as-numbers *will* be used as numbers) and `alphabetic` (letters are letters). Thus, if you really want the normal behavior, you don't need to specify a `letter-value` attribute at all.

Return of a dilemma

A couple pages back, a box such as this one followed the discussion of the `value` attribute. The point there was that when you assign nearly all these attributes to `xsl:number`, you're assigning their characteristics to the number as a whole, *not* to the individual components in a multi-level numbering scheme.

In terms of the `letter-value` attribute, if your `format` attribute has a value of `I.i`, assigning a `letter-value` attribute affects *both* parts of the "number." By default, these letters are recognized as Roman numerals. If you override the default with a `letter-value` of "alphabetic," the formerly multi-level number reverts back to a single level.

As I hinted in that earlier box, the solution is to use multiple `xsl:number` elements rather than trying to do it all at once.

---

grouping-separator

This attribute is used only with `grouping-size` (discussed next). Continue on to the information about `grouping-size` to see how this one is used, too.

grouping-size

The `grouping-size` attribute is used only with `grouping-separator` (above). If you use only one of the two, it's ignored.

"Grouping," here as in the `format-number()` function, refers to breaking up a single number into "sub-numbers," usually in groups of three (representing thousands) separated from one another by commas. Default behavior—if no `grouping-size` or `grouping-separator` attributes are specified at all, or if only one is—is to do *no* grouping. The number "one thousand" would appear as "1000". To do grouping as it usually is, specify both `grouping-separator` and `grouping-size`:

```
grouping-separator="," grouping-size="3"
```

To break the number up into four-digit chunks, separated by spaces, use this:

```
grouping-separator=" " grouping-size="4"
```

Note that, in the latter case, you might also want to ensure that the `format` attribute forces an even multiple of four (or whatever the `grouping-size` is). Thus, for instance, a numeric value like `12345` would display not as

```
1 2345
```

but as

```
0001 2345
```

This could be accomplished by an `xsl:number` element like this:

```
<xsl:number format="00000001" grouping-size="4"
  grouping-separator=" " />
```

A number of the various formatting-related attributes to the `xsl:number` element are demonstrated in this template rule:

```
<xsl:template match="cast">
  <table>
    <xsl:for-each select="leadcast|othercast">
      <tr>
        <th colspan="2" style="background-color: silver">
          <xsl:number level="any"
            count="leadcast|othercast" format="00000001"
            grouping-size="4" grouping-separator=" "/>
          <xsl:text> </xsl:text>
          <xsl:value-of select="name()"/>
        </th>
      </tr>
      <xsl:for-each select=".//castmember">
        <tr>
          <td nowrap="nowrap">
            <xsl:number format="001 &#8594; (a)"
              level="multiple"
              count="leadcast|othercast|male|female" />
          </td>
          <td><xsl:value-of select="."/></td>
        </tr>
      </xsl:for-each>
    </xsl:for-each>
  </table>
</xsl:template>
```

The "cast category" (lead or other) is numbered using the "groups of 4 separated by a space, with leading zeroes as necessary" approach I just mentioned. Individual cast members are numbered using a two-tier number—one for the `leadcast`/`othercast` and one for the `male`/`female` parent of the `castmember` element. The format for this two-tiered number is a three-digit number, followed by a space, an entity reference, another space, and a lowercase letter enclosed in parentheses. (The entity reference is the Unicode representation of a "right-ward-pointing arrow.") Notice also that the result tree for this portion of the source tree is enclosed in table rows and cells; this helps everything stay nice and aligned. (Otherwise, some of these crazy number formats—especially when using a proportional font—can shift everything which follows left or right in annoying ways.[6])

Results of this template rule (when applied to the *Criss Cross* FlixML review) display in MSIE as shown in Figure 5–18.

0000 0001 leadcast

001 → (a) Burt Lancaster
001 → (b) Yvonne DeCarlo
001 → (c) Dan Duryea

0000 0002 othercast

002 → (a) Griff Barnett
002 → (b) John Doucette
002 → (c) Percy Helton
002 → (d) Edna Holland
002 → (e) Marc Krah
002 → (f) Richard Long
002 → (g) Stephen McNally
002 → (h) Joan Miller
002 → (i) John "Skins" Miller
002 → (j) Esy Morales
002 → (k) Alan Napier
002 → (l) James O'Rear
002 → (m) Tom Pedi
002 → (n) Meg Randall

Figure 5-18 Playing games with number formatting.

---

6. Well, some of us are more prone to annoyance than others.

Miscellaneous Built-In Functions

A handful of XSLT functions don't fit neatly into one category or another.[7] Even arranging them into one kind of order versus another seems pretty arbitrary; I'll just follow the sequence in which they're covered by the XSLT spec itself.

The `current()` function

You've already seen this function in use. This was in the section, early in this chapter, on using the `document()` function. It appeared in a template rule that did a lookup in an external file, retrieving a genre's description given some genre's name as found in the source tree. Here's a compressed form of the template rule in question:

```
<xsl:template match="primarygenre">
  <h3>Primary Genre:</h3>
  ...
  <xsl:value-of select="document('genres.xml')//desc[preceding-
sibling::name=current()]"/>
  ...
</xsl:template>
```

The `current()` function returns the *current node*. Nearly always, this is the same as the *context node*. Therefore, in most cases both of the following expressions refer to the same thing:

```
.
current()
```

Where they do not necessarily represent the same value is in a location path's predicate, as in the code fragment just cited. (Note that this doesn't apply just to location paths referring to external documents; it applies to all of them.) That's because the *current node* does not change as a result of changes in the *context node* that occur simply by working your way through a location path to the predicate.

If you replace the call to `current()` in the foregoing code fragment with a simple `.`, the location path will not retrieve anything (or, if it does, it'll be completely and utterly crazily coincidental). In that case, the location path will be saying "locate the `desc` element(s) with a preceding-sibling element whose name

---

7.   Even when the attempt is made by the relentlessly categorized XSLT spec, these leftovers fall through into "miscellaneous additional functions."

is the same as *the string-value of the given* `desc` *element*." Given that the string-value of `desc` elements in this case tends to be, like, a complete sentence, finding any element at all—preceding-sibling or not—whose name is the same as that string value would seem to be a minuscule possibility.

Using `current()`, on the other hand, forces the location path to "locate the `desc` element(s) with a preceding-sibling element whose name is the same as *the string-value of the given* `primarygenre` *element*." See? The *current node* in this case is the one established by the `xsl:template` element's `match` attribute, not by the `xsl:value-of` element's `select` attribute.

Note that an `xsl:for-each` element's `select` attribute, just like an `xsl:template` element's `match`, *does* change the current node. (It's set, iteratively, to each node that matches the select attribute's value.) When the `xsl:for-each` "loop" completes, the current node is reset to whatever it was at the point where the `xsl:for-each` was entered.

The `unparsed-entity-uri()` function

You may or may not ever have occasion to use this function. Its purpose is to return the URI (as a string) which corresponds to the name of a given unparsed entity. The name of the entity you're after is passed as the function's only argument.

This is kind of an oddball XSLT feature, because it provides access to something that's otherwise invisible: the document's DTD. Specifically, it provides access to the system identifier of entities declared as type NDATA.

Why would you need this?

First, consider the way the Web handles even simple multimedia files, such as images. Such non-text data can't be physically incorporated into an (X)HTML document, of course, so the convention has sprung up to provide a URI (such as in an `href` or `src` attribute to some element) and let the browser or some plug-in determine what to do with that file.

Text-but-not-text content

One remote possibility for incorporating "non-text" content in an XML document is to *encode the binary content as if it were text*—particularly, to incorporate it inline using so-called *base64 encoding*. This is an ingenious but simple system, codified in the MIME specification (RFC 1341 and others), which represents a binary 0 as the letter A, 1 as the letter B, 26 as lowercase a, 51 as lowercase z, and so on, and the values 52 through 61 as ASCII digits 0 through 9, 62 as a plus sign, and 63 as a slash.

However, this isn't particularly applicable to XHTML, since browsers don't do anything with base64 content but display it as if it were regular text.

This Web convention came along well after SGML itself. In SGML, non-XML content is declared with NDATA-type entities, which the SGML-aware software is expected to resolve somehow.[8]

In FlixML, I've provided two attributes to an element called bees; this element is used by a reviewer to assert a B movie's essential "B-ness"—that is, how much of a B movie it is and how *good* a B movie it is. This quality is communicated in a FlixML document via a pointer to an image. The two attributes take two approaches to making the image available, via regular URI or NDATA-type entity; their declarations look like this:

```
<!ATTLISTbees
    b-ness              CDATA           #IMPLIED
    b-nesspic           ENTITY          #IMPLIED>
```

The b-ness attribute is for supplying a simple URI, and each of the B-ness rating images has a general entity defined which can be used as the value of the b-ness attribute. For example, there's an entity named BEE45URL whose value is "http://www.flixml.org/flixml/images/bees4_5.gif" (an image of four-and-a-half honeybees); my assumption is that any Web-aware application will be able to recognize this correctly when it encounters an element such as this:

```
<bees b-ness="&BEE45URL"/>
```

---

8.   SGML systems are expected to recognize the "handler" for a given NDATA entity or notation, and to forward to that handler any non-SGML content appropriate for it. In a way, this notion has been carried forward in the use of namespaces recognized by specific applications. For example, if you want to use features peculiar to the MSXML or Saxon XSLT processors, you have to include namespace declarations which alert those processors to wake up and look out, as it were, for references to such features outside the pale of XSLT proper.

As an alternative, this could also be coded (using the `b-nesspic` attribute, rather than `b-ness`) this way:

```
<bees b-nesspic="BEE45"/>
```

"BEE45" is the name of an NDATA-type entity. Thus, it has no string-value; however, it *does* have a string associated with it: its system identifier. Here's its declaration:

```
<!ENTITY BEE45 SYSTEM
  "http://www.flixml.org/flixml/images/bees4_5.gif"
  NDATA gif>
```

If this were the only way to obtain the image, even though XSLT generally recognizes no string-value associated with entity references, I could still locate the image from within XSLT using the `unparsed-entity-uri()` function.

A FlixML document can use both forms if it wants. For example,

```
<bees b-ness="&BEE45URL" b-nesspic="BEE45"/>
```

The following template rule in a stylesheet processes both of these attributes:

```
<xsl:template match="bees">
  <table>
    <tr>
      <th style="background-color: silver">Attrib</th>
      <th style="background-color: silver">Value/Picture</th>
    </tr>
    <tr>
      <td rowspan="2" valign="top" style="background-color:
silver"><xsl:value-of select="'b-ness'"/></td>
      <td>'<xsl:value-of select="@b-ness"/>'</td>
    </tr>
    <tr>
      <td><img src="{@b-ness}" /></td>
    </tr>
    <tr>
      <td colspan="3"><hr /></td>
    </tr>
    <tr>
      <td rowspan="2" valign="top" style="background-color:
silver"><xsl:value-of select="'b-nesspic'"/></td>
      <td>'<xsl:value-of select="@b-nesspic"/>'</td>
    </tr>
    <tr>
      <td><img src="{unparsed-entity-uri(@b-nesspic)}" /></td>
```

```
    </tr>
  </table>
</xsl:template>
```

The result tree from this transformation appears in MSIE as shown in Figure 5–19.

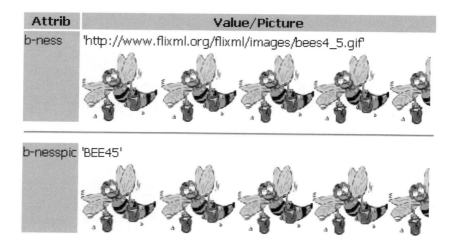

Figure 5-19 An external non-XML resource retrieved using a straight URI (the value of the b-ness attribute) and using the SYSTEM identifier of an unparsed entity (BEE45). In this grayscale version of the image. Alas, you miss the colorful yellow stripes on the honeybee's torso, and the golden color of the honey itself.

Creating unique identifiers: generate-id()

I spent a certain amount of time and energy earlier in this chapter, during the discussion of keys, trying to convince you of the inadequacy of ID-type attributes. Now I'm going to undo those efforts a bit.

The reason for undoing them isn't that any of those earlier points aren't really valid. It's that those earlier points were addressing the inadequacy of using ID-type attributes to *find something in the source tree.* There's no denying the general usefulness of a unique identifier for each element, though, especially if we didn't have to rely on having access to the document's DTD....

That's where the generate-id() function comes in.

This function takes one (optional) argument: a node-set. If the argument is omitted, its default is the context node at the point of the call to generate-id(). What comes back from generate-id() is a string—a unique identifier for the first node (in document order) in the requested node-set. (Note that if that node-set is *empty*, generate-id() returns an empty string.)

The XSLT spec lays out some interesting requirements for the returned value:

- It must consist entirely of alphanumeric characters and start with a letter.
- A given processor must always return the same value for a given node in a given document, but only for a given transformation. (That is, in a later run of the same stylesheet against the same document, the identifier for any given node may be different than it was earlier.)
- No two nodes may have the same identifier.

And there are also a couple of interesting back doors left open:

- A generated ID may or may not be equal to any *actual* ID-type attribute values in the source document.
- There's no other particular constraint on the form of a generated ID.

How might you use some arbitrary, probably completely meaningless but nevertheless unique identifier for a node?

The most obvious purpose, at least when transforming to XHTML, is to provide a unique value for the name attribute to the a element; this can then be used for intra-document linking, with counterpart href attributes to a elements elsewhere in the document. Thus (using *generated_ID* to stand in for whatever value comes back from the function), we could have a result tree that looked in part like this:

```
<a name="generated_ID" />Here's the top of the document...
[ <a href="#generated_ID">Back to Top</a> ]
```

Even if you're not transforming to XHTML, though, you can make use of the generate-id() function for creating intra-document XLinks, using XPointers instead of the XHTML fragment-identifier form. Thus, for example, the result tree might look like this (in some hypothetical XML vocabulary which uses a target element as a counterpart to the XHTML a element with an href attribute):

```
<target name="generated_ID" />Here's the top of the document...
[ <xref xlink:href="xpointer(generated_ID)">Back to Top</a> ]
```

Consider the following template rule, to be applied to a FlixML document like the *Caged Heat* review. Note that the generate-id() function is called three times, twice for the element currently being processed and once for each of that element's preceding- and following-sibling elements. Also note that this template rule does not include an `xsl:apply-templates` element; as a result, if this is invoked from the template rule processing the root `flixinfo` element, the only elements processed by this template rule are those which are children of `flixinfo`:

```
<xsl:template match="*">
  <a name="{generate-id()}"/>
  <h4><xsl:value-of select="name()"/> element here (id="<xsl:value-
of select="generate-id()"/>")</h4>
  <table cellspacing="5">
    <tr>
      <xsl:for-each select="preceding-sibling::* | following-
sibling::*">
        <td>
          <a href="#{generate-id()}"><xsl:value-of select="name()"/
></a>
        </td>
      </xsl:for-each>
    </tr>
  </table>
</xsl:template>
```

All this template rule displays are the name of the current element, its generated ID, and the names of all its siblings (other children of `flixinfo`). Those other elements' names are all contained by an a element with an `href` attribute.

Results from this template rule when run directly within MSIE are as shown in Figure 5–20.

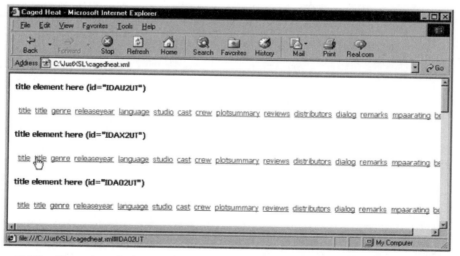

Figure 5-20 Complete index of intra-document links to "top-level elements" (`title`, `genre`, etc.) in the *Caged Heat* FlixML review, from all other "top-level elements" in it.

Note a couple of things about Figure 5–20. First, note the form of the generated IDs themselves, as displayed in the level-4 headings. MSXML always seems to construct IDs in this general way, using the letters ID followed by some other string. Also note the value currently displayed in the status bar, indicating that the title element currently being pointed to in the browser window has a generated ID whose value is IDA02UT. As you can see, this is the value associated with the next title element in the window. This establishes that MSXML is indeed generating the same value for a given node from two different places in the stylesheet.

Now let's take a look at the XHTML document generated from Saxon by this stylesheet, as shown in Figure 5–21.

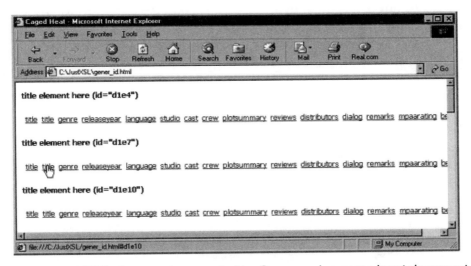

Figure 5-21   XHTML document generated by Saxon, using same input document and stylesheet shown in Figure 5–20. Everything looks like it works out identically…except the generated ID values. Processors are free to choose their own method of generating unique IDs, and any one processor may come up with a method that bears little if any relationship to another's. (Or, for that matter, to the method employed by the same processor in a different transformation.)

The system-property() function

This is a simple function. (You're probably ready for a simple one at this point.) The purpose of system-property() is to provide you with information about the XSLT processor; this information might be used in a footnote to document the environment in which the result tree was generated, for example, or perhaps to confirm that a particular processor is in use when running a given stylesheet.

The function takes one argument, a string, which has one of the following values:

- xsl:version: Function returns the version supported by the XSLT processor. Most compliant processors at this time will return "1.0"; a handful may return "2.0," although that version of XSLT isn't even close to final yet.
- xsl:vendor: Function returns a string identifying the XSLT processor's vendor.
- xsl:vendor-url: Function returns a string identifying the XSLT processor's vendor's site on the Web.

We can build a simple template rule such as the one which follows; this can be applied to any XML document, FlixML or otherwise, to report these three properties in the form of an XHTML table:

```
<xsl:template match="/">
  <table>
    <tr>
      <th style="background-color: silver">Property</th>
      <th style="background-color: silver">Value</th>
    </tr>
    <tr>
      <td>xsl:version</td>
      <td><xsl:value-of
        select="system-property('xsl:version')"/></td>
    </tr>
    <tr>
      <td>xsl:vendor</td>
      <td><xsl:value-of
        select="system-property('xsl:vendor')"/></td>
    </tr>
    <tr>
      <td>xsl:vendor-url</td>
      <td><xsl:value-of
        select="system-property('xsl:vendor-url')"/></td>
    </tr>
  </table>
</xsl:template>
```

From Saxon 6.2, this template rule produces a document which displays as shown in Figure 5–22 (left side); using the MSXML processor, results are as shown in Figure 5–22 (right side).

Property	Value
xsl:version	1
xsl:vendor	SAXON 6.2 from Michael Kay
xsl:vendor-url	http://users.iclway.co.uk/mhkay/saxon/index.html

Property	Value
xsl:version	1
xsl:vendor	Microsoft
xsl:vendor-url	http://www.microsoft.com

Figure 5-22 XSLT processor `system-property()` values for Saxon 6.2 (left) and MSXML 3.0 (right). As you can see, exactly how these values are formatted (except for the version number) is somewhat idiosyncratic and not really subject to regulation by the XSLT spec.

> **More built-in functions**
>
> I'll be covering some built-in functions in Chapter 6, "Advanced XSLT." These are functions having to do with *fallback*—that is, determining if a particular XSLT feature is available in a particular XSLT processor, and if not, taking some alternate processing path.

Extension Functions

One "feature" of the Web that has driven many folks to distraction is that vendors have been free to add support to their products for all kinds of stuff about which the official standards say nothing.

For one notorious example, an early version of the Netscape browser introduced a `blink` element. There was nothing like it in any version of the HTML spec; Netscape—which at that time owned the lion's share of the browser market—apparently just "thought it was a good idea." (Actually, it was an *awful* idea.)

The XSLT spec's authors have done something interesting in an attempt to head off the problems that arise when one vendor wants to introduce some feature not necessarily supported by others. What they came up with was the idea of *allowing* vendors to add any features (elements and functions) they want. The only catch is that they can't put those features in the XSLT namespace; they've got to declare them in their own private namespaces.[9]

I covered the use of extension elements in Chapter 3. Here, I want to address extension *functions*.

---

9. Early versions of HTML, of course, didn't have this option, since "namespacing" conventions didn't become commonplace until some time after XML 1.0 itself was finalized.

It's not practical in a book format to try covering all extension functions for all known XSLT processors; there are just too many of them (both the functions and the processors), and more are being added—and, I guess, subtracted and modified—all the time.

What I can do, though, is show you a couple of examples. One is processor-specific (Saxon 6.2); the other, although I'll demonstrate it using MSXML, is (almost) universally implemented by major XSLT processors.

Saxon 6.2: The `line-number()` function

Saxon's `line-number()` function takes no arguments at all. It returns a number which, as you might guess, is the line number *in the source document* of the node being processed at the point where the call to `line-number()` occurs.

We'll see in Chapter 6 some specific ways in which this might be useful in a practical sense. (Primarily, they relate to stylesheet debugging and issuing messages from the stylesheet.) But this is a good, simple example of the basics of using extension functions.

First, when you want to use an extension function, its name must be tagged, as it were, with a namespace prefix which maps to the given processor's namespace URI. (You'll need to consult individual vendors' documentation for this information, since it varies by product.) For Saxon, the required namespace URI for extension functions is `http://icl.com/saxon`, and we'll map this to the `saxon:` prefix by adding a namespace declaration, as follows, to the `xsl:stylesheet` element's start tag:

```
xmlns:saxon="http://icl.com/saxon"
```

Now, we can use `line-number()` (or any other Saxon extension function) wherever we need.[10] For instance, we could set up a template rule as follows for processing a FlixML document:

```
<xsl:template match="*">
  <tr>
    <td><xsl:value-of select="name()"/></td>
    <td><xsl:value-of
```

---

10. I don't think this will happen—my readers are generally a pretty intelligent bunch—but just in case: In order to use `line-number()` (or any other Saxon extension function), you must use Saxon as your XSLT processor. Simply declaring the Saxon namespace and then invoking `line-number()` will not, for example, work at all if you're using MSXML.

```
  select="substring(., 1, 10)"/>...</td>
 <td align="right"><xsl:value-of
 select="saxon:line-number()"/></td>
</tr>
<xsl:apply-templates/>
</xsl:template>
```

Assume that the beginning of the *Caged Heat* review looks like the following (with the root flixinfo element actually all on one line, not wrapped as here on the book page):

```
<flixinfo author="John E. Simpson" copyright="2001" xml:lang="EN"
xmlns:xlink="http://www.w3.org/1999/xlink/namespace/">
 <title role="main">Caged Heat</title>
 <title role="alt">Caged Females</title>
 <title role="alt">Renegade Girls</title>
 <genre>
   <primarygenre>Action</primarygenre>
   <othergenre>Prison</othergenre>
   <othergenre>Woman in Jeopardy</othergenre>
 </genre>
 <releaseyear role="initial">1974</releaseyear>
 <language>English</language>
 <studio>New World Pictures</studio>
 <cast id="castID">
 [etc.]
```

Using Saxon to process this document through the above template rule results in a document which displays as shown in Figure 5–23.

Element	Up to 10 Chars	At line #
title	Caged Heat...	2
title	Caged Fema...	3
title	Renegade G...	4
genre	Action ...	5
primarygenre	Action...	6
othergenre	Prison...	7
othergenre	Woman in J...	8
releaseyear	1974...	10
language	English...	11
studio	New World ...	12
cast	...	13

Figure 5-23 Line numbers on which element nodes begin in the *Caged Heat* review, courtesy of Saxon's line-number() extension function.

Caveats

A couple of further comments about the above:

First, if you actually want to use Saxon's `line-number()` function in your own stylesheets, be sure to specify that you want line numbers "maintained"—that is, noticed by Saxon and saved for the numbering. This is accomplished using the −l ("minus–L") command-line option. If you omit this option, the value returned by every call to `line-number()` is −1 (minus 1).

Second, note the values in the second column above, which displays "up to 10 characters" in the content of whatever element is being referred to. The source tree, as you can see, includes not only elements, attributes, and so on, but also lots of whitespace, newlines, tabs, and so on, added for legibility. That's why some of the values shown in this column seem slightly out of whack with some elements' actual content. If I wanted to strip all the extraneous whitespace-only source tree nodes, I could, of course, have used an `xsl:strip-space` top-level element in the stylesheet.

The `node-set()` function

In Chapter 4, during the discussion of variables and parameters, I talked about result tree fragments, or RTFs. As the term implies, these are portions of a result tree which are stored in an `xsl:variable` element whose value is assigned in a template rather than in a `select` attribute.

Unlike portions of the source tree—node-sets, in other words—there are only a handful of things you can do with an RTF. You can copy it to the result tree and you can treat it as a string. You can also locate specific nodes in the RTF using a location path, as in the following:

```
<xsl:value-of select="$rtf/some_node"/>
```

However, you can't do everything with an RTF that you can with a node-set. Particularly,

- you can't pass an RTF as an argument to an XPath or XSLT function (such as `sum()`, `count()`, and so on) which expects a node-set, and
- you can't use an RTF as the value of a match pattern or an `xsl:for-each` element's `select` attribute.

Consider this top-level (global) variable declaration from a FlixML-processing XSLT stylesheet:

```
<xsl:variable name="switchname">
  <xsl:for-each select="//castmember|//crew">
    <td>
      <xsl:value-of select="substring-after(., ' ')"/>
      <xsl:text>, </xsl:text>
      <xsl:value-of select="substring-before(., ' ')"/>
    </td>
  </xsl:for-each>
</xsl:variable>
```

The value of the variable declared here, switchname, is a series of td elements. In each td element is a "reversed" cast or crew member's name—switched from its form in the source tree ("Firstname Lastname") to "Lastname, Firstname" order. Now we'd like to display each of those td elements in its own row in a table, with the table as a whole sorted by the switched value. The following template rule does so (er, apparently):

```
<xsl:template match="flixinfo">
  <html>
    <head><title><xsl:value-of select="title[@role='main']"/></title></head>
    <body>
      <table border="1">
        <xsl:for-each select="$switchname/*">
          <xsl:sort/>
          <tr>
            <xsl:value-of select="."/>
          </tr>
        </xsl:for-each>
      </table>
    </body>
  </html>
</xsl:template>
```

This looks like it should work, right?

Unfortunately, any XSLT 1.0-compliant processor will complain about the xsl:for-each there. (The error message from MSXML says, "Reference to variable or parameter 'switchname' must evaluate to a node list." Recent versions of Saxon don't complain at all...but that's in anticipation of future versions of XSLT, which are expected to remove the distinction between RTFs and node-sets.) The problem is that switchname is not, of course, a node-set.

You can make it a node-set, though, using the `node-set()` function supplied with most XSLT processors. (The function is sometimes called `nodeset()`, without the hyphen. Check your own processor's documentation to be sure of the correct name.) You pass this function the RTF reference, and it returns a node-set. The latter can be operated on in any way that a real node-set can.

The first step, as with any extension function, is to declare a namespace for the processor in question. I'm going to use the MSXML processor to demonstrate `node-set()`, with an `msxml:` prefix on its name; the correct namespace URI for Microsoft extension functions is `urn:schemas-microsoft-com:xslt`. Thus, the namespace declaration in the `xsl:stylesheet` element will be this:

```
xmlns:msxml="urn:schemas-microsoft-com:xslt"
```

"You call *that* a URI?!?"

Yeah. I've tried to be careful to use the term URI (Uniform Resource Identifier) throughout *Just XSL*, and this is the sort of occasion which justifies that care.

For nearly all practical purposes, the terms URI and URL (Uniform Resource Locator) are interchangeable. However, they're not really the same; a URL (a resource identified using the classic `http://foo.com`-type syntax) is just one *variety* of URI. Another variety is a Uniform Resource Name (URN)—and that's the form in which Microsoft (ever leading the charge) has chosen to represent its extension function namespace URI. Don't worry overly much about what it "means." Practically, all it means is that the MSXML processor "recognizes" only that URI, in that format.

Having declared that namespace, we can now change the `xsl:for-each` element:

```
<xsl:for-each select="msxml:node-set($switchname)/*">
```

Now we don't get an error message. Now we get, as expected, something that looks like Figure 5–24.

"Skins" Miller, John
Barnett, Griff
DeCarlo, Yvonne
Doucette, John
Duryea, Dan
Fuchs, Daniel
Helton, Percy
Holland, Edna
J. Kent, Ted
Krah, Marc
Lancaster, Burt
Long, Richard
McNally, Stephen
Miller, Joan
Morales, Esy

Figure 5-24 A portion of the result tree output from sorting a result tree fragment, after first converting it to a node-set with the `node-set()` extension function. I first demonstrated this kind of given name-surname switching in Chapter 2, in the discussion of XPath string functions. As I said there, the algorithm isn't perfect, and this certainly demonstrates why: John "Skins" Miller and Ted J. Kent throw this supposedly "sorted" output into disarray.

How Do I ...
Drive an XSLT transformation
from an XML-based configuration file?

For this little "How Do I...?" exercise, there are two tricks to "getting" the solution.

First, probably obviously, the "XML-based configuration file" is *external* to the source document being processed by the stylesheet. And this suggests—right—that we need to use the `document()` function.

The second trick is just a little mental leap; it doesn't require any technological gimmicks. The leap is this: An external configuration file is a perfect, platform-independent substitute for passing large numbers of global parameters to your stylesheet.

I talked about passing global parameters into a stylesheet in Chapter 4. Once the stylesheet has those parameters' values, it's a relatively small matter to actually *use* them in some way. The catch is getting the parameters into the stylesheet in the first place. Static/Command-line-driven processors accept the parameters passed in as processor-specific command-line switches, whereas dynamic processors typically receive a global parameter by way of script. If you put your "parameters" into an external configuration file, on the other hand, you can use the stylesheet with any processor that understands the XSLT 1.0 `document()` function.

What you actually put into such a "config file" depends on how you need to control processing. (One of the beauties of it is that it's fairly easy to add new elements and content as your needs change, since the config file will probably be fairly small and not require validation.) But here's a sample config file that can be used to drive, in various ways, a stylesheet's processing of a FlixML document:

```
<config>
  <background-color>silver</background-color>
  <maxnames>10</maxnames>
  <maxtext>10</maxtext>
  <alt-titles>false</alt-titles>
  <legalese>Contents copyright &#169; 2001. All rights reserved.</
legalese>
</config>
```

To get to the data in the file (let's call it config.xml), we'll first load it into a variable:

```
<xsl:variable name="config"
  select="document('config.xml')/config"/>
```

Now we can locate any data item—element—from the config file using the general syntax:

```
$config/element
```

For instance, the template rule for the FlixML `title` element might now read like this:

```
<xsl:template match="title">
  <xsl:choose>
```

```
<xsl:when test="@role='main'">
  <h2 style="background-color: {$config/background-color}">
    <xsl:value-of select="."/>
  </h2>
</xsl:when>
<xsl:when test="(@role='alt') and ($config/alt-
titles!='false')">
  <h3>a/k/a <xsl:value-of select="."/></h3>
</xsl:when>
  </xsl:choose>
</xsl:template>
```

This uses two "parameters" from the config file: the background-color element, and the alt-titles element. The former it plugs into an XHTML style element (see the AVT?). As for the latter, the template rule tests to see if the value is false *and* if the current title element's role attribute has the value alt. The main title always gets displayed as a level-2 heading, on a *background-color* background; the alternate title(s), as level-3 headings (preceded by the string "a/k/a," for "also known as")...but only if alt-titles is not false.

With config.xml values as shown above, the *Caged Heat* review displays, in part, as shown in Figure 5–25 (left side); change the value of the config file's alt-titles element to true, and the display changes as shown in Figure 5–25 (right side).

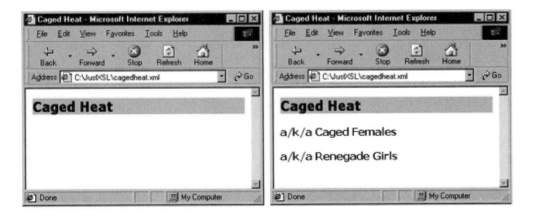

Figure 5-25 Controlling the background color, and suppressing/revealing source tree content, on the basis of values stored in an external XML-based "config file."

In a similar manner, you could use the other elements in config.xml to control how many cast/crew members' names to include in a list (the `maxnames` element); how many characters of large text nodes to display (`maxtext`); and the display of boilerplate copyright information if it's not available in the source tree itself (`legalese`).

CHAPTER 6

Beyond the Pale: Advanced XSLT

Exhausted by the last three chapters? No wonder: You had an incredible amount of information to absorb there.

The good news is that, if you *did* absorb all that information, you're well-positioned to use XSLT for the most common XML transformations: from XML to XHTML, to other (non-Web) XML vocabularies, and to *non*-XML "result trees" (such as flat files of comma- or tab-separated values).

Depending on how you look at it, it's either bad news or more good news that you don't yet know it all. That's where this chapter comes in.

The term "advanced XSLT" is kind of misleading. I'm going to start out by covering some loose-end XSLT elements and functions you may never (or only seldom) need to use; none of these elements and functions requires particularly "advanced" skills or knowledge (except, of course, knowledge of when to use them). Afterward, though, I'll include some information about using XSLT in situations and ways that may not be immediately obvious to you if you're new to XSLT. These techniques classify as "basic skills for intermediate to advanced XSLT users," not as "*advanced* skills that intermediate to advanced XSLT users have never seen demonstrated."

Including and Importing Other Stylesheets

Periodically in *Just XSL*, I've compared or contrasted XSLT with "real programming languages." And I hope you'll concur that you don't have to be a "real programmer" to use XSLT effectively.

That said, once even a rank novice has learned XSLT, she can be said to be a sort of programmer or developer. And just like programmers/developers in other languages, she's ready for the light bulb to go on over her head about the importance of *modularized code.*

(Of course, if the light bulb's already gone on over your own head—"rank novice" or otherwise—feel free to skip over this introductory passage.)

Modularized code

A module is a discrete, self-contained package of something—information, furniture, electronic components, whatever. Modularized *code* is code—XSLT or otherwise—that's been broken down into units that can be used and reused by other modules as needed.

You've already seen and used *internally* modularized code, in the form of variables, parameters, named attribute sets, and named templates. All of these are devices to minimize or eliminate the need to reinvent any wheels, even if they're wheels you yourself invented in the first place.[1] Even the "config file" gimmick that I covered in the "How Do I...?" exercise at the end of Chapter 5 is a sort of modularization of code; its vocabulary wasn't XSLT's, but the external file could be shared among dozens or hundreds of stylesheets, controlling and altering their behaviors in the same way from one stylesheet to the next.

So now we're going to extend the idea of the config file, if you will, by placing XSLT code inside an external file, and using that code not as if it were an alternate source tree but as if it were actually built into a stylesheet which references it.

B Alert!

When Dinosaurs Ruled the Earth (1970, Hammer Film Productions)

The time—somewhere around the dawn of time (as the saying goes; an ominous voice-over informs us that this is a time when "there is no moon"). The place—some unidentified tropical island or land by the sea. Three blonde virgins are

---

1.   To strain a metaphor.

about to be sacrificed to the Sun God of a prehistoric people (the "Rock People").

Suddenly, there's a huge gust of wind. In the ensuing confusion, one of the blonde virgins, Sanna, escapes by diving (well, falling) off a cliff.

Rescued by handsome, seagoing-raft-fisherman Tara, Sanna relocates to the home of the dark-haired Sand People. But trouble's brewing: Sanna and Tara have an incipient thing going on, much to the dismay of Tara's current lady. Sanna is driven inland from the Sand People's home at the beach and takes up with some strangely friendly dinosaurs.

Will Sanna live? Will she and Tara ever get back together? And what about the moon?

For me, the greatest pleasure (among many) to be had from watching this film is its dialogue. In what could be termed a leap of mad genius, the screenplay consists entirely of 27 "prehistoric" words, arranged and rearranged in various combinations. (This is a movie that is really helped by the presence of closed captions—not as a translation aid, but as a spelling aid. Who knew that cave people spelled "Neekro" that way?) This screenplay—or rather, its "story"—is credited to science-fiction author J. G. Ballard, most famous to the movie-going public as the author of the memoir on which Spielberg's *Empire of the Sun* was based.

Oh, and the stop-action dinosaurs are great, too. They garnered a Special Visual Effects Oscar nomination.

A sequel to Hammer Films' own *One Million Years B.C.*

The headline star, Victoria Vetri, had already appeared before the public as 1968's Playboy Playmate of the Year. (Her stage name at that time was Angela Dorian.) Later, she'd show up for a few minutes in *Rosemary's Baby*.

When Dinosaurs Ruled the Earth's FlixML review

(I've omitted quite a bit of this review's actual contents in this listing, marking the omissions with ellipses [. . .].)

```
<flixinfo author="John E. Simpson" copyright="2001"
  xml:lang="EN"
  xmlns:xlink="http://www.w3.org/1999/xlink/namespace/">
```

```
<title role="main">When Dinosaurs Ruled the Earth</title>
<genre>
  <primarygenre>Prehistoric Horror</primarygenre>
  <othergenre>Science Fiction/Fantasy</othergenre>
</genre>
<releaseyear role="initial">1970</releaseyear>
<language>Prehistoric</language>
<studio>Hammer Film Productions</studio>
<cast id="castID">
  <leadcast>
    <female id="VVetri">
      <castmember>Victoria Vetri</castmember>
      <role>Sanna</role>
    </female>
    <male id="RHawdon">
      <castmember>Robin Hawdon</castmember>
      <role>Tara</role>
    </male>
    ...
  </leadcast>
  <othercast>
    <male id="PHolt">
      <castmember>Patrick Holt</castmember>
      <role>Ammon</role>
    </male>
    <female id="JRossini">
      <castmember>Jan Rossini</castmember>
      <role>Rock Girl</role>
    </female>
    ...
  </othercast>
</cast>
<crew id="crewID">
  <director>Val Guest</director>
  <screenwriter>J.G. Ballard (story)</screenwriter>
  <screenwriter>Val Guest</screenwriter>
  <cinematog>Dick Bush</cinematog>
  <sound>Frank Goulding (dubbing editor)</sound>
  <sound>Kevin Sutton (sound recordist)</sound>
  <editor>Peter Curran</editor>
  <score>Mario Nascimbene</score>
  <speceffects>Jim Danforth</speceffects>
  <proddesigner>John Blezard (art director)</proddesigner>
  <makeup>Joyce James ("hairdressing supervisor")</makeup>
  <costumer>Brian Owen-Smith ("wardrobe master")</costumer>
</crew>
```

```
  <plotsummary id="plotID">The time -- somewhere around the dawn of
time (as the saying goes; an ominous voice-over informs us that
this is a time when "there is no moon"). The place -- some
unidentified tropical island or land by the sea... </plotsummary>
  <reviews id="revwID">
    <flixmlreview>
      <goodreview>
        <reviewtext>Certainly not a <emph>great</emph> movie by any
stretch of the term, this is still awfully darned enjoyable for its
sheer ludicrousness... </reviewtext>
      </goodreview>
    </flixmlreview>
    <otherreview>
      <goodreview>
        <reviewlink xlink:href="http://www.hit-n-run.com/cgi/
read_review.cgi?review=51106_daverules">Bad Movie Night (Dave
Sagehorn)</reviewlink>
      </goodreview>
      <goodreview>
        <reviewlink xlink:href="http://afm.infinit.net/chro/cine/
when_dinosaurs.htm">AstroneF Magazine (Beno&#237;t Ch&#233;nier; in
French)</reviewlink>
      </goodreview>
      <badreview>
        <reviewlink xlink:href="http://www.wsu.edu/~delahoyd/
wdrte.html">Dino-Films (Michael Delahoyde)</reviewlink>
      </badreview>
    </otherreview>
  </reviews>
  <distributors id="distribID">
    <distributor>
      <distribname>Reel.com</distribname>
      <distribextlink>
        <distriblink
xlink:href="http://www.reel.com/movie.asp?MID=10689"/>
      </distribextlink>
    </distributor>
    <distributor>
      <distribname>Amazon.com</distribname>
      <distribextlink>
        <distriblink
xlink:href="http://www.amazon.com/exec/obidos/ASIN/6302101735"/>
      </distribextlink>
    </distributor>
    <distributor>
      <distribname>Yahoo! Video Shopping</distribname>
```

```
    <distribextlink>
      <distriblink xlink:href="http://shopping.yahoo.com/
shop?d=v&amp;id=1800156177&amp;clink=dmvi-ks/
when_dinosaurs_ruled_the_earth"/>
    </distribextlink>
  </distributor>
  <distributor>
    <distribname>BlockBuster</distribname>
    <distribextlink>
      <distriblink xlink:href="http://www.blockbuster.com/mv/
detail.jhtml?PRODID=181116&amp;CATID=1020"/>
    </distribextlink>
  </distributor>
  <distributor>
    <distribname>MovieGallery</distribname>
    <distribextlink>
      <distriblink
xlink:href="http://www.moviegallery.com/
vhs_info.cgi?product_id=WHV11073.3"/>
    </distribextlink>
  </distributor>
 </distributors>
 <dialog>Most characters: Akita!</dialog>
 <remarks>A sequel to Hammer Films' own "One Million Years
B.C."... </remarks>
 <mpaarating id="rateID">G</mpaarating>
 <bees b-ness="&BEE4URL;"/>
</flixinfo>
```

Including other stylesheets with `xsl:include`

The simplest way to include other stylesheets within some "master stylesheet" is by using the (empty, top-level) `xsl:include` element. Its general syntax is this:

```
<xsl:include href="other_stylesheet_uri"/>
```

The `href` attribute is required and, you will not be surprised to learn, takes as its value the URI of the stylesheet to be included here.

The logical effect of the `xsl:include` element is that the included content replaces the `xsl:include` element itself. Note that the stylesheet to be included must be a legitimate XSLT stylesheet, in that it must have as its root element an `xsl:stylesheet` element. This `xsl:stylesheet` element itself is not "included"—only its contents are.

Let's say we have a stylesheet, xhtml_struct.xsl, that looks like the following:

```
<xsl:stylesheet version="1.0"
  <xsl:stylesheet version="1.0"
  xmlns:xsl="http://www.w3.org/1999/XSL/Transform"
  xmlns="http://www.w3.org/1999/xhtml" >

  <xsl:template name="doc_outline">
    <xsl:param name="title_param"
      select="'Title Here'"/>
    <xsl:param name="css_param">
      .std_footing {font-size: -1;
      font-style: italic;
      font-weight: bold;
      text-align: right}
    </xsl:param>
    <xsl:param name="script_param"/>
    <xsl:param name="temp_param"/>
    <html>
      <head>
        <title>
          <xsl:value-of select="$title_param"/>
        </title>
        <style>
          <xsl:comment>
            <xsl:value-of select="$css_param"/>
          </xsl:comment>
        </style>
        <xsl:value-of select="$script_param"/>
      </head>
      <body>
        <h1><xsl:value-of select="$title_param"/></h1>
        <xsl:value-of select="$temp_param"/>
        <div class="std_footing">
          [ XSLT Version <xsl:value-of select="format-number(system-
property('xsl:version'), '0.0')"/> Processed by <a href="{system-
property('xsl:vendor-url')}"><xsl:value-of select="system-
property('xsl:vendor')"/></a> ]
        </div>
      </body>
    </html>
  </xsl:template>

</xsl:stylesheet>
```

On its own, this stylesheet does (more or less) nothing. Its contents consist of a single named template—and a named template doesn't "do" anything visible until it's been called from within a regular template rule.

If this named template *were* a template rule in its own right, it would do the following:

- declare four parameters: `title_param`, `css_param`, `script_param`, and `temp_param` (the last two of which have no default values and are hence by default empty);
- instantiate XHTML `html`, `head`, and `title` elements in the result tree;
- in the `title` element (that is, in the browser window's title bar), display the value of the `title_param` parameter;
- following the `title`, but still within the `head` element, instantiate
  - an XHTML `style` element, whose contents are an XHTML comment (within which appear the contents of the `css_param` parameter), and
  - the value of the `script_param` variable;
- instantiate an XHTML `body` element, within which it instantiates
  - a level-1 heading, whose value is the value of the `title_param` parameter,
  - the value of the `temp_param` parameter, and
  - a `div` element with a `class` attribute whose value is "std_footing," and which contains a text node with various identifying information such as the XSLT version.

This is fairly unremarkable stuff so far. Now, though, we're going to associate the review of *When Dinosaurs Ruled the Earth* with the following stylesheet:

```
<xsl:stylesheet version="1.0"
  xmlns:xsl="http://www.w3.org/1999/XSL/Transform"
  xmlns="http://www.w3.org/1999/xhtml" >

  <xsl:include href="xhtml_struct.xsl"/>

  <xsl:template match="flixinfo">
    <xsl:call-template name="doc_outline">
      <xsl:with-param name="title_param">
        <xsl:value-of select="title"/>
      </xsl:with-param>
    </xsl:call-template>
  </xsl:template>

</xsl:stylesheet>
```

Note that this stylesheet is extremely simple. It has two top-level elements: an `xsl:include` (pointing to the previous stylesheet) and an `xsl:template` that matches on the source tree's root `flixinfo` element. Within that template rule is an `xsl:call-template` to instantiate the *named* template in xhtml_struct.xsl, overriding its `title_param` parameter with the value of the `flixinfo` element's child named `title`.

Results of processing *When Dinosaurs...* with this stylesheet are as shown in Figure 6–1—using MSXML (top) and Saxon 6.2 (bottom).

When Dinosaurs Ruled the Earth

[XSLT Version 1.0 Processed by Microsoft]

When Dinosaurs Ruled the Earth

[XSLT Version 1.0 Processed by SAXON 6.2 from Michael Kay]

Figure 6-1 A generic "produce an XHTML document" stylesheet, as included and invoked from within a stylesheet customized for use with a FlixML document.

This particular including stylesheet overrides a single default parameter, but it's certainly possible to override any of the others as well. For example, you could do this (showing just the template rule in the including stylesheet):

```
<xsl:template match="flixinfo">
  <xsl:call-template name="doc_outline">
    <xsl:with-param name="title_param">
      <xsl:value-of select="title"/>
    </xsl:with-param>
    <xsl:with-param name="css_param">
      .std_footing {visibility: hidden}
      h1 {text-align: right;
      font-family: Garamond,serif;
      background-color: silver}
    </xsl:with-param>
  </xsl:call-template>
</xsl:template>
```

This supplies an override value for the `css_param` parameter—hiding the informational footer and displaying level-1 headings in a particular way. The result appears as in Figure 6–2.

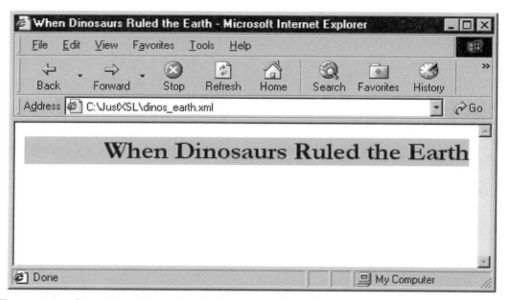

Figure 6-2 Overriding the default value not only of the `title_param` parameter (as in Figure 6–1) but also of the `css_param` parameter, with an including stylesheet. (Showing result from MSXML only.) This screen shot captures the entire browser window (see? no scrollbar at the right) to demonstrate that the `div` element's contents are indeed being suppressed by the overriding style specifications—otherwise, the standard footing would still show up at the lower right.

This generic "transform to XHTML" stylesheet also allows for the including stylesheet to contain any other template rules it needs. The generic stylesheet is useful only for creating the general skeleton of the XHTML result tree. If you want to use something like this yourself, don't forget to add one more override to your root-element (or root-node) template rule, such as this:

```
<xsl:with-param name="temp_param">
  <xsl:apply-templates/>
</xsl:with-param>
```

This allows children of that root to be processed by whatever template rules are appropriate. If the including stylesheet contains *no* other template rules, simply overriding the `temp_param` parameter in this way results in a display such as the one shown in Figure 6–3.

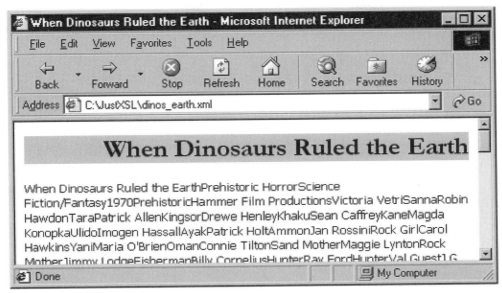

Figure 6-3   Results of processing the same XML document, with the same including stylesheet as in Figure 6–2. One difference: The including stylesheet now provides an `xsl:apply-templates` to override the default (empty) value of the `temp_param` parameter. Obviously, the including stylesheet desperately needs some new template rules as well. (But that, of course, was the subject of the previous three chapters.)

Overriding included content with `xsl:import`

In most ways, the top-level, empty `xsl:import` element functions and is used identically to `xsl:include`. Its general syntax is this:

```
<xsl:import href="other_stylesheet_uri"/>
```

which certainly looks familiar, no? The similarities don't stop there, either. For instance, the imported stylesheet must have its own `xsl:stylesheet` element, the contents of which logically replace the `xsl:import` statement in the importing stylesheet.

The most striking apparent difference between importing and including has to do with the placement of the `xsl:import` element. All `xsl:import` elements in a stylesheet must be its *first* top-level elements. (Any `xsl:include` elements, in contrast, may be mingled among the other top-level elements wherever it's convenient.) Furthermore, any `xsl:import` elements appearing in stylesheets which themselves are imported are "promoted" by the XSLT processor to the head of the importing stylesheet.

Consider four stylesheets. First, there's top.xsl:

```
<xsl:stylesheet...>
  <xsl:import href="middle1.xsl"/>
  <xsl:import href="middle2.xsl"/>
  <xsl:template match="D">
  [other content of top.xsl]
</xsl:stylesheet>
```

Then middle1.xsl:

```
<xsl:stylesheet...>
  <xsl:import href="bottom.xsl"/>
  <xsl:template match="A">
  [other content of middle1.xsl]
</xsl:stylesheet>
```

Then middle2.xsl:

```
<xsl:stylesheet...>
  <xsl:template match="C">
  [other content of middle2.xsl]
</xsl:stylesheet>
```

And finally bottom.xsl:

```
<xsl:stylesheet...>
  <xsl:template match="B">
  [other content of bottom.xsl]
</xsl:stylesheet>
```

If you apply top.xsl to an XML document, the processor "assembles" the four separate stylesheets into a single logical one in the following manner:

- The processor starts with top.xsl.
- The processor imports middle1.xsl.
- Because middle1.xsl also includes an `xsl:import` (for bottom.xsl), that `xsl:import` is "promoted" to a position in top.xsl immediately after the one for middle1.xsl itself.
- The processor imports bottom.xsl.
- The processor imports middle2.xsl.

As a result, the final "assembled" version of the stylesheet looks like this:

```
<xsl:stylesheet...>
```

```
  <xsl:template match="A">
  [other content of middle1.xsl]
  <xsl:template match="B">
  [other content of bottom.xsl]
  <xsl:template match="C">
  [other content of middle2.xsl]
  <xsl:template match="D">
  [other content of top.xsl]
</xsl:stylesheet>
```

"What imports what" is significant because of XSLT's rules for resolving conflicts in template rules: A conflicting rule in an *imported* stylesheet has a lower "import precedence" than one in its *importing* stylesheet, and this implicit priority-setting is evaluated before going on to other conflict-resolution devices (such as calculating a priority on the basis of a match pattern's specificity). Thus, in the above scenario, if

- template rules in top.xsl and either middle1.xsl or middle2.xsl conflict, those in top.xsl "win";
- template rules in middle1.xsl and bottom.xsl conflict, those in middle1.xsl "win";
- template rules in middle2.xsl and bottom.xsl conflict, those in middle2.xsl "win";
- template rules in top.xsl and bottom.xsl conflict, those in top.xsl "win";
- template rules in middle1.xsl and middle2.xsl (which have the same import precedence) conflict, the XSLT processor falls back on other means of conflict resolution.

In particular, note that this idea of import precedence supersedes the default behavior of XSLT processors—which is to let the *last* conflicting rule (in document order) win. For instance, using the "last one wins" approach, conflicting rules in bottom.xsl would override those in middle1.xsl.

Overriding imported templates with `xsl:apply-imports`

The other difference between importing and including is that the XSLT spec provides an explicit means of overriding templates in an imported stylesheet, using the `xsl:apply-imports` element. Its syntax is among the simplest in all of XSLT:

```
<xsl:apply-imports/>
```

That is, it's an empty element and takes *no* attributes. It always appears within a template in a higher-level (importing) stylesheet.

To see how you'd use `xsl:apply-imports`, consider two stylesheets for processing the *When Dinosaurs...* FlixML review. The first looks like this:

```
<xsl:import href="imported.xsl"/>

<xsl:template match="flixinfo">
  <html>
    <head><title>FlixML Review</title></head>
    <body>
      <xsl:apply-templates select="title"/>
    </body>
  </html>
</xsl:template>
```

As you can see, this simple stylesheet includes an `xsl:import` element to bring into this stylesheet the contents of one called imported.xsl. The contents of this imported stylesheet (without the `xsl:stylesheet` element) look like this:

```
<xsl:template match="title">
  <div style="border-style: solid; border-weight: 2; font-size:
18pt">
    <xsl:value-of select="."/>
  </div>
</xsl:template>
```

The result tree of the transformation as a whole will therefore consist of the basic XHTML document structure from the importing stylesheet; within the `body` element instantiated there, the movie's title will appear within a `div` element in a solid black box, in 18-point type. This is shown in Figure 6–4.

When Dinosaurs Ruled the Earth

Figure 6-4 Using `xsl:import` to style a film's title, even though the importing stylesheet doesn't include a template rule for the `title` element. At this point, we could just as easily have used `xsl:include`; all we're doing is bringing into the *importing* stylesheet the contents of the *imported* one.

If, for some reason, we need this particular film's title displayed slightly differently than the titles of other films transformed using the same pair of stylesheets, we can add a second template rule to the *importing* stylesheet, like the following:

```
<xsl:template match="title">
  <div style="background-color: silver; font-family:
Garamond,serif; font-weight: bold">
    <xsl:apply-imports/>
  </div>
</xsl:template>
```

The `xsl:apply-imports` instructs the XSLT processor to "go ahead and apply imported template rules for the current node at this point in the template, even though *this* template rule has a higher import precedence than the imported one." (Note that if you omitted the `xsl:apply-imports` element, the title wouldn't be displayed at all. That's precisely because this template rule has a higher import precedence than the conflicting imported one, and *this* template rule has no `xsl:value-of` element for actually displaying anything.)

As a result of adding this new template rule to the importing stylesheet, complete with `xsl:apply-imports`, the corresponding portion of the result tree now looks like this:

```
<div style="background-color: silver; font-family: Garamond,serif;
font-weight: bold">
  <div style="border-style: solid; border-weight: 2; font-size:
18pt">
    When Dinosaurs Ruled the Earth
  </div>
</div>
```

Thus, rather than completely superseding the imported stylesheet's template rule for processing the title element, we've (more subtly) *overlaid* its "meaning"—enclosed it within an additional result-tree `div` element, in this case. In MSIE, the result now appears as in Figure 6–5.

Figure 6-5 Adding to the "meaning" of an imported template rule by explicitly forcing a conflict, as it were, and then using `xsl:apply-imports` to subordinate the imported template rule to the importing one.

> **When overrides don't override**
>
> Note that the CSS style properties in the importing `div` element don't conflict with those in the imported one. The former includes a `back-ground-color` but not a `border-style`, and so on.
>
> If you try to "override" the `font-size` property by including, say, a 36-point specification in the enclosing `div` element, you'll find that the override doesn't take. This has nothing to do with XSLT conflict-resolution rules and everything to do with those established by CSS. The 36-point `font-size` in the result tree's outer `div` would be overridden by the 18-point `font-size` in the *inner* `div`.
>
> Fun working with multiple technologies all at once, isn't it?

`include` or `import`: Which one to use?

As a practical matter, I'd recommend using `xsl:include` rather than `xsl:import` in almost every case. Why? Maybe just a knee-jerk "Keep It Simple, Stupid" reaction. Using `xsl:import`'s rules of import precedence (with or without overriding template rules in the importing stylesheet) does allow for subtle control of which rule takes effect where (and how, if you're using `xsl:apply-imports` as well). I'll grant you that.

However, it also leaves the door open for subtle *loss* of control, in ways that you never intended and may have great difficulty fixing. The `xsl:import` facility is really provided for use in special cases; special cases, by their nature, are often fraught with additional layers of complexity. Never start out with the goal of adding complexity to such a situation—look for ways to avoid doing so, first, and embark on the more-complex path only with a clear sense of what you're getting into.

Copying

Everything you've learned about XSLT to this point has pretty much ignored one objective in particular: getting source-tree nodes (not just their string-values—the complete *nodes*) into the result tree.

It's true that you've already got two halfway-kind-of-solutions to this problem. Both require that you know *which particular source-tree node* you're processing at the time; if you know or can determine that fact, you can use either an identical literal result node or some construct such as `xsl:element` or `xsl:attribute`.

Assume your source tree looks like this:

```
<some_elem>
  <some_child>Text node 1</some_child>
  <some_child>Text node 2</some_child>
</some_elem>
```

You can therefore do this:

```
<xsl:template match="some_elem">
  <some_elem>
    <xsl:for-each select="some_child">
      <some_child>
        <xsl:value-of select="."/>
      </some_child>
    </xsl:for-each>
  </some_elem>
</xsl:template>
```

...or this (if you prefer not to use literal result elements, for some reason):

```
<xsl:template match="some_elem">
  <xsl:element name="some_elem">
    <xsl:for-each select="some_child">
      <xsl:element name="some_child>
        <xsl:value-of select="."/>
      </xsl:element>
    </xsl:for-each>
  </xsl:element>
</xsl:template>
```

Either of these approaches quickly grows unmanageable, though, as documents become more complex—particularly as elements include (or don't include) certain attributes, mixed content, optional child elements, comments and PIs, and so on.

Why copy?

Before getting into the details of *how* to copy nodes from the source to the result, it might be instructive to consider the question of *why* you'd need to do so in the first place.

To use XSLT, you need to know three things: You need to know your source tree vocabulary. You need to know your result tree vocabulary. And, of course, you need to know XSLT itself. This section of *Just XSL* has concentrated on the last part, and I've sort of sidestepped the first two kinds of knowledge. FlixML, I think, is intuitively understood by most people as a source-tree application, and most (ideally, all!) readers of *Just XSL* already know enough about (X)HTML to make it a convenient result-tree vocabulary.

The main problem I've not addressed so far is that you won't always (maybe even *ever*) be transforming from source tree to XHTML. If the result tree is similar to the source, you really need some way to get entire nodes (or sub-trees, or node-sets, even result tree fragments) into the result tree unchanged—not just as string-values but as complete nodes. At the very least, you'll need to have a sense of how to "upgrade" your XML documents to later versions of their vocabularies.[2]

And *that* is why you need to know how to copy nodes, not just string-values.

Skin-deep copies: `xsl:copy`

When all (and I mean *all*) that you want to copy is the current node, use the `xsl:copy` element. Its general syntax is this:

```
<xsl:copy use-attribute-sets="names_of_attrib_sets">
  [optional content]
</xsl:copy>
```

The `use-attribute-sets` attribute is optional; if you include it, its value is a whitespace-delimited list of the names of the named attribute sets whose attributes you want added to this node. (Obviously, if the current node is any node type other than element, specifying a `use-attribute-sets` attribute at all is meaningless.)

I emphasized earlier that the purpose of `xsl:copy` is to copy *only* the current node to the result tree. There are two implications of this.

First, as you can see from the general syntax, there's no `match` or `select` attribute to tell the processor what to copy. It always applies the `xsl:copy` to the node that is current, within the `xsl:template` or `xsl:for-each` that contains the `xsl:copy`.

Second, `xsl:copy` explicitly does *not* copy attributes or children of the current node. If the current node is itself an attribute, comment, PI, or text node, this is no great loss—none of them has attributes or children anyway. If it's an element or the root node, though, in order to copy its attributes and children

---

2.   Or to earlier versions, for that matter. Not everybody upgrades to the latest technology at the same rate—whether you're talking about computer hardware, XML vocabularies, or for that matter DVD instead of VHS versions of B films.

(including text, PI, and comment nodes) you must supply further explicit `xsl:copy` elements for them, too. All of which seems to make `xsl:copy` pretty useless, right?

Well, no. The `xsl:copy` element is useful because of that "optional content" in its general syntax. What this allows you to do is make *modified copies* of portions of the source tree—copying just the source node itself, but altering what it contains.

Consider a source tree that looks something like the following:

```
<sales>
  <sale saleno="sale0001">
    <date>2001-10-16</date>
    <salesrep id="JMarley">
      <name>Marley, Jacob</name>
    </salesrep>
    <invoice>
      <item itemno="item0001">
        <qty>12</qty>
        <unitprice>1.36</unitprice>
      </item>
      <item itemno="item0002">
        <qty>23</qty>
        <unitprice>4.75</unitprice>
      </item>
      <item itemno="item0003">
        <qty>14</qty>
        <unitprice></unitprice>
      </item>
    </invoice>
  </sale>
</sales>
```

Assume we need to pass this content to another XML-based system which, for the most part, uses the same element and attribute names. We do need to change a couple of things about it, though:

- We need to add a new attribute, `src`, to the root `sales` element. Its value should be "Scrooge and Marley, Ltd."
- Each `sale` element is to be renamed—it will now be an `invoice` element.
- The `saleno` attribute is also to be renamed, to `inv_num`.

A stylesheet to accomplish this might look like the following:

```
  <xsl:template match="*">
    <xsl:copy>
      <xsl:apply-templates select="@*"/>
      <xsl:if test="name()='sales'">
        <xsl:attribute name="src">Scrooge and Marley, Ltd.</
xsl:attribute>
      </xsl:if>
      <xsl:apply-templates select="node()"/>
    </xsl:copy>
  </xsl:template>

  <xsl:template match="sale">
    <invoice>
      <xsl:attribute name="inv_num">inv<xsl:value-of
select="substring-after(@saleno, 'sale')"/></xsl:attribute>
      <xsl:apply-templates/>
    </invoice>
  </xsl:template>

  <xsl:template match="@*">
    <xsl:copy/>
  </xsl:template>
```

The first template rule copies all elements from the source to the result tree (except for the `sale` elements, which are handled by the second template rule). Immediately within the copy of the element, all of the source *attributes* are copied as well, using an `xsl:apply-templates` to invoke the third template rule (which simply copies the attributes). The second template rule, which applies only to `sale` elements, doesn't use `xsl:copy`: It instantiates a literal `invoice` result element and gives it an `inv_num` attribute, whose value is a modified form of the current `sale` element's `saleno` attribute.

The result tree from this transformation looks like this:

```
<sales src="Scrooge and Marley, Ltd.">
  <invoice inv_num="inv0001">
    <date>2001-10-16</date>
    <salesrep id="JMarley">
      <name>Marley, Jacob</name>
    </salesrep>
    <invoice>
      <item itemno="item0001">
        <qty>12</qty>
        <unitprice>1.36</unitprice>
      </item>
      <item itemno="item0002">
```

```
      <qty>23</qty>
      <unitprice>4.75</unitprice>
    </item>
    <item itemno="item0003">
      <qty>14</qty>
      <unitprice/>
    </item>
  </invoice>
 </invoice>
</sales>
```

Effectively, we've "translated" the XML document marked up in one vocabulary to one marked up in another, not-quite-identical vocabulary. The `xsl:copy` element enabled certain nodes to be copied *with modification*, both to the node names and to their contents.

Profound copies: `xsl:copy-of`

The `xsl:copy` element, as I said, is useful for occasions when you need to copy a single node and/or to customize its contents in some way. At something like the other end of the extreme is the `xsl:copy-of` element, which copies an entire sub-tree of the source to the result.

The general syntax of `xsl:copy-of` (which is an instruction and always empty) is this:

```
<xsl:copy-of select="tree_to_copy"/>
```

The `select` attribute is required. Its value is an XPath expression (absolute or relative) indicating what sub-tree is to be copied.

Obviously, this can be of enormous help when the source and result trees are *very* close; you don't need to do any kind of crazy iteration through children and attributes, as you do with `xsl:copy`.

More importantly, `xsl:copy-of` can be used to copy result tree fragments, as well as source tree node-sets, to the result tree. This makes it valuable when you've got to instantiate content more than once.

A FlixML document typically is littered with ID-type attributes which identify major "sections" of the document. For example, the *When Dinosaurs...* review has such attributes (all named `id`) on the `cast`, `crew`, `plotsummary`, `reviews`, `distributors`, and `mpaarating` elements. You can use this information to build a sort of cross-reference table of hyperlinks which can be inserted into the result tree wherever it seems reasonable.

Here's the idea:

```
<xsl:variable name="xref_menu">
  <table>
    <tr>
      <td>
        [<a href="#{//cast/@id}">Cast</a>]
      </td>
      <td>
        [<a href="#{//crew/@id}">Crew</a>]
      </td>
      <td>
        [<a href="#{//plotsummary/@id}">The Plot</a>]
      </td>
      <td>
        [<a href="#{//reviews/@id}">Reviews</a>]
      </td>
      <td>
        [<a href="#{//distributors/@id}">Get It</a>]
      </td>
      <td>
        [<a href="#{//mpaarating/@id}">MPAA</a>]
      </td>
    </tr>
  </table>
</xsl:variable>

<xsl:template match="*[@id]">
  <h1><a name="#{@id}"/>
      <xsl:value-of select="name()"/>
  </h1>
  <xsl:value-of select="."/>
  <xsl:copy-of select="$xref_menu"/>
</xsl:template>
```

This stylesheet establishes a variable, xref_menu, whose contents are a result-tree fragment consisting of a one-row table. The table row has six cells, one for each of the major elements with an ID-type attribute; each cell contains some kind of catchword or phrase, enclosed in an XHTML a element pointfing to the location in the result tree which is tagged with the corresponding ID value.

The lone template rule applies to all elements with an ID-type attribute. It creates a level-1 heading (where the a element with a name attribute is tagged with the element's ID), followed by the element's string-value, followed by a copy of the entire result-tree fragment contained by the xref_menu variable.

The result tree from this transformation[3] looks like Figure 6–6 when viewed in MSIE.

Figure 6-6   Using `xsl:copy-of` to stamp out repeated copies of a result-tree fragment (the little "cross-reference menu" here). Note the hyperlinked address displayed in the status bar here; when I click on any of the "Reviews" labels in the result-tree fragment, the page scrolls to the list of reviews (or links to reviews) for this movie.

---

3.   Not particularly well formatted, I know—I'm just trying to show you the result of using `xsl:copy-of`, not dazzle you with a well laid-out page!

The "identity transform"

You'll occasionally see this term bandied about on XSLT- and XML-related mailing lists. The *identity transform* (also sometimes called the *identity transformation*) is simply a technique for creating a complete copy in the result tree of everything in the source tree.

I've seen a couple versions of such a beast. There's one in the XSLT spec, which uses xsl:copy:

```
<xsl:template match="@*|node()">
  <xsl:copy>
    <xsl:apply-templates select="@*|node()"/>
  </xsl:copy>
</xsl:template>
```

Basically, this says that for any source-tree node of any type, copy it to the result; then apply this same template for all children of the current node and for all attributes if the current node is an element.

This is kind of tortured; it's much simpler to use xsl:copy-of on the root node:

```
<xsl:template match="/">
  <xsl:copy-of select="."/>
</xsl:template>
```

Yeah, but *why?*

The need to copy an entire source tree to the result tree is so seldom encountered that, well, I think it's pretty much an academic exercise. (Possibly it would be useful for developers of XSLT processors, as a way of confirming that their products handle the xsl:copy and xsl:copy-of elements correctly.)

One occasion on which you may need to do this is when creating "super-documents"—or anthologies, as I referred to them in Chapter 5, under the discussion of the XSLT document() function. Say the source tree's XML vocabulary (like FlixML) permits only one "thing" to be described in a given document. You can create an "anthology"-type document doing something like this:

```
<xsl:template
  match="document(film1.xml) | document(film2.xml)">
  <super_root>
```

```
      <xsl:copy-of select="."/>
    </super_root>
  </xsl:template>
```

Again, I don't know how often you'll actually encounter that in practice. But it's possible.

How Do I…
"Re-version" a document to a newer structure/DTD?

Listen, I'll repeat what I said earlier in this chapter: To use XSLT effectively, you need to know three things: the source tree, the result tree, and XSLT itself. With xsl:copy and xsl:copy-of in your back pocket, the main things you need to focus on when transforming one version of a document to another version of the same DTD are the natures of the source and result trees.

Source tree considerations

The first source-tree concern you've got to keep before you is the nature not just of a particular source tree but of all possible source trees in the source vocabulary. Look at the content models for all elements. Just because a given element in Document X has only one child of a particular type, don't assume that all documents in this source vocabulary will follow that pattern.

Look, too, at the attributes declared in the DTD or schema, and don't trust that the attributes to a particular element in a particular document represent the full range of attributes possible.

PIs and comments are outside the scope of what can be defined in a DTD/schema, of course, but they may be critical in given applications. You may have some record in particular documents of what kinds of PIs and comments will need to be copied; more likely, you'll have to call on some outside reference material or third parties for this information.

If you've got entity references in the source tree that need to go to the result, don't worry too much about them; the XSLT processor is free to use any method it wants to create the same result, so you'll quite possibly be wasting energy on something you can't control anyway.

Result tree considerations

Again, look not just to existing documents already marked up in the target vocabulary but to formal statements—DTDs, schemas, and so on—of what the target *may* and *must* include.

When it comes right down to it, the range of things you can do in the result tree is limited to the following:

- Copy nodes from the source tree, unchanged.
- Copy nodes from the source tree, with modifications.
- Instantiate entirely new nodes, using content from the source tree.
- Instantiate entirely new nodes from scratch.

It's possible that along the way you'll need to completely eliminate content from the source tree, when there's no counterpart in the result vocabulary. (This is often a result of "dumbing down" a document to an earlier version.) In this case, it may be a good idea to put the removed content in a comment—markup and all—that will both document what you've done and facilitate later "smartening up" of the result document, should the need arise.

(Actually, don't neglect the opportunity to instantiate comments anyway. At the very least, indicate that this result tree was automatically generated from a source tree in a different dialect of the same vocabulary.)

Don't forget that your result tree may need an XML declaration, and/or a new DOCTYPE declaration as well.

XSLT considerations

At the time you sit down to code your transformation, you need to have at hand as complete a "road map" as possible, laying out all the differences between possible (or required) source-tree structure and possible (or required) result-tree structure. Given that information, "all" you've got to do is figure out what you need to do to get a given node from one point in the source to one in the result.

A good general approach, I think, is to go through the source tree's DTD or schema and include in the stylesheet a template rule for every possible node type and node. If a given node needs to be copied unchanged, including all its descendants, use `xsl:copy-of`; if copied with modifications, use `xsl:copy`; otherwise, use whatever means are suitable (literal result elements, `xsl:element` and `xsl:attribute`, and so on). If a node is to be removed from the source tree in the transformation to the result, supply an empty template rule. The main idea is to leave nothing to chance—in particular the whims of the built-in template rules. If you know you've accounted for every type of node in the source tree, you don't have to worry about the built-ins kicking in.

If you want, you can specifically override the built-in template rule for text nodes by suppressing all text, which will ensure that the only text which shows up in the result is text you explicitly put there, in some element's template.

Now that you've got a stylesheet which processes all possible forms of the source tree, go through it with a copy of the result tree's DTD or schema alongside. Check off every node type in the latter which makes an appearance in the stylesheet's result tree. (This is a bare minimum. You almost certainly need to confirm as well that this is the *only* necessary appearance of this node type.)

Anything still missing—unchecked-off—in the result tree? How and where do you need to create these missing pieces?

Messaging

This is an interesting feature of the XSLT spec. It can be almost too interesting, in fact.

The main problem is that the term "message" (and its derivatives) summons up all kinds of mental associations with user interfaces—prompts to the user, responses from him, and so on.

That's *not* what XSLT messaging is all about. (Nor is it about some of the more exotic kinds of messaging, such as so-called "Remote Procedure Calls" and so on.) All that said, maybe I should just tell you what it *is* about.

The `xsl:message` element

Issuing messages to users of a stylesheet is handled by the `xsl:message` element, which is an instruction and hence always appears as the child of some element other than `xsl:stylesheet`. Its general syntax is this:

```
<xsl:message
  terminate="yes_no">
  [template]
</xsl:message>
```

The `terminate` attribute is optional and takes a value of `yes` or `no`. (The default, if none is supplied, is `no`.) The *[template]* is the text of the message you want to issue at that point. If the value of the `terminate` attribute is `yes`, the processor halts all further processing after issuing the message.

The main point of the `xsl:message` element is to inform the user of your stylesheet that some condition has occurred during processing. This is particularly important during development of new stylesheets and new documents, and particularly in development environments using static/non-GUI XSLT processors.

Why, you might wonder, do you need a message facility at all? If something goes wrong, the processor will surely let you know, right?

The catch is that a thousand unspecified things might go wrong for every one defined by the XSLT spec, and hence found by the XSLT processor. For instance, XSLT itself doesn't care if a month element has the right number of day children, and that's kind of a difficult constraint for a DTD to specify. (If your source document is merely well-formed, of course, whether it's easy or difficult for a DTD or schema to specify is immaterial.) You could test for this kind of condition with a template rule like the following:

```
<xsl:template match="month">
  <xsl:if test="count(day) & gt; 31">
    <xsl:message>
     Sorry -- number of days in a month must be less than or equal
to 31. (Month=<xsl:value-of select="."/>, number of
days=<xsl:value-of select="count(day)"/>)
    </xsl:message>
  </xsl:if>
</xsl:template>
```

If the source document has a month element with a string-value of JUNE and 35 day children, this template rule causes the XSLT processor to emit the message:

```
    Sorry -- number of days in a month must be less
    than or equal to 31. (Month=JUNE, number of days=35)
```

A notable holdout among XSLT processors for its "handling" (or lack thereof) of the `xsl:message` element is Microsoft's MSXML. Even a simple template rule like the following fails completely to do anything at all with this processor:

```
<xsl:template match="flixinfo">
  <xsl:message>
  Found a flixinfo element!
  </xsl:message>
</xsl:template>
```

That is, the MSIE browser simply displays a blank screen. I guess the idea is that if you're transforming on-the-fly into XHTML, which is what MSIE does with

XSLT, you don't need to emit messages. You can simply replace the above with an "XHTML message," as in this:

```
<xsl:template match="flixinfo">
  <h1>Found a flixinfo element!</h1>
</xsl:template>
```

> ### Schematron
>
> Later in this chapter, I'll introduce you to Schematron—a tool for simplifying the "validation" of XML documents using XSLT.

Fallback Processing

When a military commander orders his or her troops to "fall back," everybody kind of takes a step backward, away from the line of fire, and regroups. It's not a retreat, certainly not a rout, just a means of recovering from what would otherwise be a hopeless situation.

That's what XSLT's fallback feature is for. There's a built-in extension mechanism for vendors to add elements and functions not provided by XSLT itself; fallback is the other side of this mechanism—a provision for handling the case in which some expected feature isn't available at all.

The first ingredient in building "fallback smarts" into your spreadsheets is the xsl:fallback element, whose general syntax is this:

```
<xsl:fallback>
  [template]
</xsl:fallback>
```

The *[template]*, of course, provides some mixture of instructions and result-tree content that will be instantiated when the fallback is triggered.

As for what triggers the fallback in the first place, it happens when the xsl:fallback element's parent element is not known to whatever XSLT processor is currently running. This makes xsl:fallback useful not only for guarding against the unavailability of vendor-specific features but also for covering yourself if you're using some feature available only in a "beta version" of the XSLT spec itself.

Suppose XSLT 2.2 is being worked on by the W3C, and there's a really cool feature defined in that version of the spec that you'd like to take advantage of. It's an xsl:date element, say, that works like xsl:number but for generating a sequence of dates. There are only a handful of processors that implement this experimental `xsl:date`, so—just to be sure your stylesheet won't break if it's being processed by one of the non-bleeding-edge processors—you work some fallback into the stylesheet:

```
<xsl:template match="calendar">
  <xsl:date [xsl:date attributes, whatever they are]>
    <xsl:fallback>
      [some template that builds the dates
      "manually," without being able to take advantage
      of xsl:date's cool features]
    </xsl:fallback>
  </xsl:date>
</xsl:template>
```

If the processor implements `xsl:date`, it ignores the `xsl:fallback` element. If it doesn't recognize the `xsl:date`, it simply does whatever `xsl:fallback`'s template tells it to do. This might be issuing a message with `xsl:message` ("Sorry — xsl:date needed to run this stylesheet"), or it might be (as hinted at above) some traditional XSLT process that does sort of the same thing as `xsl:date`.

Falling back with `element-` and `function-available()`

You can also take advantage of two XSLT functions that provide finer control over the fallback condition. These are the `element-available()` and `function-available()` functions. Each takes a single argument, a string, which is the name of the XSLT element (instructions only) or function for which you want to test.

Using `element-available()`, for instance, you could re-code the above template rule for a hypothetical `calendar` element as follows:

```
<xsl:template match="calendar">
  <xsl:choose>
    <xsl:when test="element-available('xsl:date')">
      <xsl:date
        [xsl:date attributes, whatever they are]/>
    </xsl:when>
    <xsl:otherwise>
      [some template that builds the dates
      "manually," without being able to take advantage
      of xsl:date's cool features]
    </xsl:otherwise>
  </xsl:choose>
</xsl:template>
```

If you've only got two conditions to test for—the element is available, or it's not—using `xsl:fallback` (versus an `xsl:choose` block laying out the two alternatives with an `element-available()` function call) is pretty much a matter of taste. If there are more than two alternatives ("If this element isn't available, then use this element; and if that one's not available, then use this one," and so on), the `xsl:choose` block is clearly the way to go.

And if you need to test for the availability of a function, what you're after is not `element-available()`, but `function-available()`. For instance:

```
<xsl:template match="some_elem">
  <xsl:message>
    Found a some_elem element
  </xsl:message>
  <xsl:if
      test="function-available('saxon:line-number')">
      <xsl:message>
        at line #<xsl:value-of
        select="saxon:line_number()"/>
      </xsl:message>
  </xsl:if>
</xsl:template>
```

This template rule locates a `some_elem` element and informs the stylesheet's user that it has. If the `saxon:line-number()` function (discussed in Chapter 5) is available, though, the template rule *also* identifies the line in the source document where the `some_elem` was located.

"Advanced XSLT" #1: Table Structures

In the next three sections, we're going to take a look at a handful of common situations that trip up XSLT newcomers, and sometimes even intermediate-level stylesheet developers.

The first puzzle has to do with creating a table from some regularly occurring structure in the source tree.[4] This is fairly simple if the table to be instanti-

---

4. I'm using the term "table" kind of loosely here. What's important isn't whether the intended result is a physical/geometric arrangement of rows and columns; what's important is that the intended result has some kind of regularly recurring structure. The most familiar analogue to this in most people's minds is a table structure, that's all.

ated follows the structure of the source tree exactly. For instance, using a FlixML document as the source tree, you might have a template rule such as this one:

```
<xsl:template match="crew">
  <table>
    <xsl:for-each select="*">
      <tr>
        <td><xsl:value-of select="name()"/></td>
        <td><xsl:value-of select="."/></td>
      </tr>
    </xsl:for-each>
  </table>
</xsl:template>
```

This creates a two-column table, with the given crew member's position (director, editor, and so on) in the first column and his or her name in the second.

The problem that seems to confuse everyone comes about when the table structure is not directly related to the data structure. In a simple case, if you're laying out a month's calendar for printing, say, you need to allow a grid of seven columns wide by up to six rows high, and then fill it starting at one of the cells in the top row, for a length of however many days there are in a month.

What nearly everyone, at some point, thinks of doing in a case like this is a solution that involves "turning on" a new row, filling it for however many columns are needed, then "turning off" the row and "turning on" the next one. In pseudo-code, such a solution might look something like the following

```
For each month:
  For each day:
    If this is the start of a new week
      End the previous row
      Start a new row
    End If
    Put the day's data in a cell
    Get the next day
  Get the next month
```

See the problem? Think of the "end a row" and "start a row" instructions as XHTML `</tr>` and `<tr>` end- and start-tags, respectively. Right: The stylesheet is no longer well-formed.

The main thing you've got to do to get around this problem is to stop thinking in terms of turning on/turning off *anything*. Think instead of (1) instantiating something in the result tree for something in the source; of (2) the "every nth something" problem (such as "coloring every other table row") which the position() function and mod XPath operator solve; and, finally, of (3) the creative use of XPath axes other than child and self.

The general solution to this problem involves nesting two xsl:for-each elements. The outermost one represents each table row; the innermost, each cell (column) within the row. Let's tackle the outermost first.

Recall the use of position() and the mod operator to process every other row in a table differently. An expression such as

```
position() mod 2 = 0
```

results in the value true if the remainder, after dividing the current node's position by 2, is 0. That is, this expression is true for *even*-numbered nodes. Odd-numbered nodes (the first, third, etc.) could be tested for with the similar

```
position() mod 2 = 1
```

That—the odd-numbered position test—provides the germ of a solution to the outermost loop. The 2 in that expression (or the preceding one, for that matter) is the *n* in a phrase like "every *n*th something." Testing for a remainder of 1 always gets the first position, the *n*th-plus-1 position, and so on.

With me so far? Now let's take a look at, say, putting a FlixML document's crew members' names into a table like this, as a practical example. The table in question is going to be five columns wide by however many rows we need. Here's the start of a template rule for building it:

```
<xsl:template match="crew">
  <table border="1">
    <xsl:variable name="cols" select="5"/>
    <xsl:variable name="pct"
      select="concat(100 div $cols, '%')"/>
    <xsl:for-each select="*[position() mod $cols = 1]">
      <tr>
        [inner for-each for table cells]
      </tr>
    </xsl:for-each>
  </table>
</xsl:template>
```

There's a little fooling around with variables going on here. The value of the first one, cols, is just for you to replace with the number of columns you want to use. The second one, pct, builds a string by dividing 100 by cols and tacking a percent sign onto the end. This pct variable will be used to allocate space evenly among the table cells; when `cols` is 5, for instance, each column will take up 20% of the table width.

But the real heart of this code is the `xsl:for-each` element. Its `select` attribute locates "every child of the `crew` element which yields a remainder, when the current node's position is divided by the desired number of columns, of 1." Referring a few paragraphs back, in other words, this `select` attribute (given the value of the `cols` variable above) says, "Every fifth child of the `crew` element." And, as you can see, what's being instantiated for every fifth child is a table row. (In other words: Add a new row *after* child #5, *after* child #10, and so on.)

Now, within the table row, we need to include a table cell for the current node (which, because of the `xsl:for-each` above, is going to be the first child of the `crew` element, the sixth, the eleventh, and so on) *and* for each following sibling of the current node up to the total number of columns desired. (We don't want to include *all* siblings of the current node, since the ones before it will have already been placed into their own cells.) That is, in place of the italicized portion of the above template rule, we'll do this:

```
<xsl:for-each
  select=
    ".|following-sibling::*[position() &lt; $cols]">
  <td valign="top" width="{$pct}">
    <xsl:value-of select="."/>
  </td>
</xsl:for-each>
```

The main thing to notice here, once again, is the value of an `xsl:for-each` element's `select` attribute. This one uses the "union" operator—the | character—to tell the processor to construct a node-set consisting of the current node (.) plus all of its following siblings up to one less than the desired number of columns. If `cols` is 5, as in this example, this creates a node-set consisting of the current node plus up to four of its following siblings.

Results appear as shown in Figure 6–7.

Val Guest	J.G. Ballard (story)	Val Guest	Dick Bush	Frank Goulding (dubbing editor)
Kevin Sutton (sound recordist)	Peter Curran	Mario Nascimbene	Jim Danforth	John Blezard (art director)
Joyce James ("hairdressing supervisor")	Brian Owen-Smith ("wardrobe master")			

Figure 6-7 Fitting the values of a variable number of nodes into a table of fixed size. Note the incomplete third row; see the box titled "Leaving something for you" for some comments about this effect.

> **Leaving something for you**
>
> The solution in Figure 6–7 presents a general model for solving the problem at hand. It's notable, though, for some of the problems it *doesn't* solve.
>
> First, it works only as long as the source-tree elements to be placed in the *n*-column table are all siblings. It's *adaptable* to other structures, just a bit trickier. If you want to work on the problem yourself, try adapting the above to produce a five-column table in which each cell contains a *cast* member's name.
>
> Second, it ignores a problem with unbalanced tables as displayed in some browsers. In the case above, we've got 12 crew members to fit into a five-column table. This means we'll have two full rows plus, in a third row, two cells with data. Cells 3, 4, and 5 in that row are simply not created, as shown in Figure 6–7. This difficulty is a little easier to solve than the first one. The general idea is to nest within the second `xsl:for-each` element a *third* one, which is "fallen into" only if the number of nodes left to process (that is, the number of following siblings plus one) is less than the number of columns in the table. Instantiate an empty cell for every one of these "missing nodes."

"Advanced XSLT" #2: Grouping

Here's the problem: As marvelous as XML is for structuring data into a hierarchy, a given document—indeed, a given document *type*—can have only one structure.

Consider the case of a simple document such as the following:

```
<books>
  <book edition="2">
    <title>Just XML</title>
    <author>John E. Simpson</author>
    <subject>XML</subject>
  </book>
  <book edition="3">
    <title>Tristram Shandy</title>
    <author>Laurence Sterne</author>
    <subject>Fiction</subject>
  </book>
  <book edition="1">
    <title>XML by Example</title>
    <author>Sean McGrath</author>
```

```
    <subject>XML</subject>
  </book>
  <book edition="1">
    <title>Catch-22</title>
    <author>Joseph Heller</author>
    <subject>Fiction</subject>
  </book>
</books>
```

Pretty clear, right?

Now, suppose we need to kind of turn the structure inside-out and do something like the following:

```
<shelves>
  <shelf subject="Fiction">
    <book edition="3">
     <title>Tristram Shandy</title>
     <author>Laurence Sterne</author>
    </book>
    <book edition="1">
     <title>Catch-22</title>
     <author>Joseph Heller</author>
    </book>
  </shelf>
  <shelf subject"XML">
    <book edition="2">
     <title>Just XML</title>
     <author>John E. Simpson</author>
    </book>
    <book edition="1">
     <title>XML by Example</title>
     <author>Sean McGrath</author>
    </book>
  </shelf>
</shelves>
```

That is, some content that was formerly *subordinate*—the content of the subject elements, in this case—has been elevated, made more important. It's become a *category*, in short, on which you need to group the data.

There are a number of solutions to this problem, some quite ugly. Among the most obvious of these is a multiple pass through the source tree: once to get all the group values, once to get each "record" with that value. If the source tree is short, this works well. But it's extremely slow if the source tree is large, with many nodes.

When you hear the phrase "extremely slow" in an XSLT context, you may leap to the conclusion that the answer lies in using keys and/or IDs. Not a bad leap to make; that's exactly the approach to follow.

Suppose we're working for a film production company doing a remake of *When Dinosaurs Ruled the Earth.*[5] We need to produce two separate casting lists, one for the female roles and one for the male. We don't care primarily whether a role is a lead or supporting one; we care primarily whether it's a male or female one.

So again, the problem is the same. We've got a structure that looks as follows (in part):

```
<cast>
  <leadcast>
    <female id="VVetri">
      <castmember>Victoria Vetri</castmember>
      <role>Sanna</role>
    </female>
    <male id="RHawdon">
      <castmember>Robin Hawdon</castmember>
      <role>Tara</role>
    </male>
  </leadcast>
  <othercast>
    <male id="PHolt">
      <castmember>Patrick Holt</castmember>
      <role>Ammon</role>
    </male>
    <female id="JRossini">
      <castmember>Jan Rossini</castmember>
      <role>Rock Girl</role>
    </female>
  </othercast>
</cast>
```

We need to invert the relationships among some of this content, making it usable as if the structure were actually something like this (and note that we really don't care who starred in the original at this point):

---

5. This isn't as implausible as it might sound. For one Hollywood reason or another, B movies *do* get remade. To take one recent case, the Nicolas Cage car-crash extravaganza *Gone in 60 Seconds* was generally regarded as worse than the cult film on which it was based.

```
<cast>
  <female>
    <role type="lead">Sanna</role>
    <role type="other">Rock Girl</role>
  </female>
  <male>
    <role type="lead">Tara</role>
    <role type="other">Ammon</role>
  <male>
</cast>
```

What I'm going to show you is how to create one XHTML table for the female roles and one for the male. Each table is only one column wide, and in that column is a simple list of the appropriate characters' names.[6]

We'll start out with a handful of top-level elements to do some general "housekeeping." First is a named template, whose only purpose is to convert a parameter's value to uppercase. It looks like this:

```
<xsl:template name="ucase">
  <xsl:param name="value"/>
  <xsl:value-of select="translate($value,
    'abcdefghijklmnopqrstuvwxyz',
    'ABCDEFGHIJKLMNOPQRSTUVWXYZ')"/>
</xsl:template>
```

We'll need a template rule to establish the basic structure of an XHTML document:

```
<xsl:template match="flixinfo">
  <html>
    <head>
      <title>
        Casting Lists: <xsl:value-of select="title"/>
      </title>
    </head>
    <body>
        <xsl:apply-templates select="cast"/>
```

---

6.   This technique is one approach to the grouping problem devised by Steve Muench and promulgated on the public XSL-List mailing list. It's popularly called "the Muenchian method."

```
    </body>
  </html>
</xsl:template>
```

Note that the only child of the `flixinfo` element which will be processed from this point, per the `xsl:apply-templates` element, is `cast`.

And because we're using a key to speed things up, of course we need a top-level `xsl:key` element:

```
<xsl:key name="gender" match="role" use="name(..)" />
```

When this `gender` key is referred to in the body of a template, it will assemble a node-set consisting of all `role` elements (the value of the `match` attribute) whose parent elements have the same name (that's the `use` attribute's value). Looking at the source tree, you should see that each `role` will therefore belong to a node-set based on whether its parent is a `male` or a `female` element.

Now we need the skeleton framework of a template rule for processing the film's cast in the way we want to. I'll use comments temporarily as placeholders for the "funky" bits to come.

```
<xsl:template match="cast">
  <!-- Placeholder 1: Outermost xsl:for-each to process
  each "category." -->
    <xsl:sort select="name(..)"/>
    <table border="1" width="20%">
      <tr>
        <th>
          <xsl:call-template name="ucase">
          <xsl:with-param name="value"
           select="name(..)"/>
          </xsl:call-template> Roles
        </th>
      </tr>
      <!-- Placeholder 2: Innermost xsl:for-each to
      process each character within this category -->
        <xsl:sort select="." />
        <tr>
          <td>
          <xsl:variable name="backstyle">
            <xsl:choose>
              <xsl:when
                test="name(../..)='leadcast'">background-
                color: silver</xsl:when>
              <xsl:otherwise>background-color:
```

```
          white</xsl:otherwise>
        </xsl:choose>
      </xsl:variable>
      <span style="{$backstyle}">
      <xsl:value-of select="." />
      </span>
    </td>
  </tr>
  <!-- End Placeholder 2 -->
  </table>
  <p />
 <!-- End Placeholder 1 -->
</xsl:template>
```

Disregarding for now the two "placeholders" standing for the xsl:for-each elements, we see that this template rule does the following:

- Sorts the "categories" on the basis of the corresponding elements' names. This will cause the content for female elements to come first, male second.
- Instantiates a table for this category's data.
- In the first row of the table, instantiates a header containing the upper-cased form of the category's name (that is, the name of the corresponding elements). The table headers will read FEMALE Roles and MALE Roles.
- Within each category's table, instantiates for each character a new table row with one cell. In that cell will be the character's name; the name appears on a silver background if the character is a lead role, or a white background otherwise.
- After each category's table, instantiates an empty paragraph (p) element. This is just to separate the categories' tables a bit.

Nothing really dreadful so far. But now let's take a look at the start tag of the xsl:for-each element which will take the place of the comments marking the start of Placeholder 1 (hold your breath):

```
<xsl:for-each
  select=".//role[generate-id()
  = generate-id(key('gender', name(..))[1])]">
```

Start by remembering that, at the time the processor hits this xsl:for-each, the context node is simply the one established by the template rule's match pattern—that is, the cast element. Thus, the location path—not getting into the predicate details for a moment—is going to select all role descendants of the cast element which meet some condition, as specified by the predicate. But what a predicate!

It starts by saying that the ID generated by the processor for this role element must be equal to…something else. The "something else" is another generated ID, this one generated using the node-set consisting of *the first node* (that's the [1] at the end of the predicate) *in the node-set of all the elements which have a parent with the same name as this* role *element's parent.* (See? We're passing to the key() function the name of the key in question—gender, in this case—and a key value of either "female" or "male.")

In short, the question this predicate asks is this: "Is this the first node in the keyed node-set?" For each such first node, a new table is set up.

(Note the similarity to the previous "Advanced XSLT" tip. As with that tip, basically what's happening here is that we're identifying a handful of things to be processed *en masse.* For the first thing in the handful, we're starting off a new logical division of some kind. There, it was starting a new row; here, it's starting a new table.)

After you've digested the outermost xsl:for-each, the inner one—taking the place of Placeholder 3—will be like a light dessert. Its start tag looks like this:

```
<xsl:for-each select="key('gender', name(..))">
```

That is, it processes each member of the gender keyed node-set whose parent element has the same name as the parent of this *first* node (the one selected by the outermost xsl:for-each). If the first node's parent is a female element, this xsl:for-each selects all members of the gender node-set whose key value is "female." Note that this will get the current node as well as all the others which match the key.

The result tree output by Saxon from this transform looks as follows:

```
<html>
  <head>
    <title>
       Casting Lists: When Dinosaurs Ruled the Earth
    </title>
  </head>
  <body>
    <table border="1" width="20%">
      <tr><th>FEMALE Roles</th></tr>
      <tr>
        <td>
```

```
          <span style="background-color: silver">Ayak</span>
        </td>
      </tr>
      <tr>
       <td>
         <span style="background-color: white">Oman</span>
        </td>
      </tr>
      <tr>
       <td>
         <span style="background-color: white">Rock Girl</span>
        </td>
      </tr>
      [etc.]
    </table>
    <p/>
    <table border="1" width="20%">
      <tr><th>MALE Roles</th></tr>
      <tr>
       <td>
         <span style="background-color: white">Ammon</span>
        </td>
      </tr>
      <tr>
       <td>
         <span style="background-color: white">Fisherman</span>
        </td>
      </tr>
      [etc.]
    </table>
    <p/>
  </body>
</html>
```

Whether you view this Saxon-generated XHTML result tree or look at the raw FlixML review itself, it looks like Figure 6–8 in the MSIE browser.

FEMALE Roles
Ayak
Oman
Rock Girl
Rock Mother
Sand Mother
Sanna
Ulido
Yani

MALE Roles
Ammon
Fisherman
Hunter
Hunter
Kane
Khaku
Kingsor
Tara

Figure 6-8 Two cast lists generated from the *When Dinosaurs Ruled the Earth* FlixML review, grouped by gender. This grouping effectively inverts the structure of this portion of the source tree, in which a character's gender is subordinate to the "cast category" (lead or other). In fact, the only indication of a character's lead/other status is the silver background (applied to the former).

"Advanced XSLT" #3: Validating

I've mentioned this notion a few times—that XSLT naturally lends itself to confirming that a given document does or does not meet certain criteria. Whether you use the `xsl:message` element as described in this chapter or simply an XHTML result tree, giving error messages about the document's contents is pretty straightforward.

It's so straightforward, in fact, that you might be tempted to overlook its potential power. Hidden within XSLT (particularly, within XPath) is the germ of a really *slick* "validation" mechanism.

Of course, validating XML with XPath/XSLT may seem like a pursuit for fools and madmen. You can already validate it *per se*, using a DTD, an XML Schema, or a combination of both; why would you bother adding another layer of complexity on top of those built-in, officially blessed approaches? The reason you might even think about doing so is a restatement of the Goldilocks story. DTDs just don't do enough, and Schema requires way too much effort for many purposes. You really need something, well, *just right*.

Consider one of the simplest elements that can appear in a FlixML document, `title`. Here's its declaration (including those for its attributes) in the FlixML DTD:

```
<!ELEMENT      title (#PCDATA) >
<!ATTLIST      title
  role         (main | alt) "main"
  xml:lang     NMTOKEN "EN"
  id           ID #IMPLIED>
```

I'll tell you a couple of things that have always annoyed me about this:

- The `role` attribute: As you can see, it takes a value of `main` or `alt`; and if no value is explicitly provided in a given document, the default is `main`. What's the problem? There's no way to specify in a DTD that *one and only one* `title` element has a `role` attribute whose value is `main`. A document might have only a single `title` element, with `role="alt"`; or it might have more than one `title` element with `role="main"`...even if this doesn't make a lot of sense in terms of the real *things* represented by this element and attribute.
- The ID-type attribute, `id`: When I was first learning XML, I recognized immediately (like most people) that IDs could be used for constructing intra-document tables of contents. I *really* wanted to make the IDs have fixed values for elements that can occur only once. (So the `flixinfo`

element would have `id="flixinfo"`; the `genres` element, `id="genres"`; the `cast` element, `id="cast"`; and so on.) This would mean that these intra-document targets could always be counted on to be present, even if a specific document instance omitted them. Unfortunately, the XML spec forbids assigning fixed values to ID-type attributes.

Rick Jelliffe, a member of the W3C Working Group on XML Schema, wondered about these kinds of limits to DTDs, too. Although conceding to DTDs the near-universality of their support and to XML Schema its comprehensiveness, Jelliffe came up with a nifty little just-right solution he calls *Schematron*.

Finding Schematron

The home page for all things Schematron-related is this:

```
www.ascc.net/xml/schematron/
```

This page (and the ones to which it links) provide plenty of details, tutorials, examples, and so on. Trust me, all I'm providing in this section is the tip of an iceberg.

At one level, Schematron starts out as a simple XML vocabulary consisting of a handful of elements and attributes. Their purpose is to assign a text string to each of however many conditions you want to test a document for; the conditions themselves are tested using XPath expressions of any kind. Once you've built your "Schematron file" using this vocabulary, you run it through an XSLT processor to produce an XSLT stylesheet. When you apply this stylesheet to any document marked up in whatever vocabulary your conditions test, it displays whatever things it found wrong (and, if you've coded the Schematron file this way, the things it found right as well).

Notice a couple advantages of this approach to validation versus using a DTD.

First, and maybe most obviously, you don't need to validate against a DTD at all. You can test for pretty much any condition a DTD can test for, even when the source document is simply well-formed.

Second, while validating with a DTD goes belly-up at the first sign of rebellion from a document instance, "validating" with Schematron can continue until the entire document has been checked. This makes Schematron-checking a document infinitely more productive than validating it.

The Schematron language

Here's a Schematron document to check the `role` attribute to a FlixML document's `title` elements as I described above:

```
<schema xmlns="http://www.asc.net/xml/schematron">

  <pattern name="Structures">

    <rule context="/">
      <assert test="flixinfo">Document must have a flixinfo
element</assert>
    </rule>

    <rule context="title">

      <assert test="count(.) &gt;= 1">Structural error: Your FlixML
document must have at least one <name/> element.</assert>
      <assert test="count(.) = 1 and @role[.='main']">Structural
error: Your FlixML document has one <name/> element; its role
attribute needs to have a value of 'main'.</assert>
      <assert test="count(.) &gt; 1" and count(.[@role='main']) !=
1">Structural error: Your FlixML document has multiple <name/>
elements; one and only one may have a role attribute whose value is
'main'.</assert>

    </rule>

  </pattern>

</schema>
```

The root element of a Schematron file is the `schema` element, which here simply declares the default namespace for all unprefixed elements in the document. Within a `schema` element are one or more `pattern` elements, which themselves contain one or more `rule` elements, which in turn contain any number of `assert` and `report` elements. The roles played by each of these descendants of the root `schema` are listed here:

- `pattern` elements: Each `pattern` element contains one or more related rules. You can name your `pattern` elements whatever you want, using their `name` attributes, and group their `rules` however you want as well. Typical patterns might be a set of rules for verifying the legitimacy of document structure (like the pattern above), another for verifying document contents by datatype (numeric or alphabetic, for instance), and maybe a third for verifying the actual *values* of various elements and attributes.

- `rule` elements: Each `rule` takes a `context` attribute, the value of which is an XPath expression locating some node in a source document. Note that these expressions need not be absolute; and, when they're relative, they aren't relative to anything in particular.
- `assert` elements: Within the context established by each `rule` element, an `assert` element tests (via its `test` attribute) some condition. If the result of the test is *false* when the Schematron file is applied to the document, the message whose text is contained by the `assert` element will be output.
- `report` elements: Within the context established by each `rule` element, a `report` element tests (via its `test` attribute) some condition. If the result of the test is *true* when the Schematron file is applied to the document, the message whose text is contained by the `report` element will be output. (The example above obviously contains no `report` elements.)

The above Schematron file has only one `pattern`, containing two `rules`. The first `rule` simply confirms that there's a `flixinfo` child of the root node; if not, the corresponding message is cranked out.

The second `rule` is the important one for testing the `title`'s `role` attribute. It conducts three tests—if a document fails any of them, the corresponding message is output. Note that the `assert` (and `report`) elements have mixed content models. They may contain text nodes, various simple XHTML-like elements—`p`, `emph`, `span`, and `dir`—and a special `name` element if desired, as shown in the example. The `name` element represents the name of the element being evaluated at that point and will be plugged into the message as needed. (This enables you to construct rules matching multiple element types.)

Creating and running a Schematron "validation"

You don't apply your Schematron file—the one containing all the `pattern`, `rule`, and other elements above—directly to documents. Instead, you first "compile" it into a form which may then be applied to documents.

One of the forms into which you can compile a Schematron file is an XSLT stylesheet. To do so, you run an XSLT processor against the Schematron file, using as the "stylesheet" a special so-called skeleton file. The skeleton file is an XSLT stylesheet which Jelliffe provides at the Schematron Web site and which you need to import and override—or hand-tweak—in various simple (and reasonably well-documented) ways. Once tweaked or overridden, the skeleton file drives the transformation of your Schematron file into a full-fledged XSLT stylesheet.

The skeleton file (at least in version 1.5 of Schematron, which is current as of this writing) consists of over 500 lines of XSLT code, which uses the Schematron document you've created as its source tree. Much of the work of this skeleton file would take place in named templates to process the various element types in the source tree; for example, there's a template named `process-rule`, one named `process-pattern`, and so on. These named templates are where most of your customization will occur, because they're often *empty*. For instance,

```
<xsl:template name="process-rule"/>
<xsl:template name="process-pattern"/>
```

The Schematron site includes several testing tools that demonstrate how you might perform these overrides. There's one tool, for example, that creates a framed XHTML document. In the top frame is a list of Schematron's error messages; in the bottom, a reproduction of the document (such as a FlixML review) being analyzed. The messages in the top frame are hyperlinked to specific lines of code in the bottom, so when you click on a message the lower frame "jumps" to the line of code in the source document responsible for the message.

This demonstrator (which was developed by David Carlisle) contains an override for the `process-pattern` named template:

```
<xsl:template name="process-pattern">
  <xsl:param name="icon" />
  <xsl:param name="name" />
  <xsl:param name="see" />
  <xsl:choose>
    <xsl:when test="$see">
      <a href="{$see}" target="SRDOCO"
        title="Link to User Documentation:">
        <h3 class="linked">
          <xsl:value-of select="$name" />
        </h3>
      </a>
    </xsl:when>
    <xsl:otherwise>
      <h3><xsl:value-of select="$name" /></h3>
    </xsl:otherwise>
  </xsl:choose>
  <xsl:if test="$icon"><img src="{$icon}" />
</xsl:if>
</xsl:template>
```

The `icon`, `name`, and `see` parameters are all set by the template rule in the skeleton file which calls this named template; they're the values of *attributes* to the `pattern` element in the Schematron file. As you can see from the above, in this overriding version of the `process-pattern` named template, they're used, respectively, to do the following:

- Set the value of an `img` element's `src` attribute (to the URI of an image that will appear in the result tree).
- Transfer, to a level-3 heading in the result tree, the value of the `pattern` element's `name` attribute (such as `Structures` in the Schematron document I showed you a few pages back).
- Set the value of an `a` element's `href` attribute, which will be the target of a hyperlink in the lower frame allowing you (in this case) to jump to all messages pertaining to "Structures" (per the pattern's `name` attribute).

To demonstrate how this might work, I used the Schematron document I presented earlier. I also recoded the `title` element in the *When Dinosaurs Ruled the Earth* FlixML review, so that—although still valid in the DTD's terms—it flunked the second `assert` element's test in the Schematron file's rule for processing `title` elements: If a document has only a single `title` element, its `role` attribute must have a value of `main`.

The result from this run of the Schematron process is shown in Figure 6–9.

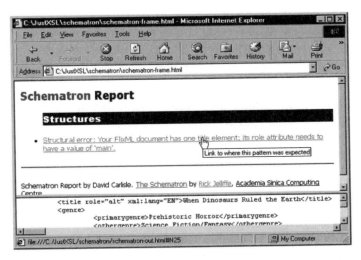

Figure 6-9   Using the Schematron "output to framed XHTML" report demonstrator, with a broken title element (lower frame). This causes the Schematron document I wrote to create the message in the upper frame; when you click on the hyperlinked message text, the lower frame scrolls to the point in the document where the error occurs. (Note the "tool-tip" label associated with the message in the top frame, which is a nice touch. This is set by the Schematron demonstrator itself, developed by David Carlisle.)

How Do I...
Transform a document for use with the Open eBook standard?

The Open eBook standard—developed by a consortium of software vendors, publishers, non-profit groups, and others—is an XML-based markup language for containing a book's contents in ways that can be rendered on PDAs and other hand-held devices, specialized eBook readers, desktop and other computers, even Web browsers.

Transforming documents from your own XML vocabulary to OEB (as I'll refer to it) isn't that great a challenge if you've stuck with me this far. That's because OEB is based on XHTML, which is the result-tree vocabulary I've used in almost all of *Just XSL*'s examples to this point. There are h1, p, and div elements, for example, and the "look" of an eBook's page is constrained using CSS. The XHTML-based OEB language is referred to as "basic OEB."

But like I said, OEB is *based on* XHTML, it's not a clone of it. Some features of the Web-page language have been dropped, either because they're unsuitable for these kinds of output devices or because there are better, CSS-based alternatives.

The other main difference with XHTML is that all the familiar XHTML markup which has been retained in basic OEB is used for only a part of an OEB "publication." This is the marking up of the book's text, chapter titles, and so on—arguably the most important part, of course. But there's another, separate vocabulary for describing the publication as a whole. This XML code goes into a completely separate file, called the package. (More formally, it's referred to as the OPF: Open eBook Package File. This file is supposed to have a filename extension of .opf as well, although hard-wired filename extensions seem more an indication of ties to the Microsoft Windows world than of "openness.")

The package file

What goes into an OEB package file are elements and attributes *about* the data contained in an entire publication, which may consist of more than one basic OEB document. This information includes some descriptive elements, a list of all the files which make up the publication, a list of the sequencing of those files, something like a table of contents, and optional "tours" which can be used to lead a reader (prospective or otherwise) through one or more customized views of the contents.

The root element of the package file is package. It has three required children:

- metadata: Descendants of this element include various labels and descriptors, such as the publication's title, its "creator" (author), publisher, and so on.
- manifest: This element's contents list all the basic OEB documents, image files, and so on, which the publication comprises.
- spine: Here's where you spell out the order in which the publication's contents are normally read through.

For instance, a package file for an OEB anthology of B-movie reviews might look something like this:

```
<package unique-identifier="FromBToB">

  <metadata>
     xmlns:dc="http://purl.org/dc/elements/1.0/">
     <dc-metadata
     <dc:Title>From B to B: Second-Tier Movie Reviews</dc:Title>
     <dc:Identifier id="FromBToB"
       scheme="FlixMLTitle">From_B_to_B</dc:Identifier>
     <dc:Creator role="aut"
       file-as="Simpson, John E.">John E. Simpson</dc:Creator>
     <dc:Date>2001</dc:date>
   </dc-metadata>
  </metadata>

  <manifest>
   <item id="foreword" href="foreword.html"
     media-type="text/x-oeb1-document"/>
   <item id="cagedheat" href="cagedheat.html"
     media-type="text/x-oeb1-document"/>
   <item id="crisscross" href="crisscross.html"
     media-type="text/x-oeb1-document"/>
   <item id="dinos_earth" href="dinos_earth.html"
     media-type="text/x-oeb1-document"/>
   <item id="contents" href="toc.html"
     media-type="text/x-oeb1-document"/>
   <item id="cover" href="cover.html"
     media-type="text/x-oeb1-document"/>
   <item id="bees4" href="bees4_0.jpg"
```

```
      media-type="image/jpeg"/>
    <item id="bees45" href="bees4_5.jpg"
      media-type="image/jpeg"/>
    <item id="stylesheet" href="flixml_in_html.css"
      type="text/x-oeb1-css"/>
  </manifest>

  <spine>
    <itemref idref="cover"/>
    <itemref idref="contents"/>
    <itemref idref="foreword"/>
    <itemref idref="crisscross"/>
    <itemref idref="dinos_earth"/>
    <itemref idref="cagedheat"/>
  </spine>

</package>
```

Most of this should be pretty straightforward and easy to understand. The following are some things to note in particular about it:

- The `dc-metadata` child of the `metadata` element declares a namespace associated with the `dc:` prefix. This namespace is that of the so-called Dublin Core initiative, which is a (yet another) consortium of organizations with an interest in standardizing the ways in which "data about data" can be represented. (The term *metadata* is generally defined as "data about data.") The children of this `dc-metadata` element are all elements as defined by Dublin Core.

- The `manifest` portion of the package doesn't simply list the URIs of the publication's content. It also assigns to each an ID-type attribute and gives its media (MIME) type. Aside from the basic OEB documents (which have a media type of `text/x-oeb1-document`), a publication can include various other kinds of content, such as JPEG and PNG images. If there's a CSS stylesheet to be used with the publication, it's assigned a media type (as you can see above) of `text/x-oeb1-css`.

- The `spine` element's `itemref` children appear in the order in which the publication is typically read. Each `itemref` element has an `idref` attribute, which points back to the `id` attribute of some `item` element in the `manifest`. Images and the stylesheet don't appear in the spine. (If an image from the `manifest` is needed in a particular OEB document, its presence is simply signaled with an `img` element, just as in XHTML. The stylesheet is associated with a document just as a CSS stylesheet is normally associated with an XHTML element: by way of a `link` element in the document's `head`.)

"Publishing" an OEB publication

So far, little software seems to exist for reading raw OPF and basic OEB documents *per se*. Instead, you have to process them through a software application that "compiles" them into a binary or other form readable by a particular type of device, such as an Open eBook reader, a PDA, and so on. These compiled forms of the contents are not portable across devices; you've got to compile the publication once for each desired device type.

Now, I don't own a PDA, eBook reader, or whatever.[7] Luckily, there are a number of free "emulators" for such devices, as well as free (or evaluation versions of) software to *publish* (that is, compile) eBooks from their raw XML-based OPF and basic OEB formats to one device's format or another.

A reasonably good example of the latter is the MobiPocket Publisher. It's capable of compiling OEB documents to the Palm OS format (for PalmPilot and Handspring PDAs), to Windows CE (for PDAs based on that operating system from Microsoft), and to Microsoft Reader format (for eBooks readable on a Windows-based PC).

MobiPocket Publisher (at least Version 3.0, which is what I'm using here) doesn't seem to handle all the features of the OPF file format; and those it does use sometimes have little "gotchas" that aren't always obviously resolvable.

After you've built your OPF through the package's user interface (which ensures that you'll use only those features the MobiPocket supports), you see the manifest portion of the OPF, like the one shown in Figure 6–10. (Note that this is actually like a combined manifest/spine view, since the contents of this publication are actually read in the order in which they appear in the manifest.)

Note in Figure 6–10 the button along the top labeled "Publish…" Clicking this button gives you a choice of publishing (compiling) to one of the various PDA-readable forms or to the Microsoft Reader form (referred to as "LIT files,"

---

7.   Yeah, I know. Last of the Philistines.

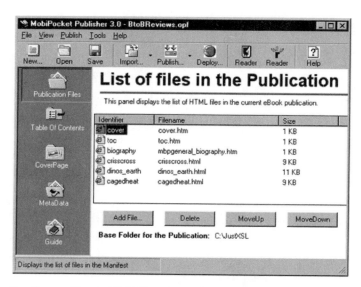

Figure 6-10   An Open eBook OPF file, viewed with MobiPocket Publisher. All the contents here are XHTML files of one kind or another, which means you must have transformed your raw XML to XHTML before getting to this point. Also note that this "manifest" doesn't include images or a stylesheet. If you try to add them, using the Add File…button, MobiPocket will allow it; however, if you then try to *compile* the OPF file to a real device-readable eBook file, you get one or another of various unpleasant error messages.

after their filenames' extension, which is .lit). I chose to publish my "B to B Reviews" anthology to a LIT file. Figure 6–11 shows the "cover" of the resulting eBook.

Figure 6–12 shows you page 1 of the document itself—a title page. Because these documents are XHTML, they're easily edited to include features like the image shown here.

Finally, Figure 6–13 shows you a page from one of the reviews contained by the book. Although the OEB standard is based on XHTML *and* uses CSS for styling, it—or at least MobiPocket Publisher's compile step and/or Microsoft's LIT format—doesn't honor all the markup and styles you think you may have specified in your transformation from XML to OEB.

Figure 6-11 Cover of an eBook published by MobiPocket Publisher. Supposedly there's a way to customize the cover *image*, which by default is a kind of dark red, leatherish-looking texture appearing here as the border down the left edge. Supposedly. I still haven't figured out how to make that happen, though.

Figure 6-12 An eBook component (cover.htm, according to the manifest shown in Figure 6–10) including an image. Ugly observation: The publication's title as it appears here ("B to B Reviews") doesn't match its title as it appeared in Figure 6–11 ("BtoB Reviews"). That's because the title isn't automatically controlled by MobiPocket Publisher: You have to enter it twice, with all the chances for error that implies.

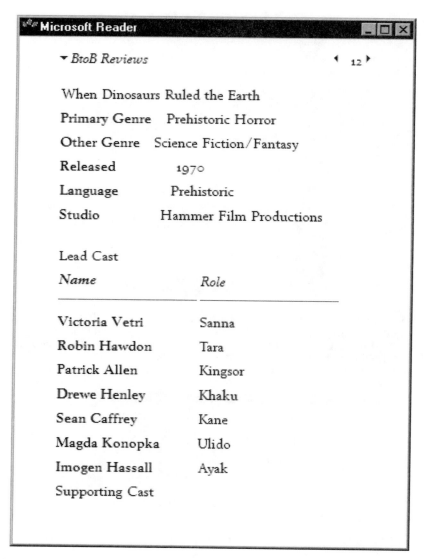

Figure 6-13   A single page of a FlixML review, as seen in Microsoft Reader following the "compile" from MobiPocket Publisher. Note the rather wavery layout of the table (Primary Genre, Other Genre, etc.) at the top—not exactly an attractive "table," is it? Also, although the CSS for this page specifies that section headings (like "Lead Cast," here) will display in a shaded box, in all lowercase letters, this doesn't translate well to the OEB format. Compare this view with a Web browser's view of the same XHTML file (shown in Figure 6–14).

When Dinosaurs Ruled the Earth

Primary Genre	Prehistoric Horror
Other Genre	Science Fiction/Fantasy
Released	1970
Language	Prehistoric
Studio	Hammer Film Productions

lead cast

Name	*Role*
Victoria Vetri	Sanna
Robin Hawdon	Tara
Patrick Allen	Kingsor
Drewe Henley	Khaku

Figure 6-14　A portion of the same XHTML file shown in Figure 6–13 in its MobiPocket-"compiled" form within Microsoft Reader; shown here within the MSIE browser window. Maybe it's unfair to compare the behavior of a CSS-smart browser to the behavior of software supporting the first version of the OEB standard.

CHAPTER 7

Getting There:
XSLT Software

I've been implicitly demonstrating XSLT software all along; no surprise there. But it's time to put the spotlight on *the tools available* to support your "doing XSLT," rather than on the doing-XSLT itself.

Even while I was working on *Just XML*'s second edition, in mid-2000, the state of XSLT software was promising but still a little rough around the edges. It (most of it) was like a newborn bird or mammal in one of those animal-channel cable TV documentaries: still a little wet, staggering and crashing into objects and walls, blinking its eyes as if to say, "Where the heck *am* I?" Of course, at that point the ink was still drying on version 1.0 of the XSLT standard itself, so the tool makers could hardly be blamed. But in the time since then, XSLT software has really burgeoned into something like late adolescence or early adulthood.[1]

The good news is that this gives me lots of choices for what to cover in this chapter. The bad news, needless to say, is that there's no way I can cover it all.

This chapter is broken into two main sections. The first covers XSLT software you use locally, on a desktop computer or workstation, even if the software is housed and actually running on some remote machine. (I'll call this client-side software—not to imply that you *must* at some point consider doing server-

---

1.   As with human adolescents, XSLT software runs the gamut from functionally adult at the top end, to blunderingly immature at the bottom.... And with that, maybe it's a good idea to say farewell to *this* metaphor.

side as well, but simply to contrast it with serving live XSLT transformations to others.) Products in this category include XPath utilities, XSLT editors/ authoring aids, processors, and client-side browser support for XML-to-XHTML transformations.

The second section takes a brief look at some of the options available in processing XSLT transformations on a Web server. Given the nature of the beast, of course, this will pretty much be limited to XML-to-XHTML transforms.

Regardless of which packages I show here, be aware that there are plenty of others available. Also don't forget that I'm not writing a user manual or even providing a list of all of each product's features; my intention is just to give you a feel for the general state of the art.

Where to get them

Whether you're an application developer, an application user, or somewhere in between, the easiest way to locate XPath and XSLT software is by way of one of the common directories of XML software, including XPath/XSLT categories as well as others. Probably the most popular directories are these:

www.xmlsoftware.com: One of James Tauber's array of XML-related sites, this one (obviously) focuses on software. Select from the menu the specific category in which you're interested. Each category has its own Web page, and each product listed on the page includes a capsule description and links to the vendor's own site, to the product's specific page on the vendor's site, and/or to an email address for more information.

www.xml.com: This is a terrific place to begin learning about almost anything XML. (And it was that way long before I started contributing a monthly column, and it will be that way for long afterwards.) For software, begin at the page that heads the "resource guide," www.xml.com/resourceguide, and work your way down through the category in which you're interested.

Robin Cover's "XML Cover Pages": The root of the site is xml.coverpages.org. Nearly everything anyone has ever said about XML, for public consumption anyway—on the Web, in mailing lists and newsgroups, in print—seems to be indexed here, and the site is updated daily (sometimes even more often). Follow the "Software" link for information on specific categories, including product release announcements, links to vendors' pages, and so on.

Client-Side XSLT

Much of the attention XSLT has gotten is misleading: It's based on the narrow-minded notion that XML is meant to replace HTML. In this view, XSLT is useful mostly—even solely—as a means of turning your XML into Web-viewable markup. I hope you, at least, don't suffer from that misapprehension. Except for the last topic in this section ("Web browser support for XSLT"), I will address products that can be used with XPath and XSLT *regardless* of the result tree's vocabulary.

The Microsoft effect

A number of the products in this section owe their existence to Microsoft's release of its MSXML 3.0 XML/XSLT processor in October 2000—or rather, not just to that processor's release but to its *availability*. Because developers can easily use it within applications developed for the Windows environment, and of course because of the high XML/XSLT interest factor, developers have flocked to it.

Although I use Microsoft's application and development products in my everyday work and greatly appreciate how easy it is to make any one of these products integrate with another, I confess that I've got grave reservations about recommending them as the solution to fit all problems. But MSXML 3.0 is a terrific product by almost every measure: the ease of embedding it within Windows applications, its compliance with the standard, and its speed.

It has two severe drawbacks, neither of which is likely to change anytime soon. First, of course, it runs *only* under Windows. This puts it out of reach of a substantial audience who can't or won't run the Microsoft OS. Second, in the context in which most users will experience MSXML (that is, within the MSIE browser), it transforms only to (X)HTML—and that, only "virtually."

What that means is, you don't conclude an MSXML-in-MSIE transformation with a physical document containing the result tree; the result tree is just an in-memory representation of the result tree as displayed by the browser. Of course, with a little work on your part, you can then write this or any other result tree out to an actual document; but that capability isn't built into MSIE, where any result-tree vocabulary other than XHTML is of little use.

I'll cover MSXML more specifically in the sub-sections on XSLT processors and XSLT support in Web browsers. Just understand that if an application is Windows-based, and Windows-based *only*, it's almost certainly using MSXML under the hood.

XPath utilities

XPath is a strange little standard. Although critically important to certain other standards, it's not useful on its own. (If XSLT is the language you're speaking, XPath might be considered the *voice*.)

Most of the software that falls into the XPath utilities category thus isn't generally meant to be run in standalone mode. Rather, it's meant to provide "XPath awareness" at the application level. For example, if a Perl developer needs to tease out the meaning of an XPath expression, there's little sense in building her own module to do so if she can use Matt Sergeant's XML::XPATH instead. Likewise, developers using Python can fall back on FourThought's 4XPath library; and those using PHP can rely on Michael P. Mehl's phpXML class.

If you're not an application developer, but simply want to see the effects (say) of one form of an XPath expression versus another, you're not necessarily shut out of the action. A handful of tools are in the category of XPath *visualizers*—visually highlighting in some way the node(s) addressed by a particular XPath expression. In the sections following, I'll cover a couple of these tools.

XPath Tool

Developed by Khun Yee Fung in support of his book, *XSLT: Working with XML and HTML* (Addison-Wesley, December 2000), this Java/Swing tool can be downloaded from its creator's Web site at www.wireoptional.com/XML/xslt.html. The low version number (0.3 as of this writing) might lead you to believe that the product is tentative and prone to crashing, but that doesn't seem to be the case at all.

Indeed, at first the only challenge in using it is figuring out just what it does. Figure 7–1 shows you the main XPath Tool window, with the *Criss Cross* FlixML review loaded and a couple of selections made. What's going on here?

Not much, in fact, is going on at this point. We can see a document tree, and the next two sub-windows to its right show something mysteriously called the "Syntax Tree" and (probably a bit more intuitively understood) the "Context Tree." Both of these sub-windows refer to the document root at this point, which should make sense. We haven't actually navigated anywhere in the document yet, simply opened it up. The main thing *you* need to do to get the *package* to do something meaningful is to enter an XPath expression in the area immediately above the document tree.

Figures 7–2a through 7–2d show the effects of doing so.

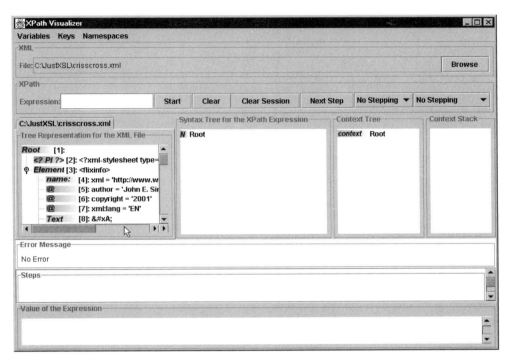

Figure 7-1 The "XPath Tool" Java-based XPath visualizer. So far, all I've done is load an XML document (the *Criss Cross* review, from earlier in the book) whose content I'm interested in accessing via XPath. Consequently, most of the window is still empty. The document tree is shown (in collapsible/expandable form) in the little sub-window to the left, pointed to by the cursor in this screen shot. (Note that all the nodes are numbered, including the newline—the text node, value
, shown here as node number 8— which follows the flixinfo element's start tag. Namespace nodes are identified with the keyword "name:" and attribute nodes, with an "@" character.) Other sub-windows will acquire contents as we work with the tool.

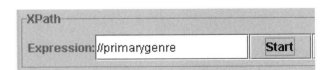

Figure 7-2a Simply typing an XPath expression into the appropriate text field and clicking the Start button kicks off an XPath Tool session. This has no effect on the document tree window originally opened with the document itself (after all, the document tree doesn't change when you simply locate something in it). But it does have an effect on some other portions of the XPath Tool window, as shown in the following figures.

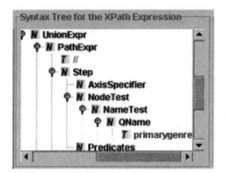

Figure 7-2b   The sub-window or pane immediately to the right of the document tree now displays an expandable/collapsible "syntax tree," at the bottom level of which is the result—so far—of the XPath expression. The tree view represents an Extended Backus-Naur Format (EBNF) view of the XPath expression—that is, a formal statement of everything in the XPath expression to this point.

Figure 7-2c   The "Context Tree" pane has also changed, subtly. Instead of just showing the root node, it's now added a namespace node (pointing back to node #4 in the document tree pane) to show that "where we are" as a result of this XPath expression is being assessed in terms not just of the document root but also of the indicated namespace node.

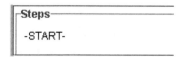

Figure 7-2d   The "Steps" pane near the bottom of the XPath Tool window simply shows that we've hit the Start button. XPath Tool can be used as a "stepping XPath visualizer"—that is, it can evaluate an XPath expression a little bit at a time.

If you'd prefer, you can select from the pick lists at the right of the XPath Tool window, enabling you to step through the XPath expression you've entered. For instance, you can change the XPath expression as shown in Figure 7–3a, using values selected as in Figure 7–3b, and every time you hit the "Next Step" button a new leaf is added to the Syntax Tree pane (as shown in Figure 7–3c, after advancing three steps into the tree); when you're not doing stepping, the Syntax Tree pane opens the entire EBNF syntax tree at once, expanded all the way to its lowermost leaf.

Figure 7-3a   Adding a bit of a spin to the XPath expression entered earlier…

Figure 7-3b   …and selecting "stepping" options rather than the "no stepping" defaults…

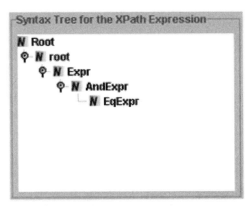

Figure 7-3c   …permits walking through the XPath expression, a fragment of EBNF at a time.

XPath Tool, I have to say, isn't the best-documented tool I've ever seen— not by a long shot. The "readme" file that comes with the download tells you how to install and run it; however, it doesn't explain any of the options, like what to expect different areas of the main window will contain or how they'll behave (especially when you interact with other areas of it). The author's Web site doesn't offer any additional explanation; perhaps you have to consult his book (which I don't have) in order to learn the software's secrets.

On the other hand, it's free, the source is openly available, and if you need to understand EBNF—the language in which not only XPath but also XSLT, XSL-FO, and even XML itself are formally defined—it's probably just the ticket.

XPath Visualizer

Dimitre Novatchev's Windows-based package is available from the VBXML site for developers of Visual Basic/XML applications—at www.vbxml. com/downloads/files/xpathvisualiserseptember.zip. Of course, it requires the use of Windows and the MSXML processor—and the Internet Explorer browser. That's because this application is really a combination of (X)HTML pages and JavaScript code which invokes MSXML in various ways to interpret the XPath expression you're interested in. Figure 7–4 shows the main XPath Visualizer window.

Figure 7-4 XPath Visualizer's main window. This is an HTML frameset with a large, scrollable frame at the bottom, where the source code of the XML document (the *Caged Heat* FlixML review, here) appears. Text fields and buttons at the top of the form let you select an XML document, enter an XPath expression, etc. All nodes in the document which match the XPath expression are highlighted in yellow; nodes which do not match still appear in the scrollable area, but aren't highlighted. The package also tells you how many nodes in the document match (all 90 element nodes in the document here, of course, matching the expression "//*"—the default when a document is first loaded).

If you enter a specific expression in the text field to override the default of //*, and hit the "Select Nodes" button, all non-matching nodes are deselected; any that match are highlighted, as shown in Figure 7–5.

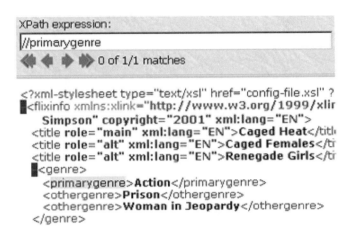

Figure 7-5 Entering a specific XPath expression through the XPath Visualizer interface deselects all nodes but those that match. (That is, in this case, it deselects all but the document's sole `primarygenre` element.)

Element nodes aren't the only kind of nodes you might want to select, of course; Figure 7–6 demonstrates that you can enter XPath expressions as complicated as you want, in this case with the objective of locating all *attributes* of all descendants of the `cast` element (which, in turn, is located by way of the `primary-genre` element).

Figure 7-6 Results of jazzing up the XPath expression from Figure 7–5, to locate some other nodes (attributes, in this case) relative to the node selected by that earlier expression. As you can see from the message area below the XPath expression field itself, there are 12 nodes that match this condition. But what does the "0 of 12" portion of this message mean? See the text.

```
◀◀ ◀ ▶ ▶▶ 1 of 12/12 matches

 -<genre>
    <primarygenre>Action</primarygenre>
    <othergenre>Prison</othergenre>
    <othergenre>Woman in Jeopardy</othergenre>
  </genre>
  <releaseyear role="initial">1974</releaseyear>
  <language>English</language>
  <studio>New World Pictures</studio>
 <cast id="castID">
   <leadcast>
    -<female id="EGavin">
       <castmember>Erica Gavin</castmember>
       <role>Jacqueline Wilson</role>
```

Figure 7-7   Selecting the "next matching node" when you've started from Figure 7–6's "0 of 12" changes the display subtly. The label changes to indicate "1 of 12," and this attribute and its value are now highlighted in lavender. All the other matching nodes (like id="EGavin" here) are still highlighted in yellow, however.[2]

You may have noticed the little left- and right-pointing arrows just below the XPath expression's text entry field. These are used for moving back and forth among the selected nodes; the four arrows add extra highlighting to the first, previous, next, and last nodes in the selected node-set, respectively. For instance, when you start out with the "0 of 12" nodes shown in Figure 7–6 and click on the "next" arrow, you see a result like that shown in Figure 7–7.

---

2.   I'm not particularly crazy about XPath Visualizer's default color scheme—especially when trying to do screen captures for a book printed in black and white (ahem). For the screen shots here I've changed only the background color, from a kind of aqua blue to plain old white. Changing the look of the display requires that you edit the myDefaultss70.xsl stylesheet which comes with the download; be sure to save a backup copy before doing so, as changing the wrong line, or the right one in the wrong way, will make the tool pretty much unusable!

XSLT editors/authoring tools

Deciding what to use to create XSLT stylesheets can be a simple subset of a larger question: What do you want to use to create XML documents in general? After all, if you've found a tool you like to use for authoring XML Vocabulary A (whatever A is), it's probably just as good for authoring XSLT.

The most important consideration is that you want an editor or authoring aid which knows the XSLT vocabulary. At a bare minimum, this means it won't let you insert into the stylesheet any elements using the `xsl:` prefix *other* than those which indeed belong to the XSLT vocabulary. Better, you want a tool which will allow you to use legal elements only in legal contexts. For example, given that `xsl:template` is a top-level element only, you don't want to be able to use it as a child of any element other than `xsl:stylesheet`.

Best of all would be a tool which not only controls what you can enter into the stylesheet when editing it but also helps you confirm that the result tree will be as expected (using some arbitrary document as the source tree).

In the next sections, I'll take a look at a couple examples of this last level of support.

XSLT context-aware editing with XML Spy

XML Spy, from Altova, is one of the best-selling commercial XML source editors. It runs on Windows platforms and allows you to do all the usual sorts of GUI-based operations to manipulate a source document. You can also switch to a raw text-based editing mode, if that's your preference.

Figure 7–8 depicts the XML Spy 3.5 window, with a portion of the FlixML review of *When Dinosaurs Ruled the Earth* opened in the main pane.

With a source document open, when you pull down the XSL menu at the top of the window you have three choices, as shown in Figure 7–9.

If you opt to view/edit the stylesheet, a second "main pane" opens over the source document pane itself. Initially, this is a raw, editable source view, which you can edit however you want just as if you were in an XSLT-ignorant text editor. A more foolproof approach is to switch to the so-called Enhanced Grid view—the same one employed by default to edit the XML source document itself. When you do so, you see something like what's shown in Figure 7–10.

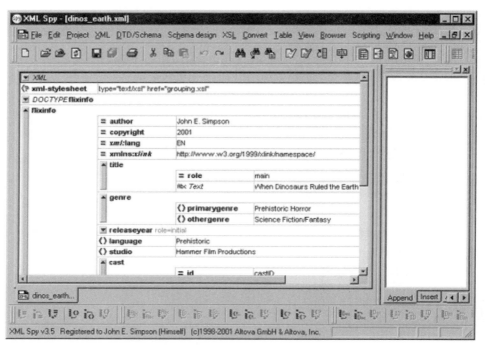

Figure 7-8 A FlixML review opened from within XML Spy. Note, per the `xml-stylesheet` PI at the top of the main pane, that this document is currently associated with a stylesheet called grouping.xsl. (This is the stylesheet used to demonstrate grouping as one of the "advanced XSLT" techniques in Chapter 6.)

Figure 7-9 XML Spy lets you do three things with an XSLT stylesheet and an open source document: (a) You can apply to the source the stylesheet with which it's already associated, via its `xml-stylesheet` PI. (b) You can associate a stylesheet with the document (which will replace the `xml-stylesheet` PI with another one). Or (c) You can select the "Go to XSL" option (highlighted here) to view and/or edit the stylesheet itself.

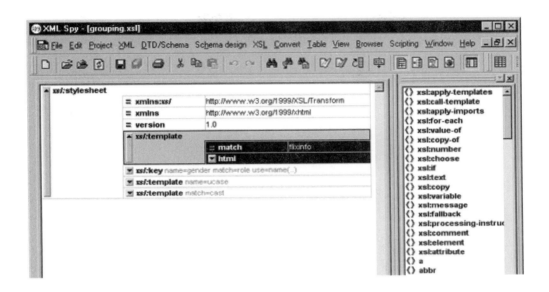

Figure 7-10 Enhanced Grid" view of the grouping.xsl XSLT stylesheet. Note that an `xsl:template` element is currently selected in the main pane. The narrow pane to the right shows you the elements you can add here, as children of the selected element. There are no top-level XSLT elements visible in this scrolling list, which is as it should be; you should *not* be allowed, for example, to add an `xsl:import` as a child of an `xsl:template`. As you can see, there are also elements in the list from the one *result-tree* vocabulary XML Spy knows about: (X)HTML. The product's not quite so clever about these elements. For instance, if you select the `html` element in the main pane, the list at the right includes not only all XSLT elements (including `xsl:import`, `xsl:stylesheet`, and so on) but all the same ones from the (X)HTML namespace— including the `html` element itself.

With the source document open, if you pull down the XSL menu and select XSL Transformation (or just click the F10 key), a different pane opens. This is, effectively, a mini-browser window—the browser, unsurprisingly, being MSIE. Figure 7–11 shows you how this pane looks when transforming the *When Dinosaurs Ruled the Earth* review to XHTML, using the grouping.xsl stylesheet. Looks a lot like Figure 6–8, doesn't it?

Given the "XSL Output" pane shown in Figure 7–11, you might be curious how XML Spy handles result trees in vocabularies other than XHTML. I can say this: It handles them. Not optimally, but it works...sort of.

Figure 7-11   XML Spy's "mini-MSIE" pane for the current transformation.

For instance, you could change the `xml-stylesheet` PI (manually, or using the "Assign XSL..." menu choice as shown in Figure 7–9) to point to one of the stylesheets from Part 2 of this book, which transform FlixML documents to XSL-FO documents. The mini-MSIE pane in XML Spy doesn't know quite what to make of this, as you can see in Figure 7–12. It's equipped to deal with the presentation elements from the XHTML namespace, not from any other.

XML Spy 3.5 retails for $199 per single-user license, from its Web site at www.xmlspy.com. A free but time-limited (30 days) evaluation version is also available.

XSLT stylesheet generation with XSLWiz

Depending on your perspective and needs, the approach taken by EBProvider's XSLWiz 2.0 product is either exactly the right way to go or an enormously painful solution to a painful problem. (The same debate swirls around the Frankenstein monster.) By any measure, though, it must be counted as extremely interesting.

XSLWiz attempts to insulate the user entirely from a need to know XSLT code. The general idea is that you feed it information about your source and result trees' structures, then use a GUI-based drag-and-drop approach to establish connections between the two trees. (This may recall for you the illustration of the backyard-burger-flipper-to-executioner transformation way back in Chapter 1.

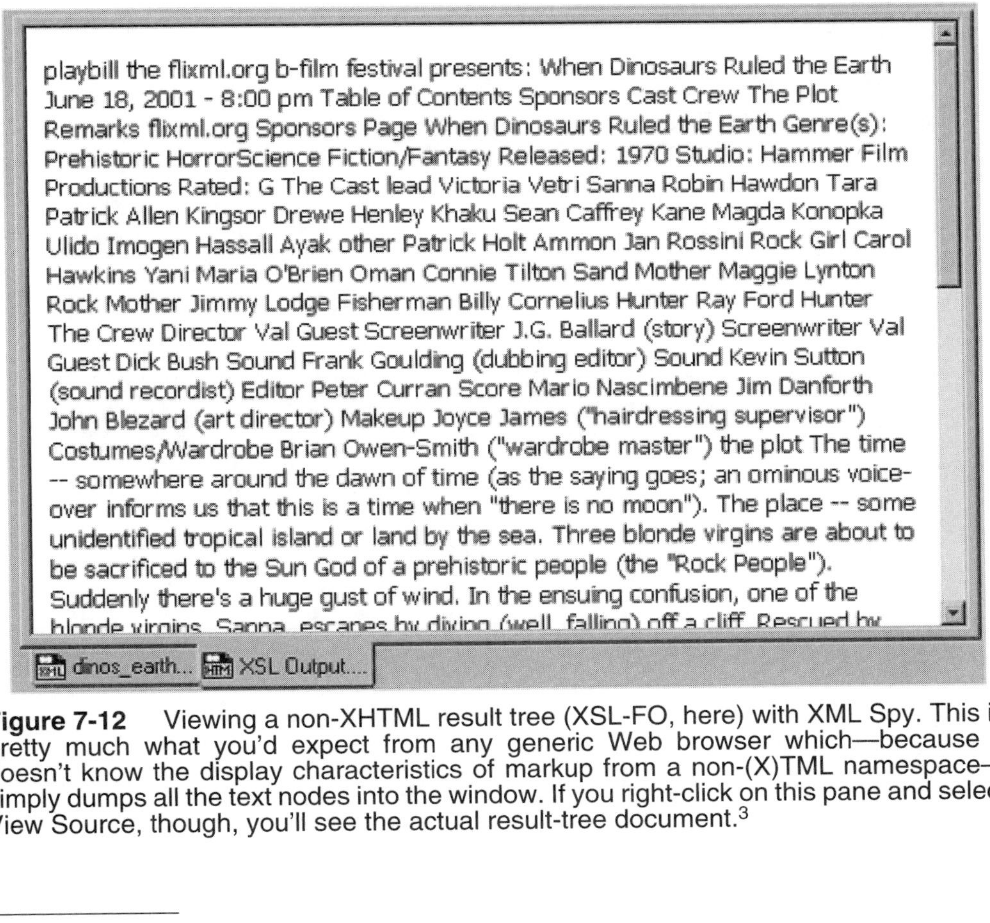

Figure 7-12 Viewing a non-XHTML result tree (XSL-FO, here) with XML Spy. This is pretty much what you'd expect from any generic Web browser which—because it doesn't know the display characteristics of markup from a non-(X)TML namespace—simply dumps all the text nodes into the window. If you right-click on this pane and select View Source, though, you'll see the actual result-tree document.[3]

---

3.   However, if your XSLT stylesheet does not specify the result tree's encoding, XML Spy seems to assume UTF-16—that is, with each character represented in two bytes instead of the more common (in Western languages) UTF-8's single-byte representation. If you are viewing the source in a UTF-16-ignorant application, this makes the document look extremely strange—every character is followed by a space.

You provide information about the source and result trees in any of a variety of ways. You can feed XSLWiz the DTDs for the two vocabularies, you can feed it their XML Schemas, or you can feed it two actual documents and let XSL-Wiz infer the corresponding structures. (You can also mix-and-match—using the DTD of the source tree and a sample result document, for instance.)

I experimented with XSLWiz to try generating a stylesheet to transform FlixML to XHTML. Of course I had the FlixML DTD handy, and I downloaded the XHTML 1.0 Transitional DTD from the W3C Web site. (XSLWiz seems to accept only local files as input—not URIs.) I immediately got into trouble.

First, some odd little glitch in the program kept insisting that I hadn't loaded a valid document. This glitch popped up no matter whether I tried loading actual documents or DTDs, or mixing-and-matching. Eventually, somehow, I got it to stop whining about this imagined problem. Second, the program has some kind of limit that I seemed to be exceeding—complaining there were too many "mappings" between the source and result, even when I'd connected only one element from one tree to one element from the other.

Now, the tutorial that comes with XSLWiz includes what to me is extremely simple sample input—two XML documents, each consisting of just a handful of elements. So I scaled my expectations way back and created two stripped-down sample documents of my own. First, there was a mini-mini-FlixML review:

```
<flixinfo>
  <author>John E. Simpson</author>
  <title>Carnival of Souls</title>
  <genre>Horror</genre>
</flixinfo>
```

Then there was a mini-mini-XHTML document to be used as the sample result tree:

```
<html>
  <head>
    <title>author</title>
  </head>
  <body>
    <h1>title</h1>
    <h2>genre</h2>
    <h3>language</h3>
```

```
    </body>
</html>
```

The actual element content in this sample result document is immaterial; I've used the content here just so you can see how I planned to connect the two trees. Note that there wasn't a one-to-one correspondence between the two, either. For instance, what's the source of the result tree's `h3` element? It's not available from this source tree.

After laying that groundwork, I used XSLWiz to start a new "project" (as a given source-to-result mapping is called). I identified the two source files as part of the project; what I had at this point appears here as Figure 7–13.

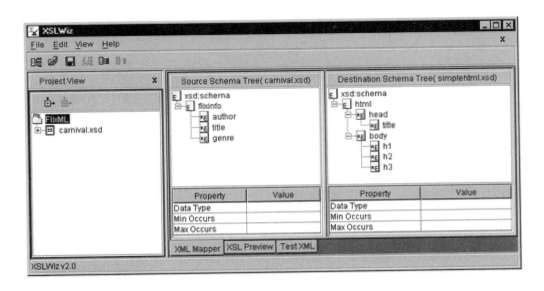

Figure 7-13 The start of generating a (greatly simplified) FlixML-to-XHTML XSLT stylesheet with XSLWiz. I've expanded the two trees, source and result (called "destination" by XSLWiz), so you can see all their elements available for mapping. Among the most interesting things this illustrates—see the file names at the top of the source and result "schema tree" panes?—is that no matter what kind of input you actually feed it, XSLWiz always works from XML Schemas. My input was two sample XML document instances, but I somehow ended up with .xsd files (their assumed schemas). This suggests that, even if I can't get XSLWiz to generate a useful XSLT stylesheet, I can still use it to generate at least the skeleton of an XML Schema!

The connections—mappings—between source and result are accomplished by selecting a node from the source tree and dragging-and-dropping it to a node in the result. When I'd done this for my sample data and made the mappings visible (they aren't shown, by default), I had something that looked like Figure 7–14.

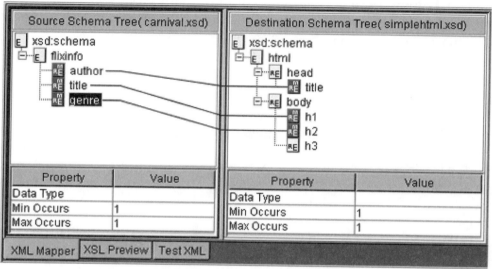

Figure 7-14   Mapping source to result tree nodes using XSLWiz. In constructing the XML Schema corresponding to the sample documents (as described in the caption for Figure 7–13), XSLWiz isn't a mind-reader: It can extrapolate only so much from a limited sample. Here, with the genre element selected on one side and the h2 element selected on the other, XSLWiz (per the property boxes at the bottom) has determined that the genre element can occur once and only once in a FlixML source tree, and that an h2 element in the result is also limited to a single occurrence.

To actually create the XSLT to accomplish the transformation, XSLWiz does not provide a "transform it!" button or menu command. You just select the "XSL Preview" tab below the source tree, at which point you see a pane containing the XSLT code. Well—as you can see in Figure 7–15—at least, you see that in theory.

So I went back to the "XML Mapper" tab. There was no content *in* the source tree to map to the orphaned h3 in the result, which may have been a problem. However, XSLWiz also includes something called the Funclet Wizard. This little pop-up dialogue (see Figure 7–16) lets you operate on literal strings and numeric values and/or concatenate, substring, and perform other functions on pieces of the source tree. In Figure 7–16, I'm attempting to convince XSLWiz to map a simple text string (the word "English") to the h3 element.

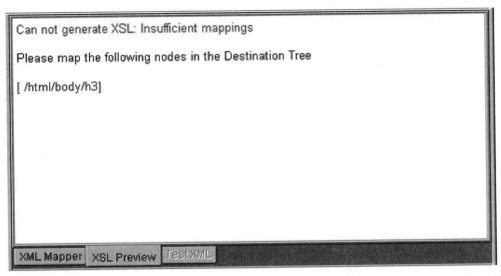

Figure 7-15 Result of the first-cut mapping between the sample source and result trees. Whoops. Looks like I'll need to back up and map that stray h3 element after all.

Now the generation of XSLT worked just fine. When I clicked on the "XSL Preview" this time, I was greeted with the following code (extra newlines added for clarity):

```
<?xml version="1.0" ?>
<!--Generated by XSLWiz, the XSLT generator from EBProvider Inc.-->

  <xsl:stylesheet
    xmlns:xsl="http://www.w3.org/1999/XSL/Transform"
    version = "1.0">

  <xsl:template match = "/">

    <xsl:variable name = "title_2_var1"
      select = "/flixinfo/author"/>
    <xsl:variable name = "title_2_position_var1"
      select = "position()"/>
    <xsl:variable name = "h1_3_var1"
      select = "$title_2_var1/ancestor-or-self::flixinfo/title"/>
    <xsl:variable name = "h1_3_position_var1"
      select = "position()"/>
    <xsl:variable name = "h2_3_var1"
      select = "$title_2_var1/ancestor-or-self::flixinfo/genre"/>
```

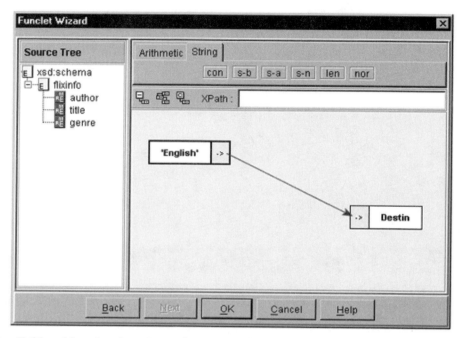

Figure 7-16   Mapping (or attempting to map!) a literal string to a result-tree node. An earlier step in the Funclet Wizard let me select the result-tree node in question.

```
<xsl:variable name = "h2_3_position_var1"
  select = "position()"/>

<xsl:element name = "html">

  <xsl:element name = "head">
   <xsl:element name = "title">
    <xsl:value-of select = "$title_2_var1"/>
   </xsl:element>
  </xsl:element>

  <xsl:element name = "body">

   <xsl:element name = "h1">
    <xsl:value-of select = "$h1_3_var1"/>
   </xsl:element>

   <xsl:element name = "h2">
    <xsl:value-of select = "$h2_3_var1"/>
```

```
      </xsl:element>

      <xsl:element name = "h3">
        <xsl:value-of select = "'English'"/>
      </xsl:element>

    </xsl:element>

  </xsl:element>

  </xsl:template>

</xsl:stylesheet>
```

This might not be the way you or I would code the transformation—encapsulating it all within a single `xsl:template` element—but it does work. There's even a feature built into XSLWiz which lets you confirm this for yourself: the "Test XML" tab at the bottom of the main (schema tree) window. When you select this tab, you provide XSLWiz with the name of a sample document; it feeds the document through the generated transformation to a result tree, as shown in Figure 7–17.

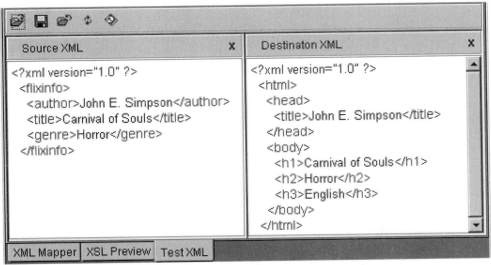

Figure 7-17   Testing XSLWiz's generated XSLT code against a sample source document (the same as the one used to initiate the whole project in the first place).

XSLWiz has one other interesting little feature, technologically speaking. Although it's a Java application, it runs only on Windows platforms. I don't know, but I suspect that the reason this is so is that both the XSL Preview and Test XML tabs use the MSXML XML/XSLT processor to generate their windows. The views of the XML documents and XSLT stylesheets provided there aren't 100% like those provided by, say, Internet Explorer—but they're awfully close.

The product's got a pretty stiff price tag—$995 per license. (A seven-day time-limited evaluation version is also available, for free.) Of course, if you can actually use it to do what the product promises, this may be a thousand dollars well spent.

XSLWiz's home page is at www.ebprovider.com/products/xslwiz.html.

XSLT processors

This is easily (in my view) the most important category of XSLT software, comprising those products that actually do the work of converting a source tree to a result tree according to the instructions in an XSLT stylesheet.

All other things being equal, you've essentially got two platform-specific choices here. Either you'll use the MSXML processor or you'll use any of a dozen others.

If you opt for MSXML, you'll be mostly limited (as I've said) to generating XHTML result trees, and you can't run that processor on any platform other than the various flavors of Microsoft Windows, from 95 on up. In exchange, you get a high level of compliance with the XSLT spec, speed, and ease of use (including simple integration with the MSIE browser).

If you opt to use one of the other processors, naturally the principal benefit is (mostly!) platform independence. These are generally not slouches when it comes to performance, either, and nearly all of them are fully XSLT 1.0-compliant as well. The only thing MSXML has that the others haven't, in my opinion, is its integration with MSIE and other Microsoft-based products.

I'm going to look at two processors in this section, both of which you've seen throughout this part of *Just XSL*: MSXML and Saxon.

Processor performance

A somewhat controversial issue has to do with the speed at which different processors transform a given source tree to a "correct" result tree.

The controversy derives from two difficulties: the enormous range of conditions to be tested and the usual apples-vs.-oranges dilemma. For example, consider Processor A; it's fully compliant with XSLT 1.0 and includes some convenient extensions of its own. On the other hand, Processor B complies with all but a couple of seldom-used XSLT 1.0 features and offers no extensions of its own. B is blazingly fast, whereas A's performance is, er, adequate. Selecting a processor purely on the basis of speed is almost certain to cost you something over the long run.

As always, consider the full range of your foreseeable needs—not just how fast a software package runs (although for your purposes, that may well be the most important need).

In any case, for a reasonably good comparison of different processors' performance in a variety of conditions, consult the DataPower "XSLTMark" benchmark results at www.datapower.com/XSLTMark/.

MSXML 3.0

It took Microsoft a goodly number of tries, but they finally got it right. Within the scope of what it's useful for, MSXML 3.0 is a great product.

First, what do I mean about a "goodly number of tries"? Microsoft released the first version of MSXML in 1998. This was kind of exciting to use, because it transformed XML to HTML directly inside the MSIE browser. Unfortunately, it also complied with what was then just a working draft of the XSLT spec. Even more unfortunately, Microsoft said that its XSLT-compliant processor was compliant with "XSL," leading to countless confusing iterations over the next three years of mailing-list messages like this:

```
Sigh. No. If you're using MSXML you are *not* doing
XSLT, and you're not doing plain-old XSL. You're doing
the language-formerly-known-as-XSL-but-no-longer-
recognized-formally-by-anyone (including Microsoft).
```

Compounding the confusion, of course, was the surge of interest in XML technologies in that first year or two—especially as expressed in books that continued to sell and be used long after the W3C had driven a stake through the heart of the language-formerly-known-as-XML. Worse, in a way, is that MSXML continues to support the old flavor of the spec even now.

At its simplest, using MSXML is almost embarrassingly easy: Just point the MSIE browser at a file with an .xml extension and, bingo, there you are. If the source document doesn't include an xml-stylesheet PI, MSIE displays it as a generic tree structure, as in Figure 7–18.

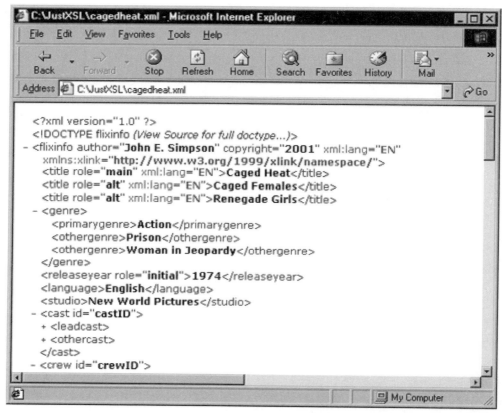

Figure 7-18   The MSXML 3.0 processor hard at (invisible) work, within the bowels of the MSIE browser. Note (per the "Address" field) that the XML document doesn't have to be *served* as XML—over an HTTP connection—in order to be *recognized* as XML.

Because MSXML is really meant for use within the framework of MSIE, I'll cover some other aspects of using it below, in the discussion of browser support for XSLT.

Saxon 6.2

Saxon, developed and maintained by Michael Kay of ICL,[4] is a speedy, versatile, highly compliant XSLT processor. Because it's written in Java, it's suitable for use on a wide variety of platforms, and Kay has even packaged it as an easily usable executable (.exe) file, called Instant Saxon, which runs as a command-line processor on Windows machines. The current version, 6.2, is available from the Saxon home page, users.iclway.co.uk/mhkay/saxon/.

I'd be hard pressed to cite something that Saxon doesn't do right, for the Java programmer or the Windows user who likes to work from the command line. Everything from the XSLT 1.0 spec is in there, and it behaves the way you'd expect it to. Furthermore, Kay has kept the package up to date with enhancements to XSLT that, at this point, are merely in the talking stages as an XSLT 2.0 Requirements document.

You can run Saxon from the command line, as a servlet from a Web site, or in any of a number of other configurations. You can get a sense of the options available at run time from Figure 7–19.

Figure 7-19   The run-time options available to a Saxon user. This screen shot shows the way the options are invoked from the command line, running the Instant Saxon package for Windows computers, but the options are available in other execution modes as well.

---

4.   Kay is a widely respected member of the XSLT community, and author of *XSLT: Programmer's Reference* (Wrox Press, 2000–2001).

The options from Figure 7–19 which I use most often are these:

- -a: Saxon doesn't require that the XML source document include an xml-stylesheet PI; by default, you supply the name of the source document *and* the name of the stylesheet as command-line options. (They appear in Figure 7–19 as *source-doc* and *style-doc*, respectively.) This default mode is a useful feature, especially when you're developing a stylesheet and prefer (for example) to test just a single template rule at a time. Nevertheless, for the occasions when you want Saxon to read and process the xml-stylesheet PI in the source document, use the -a switch. Obviously, if you do so, you omit the *style-doc* command-line option.
- -o *filename*: By default, Saxon dumps its output—the result tree—to what's commonly called "standard output,"—which, by default, is the console (i.e., if you're running under Windows, the "DOS window"). If you want Saxon to write the result tree to an output document instead, use the -o switch, followed by the name of the file to create. Note that if the file already exists, Saxon overwrites it without comment—so be sure that's the effect you want.
- *param=value*: Passing the value of a global parameter into your stylesheet with Saxon is just a matter of supplying the parameter name (without the $ prefix character), followed by an equals sign and the parameter's value. If the parameter value contains embedded spaces, enclose it in double quotes.

Assume you've got a hypothetical source document named crisscross.xml. This document contains an xml-stylesheet PI, which you want to use for this transformation, and you want Saxon to write out its XSL-FO result tree to a document named playbill.fo. The stylesheet takes one global parameter, internally referred to as $date, used to capture a date (obviously) for some purpose, and the date should be in dd Month, yyyy format. You could invoke Saxon from the command line under these circumstances as follows (note that the command line wraps as reproduced here, although it should be entered all on one line):

```
saxon -a -o playbill.fo crisscross.xml
  date="18 June, 2001"
```

If the stylesheet didn't have an xml-stylesheet PI, or for some reason (such as testing) you wanted to override it, the command line might be this:

```
saxon -o playbill.fo crisscross.xml playbill.xsl
  date="18 June, 2001"
```

If Saxon encounters any errors, it writes them to the console (including line and character number in the document where it found the error). If there are no errors, it simply performs the transformation—there's no "Success!" or any such message.

Web browser support for XSLT

As I've said repeatedly, there's nothing about XSLT that requires it to create (X)HTML result trees and nothing but. Nevertheless, naturally enough, this is an area of tremendous interest both to developers and to that part of the general populace that knows anything at all about XML.

I'll start by discussing Microsoft Internet Explorer, then move on to Netscape, followed by Opera.

MSIE

In Figure 7–18, you saw how Internet Explorer displays an XML file that doesn't have an `xml-stylesheet` PI. What interests me most about this is that this default display is nonetheless entirely dependent on the presence of a stylesheet. That is, IE comes with its own *default* stylesheet for displaying an XML document, in the absence of another. From within IE, you can examine this stylesheet for yourself, by entering this URL into the Address field: res://msxml.dll/defaultss.xsl.

Here's how the stylesheet begins:

```
<?xml version="1.0" ?>
<x:stylesheet xmlns:x="http://www.w3.org/TR/WD-xsl"
  xmlns:dt="urn:schemas-microsoft-com:datatypes"
  xmlns:d2="uuid:C2F41010-65B3-11d1-A29F-00AA00C14882">

<x:template match="/">
  <HTML>
    <HEAD>
      <STYLE>[CSS style specs]</STYLE>
      <SCRIPT>[Script code]</SCRIPT>
    </HEAD>
    <BODY class="st">
      <x:apply-templates />
    </BODY>
  </HTML>
```

```
</x:template>

<x:template match="node()[nodeType()=10]">
  <DIV class="e">
    <SPAN>
      <SPAN class="b">
        <x:entity-ref name="nbsp" />
      </SPAN>
      <SPAN class="d">
        &lt;!DOCTYPE
        <x:node-name />
        <I>(View Source for full doctype...)</I>
        &gt;
      </SPAN>
    </SPAN>
  </DIV>
</x:template>
... etc. ...
```

At first glance, this looks kind of straightforward. There's an `xsl:stylesheet` element (even though they use an `x:` namespace prefix instead—which is perfectly legal as long as they associate a namespace URI with it), and there are a couple of template rules.... But when you look at it more closely, little anomalies start to crop up.

Look, for instance, at the URI associated with the `x:` prefix. Isn't that supposed to be "http://www.w3.org/1999/XSL/Transform"? Where'd the "http://www.w3.org/TR/WD-xsl" come from? And where's the required `version="1.0"` attribute? What's that `node-type()` function call, and what about the `x:entity-ref` and `x:node-name` elements...?

In short, do *not* try to figure this code out in terms of what I've told you about XSLT in this book. The reason: This code conforms (and not completely, at that) to a version of the XSLT spec long ago superseded by *later* versions—including, of course, the XSLT 1.0 Recommendation itself. It is, in fact, the outdated "XSL" version I mentioned in the section on XSLT processors.

(Personally, I suspect that this default stylesheet is the main reason IE hasn't completely abandoned support for the earlier version of "XSL": The stylesheet is just too hard to rewrite as XSLT 1.0. Some things which this Microsofted version of "XSL" does are downright impossible with true XSLT. For instance, that second template rule is used to match the document type declaration in the source tree—that's what the `nodeType()=10` in its match pattern's predicate means. But the document type declaration isn't really part of the document tree, so there's no way for a compliant XSLT stylesheet to access it.)

Other surprises... I've made much of what a good product I believe MSXML to be—and indeed it is. Its compliance with the XSLT standard is excellent (notwithstanding all I just said about the default, built-in stylesheet).

That said, there are a few surprises that come with it.

One of the most surprising of these surprises is that MSXML—left to its own devices—does *not* preserve whitespace in the source document; by default, it normalizes an XML document's whitespace, just as it does for an HTML document. This may strike you (as it struck me) as...how to put this politely...retrograde, let's say. One of the advantages of XML over HTML, after all, is that you can reliably expect the processor by default to *preserve* whitespace.

Microsoft's explanation of this behavior is that MSXML is not an XML processor (parser), nor an XSLT processor; it contains *both*. The parser within MSXML does, indeed, preserve whitespace. However, it then hands the parsed document off to a "downstream application," the XSLT processor...which just happens to be built into the same DLL.

If preserving whitespace is important to you, you can signal to MSXML that it should retain all whitespace in the source document, from one end to the other of the XML-to-result tree. Unfortunately, the only way to signal this is by way of script or program code.

For more information about this behavior and how to control it, see msdn.microsoft.com/library/psdk/xmlsdk/xslp1n3m.htm.

Netscape/Mozilla

Viewing XML with a browser has been mostly an MSIE affair ever since the XML 1.0 Recommendation appeared. As for the more advanced task—viewing a document whose contents were transformed on the fly to (X)HTML—well, there just weren't any other kids on the block. By the time you read this, though, that situation should have changed.

As you probably know, Netscape—now owned by America OnLine—has for the last few years been undergoing a massive, public reworking of its code. That effort, known as Mozilla, finally bore stable fruit in 2000 with the release of the Netscape 6.0 browser. (At the time I write this, there's since been a minor upgrade, to version 6.01.) Netscape 6.0 includes good support for styling XML documents using CSS stylesheets.

Meanwhile, work has continued on various components that can be folded into later Netscape releases. This work is organized into what the Mozilla team refers to as *projects*—one of which will result in Netscape's finally being able to apply XSLT transformations to an XML document viewed in the browser.

The central component of this effort is an XSLT processor called Transformiix, developed by the Mozilla team. Like Saxon, Transformiix can run as a command-line processor, and has been able to for some time. But like MSXML, it can *also* run within a browser. (The browser, in this case, is of course Mozilla/ Netscape, not MSIE.)

The Mozilla developers have always been forthright about their deadlines for new features and the possible problems that may prevent a deadline from being met. Unfortunately, at this writing I can't show you screen shots of Transformiix in action within Netscape; the targeted deadline for integration with the browser is still a month away.

Opera

Anytime a discussion of Web browsers comes up, the careful author of computer or Internet books deals with Microsoft and Netscape and then says, "But those aren't your only choices...!"

XML itself is being tackled by a number of other browsers, not all of them exactly household names. But XSLT-on-top-of-XML is a whole different matter. Here's a brief look at the position taken by "the other browser," Opera.

The Opera browser is small, fast, and historically standards-friendly.[5] But when it comes to XSLT, the vendor, Opera Software (www.operasoftware.com), seems to have drawn a line in the sand—as much as saying, "We *never* expect to support XSLT."

I'm not sure exactly what the problem is. At the least, you'd think a browser that does such an excellent job of rendering CSS-styled (X)HTML would eventually (like MSIE and Netscape) support XML-to-XHTML transformations. I do know that the people at Opera seem very much opposed to transforming XML

---

5.   And recently, Opera finally took the plunge into freeware. It was always worth the small price to register, but with both Netscape and MSIE available for free—and increasingly standards-compliant themselves—the fact that Opera actually cost something was becoming a sticking point. The freeware version is now advertiser-supported; you can still buy Opera, in exchange for which you suppress all the advertising.

to XSL-FO for delivery over the Web; that's okay, I'm kind of ambivalent about it myself. But the aversion to XSLT doesn't make a lot of sense, in my opinion. We can just hope they'll get over it at some point.

Server-Side XSLT

Much of the media attention paid to XSLT derives, rightly or wrongly, from its use in a Web client (such as a browser). The drawback of following this approach should be obvious: If a site visitor's Web client doesn't know how to associate an XML document with a stylesheet—assuming it can handle XML at all—you might as well try to serve him chicken-noodle soup over his Internet connection.

A far more robust solution, particularly when you can't lock site visitors into a particular client, is to *serve* them the transformed XML in the form of generic XHTML.

Active versus passive serving

If your XML content for Web presentation doesn't change very often, don't overlook a rather dull but very effective option: transforming the XML to static XHTML documents, which you then place on your Web site just as if they'd been hand-coded or cranked out by FrontPage, DreamWeaver, or what-have-you.

I think of this as "passive serving" of XML. It stands in sharp contrast to the "active serving" this section of the chapter addresses. Under the latter scenario, XML documents are transformed on the fly and delivered to browsers and other clients.

If you want to serve XML, transformed on the fly, to Web clients, you've effectively got two platform-specific alternatives. One choice is Microsoft Active Server Pages; the other, for non-Microsoft environments, is the Apache Project's Cocoon.

(Note that I'm not going to detail setting up and running Web servers running these two products. Nor am I going to provide you with pages of running code samples. These are huge topics, to which many entire books—to say nothing of magazine articles, newsgroups, and Web sites—have been devoted. All I want to do here is give you a sense of how the two environments work to transform and deliver XML content to a Web browser.)

XML-to-XHTML with Microsoft Active Server Pages

If your Web site is hosted on a machine running Microsoft's Internet Information Server (IIS), this is probably the way to go.

Active Server Pages, or ASP, is a separate add-on component to IIS. (You can also add ASP support to the Microsoft Personal Web Server product used for local FrontPage 2000 site development.) A page coded in the ASP language contains a mixture of HTML, ASP directives, and script—that is, a mix of data, presentation, and logic.

If you're a dyed-in-the-wool XML purist, this mishmash-seeming stew of data and instructions to *do* things with that data may make your blood run cold. If you can stop shuddering long enough to spend some time with ASP, though—particularly how it works to apply XSLT code to an XML source document—you should develop an appreciation for the practical benefits (particularly convenience) of this approach.

An ASP-based page which applies an XSLT stylesheet to an XML document works pretty much like a script running inside the MSIE browser which does the same thing. A simple example of such a page looks like this:

```
<%@ LANGUAGE=JScript %>
<html>
  <head><title>XML Served a la ASP</title></head>
  <body>
    <%
    var xmlSource =
      Server.CreateObject("Microsoft.XMLDOM");
    var xslXform =
      Server.CreateObject("Microsoft.XMLDOM");
    xmlSource.load(Server.MapPath("crisscross.xml"));
    xslXform.load(Server.MapPath("flixml.xsl"));
    Response.Write(
      xmlSource.transformNode(xslXform));
    %>
  </body>
</html>
```

Instructions to the ASP processor are enclosed within <% and %> delimiters. The heart of the page is the JScript code appearing within those delimiters in the document's body element. This code creates two XML objects, one for the source tree and one for the stylesheet, and applies the latter to the former with the transformNode() method. The result tree from the transformation replaces the entire content of that <%/%>-delimited block, including the delimiters themselves.

The Microsoft Web site is well-stocked with sample code, white papers, technical documentation, and other resources on using ASP with XML and XSLT. Undoubtedly, the best place to start browsing is the root of their XML technical information site, at msdn.microsoft.com/xml. If you'd like to dive straight into some more code, try the page located at msdn.microsoft.com/downloads/samples/internet/xml/asp_samples/sample.asp.

XML-to-XHTML with Apache Cocoon

The Apache open-source Web server is consistently the most widely used Web server in the world—giving Microsoft IIS a run for its money even on Microsoft platforms.

In addition to the resources provided by a loyal, hardworking, extremely clever community of developers, Apache has also been the beneficiary of numerous contributions in kind from corporate donors. This has been especially true in the XML arena, and most especially true of IBM. The hardware/software giant has turned over the code to Apache not just for its XML parser but also for its XSLT processor. These two products live on in Apache as the Xerces parser and the Xalan XSLT processor, respectively.

Like many open-source efforts, the Apache work is divided into projects, each of which focuses on a problem of one kind or another. One of the most successful projects, aside from the server itself, has been the Cocoon XML "Web publishing" platform.

Cocoon, which resides in a single Java servlet, treats the problem of making XML data Web-ready as a three-stage problem: creating the data, processing the data, and rendering the transformed result. The last two stages are heavily XSLT-dependent. (The Cocoon documentation refers to the XSLT documents involved in Step 2 as "logicsheets" rather than "stylesheets," but they *are* XSLT.)

Cocoon's two-stage transformation suggests an interesting *iterative* (or "chained") transformational process. For example, you might apply one transformation to the data to put it into raw XHTML form, say as a table; a second transformation to add a menu or other navigational "chrome" to the page; and a third to add DHTML scripting. All of this happens on the fly, simply as a result of a browser's having requested some XML document.

Cocoon has answered the Microsoft ASP model of adding logic to a page with one of its own, called (and somehow, I don't think this is coincidental) XSP, for eXtensible Server Pages. An XSP page—unlike an ASP page—consists of well-formed XML. The XSP code itself comprises XML elements in the XSP namespace (http://www.apache.org/1999/XSP/Core is the namespace URI), which instructs the XSP processor to perform one action or another. For instance:[6]

```
<xsp:page language="java"
  xmlns:xsp="http://www.apache.org/1999/XSP/Core">

  <page title="Time of Day">

    <xsp:logic>
      // Define a variable to hold the time of day
      Date now = new Date();
    </xsp:logic>

    <p>
      To the best of my knowledge, it's now
      <!-- Substitute time of day here -->
      <xsp:expr>now</xsp:expr>
    </p>
  </page>

</xsp:page>
```

Here, the XSP page includes a script, embedded in the xsl:logic element. This script is written in Java (per the language attribute to the root xsp:page element) and includes a function, named now, which returns the current date and time. The value returned by this function replaces the xsp:expr element (including the start and end tags) that refers to it. Transformed by the Xalan XSLT processor, what the user actually sees as a result is this result tree:

```
<html>
  <head><title>Time of Day</title></head>
  <body>
    <h3 style="color: navy; text-align: center">Time of Day</h3>
    <p>It's now Thu Dec 23 20:11:18 PST 1999</p>
  </body>
</html>
```

---

6.   I've cribbed the following example straight from the Cocoon XSP page, at xml.apache.org/cocoon/xsp.html. As an example, it's hard to improve upon.

The Cocoon home page is at xml.apache.org/cocoon/index.html. It's definitely worth a look—even if you're locked into a Microsoft platform. (Requiring only the right level of Java support, not a particular server—not even Apache—Cocoon has been successfully run on all kinds of Windows machines, from Win98 through 2000.)

How Do I...
Use XSLT with a database?

One of the annoying facts of life you encounter when you start sniffing around the mixing of database and Web technologies is how much of the material out there is Microsoft-focused.

Now, I'm no Microsoft basher—I use (and I *like* using) their products on an everyday basis, and I'm on cordial terms with any number of Microsoft employees. (And for that matter, heck, just look at the screen shots in this whole part of *Just XSL*.) But as easy as Access is to use, and as powerful as SQL Server is, when it comes to databases (like Web servers) Microsoft is by no means the only show in town.

General principles

If you think about it, a database back end and an XSLT "intermediary" to the outside world are a natural combination. After all, a standard part of any database platform is a report generator—something capable of taking the raw data retrieved by the database engine and (dare I say it?) transforming the data for output. If you're "reporting" to the Web, or for that matter to print (via PDF), there's no reason at all why you need to learn multiple report generators for each kind of back end (Oracle, SQL Server, Sybase, or what-have-you). Just use XSLT.

The only piece missing from this scenario is how to feed the XSLT processor in the first place. XSLT can't do anything with *any* input (source tree) that's shaped like anything but XML.

Luckily, such tools are becoming common. Oracle, in particular, has taken a strong lead in XML- and XSLT-enabling their products. Of course, the underlying storage and retrieval mechanisms aren't going to change anytime soon, for Oracle or any other big player. In the first and maybe most obvious place, commercial vendors are highly unlikely to suddenly expose their storage, indexing, and retrieval structures in the totally open (and totally text-based) way demanded of XML data. Second, good reasons exist for not actually storing large databases *as* XML, reasons that have nothing to do with protecting a vendor's competitive advantage. Database vendors know a *lot* about optimizing data retrieval, and these optimization methods commonly rely on platform-specific tricks, using binary data, internal lookup tables, and so on; these methods just won't work for large XML data sources.

What does work, though, is using a general-purpose intermediary between the database and the XSLT processor—something capable of making the database's native data look like XML.

Database connectors

You may have encountered the acronyms ODBC or JDBC. The O stands for Open, the J for Java, and the DBC in both cases stands for Database Connectivity. Both of these are standards for making a variety of back-end data sources look the same to middleware and front-end applications. As long as a particular type of data source has had an ODBC or JDBC driver developed for it, it makes little difference in most respects if the data source is an Oracle database, a mySQL database, a Microsoft Access database, a comma-delimited flat file, or a spreadsheet. All these data sources are capable of responding to a query with a two-dimensional table of results.

What makes all this work is that the query language in question has been standardized: Structured Query Language (SQL).[7] With minor variations, an SQL query on one platform is identical to one on another; and, on a given platform, an SQL query to interrogate one back-end data source is structured identically to an SQL query interrogating a different one. Thus, you can do things like this:

```
SELECT * from EMPLOYEES
```

regardless of the data source, in this case retrieving all the data from some two-dimensional (row-and-column) resource named "EMPLOYEES." If you need to select more carefully, you can do something like this:

---

7.   The "SQL" is sometimes pronounced like that, as a sequence of three letters—ess-cue-ell—and sometimes as "sequel." I tend to prefer the former. So if I keep speaking of "*an* SQL query" where you'd expect to see "*a* SQL query," you'll know why.

```
SELECT * from EMPLOYEES
  WHERE emp_region = "NW"
```

You don't have to stare too hard at this to recognize how tempting a target SQL has been for those familiar with XSLT, or vice versa. Consider this:

```
<xsl:template
   match="EMPLOYEES[emp_region = 'NW']">
   ...
</xsl:template>
```

From database to XSLT, via ESQL

I don't want to dwell further on SQL itself. All I meant to do was lay a common groundwork of understanding, to prepare the way for discussing ESQL,[8] yet another Apache open-source project. (In fact, it's included in Cocoon versions 1.8.1 and later.)

At root, ESQL is simply an Apache "logicsheet" as I briefly described it above: an XSLT-based transformation intended to manipulate data somehow. Particularly, the ESQL logicsheet allows you to embed an SQL query in the transformation; this query is passed through a JDBC middle layer to the database, where the retrieval (or other operation) is performed.

As is often the case, in order to take advantage of an XML-based feature (ESQL in this case), you simply associate a namespace prefix (esql:, by convention) with a unique URI. The URI for ESQL is http://apache.org/cocoon/SQL/v2. Thus, to embed an ESQL query in a Cocoon XSP page, you'd use a framework like this:

```
<xsp:page language="java"
  xmlns:esql="http://apache.org/cocoon/SQL/v2"
  xmlns:xsp="http://www.apache.org/1999/XSP/Core">
  ...
</xsp:page>
```

Within this root xsp:page element, you'd include the guts of the "query"—like this:

```
<esql:connection>
  <esql:driver>org.gjt.mm.mysql.Driver</esql:driver>
  <esql:dburl>
```

---

8. The "E" there stands for "Extended." They couldn't use the more conventional X, because XSQL had already been claimed by a competing standard.

```
    jdbc:mysql://www.flixml.org/bfilms
  </esql:dburl>
  <esql:username>anonymous</esql:username>
  <esql:password></esql:password>

  <esql:execute-query>

    <esql:query>
      SELECT * FROM castmems order by surname limit 10;
    </esql:query>

    <esql:results>
      <ROWSET>
        <esql:row-results>
          <ROW>
            <esql:get-columns/>
          </ROW>
        </esql:row-results>
      </ROWSET>
    </esql:results>

  </esql:execute-query>

</esql:connection>
```

Pay particular attention to the elements prefixed `esql:` in this example. The general sequence of steps is this:

1. Declare the data source *type* with the `esql:driver` element.
2. Tell the Cocoon ESQL processor where to find your particular database, using the `esql:dburl` element.
3. Provide any other necessary parameters to establish a connection, such as a login username/password combination.
4. Wrap the query and its results within an `esql:execute-query` element. The actual SQL statement goes into the `esql:query` element, and the results are returned into the `esql:results` element.

(Note, by the way, the `esql:get-columns` element, which actually causes the query results to be placed at that point. The term "columns" is used here in its database sense—the synonymous term "fields" may be more familiar to you— not in its table-layout sense.)

This query is transformed by the esql.xsl stylesheet (all right, *logic*sheet) that comes with Cocoon into an actual working JDBC call to what (in this case) is a mySQL database named `bfilms`. Results of the query are displayed in the form of an XHTML table. If you want, you can pass them through a secondary transformation to customize the look and feel of the resulting page.

If you're interested in serving database data to Web clients, you could do a lot worse than using Cocoon/ESQL.[9]

---

9.   In the not-too-far-off future, as I write this, there's also the possibility that you'll be able to use XML Query for this purpose.

CHAPTER 8

Just Around the Corner: Future XSLT

In the couple years since the XSLT 1.0 Recommendation's publication, XSLT users have had ample time to get used to the language's little quirks and foibles, endearing and otherwise. More importantly, they've had time to identify and verbalize true problems with the original language.

Concurrently, of course, lots of other activity has been taking place within the W3C in a number of other Web/markup arenas. XML Schema, particularly, has the potential to have a profound impact on nearly everything XML-related[1]—XSLT as well as all the rest.

On the horizon as of this writing are two amplifications to the XSLT 1.0 Recommendation. The first, XSLT 1.1, addresses a handful of language "features" no one has ever been completely happy with. The second, although still a way off, will represent deeper, more fundamental change (for the better, one hopes!)—and has thus been dubbed XSLT 2.0.

This chapter provides a survey of some of the more significant components of these further stages in XSLT's evolution.

---

1.   Boy, is *that* probably going to be the understatement of the decade. XML Schema is like a proof of Einstein's general relativity; it squats like a gigantic super-dense star at the center of the galaxy, distorting the behavior of everything that so much as looks in its direction.

Late-breaking news
While I was working on this chapter, the XSLT Working Group (WG) reported that they would do no further work on the XSLT 1.1 WD, but would concentrate instead on XSLT 2.0. Except for some of the more controversial or technically unfeasible features of the XSLT 1.1 spec, it's expected that XSLT 2.0 will incorporate not only those things set forth in the XSLT 2.0 Requirements but also all the features of XSLT 1.1. In the balance of this chapter, I'll continue to refer to the two specs as if they were actually separate documents. Just understand that they'll probably be merged, finally, under the 2.0 umbrella.

XSLT 1.1: Taking in the Seams

As of this writing, the XSLT 1.1 spec is still a Working Draft. (You can find it at www.w3.org/TR/xslt11/.) It codifies requirements set forth in August 2000, in a document located at www.w3.org/TR/xslt11req.

The document established five general requirements:

- Upward compatibility
- Portable extension functions
- Multiple output documents
- Automatic conversion of result-tree fragments (RTFs) to node-sets
- XML Base support

I'll look briefly at each of these general requirements as they seem to be spelled out in the XSLT 1.1 Working Draft.

Degrees of "requirement"
The XSLT 1.1 requirements document distinguishes between a couple of terms which describe the importance of the "requirement": MUST (NOT) and SHOULD (NOT). If the new version of the spec absolutely, unequivocally needs to address the requirement, the requirement falls into the MUST category; otherwise, it's considered a SHOULD. The XSLT 2.0 requirements document, being at a more tentative stage, adds yet another level, COULD. I'll indicate at the time I discuss each requirement which category it falls into.

Upward compatibility

This is easy: It simply asserts that things which worked in XSLT 1.0 MUST still work in XSLT 1.1. That is, even if a processor supports XSLT 1.1, it should still support features carried over from 1.0. The XSLT 1.1 WD notes that the proper value for the `xsl:stylesheet` element's `version` attribute is `1.1`, which can be used to unambiguously indicate that a given stylesheet makes use of features requiring compliance with version 1.1 (as opposed to 1.0) of the spec.

I confess that the term "upward compatibility" bemuses me. It seems interchangeable with the term "forwards compatibility" (as it's called in the XSLT 1.1 WD)—and, for that matter, "backwards compatibility" (as it's often heard in everyday usage). Whatever you call it, the central point is that XSLT is trying to "future-proof" stylesheets; as long as a given stylesheet identifies itself with a particular version, processors are bound to treat it as that version.

(This is not quite the same as requiring processors to support *all* prior versions. If I set out tomorrow to build an XSLT 1.1-compliant processor, I don't have to retrofit it with XSLT 1.0-specific compliance.)

Portable extension functions

As you know, XSLT 1.0 lays out a framework for developers and vendors of specific processors to provide extension functions—those offering functionality beyond the ones built into XSLT and XPath. The only catch is that these extension functions must be identified with a vendor's unique namespace URI.

Portable extension functions are a more ambitious goal. The idea is that extension functions could be made available which worked *across platforms and processors*, obviating the need to qualify their names by namespace.

Importantly, to provide this capability, the XSLT 1.1 spec would have to allow for a new datatype (beyond the basic XPath four: number, string, Boolean, and node-set). This is because the languages in which these portable extension functions are coded may need to accept—or return, for that matter—datatypes specific to those languages. For instance, a language might make efficient use of bit, word, and double-word datatypes; or packed decimal; or date/time values. Rather than attempt to provide analogs for all these other datatypes, XSLT 1.1 lumps them together as a new *external object* datatype.

The spec declares limitations on what a stylesheet may do with an external object. In general, the idea is that an external object may be used only in communicating with an extension function. You can't place its value in the result tree, for instance. (I'm not in the business of forecasting the future, but this sounds to me a lot like the kind of restrictions currently placed on RTFs. It sounds, in short, like a restriction a lot of people will squawk about, with reason.)

The `xsl:script` element

Boy, has *this* one stirred things up....

The XSLT 1.1 WD proposed the addition of a new top-level element, called `xsl:script`. Its function—and general syntax—would be like the XHTML `script` element's, allowing code like this:

```
<xsl:script
  language="javascript">
  function DoSomething () {
  ...etc....

</xsl:script>
```

To say this unleashed a firestorm might be exaggerating a little, but only a little. People who'd invested a couple years of time and anxiety learning—and growing to appreciate—the XSLT way of problem solving foresaw a real danger here: namely, the danger that newcomers to the language would simply use `xsl:script` as an escape hatch into old, non-XSLT solutions at the first sign of resistance from the stylesheet language.

Again, I don't know what the future holds. I do know that a *lot* of XSLT practitioners[2] signed a petition asking for the elimination of this "requirement." (And the string s, c, r, i, p, t appears nowhere in the XSLT 2.0 requirements, for what that's worth.)

Multiple output documents

A couple of XSLT 1.0 processors introduced a useful idea: that of generating *more than one result tree* from a given source tree. The mechanism to do so is a new proposed `xsl:document` element, the most important attribute of which is `href`— for specifying the URI of a document to be created. Thus, this new element would work something like the inverse of the `document()` *function*, which allows you to access multiple source trees.

One example of where you'd use this is given in the XSLT 1.1 WD: simultaneously creating both an XHTML frameset *and* a document to be included in

---

2.   Including Yours Truly (in the interest of full disclosure).

one of its frames. Another case where it would come in handy would be as a kind of "disaggregator" (for lack of a better term). Think of an XML document describing multiple instances of some general class of objects: multiple employees, region and sales results, books, or—oh, heck—B movies. You could use the `xml:document` element to "burst apart" this original document into instance-specific documents.

Finally, one of my favorite uses for this multiple output documents feature would be as a fast way to initialize an XHTML-based Web site or other collection of XML documents using as a source tree an RDF/XML Schema document. Basically, you'd use the Schema as a road map to drive the generation of generic "placeholder" outputs.

Automatic RTF to node-set conversion

One of the most inscrutable back corners of the XSLT 1.0 Recommendation is almost everything to do with the result-tree fragment (RTF) datatype. What's inscrutable about it is that, in all respects but one, an RTF is exactly like a node-set. And that one respect is that the XSLT 1.0 standard simply asserted—rather unconvincingly, at that—"In the following cases, an RTF is different from a node-set...."

This arbitrary distinction will almost certainly be removed in XSLT 1.1, resulting in the elimination, in fact, of the RTF datatype. Where `xsl:variable` elements are assigned a value in element content, rather than via a `select` attribute, the datatype of the result will simply be a node-set.

XML Base support

The XML Base standard is one of the recent torrent of XML-related specs from the W3C. It lays out the rules by which relative URIs are to be resolved.

In the context of an XSLT stylesheet, the question has been along these lines: Let's say you have a call to the `document()` function (or the new `xml:document` element, for that matter) that locates the document it's referring to by way of a relative URI. What is the relative URI relative *to*?

Common sense generally applies. That is, in the absence of any other clue, it's relative to the URI of the document in which the relative URI reference appears—the stylesheet, in this case. But the XML Base standard allows this so-called "base URI" to be overridden for any sub-tree of the document, using an `xml:base` attribute. Like other attributes in the `xml:` namespace—`xml:lang` and `xml:space`—the value of the `xml:base` attribute is inherited by descendants of the element which declares it. Furthermore, a descendant can refine the value of an `xml:base` attribute established by an ancestor with its own `xml:base` attribute, which applies any of various forms of relative URIs to alter the implicit base URI from there down in the tree.

For more information about XML Base, see www.w3.org/TR/xmlbase. (This is a fairly concise and—as W3C specs go—fairly lucid document.)

XSLT 2.0: The Broader Future

In the world of XML and related specs, the W3C sometimes seems to be tripping over its own feet in releasing new versions, immediately followed by (and sometimes overlapping) even newer ones. So it is with XSLT. At this writing, the most recent WD of the XSLT 1.1 spec was published in December 2000; just a couple months later, in mid-February, the XSLT 2.0 Requirements WD appeared.

According to the latter, XSLT 2.0 will meet the following goals:

- Simplify manipulation of XML Schema-typed content.
- Simplify manipulation of string content.
- Support related XML standards.
- Improve ease of use.
- Improve interoperability.
- Improve i18n[3] support.
- Maintain backward compatibility.
- Enable improved processor efficiency.

This list suggests that the remainder of the document will be organized accordingly, most obviously into eight sections. In fact, though, there are only four major sections: support the XML "family" of standards, improve ease of use, support XML Schema, and simplify grouping. Note that supporting the XML family of standards and supporting XML Schema probably classify as a single goal, and that improving grouping seems like a special case of improving ease of

---

3.   "i18n" is the clever popular shorthand for *internationalization*. Why "i18n"? Just count the number of letters between the starting "i" and concluding "n." Maybe "clever" isn't really the word I'm looking for here.

use—so there are really only a couple of major goals. (But this is, after all, just a first-cut WD.)

The Requirements WD also says that the following are explicitly *not* goals of XSLT 2.0:

- Simplifying the ability to parse unstructured information to produce structured results: This would enable you to use non-XML source trees. It's an interesting idea, but I, for one, am glad it's not on the radar (yet, if it ever ends up there); it would just move XSLT off its central focus.
- Turning XSLT into a general-purpose programming language: Likewise, the world probably does not at this point need another programming language—and if it does, it probably doesn't want something like XSLT.

I'm not going to cover either of these "what XSLT 2.0 will *not* do" goals further. As for the others, I'll list (with commentary) the specific objectives currently listed under the MUST category.

What XSLT 2.0 "MUST" do

As I mentioned earlier, the version 2.0 spec uses language like MUST, SHOULD, and COULD to identify which objectives are most important. Of 31 specific objectives, only 8 are MUSTs. (The "simplify grouping" category isn't broken down further into specific objectives, simply treated on its own. However, that item does have 13 specific *use cases*—rationales for why it's important—far more than any other.)

Support XML "family"

Objectives in this category are meant to ensure that XSLT 2.0 integrates well with other W3C-sponsored XML-related standards

- Maintain backwards compatibility with XSLT 1.1: Yes—the forwards compatibility of XSLT 1.1 has become backwards compatibility in 2.0. Same general idea, though. (As I said, it would still be the same general idea even if they called it up- or downwards compatibility.)
- Match elements with null values: This gets at one of the classic computing problems—distinguishing data values which are explicitly null from those which are merely empty. XML Schema permits the declaration of an element or attribute as "nullable"; that is, such an element or attribute may be

assigned an explicit null value. The way you do so is with a special attribute, xsi:null, whose value is either true or false (true meaning "this element/attribute actually has a null value, even though it looks like it's simply empty"). This XSLT requirement would permit locating elements (and attributes) that are explicitly null-valued.

Weird but true

Given that the xsi:null="true" attribute is the trigger for this condition, it's easy to locate *elements* that are explicitly null. (You just use a predicate like [@xsi:null="true"].) The problem apparently arises because attributes, too, can be assigned a null value. Given markup like this,

```
<some_elem some_attrib=""
    xsi:null="true"></some_elem>
```

...well, is the attribute null? The element? *Both?*

Improve ease of use

Items in this category would help minimize confusion among newcomers to XSLT and simplify life in general for *all* the language's users.

- Allow matching on default namespace without explicit prefix: So you're feeling pretty cocky and think you've got the hang of this namespace business. In your xsl:stylesheet element, you've declared a default namespace (one with no prefix) to be applied to source tree nodes in your match patterns. Unfortunately, under XSLT 1.0 and 1.1, you *won't* match any nodes this way. Instead, you've got to declare a completely bogus namespace prefix and match on the prefixed node name, instead. (Note that this applies to default namespaces in the source tree, *not* to those in the result tree—where the problem doesn't come up.)

- Add date formatting functions: This is related to XML Schema, like the "null elements and attributes" item I discussed earlier. Because XML Schema provides a date datatype, XSLT will need to be able to represent this datatype in various ways. (By default, the date datatype's representation will be unambiguous but not what you need in many cases—e.g., "2001-06-18" instead of the more colloquial "June 18, 2001.")

- Simplify accessing IDs and keys in other documents: Although you can currently use the XSLT `id()` and `key()` functions to get at these values in external documents (retrieved using the `document()` function), it's dreadfully awkward. Meeting this goal will help ensure the continued usefulness of `document()` in more complex scenarios (involving dozens of external documents, say).

Support XML Schema

As I'm writing this, the XML Schema spec has just become a full-fledged Recommendation. No matter how you feel about this fact (excited and happy or profoundly ill at ease), there's no doubt that the implications are huge. XSLT 2.0 objectives in this category are meant to soften the blow (and hence lessen the angst) for XSLT developers.

In particular, these objectives are meant to make XML Schema *datatypes* useful in an XSLT context. This means exposing to XSLT knowledge of whether a bit of content is string, numeric, Boolean, or one of the more exotic datatypes such as "anyURI."

- Simplify constructing and copying typed content: When you place content into an XSLT result tree, of course it could have originated from the source tree *or* from some calculation available to the stylesheet at run time. XSLT will need the ability, though, to assign a datatype to result-tree content—or, if the content is copied from the source tree, to *copy* the datatype of the source content. This may not be important if the target vocabulary is something like XHTML, which itself is more or less "typeless"; it will be supremely important if you're instantiating content in a "typed" vocabulary. For instance, if the source data is floating point, failing to notify the target of that fact may result in truncation or rounding errors.
- Support sorting nodes based on XML Schema type: Right now, XSLT can sort content identified as text or numeric. It can sort other datatypes only to the extent they can be represented as one of those two. However, many of these other datatypes—float, double, datetime, duration, and so on—have sort orders unique to themselves. If XSLT is going to encounter such data in source trees, it needs to know how to sort them.

Simplify grouping

Although there are no specific MUST-type objectives listed under this category, the category as a whole is labeled that way in the XSLT 2.0 Requirements WD.

The problem now is that—as you saw at the end of Chapter 6—you've got to jump through hoops to make your stylesheet group data. You sort it, then go through various gyrations comparing one data value to those preceding or following it to determine if it's in the same group. Crazy.

This goal for XSLT 2.0, says the WD, will ensure that users can group data according to some common string-value (e.g., "group by the first letter of the glossary term"), by a node name ("group all the castmember elements together"), and by—well, by any *other* value a group of nodes might have in common ("put all surnames 8 characters or less in one group, then all those of 9 through 16 characters in the second group, and all those of 17 or more characters in the third"). The spec goes one step further and asserts that simple grouping must be possible on the basis of nodes' *positions*. For example, maybe you want to group every five nodes of some collection into a row of a table. (Sound familiar?)

A clutch of "SHOULDs" and "COULDs"

I don't want to leave you with the impression that the XSLT 2.0 spec aims to be no more than an incremental improvement over 1.0/1.1. A good number of other possibilities are also mentioned in the "requirements," although they have the general feel of "This would be nice" rather than "We gotta have this." Here's a small sampling.

Encapsulating local stylesheets

Here's the scenario: You've got a source document, call it main.xml, which is to be transformed by some XSLT stylesheet—main.xsl, say. Among the other tasks performed by main.xsl is opening up a secondary document (alt.xml) for obtaining some content not available in main.xml.

With me so far?

Okay, now imagine that the secondary document *itself* has an XSLT stylesheet associated with it. Might it not be useful to allow alt.xml to be transformed by its stylesheet before its content is included in the main.xsl transformation?

Calling a feature such as this "encapsulating local stylesheets" seems kind of perverse—yet another layer of jargon for the uninitiated to scratch their heads over, you know. Whatever it ends up being called, the feature itself could be very powerful. Depending on how it's implemented, it also could contribute to, well, call it civility for lack of a better term (jargon or otherwise). A document's developer could make her information available with a stylesheet as much as if to say, "Use this content if you want, but *only* transformed in the following way...."

This is a SHOULD objective.

Permit computed namespace nodes

This would provide an analog, for namespace nodes, to the existing `xsl:element` and `xsl:attribute` elements: an `xsl:namespace` element, say, whose associated prefix and/or URI were computed at run time.

This is a COULD objective.

Allow authoring XSLT extension functions

I mentioned that XSLT 1.1 opened up a controversial subject in its proposed `xsl:script` element. This SHOULD objective in XSLT 2.0 is much less controversial, although it's related. The reason? It proposes developing some kind of mechanism for building extension functions *written in XSLT itself.*

There's no telling what form this mechanism might take. But I could develop, say, a library of such extension functions, which could then be simply invoked as needed by full-blown stylesheets, in much the same way that a vendor's *nsprefix*:`node-set()` extension function is now.

Not standing or waiting

An extremely cool recent development, in my opinion, has been something called EXSLT. (Nowhere is it made explicit, but the "E" stands for "extensions to," I believe.) According to its home page, www.exslt.org, "EXSLT is an open community initiative to standardize and document extensions to XSLT."

That is to say, EXSLT is a community effort to collect and make available for download *lots* of XSLT-only "functions." This short-circuits this XSLT 2.0 objective by making use of an existing, thoroughly satisfactory XSLT 1.0 technique: stylesheet inclusion. Port to your location the library of "functions" (actually, just named templates) which you need and include them in any stylesheet which needs them.

Currently, EXSLT offers four modules: EXSLT Common, EXSLT Math, EXSLT Sets, and EXSLT Functions. You assign a namespace prefix to the URI `http://www.exslt.org/module-name`, substituting `common`, `math`, `sets`, or `functions` (as appropriate) for `module-name`. Then just include the module you need and call the named templates you need, where you need them.

The people behind EXSLT are a great group. I encourage you to make suggestions and—who knows?—even offer your own general-purpose named templates as candidates for the EXSLT library.

PART 3

XSL Formatting Objects

So now, having slogged throught Part 2, you know how to use XSLT to translate a given source tree to an arbitrary result tree.

That part of *Just XSL* focused heavily, in its example code and screen shots, on transforming to XHTML. It was convenient to do so, because in all likelihood you're already familiar with that XML vocabulary. You needed to focus on the means—XSLT—and not on the end.

Now it's time to turn your attention to what is probably an unfamiliar result-tree vocabulary: XSL Formatting Objects. While it and XSLT sprang from the same root, the same W3C Working Draft standard now three years old, they have grown up in two entirely different directions...as you're about to see!

CHAPTER 9

The "What" of XSL-FO

Somewhere out there, I guess, somebody still believes the paperless office is right around the corner. I don't know *where*, exactly, this person is—certainly nowhere within shouting distance of any of the offices I've ever been in.[1]

There's no question that reducing paper is a worthwhile goal. It really is. Unfortunately, the world is still a long way off from *recognizing* that goal. Even in the Internet age, we're not ready to shrug off the shackles of paper. And that's probably the main reason you need to care about the XSL Formatting Objects standard.

You may recall Chapter 2, similarly titled "The 'What' of XSLT." This chapter, like that one, will cover some of the basic concepts of XSL-FO, including some basic (but by and large unexplained) code. Subsequent chapters in *Just XSL* will delve much deeper into the specifics of the XSL-FO language.

---

1. Actually, I do know where this person is. He's moved in right next door to the woman who has placed the first order for a gleaming, brushed-aluminum sidewalk in the sky. If they got married and had kids, the kids would all use Buck Rogers–style jetpacks instead of skateboards.

First, The "Why"

I covered some of this earlier. But now might be a good time to revisit the question of why an XML-based formatting standard is even worth, er, the paper it's printed on.

The alternatives

If you want to format your documents and data for print, and you *don't* want to do so in a platform-dependent way, you've generally got any number of choices. Among the most common are PostScript and CSS. Each has its advantages and drawbacks.

(Just remember that "platform-(in)dependent" actually means much less than a visitor from another planet might think, given the amount of media attention the phrases receive. PostScript and CSS both "run" on a variety of platforms (in the sense of operating systems), so you might consider them platform-independent. On the other hand, the PostScript specification is owned by Adobe, whereas CSS runs in only a single kind of application—a Web browser—on any of its "platforms." Whether this makes these two formatting languages platform-independent in any real sense is debatable!)

The operative word is "common"

Numerous other (some exotic, some quite powerful) options are available. For instance, the LaTex document-preparation language is widely used among the academic community. Old-line Unix techies still favor the troff command-line facility for formatting print documents.

Other options aside, I believe PostScript (in one form or another) and CSS are probably the most widely used print-formatting languages.

PostScript

PostScript is a text-based language developed by Adobe Systems for creating vector-based "images" (including text) on any output device that understands the language. Here's an example of PostScript code:

```
/Courier findfont                    % Get the font
```

```
24 scalefont          % Scale it to 24-point size
setfont               % Make it the current font
newpath               % Start a new "path"
40 65 moveto          % Set lower left corner (40,65)
(B Alert!) show       % "Print" string "B Alert!"
```

Without knowing anything at all about the language, it's pretty easy to guess what's going on in this code fragment. For instance, the percent signs evidently mark the start of inline comments. (And, duh, the comments explain the rest!)

There's also some stuff that *isn't* quite so obvious. One example is the slash at the beginning of the first line, the function of which is to put something (a font, in this case) on the so-called "stack" for later use. (The font on the stack here is used by both the `scalefont` and `setfont` operators.)

PostScript is in wide use, across all kinds of platforms. *Lots* of devices support PostScript—printers, plotters, monitors, and so on. It has two main drawbacks for our purposes here: It's property of Adobe Systems (although Adobe is generally amenable to new implementations), and it's not at all markup-aware.

That second point may be fatal for many applications. Not only does PostScript not process marked-up documents, it's not even in markup form itself. Thus, you couldn't for example develop an XSLT stylesheet to manipulate a PostScript document (although, with a great deal of work, you could transform XML *to* PostScript).

PostScript and PDF

In the mid-1990s, Adobe announced its Portable Document Format (PDF) standard. This was intended to make PostScript "Web-friendly" by eliminating one other significant problem of PostScript files: They can be *enormous.*

PDFs are created from PostScript using a "distiller" process that boils down the text-only raw PostScript into a combination of text and binary data. You can embed PostScript fonts in a PDF, too, which greatly increases the chances that a document will print exactly as it was formatted.

More importantly for our purposes, you can use various software packages to generate PDF directly from XSL formatting objects. This eliminates various difficulties involved in handling raw PostScript code, and at the same time allows you to take advantage of features unique to

> XSL-FO (primarily, the ability to generate the latter from raw XML using XSLT stylesheets).[2]

CSS

I talked about CSS versus XSL-FO in Chapter 1. There, I said that CSS's chief drawback as a formatting language is that it's Web-bound. Even with cursory, latter-day nods in the direction of print publication needs, CSS is (and will probably remain) almost exclusively a Web technology.

On the other hand, of course, there's one of XSL-FO's chief drawbacks: It's oriented almost exclusively toward support of *print* applications. This doesn't make XSL-FO any better or worse, *per se*, than CSS. As always, you pick the right tool for the job (i.e., avoid the "when all you have is a hammer, everything looks like a nail" trap).

Political unrest

A sometimes heated argument has been swirling in the air for a couple of years now, and this is a good time to bring it up. The argument goes like this: "Why do we need another formatting language blessed by the W3C? We've already got CSS; shouldn't we just focus on improving *that*, rather than developing a competing standard?"

It's really not an unreasonable question. Unfortunately, some of those asking the question are asking it rhetorically. They already know the right answer. Which is, in short, that there's nothing wrong with CSS that can't be fixed.

This argument has gone through several stages. At first, it was "All XSL, including both XSLT and XSL-FO, is redundant. You can use scripting languages for the former and CSS for the latter." In fairness, that form of the argument predominated before the one XSL spec

---

2.   While on the subject of PDF, here's one important note: These mixed binary-and-text documents have a certain *legal* standing which is unlikely ever to be attained by text-only documents (including those coded in XSL-FO or other markup vocabularies). The reason is that a document's physical form—including such seemingly non-substantive characteristics as layout, headings, and so on—is considered "information" in a legal sense. A PDF document captures all that information and locks it down in electronic form exactly as it appears when printed.

split into the two separate ones. Since the split, and especially since XSLT has become such a successful technology on its own, you hear much less grumbling about that half of "XSL."

But XSL-FO still raises hackles. A few arguments are put forth most often for its undesirability.

The first is philosophic, and has to do with the notion that XML is all about semantics—about *meaning*—and not about presentation at all. In these terms, an XML vocabulary whose only "meaning" is presentation characteristics may seem a perverse, heretical abomination. I take the point here, in a way: Start with a document in a nice, richly meaningful source vocabulary such as MathML or DocBook or (egad) FlixML; to it, you apply an XSLT transformation whose function is to strip its contents of all meaning *except* presentation. Yeah, in a way that does seem bizarre. On the other hand, it seems to me that "how to present something" is a problem domain profoundly in need of its own structured vocabulary. When you want to send XML to a printer, what language *should* you speak? What's a printer supposed to do with an element named invoice or one named EmpNum? Saying, "No! No! XML may be used to construct vocabularies for every problem domain *but* presentation!" seems a tad arbitrary and selective (to say nothing of silly).

(This argument against XSL-FO really ignores one central point: that the "meaning" inherent in any XML document is meaning *ascribed to it by humans*. That is, the XSL-FO spec, or any other, chooses element and attribute names on the basis of their usefulness to human readers of documents marked up in that vocabulary. If the human readers see meaning in the markup, then it's meaningful. *There is no inherent meaning in an XML document.*)

Next is the argument that XSL-FO is too explicitly print-bound—in particular, that it's a giant step backward in terms of accessibility of content to vision-impaired users. This may well be true, at least in the sense that XSL-FO continues to place the same emphasis on "reading" that CSS does. XSL-FO, like CSS, specifies quite a few aural properties for spoken (text-to-speech) content, but the lion's share of attention is inarguably on text.

The third argument is the one I've seen presented most recently, and it goes something like this: "Oh no no no! We weren't saying that XSL-FO *as such* is a problem. We were saying that XSL-FO as a formatting vocabulary for content presentation *on the Web* is a problem." I can only scratch my head at this argument. Maybe I'm hanging out with the wrong people, but no one I know *wants* to use XSL-FO for presentation on the Web. We have CSS for that.

> Harder to shoot holes in is the argument that, at one level, XSL-FO is no more than CSS properties recast in XML-based form. (If that were *all* it were, I'd have more sympathy for the "Who needs XSL-FO?" point of view.) Also, as you'll see soon enough, XSL-FO is unbelievably verbose. It's not too great a stretch of the English language to say that XSL-FO can be downright ugly. I've got some feelings about this last point, but I'll hold them for now. (Just for now, though!)
>
> (Note that although XSL-FO can be considered ugly, the spec has been developed—as such things go—fairly quickly. As a general rule, the longer a spec incubates before its completion, the uglier its tenets become.)

Key XSL-FO Concepts

Before getting into all the specific bits of the XSL formatting model, let alone the vocabulary itself, let's clear the air of some terms and concepts you'll need to have a grip on.

What XSL-FO *is*

XSL-FO is an XML vocabulary that serves one purpose: unambiguously describing block layout, inline formatting, and other presentational characteristics that one bit of content has versus another.

Where's the spec?

The XSL-FO standard is available on the W3C Web site, at

`www.w3.org/TR/xsl/`

This is a W3C *Candidate Recommendation* (CR), which means it's not yet final but expected to become so. (The next stage in its "acceptance," if it follows the normal path for such documents, would be Proposed Recommendation, followed by plain-old Recommendation.) The CR "review period" supposedly ended a few weeks ago (as of this writing), which in theory means that the W3C Working Group responsible for the standard is mulling over any comments received before moving it along to the next stage. Since W3C Working Groups deliberate in private, there's no way of knowing for sure which way the wind will blow... just that it's *likely* to be in the direction of the CR.

As you know, the content of an XML document consists of text—letters, digits, punctuation, and whitespace—optionally including pointers to non-XML content (images and what-not) that lies outside the document itself.

So think about it, then: If you were designing a formatting vocabulary for presenting content such as this, what would that vocabulary have to know about and deal with?

- Any vocabulary (or other means) for presenting such content must account for common characteristics of the individual letter-forms themselves (font family, weight, "posture," and so on). If it's intended as a *non-trivial* formatting mechanism, it needs to address the less common characteristics as well, such as spacing between letters, sub- and super-scripting, and the like.
- It must also handle *groups* of letters—spans and paragraphs—in ways appropriate to the language and writing system in which the text will appear. (For example, how much space appears between lines of text? Does the text flow from left to right or right to left, top-to-bottom or vice-versa? What special classifications of text need to be addressed—headings, footnotes and endnotes, callouts, tables?)
- And it must provide facilities for positioning and sizing blocks of content (whether the content in question is text or something else, such as images, which an output device can handle). You'll want to be able to draw a box around such content if desired, for example, or position it to the left, right, top, or bottom of the output medium (irrespective of the alignment of text *inside* the block). You'll probably want the ability to "anchor" such a block of content to a particular piece of text—or, alternatively, to force the block to appear at a certain position regardless of the text around it. And you'll want to be able to use content (again, text and/or images) as a watermark—that is, repeated content floating in the background, behind any "real" content.

Beyond these requirements to style and present the actual content, though, a fully functional formatting language must be able to "understand," even *manipulate*, the format of the output medium in which the content will be presented.

In terms of print, this requirement includes obvious considerations such as paper size and margins. It also covers how to break up the physical page into sub-pages—regions or areas on the page—reserved for particular purposes, such as running page headers and footers. It addresses matters of text flow from one page to the next, including widow and orphan[3] control, and whether the "content" area of each page text will appear in single- or multi-column format (and, if the latter, whether the columns need to appear "balanced").

Finally, a print-formatting vocabulary needs some way of expressing the structure of an entire publication—as a collection not just of pages but of *types* of pages. There's one page type for the title page, a different one for the table of contents, one for regular text, one for the index, and so on. (Within each of these *types* there might be, yes, one or more pages.) And note as well that the language in question must be able to spell out what *sequence of page types is acceptable.* Do the glossary pages precede or follow the appendix? Does the title precede or follow the dedication? And so on.

(Of course, if the formatting vocabulary is, like XSL-FO, meant to cover *aural* presentation of the content as well, there's a whole raft of additional issues: pacing, volume, inflection and intonation, pauses, orientation—sounds coming from the left or right, up or down, front or back [the so-called "Z-axis" or "Z-coordinate"]—and so on. I wish I could demonstrate some of these capabilities of XSL-FO; I guess you'll just have to wait for the audio-book edition of *Just XSL.* Or, for that matter, the VRML edition—VRML also provides fully spatialized sound—even if the likelihood of a VRML edition is even more remote than an audio-book!)

XSL-FO's "verbosity"

Given the number and variety of types of presentation XSL-FO is meant to support, it's no wonder that the spec's table of contents alone is 8 or 9 pages long, that the spec itself (depending on how it's formatted) is nearly 400 pages long, and that even a "simple" fragment of XSL-FO code can run to a couple of pages.

---

3. Just in case you haven't seen these terms before, a *widow* is the last line of a paragraph which, without widow control, appears by itself at the top of a page. Depending on a number of factors, this may be merely unattractive or actually problematic (as when the widow consists of an entire sentence, which may cause the reader to miss it altogether). With widow control, a page break is inserted by the software so that more than one line of the paragraph will be bumped to the new page. An orphan presents the opposite problem: The first line of a paragraph is stranded by itself at the bottom of a page. The software-controlled page break will be placed before the orphan, if orphan control is on.

> You'll soon see that not only are XSL-FO's "sentences" quite long but so are many of its individual "words." Again, this makes a kind of sense; any full, formal, and unambiguous statement of something—from space-shuttle documentation to human-resource policies to legislative acts to document structure and format—always seems to take lots of big, complicated words to state it. Short words and sentences work best for generalizations.
>
> Given all this, I'm not terribly bothered by XSL-FO's "verbosity"... aside from the fact that I'm in a position to profit from explaining it (cough).

Namespaces and XSL-FO

If you understand the general concept of namespaces, namespace prefixes, and so on, all you need to know about them in an XSL-FO context is the namespace associated with elements and attributes in the XSL-FO vocabulary. The URI is http://www.w3.org/1999/XSL/Format, and (by convention) the prefix is `fo:`. Therefore, in a document containing these elements and attributes, you'd need the following namespace declaration:

```
xmlns:fo="http://www.w3.org/1999/XSL/Format"
```

Of course, this declaration needs to be in scope at the time an element or attribute with that prefix occurs. Typically, this means the namespace declaration will appear in an XSLT stylesheet's `xsl:stylesheet` element.

No "hand-editing" of XSL-FO documents

Maybe that's a little extreme. There's nothing at all to prevent your building from scratch an entire XSL-FO document, if you're so (masochistically) inclined. After all, XSL-FO is just another XML vocabulary. As long as you've got the right attributes on the right elements, and all the elements and text conforming to the right context models, who cares whether the document was authored and edited by a human or generated by software?

The answer is, *you'll* care—once you've tried to create even a simple XSL-FO document yourself. The reasons are the language's verbosity *and* its problem domain, both of which I addressed above. Even if your XML authoring/editing software is quite happy auto-generating the lengthy element and attribute names for you, freeing you just to enter the content, the content is really devoid of "meaning." This is a tedious and confusing way to work.

Much simpler is to author your documents in a real XML vocabulary, one which truly describes and structures the documents' contents in a meaningful way, and then transform the documents to XSL-FO with XSLT stylesheets. The XSLT processor doesn't grow bored typing and re-typing lengthy element names, and it does so consistently, one transformation after another. Any sensible use of XSL-FO simply will not require hand-coding of XSL-FO "stylesheets." In fact, the only way you may ever need to see XSL-FO code is in the context of templates in an XSLT stylesheet.

Practicing what I preach

In this part of *Just XSL*, I'll be showing you many code fragments as if I'd hand-coded them myself. This is an illusion. Although I do need to show you, for instance, how one element fits inside another, the XSL-FO code fragments I'll demonstrate here are always the result trees from XSLT transformations. I may hand-tweak them for presentation purposes—making sure their indentation is reasonable, for example, and replacing lengthy sections of repeated or irrelevant code with ellipses. But creating XSL-FO code by hand is just crazy.

Oh, I know—there are always obsessive-compulsive types who will insist on building things by hand rather than using the equivalent of power tools. When this book was in production, I heard of someone who'd coded by hand, in VRML, an incredibly complex world called the Tralee Mars Colony. VRML, like XSL-FO, is not a language for the faint of heart even when power-assisted. When one hears of such people, one just has to shake his head in amazement.

The `fo:root` element

The root element of an XSL-FO result tree or document must be `fo:root`. This element's syntax is very basic; it's used, minimally, as the container for the rest of the document and as a repository for namespace declarations. (There are quite a number of "inheritable" properties—inheritable in the same sense that a namespace declaration is—that can be assigned in the `fo:root`, as well; I'll cover them in Chapter 10.)

Within the `fo:root` element are any number of other elements. Roughly, these fall into two categories: elements that describe the types of layouts in a publication and elements that make up the actual content. These two categories of the `fo:root` element's descendants together reflect the XSL-FO *formatting model*.

The XSL-FO Formatting Model

A content model in XML is an expression of how the various elements and text contents fit together when represented in a given XML vocabulary.

Similarly, XSL-FO can be said to have a *formatting model* describing the interrelationships of different kinds of formatting. The spec itself is replete with a dizzying constellation of graphical illustrations of this formatting model and the steps a formatting processor takes to implement it. I'm not going to try reproducing most of these illustrations here; after you've stared at each one for a few minutes, you'll probably come to suddenly think (as I did), "You mean *that's* all this thing illustrates?"

A few of the illustrations are essential, though, and I'll provide my own versions of them when the time comes.

XSL-FO's view of a publication

In the XSL-FO world, a document—in its as-output form—somewhat resembles an Open eBook document, as I described at the end of Chapter 6: You spell out not only the individual chunks of content but also the sequence in which they appear. The overall structure of an XSL-FO publication is defined in the portion of the XSL-FO document called a *layout master set*; the content goes into a series of *page sequences*. Thus, the general structure of an XSL-FO document (result tree) is something like this:

```
<fo:root>
    [...layout master set...]
    [...page sequence(s)...]
</fo:root>
```

Within the layout master set are specifications for one or more *types of pages*, and there's a *sequence* in which those types of pages may appear. Each type of page is referred to as a *simple page master*; the order in which each may appear, as *page sequence masters*. So we can expand the general structure of an XSL-FO document to something like this:

```
<fo:root>
    [...layout master set:
      simple page master(s)...
      page sequence master(s)...]
    [...page sequence(s)...]
</fo:root>
```

Now, before going any further, note the use of the word "master" in all these terms. The XSL-FO spec uses the "master" designation to denote a class of objects. Thus, for instance, a simple page master does not describe a specific page; it describes a *class* or type of page. One or more specific pages will have the characteristics of that master, but their contents will differ.

The second point I wanted to raise here is that the XSL-FO vocabulary just *loves* hyphens. Most of these terms actually appear in the spec as hyphenated phrases: layout-master-set, simple-page-master, page-sequence-master. The significance of this is that these are generally the *names* of element types in the XSL-FO language; if you understand the nesting of the concepts, you also understand at least the rudiments of the language's content model. Thus, an XSL-FO result tree will include a structure something like this:

```
<fo:layout-master-set...>
    <fo:simple-page-master...>
    <fo:simple-page-master...>
    <fo:simple-page-master...>
    <fo:page-sequence-master...>
    <fo:page-sequence-master...>
    <fo:page-sequence-master...>
</fo:layout-master-set>
```

Simple page masters

Each simple page master considers a page to consist—at least potentially—of five *regions*. Each region (as the term implies) is a rectangular portion of the page within which content of one kind or another can appear. The five regions are listed below:

- region-body: This is the main area of a page—the part where the bulk of the content will be placed. The other four regions surround it.
- region-before: In Western writing systems, this corresponds to a "page header" area (that is, a rectangular area that occurs *before* the body itself).
- region-after: In Western writing systems, this corresponds to a "page footer" area (that is, a rectangular area that occurs *after* the body itself).
- region-start: In Western writing systems, this corresponds to a "left margin" area (that is, a rectangular area that occurs before the *start* of individual lines).
- region-end: In Western writing systems, this corresponds to a "page header" area (that is, a rectangular area that occurs after the *end* of individual lines).

Notice that the terms for the "surrounding" regions don't explicitly refer to directions such as top, bottom, left, and right. They're named in ways whose actual meanings differ from one language or writing system to another. Throughout the rest of *Just XSL*, I'll fall back on the more common Western terms—"before" means "top," "after" means "bottom," "start" means "left," and "end" means "right"— but remember that the results as formatted in one part of the world may be quite different from those as formatted somewhere else.

Figure 9–1 depicts the relationships of these regions within a simple-page-master (again, assuming a Western orientation).

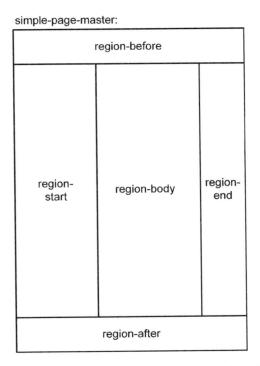

Figure 9-1   Breakdown of an XSL-FO simple-page-master into its constituent regions. The simple-page-master itself isn't the entire physical page; it's the entire area which may contain content, the area *within the page margins*. In certain non-Western writing systems, the region-start and region-end, and/or the region-before and region-after, may switch positions.

As before, you wouldn't be far off the mark if you guessed from this that an XSL-FO result tree might contain something like the following:

```
<fo:simple-page-master...>
   <fo:region-body...>
   <fo:region-before...>
   <fo:region-after...>
   <fo:region-start...>
   <fo:region-end...>
</fo:simple-page-master>
```

About that "simple"...

The simple page master is only one kind of *page master*—the only kind, as it happens, described by the XSL-FO spec. Without offering much discussion of the alternative, the spec says only that future versions of the standard "will support more complex page layouts." This will undoubtedly be accompanied by a fresh crop of graphics showing boxes-within-boxes.

The `fo:simple-page-master` element takes one interesting (and optional) attribute: `media-usage`. This attribute controls the overall way in which the output medium or device (referred to as the "User Agent") presents the XSL-FO document's content. It can take one of four possible values:

- `auto` (the default): How the output is presented will behave as if one of the other three values were assigned, depending on circumstances the User Agent can assess.
- `paginate`: Both the height and width of the output medium are fixed. (This is the most common value for print publications, of course.) Note that the effect of fixing the height and width of the medium is that, every time that two-dimensional area gets filled up, another instance of it is presented for filling. It's paginated, in other words, and hence this value for `media-usage`.
- `bounded-in-one-dimension`: The most obvious example here is a browser window or other "scrollable" area. One dimension is nailed down, and the other simply grows or shrinks to accommodate it.
- `unbounded`: As the value implies, there are no limits to either height or width. This presumes that text will not wrap, and that there are no line-feed characters in the content to *force* the wrapping. Each chunk of text simply takes up as much "width" as it needs, and the number of chunks determines the "length."

A reach, to be sure

This last value for the `media-usage` attribute seems to be of really limited usefulness (with one exception, which I'll get to in a moment). In a way, it seems a good example of why the XSL-FO spec is as long as it is—the editors are determined to cover all bases, even the implausible ones. ("Hey, we provided bounded in both directions, bounded in one direction but unbounded in the other...so we *have to* cover the 'bounded in neither direction' case too!")

The one case I can see where `media-usage="unbounded"` might be of any importance would be for *aural* media. For instance, you wouldn't want the text-to-speech synthesizer reading your XSL-FO document to say, "line break," "word-wrap," or "page break" when each of those events occurs. This is still kind of a stretch, though; to make it reasonable, one would have to assume that by default a synthesizer would, in fact, note those events. I don't use a text-to-speech synthesizer, but I think I'd shoot it if it by default pursued such an insane course of action.

All of which doesn't even begin to address the insanity of using a visual metaphor, such as the one provided by flow objects, to represent an aural experience....

Page sequence masters

The page sequence master describes the order in which pages of a certain kind (i.e., a page master) may appear. Three sequences are available:

- `single-page-master-reference`: This particular kind of page appears once within the layout master set. Examples in a book might include a title page, a dedication page, the page showing the book's ISBN and Library of Congress classification information, and an "About the Author" page appearing as the last page of a novel.
- `repeatable-page-master-reference`: This is a way of asserting that a particular page master appears over and over and over, until all content for that page master is exhausted. The most obvious kind of repeatable page master is, well, just about any page in just about any publication. A book's content consists of page after page after page, formatted the same way. Except for its contents, every page in the index looks the same as every other page in the index. And so on.

- `repeatable-page-master-alternatives`: This kind of page sequence is most commonly exemplified by the left- and right-hand pages of a book or magazine. Page headers and footers commonly have different content depending on whether a given page is odd- or even-numbered, and even the page margins may be different to allow for the binding (the edge of the page closest to the staples, stitching, and/or glue holding the publication together). Like the `repeatable-page-master-reference`, this kind of page sequence just goes on and on (in this case, cycling through the alternative layouts) until all its content is exhausted.

Given these three kinds of page sequences, then, a typical page sequence master might be coded in XSL-FO like the following:

```
<fo:page-sequence-master...>
   <fo:single-page-master-reference...>
   <fo:repeatable-page-master-alternatives...>
   <fo:repeatable-page-master-reference...>
</fo:page-sequence-master>
```

This might indicate that this page sequence master describes (respectively) a book's title page, any number of pages laid out differently for left- and right-hand pages, and an index whose pages are all laid out identically, regardless of which side of a two-page spread they fall on.

Page sequences

A *page sequence* is an instance of actual pages with content, not simply a *type* of page. Thus, this is where most of the content from your source tree will wind up, formatted in a way that is controlled by a page master and page sequence master working together.

Each `fo:page-sequence` element contains at least one and up to three (or more) children:

- `fo:title`: An optional element used to assign a title to a document, this serves the same purpose as an XHTML document's `title` element. Depending on the User Agent, this might end up being reproduced in a window's title bar, as a watermark or running footing, and so on.
- `fo:static-content`: Also optional, this element can occur as many times as you need it. Its purpose is to declare (as the name implies) content that does not change—or, rather, that does not change according to some

condition in the source tree. For instance, you might put the literal text "First Edition" in the region-after area of every page. Or you might put "Page *n*" on every page (where *n* is replaced by a special `fo:page-number` element); even though the page number varies from one page to the next, this kind of content always appears at the same place in a page sequence defined by this `fo:page-sequence` element.

- `fo:flow`: Here's where your actual content appears, and this is the only required child of each `fo:page-sequence` element. The content is not contained directly by the `fo:flow` element; this serves just as a "wrapper" for the contents of the page sequence as a whole.

Bottom line

In Chapter 10, I'll cover the details of the XSL-FO elements I've mentioned so far. For now, though, you already know the rough framework of describing a publication's overall layout and structure using XSL-FO:

```
<fo:root media-usage="type">

  <!-- The one layout-master-set in each XSL-FO
    document describes the overall structure which the
    publication will have. -->
  <fo:layout-master-set>

    <!-- Every simple page master describes a different
      type of page in the publication. -->
    <fo:simple-page-master>
      <fo:region-body/>
      <fo:region-before/>
      <fo:region-after/>
      <fo:region-start/>
      <fo:region-end/>
    </fo:simple-page-master>

    <!-- Every page sequence master describes a
      different *sequence* of pages within the
      publication. -->
    <fo:page-sequence-master>
      <fo:single-page-master-reference...>
      <fo:repeatable-page-master-alternatives...>
      <fo:repeatable-page-master-reference...>
    </fo:page-sequence-master>
```

```
    </fo:layout-master-set>

    <!-- Publication's content is all poured into
     a series of fo:page-sequence elements. -->
    <fo:page-sequence>...</fo:page-sequence>
    <fo:page-sequence>...</fo:page-sequence>
    <fo:page-sequence>...</fo:page-sequence>
     [etc.]
</fo:root>
```

Formatting objects and properties

The XSL-FO spec seems to waver on exactly what the term "formatting object" refers to. (This is surprising in that the term is built into the vocabulary's very name.) At one point, it says that all the elements in the result tree of an XML-to-XSL-FO transformation are formatting objects. At other points, it indicates that only *some* of these result-tree elements are formatting objects.

As a practical matter, I think it's safe to consider a formatting object to be any element which either is itself subject to formatting *or* provides that formatting. For example, the various regions described in the previous section are all formatting objects (FOs); they may assume various presentational characters and hence fall into the first category—objects to which formatting may be applied. There's also a color-profile FO, which is used (as you might guess) to declare the coloring scheme to be used in a document. This isn't itself—unlike one of the regions—something that is actually rendered in a document or something that "has content." It simply assigns formatting characteristics to other FOs, and hence is an example of the second FO category.

Categories of FOs

Formatting objects can be placed in one of five general categories, as summarized in Table 9–1. The categories are assigned based on where in a page sequence (or, more precisely, where within an fo:flow element) you may use the FOs within that category.

A block FO is a contiguous area of content derived directly from the source tree. An out-of-line FO is, in some ways, similar to a block FO—like the latter, it's a single "thing"—but it operates independently of the flow of content. For instance, a callout (an excerpt from the content, placed above or to the side of a

Table 9-1 Formatting-Object Categories

Category	Description
block	Block FOs work similarly to XHTML's div element. They're single *things* (or clusters of things) which can be manipulated (formatted) as a unit. Among the block FOs are an element called fo:block, one called fo:table, and so on.
inline	Inline FOs are analogous to XHTML's span element, in that they assume some characteristic(s) apart from those of the containing block or other FO. There's an inline element named fo:inline, one named fo:character, one named fo:page-number, and so on.
neutral	These FOs may be used anywhere that text (#PCDATA), inline FOs, or block FOs may be used. Among the "neutral" FOs are one called fo:wrapper and one called fo:retrieve-marker.
out-of-line (1)	There's only one FO in this category, fo:float. It may be used anywhere that text, inline FOs, or block FOs may be used, *except* as a descendant of an out-of-line FO.
out-of-line (2)	Likewise, there's only one FO in this category, fo:footnote. It may be used anywhere that text or inline FOs may be used, *except* as a descendant of an out-of-line FO.

paragraph in which the excerpt appears) might be considered an out-of-line FO. Footnotes are out-of-line FOs because they, too, appear outside the normal flow of content.

Properties

Properties are characteristics (generally presentation-related) which formatting objects may have. There's a huge overlap between CSS's properties and XSL-FO's, and where the overlap exists the properties even share the same name. For instance, the XSL-FO equivalent of the CSS font-size property is also called font-size.

Of eight main numbered sections in the XSL-FO spec, the last, titled "Conformance," is a page or less long when printed out. Section 7 describes the XSL-FO properties, and begins before the half-way point—easily the biggest single portion of the standard. (If you threw out Section 7, in other words, the spec would be half its present length. Of course, in that case XSL-FO would be much more lightweight in more ways than one!)

There's no reasonable way to cover *all* FO properties in *Just XSL*. You can probably safely assume, though, that if there's some formatting characteristic imaginable, it's covered somewhere in the spec.

Properties are used in an XSL-FO document as *attributes* placed on the FO element(s) desired. For example, the `text-align` property can be assigned to the `fo:block` element, as in this example:

```
<fo:block text-align="right">Text</fo:block>
```

(You can probably guess that this element formats the word "Text" as right-aligned text within the block FO.)

Properties, traits, attributes...

One incredibly annoying feature of the XSL-FO spec—at least in its Candidate Recommendation form—is that it seems determined to invent new words where perfectly good ones already exist, in the general XML universe of discourse.

This business about properties being represented as what are more commonly called attributes is just one example. Another is the term "trait," which seems to appear in the text almost as often as the phrase "formatting object" but is defined nowhere. (Not that "formatting object" is, either.) If you read closely enough, though, it appears that the terms "property" and "trait" are interchangeable. For instance, `line-height` is sometimes referred to as "the `line-height` property" and sometimes as "the `line-height` trait."

If I were you, I wouldn't lose too much sleep over any of this. I'll try to stick to the word "property" to refer to some characteristic of an FO, and "attribute" to refer to what you put on an element representing the FO.

Transforming to an XSL-FO Document

I've pretty much given you the basics of this, especially in the earlier section titled "Bottom line."

What I'm going to give you now is a bare bones overview of an XSLT stylesheet for transforming a FlixML document to an XSL-FO document. All this XSL-FO document will contain, at first, is the title of a reviewed movie. Then I'll show you how to view the results (given that we won't be able to look at it in a Web browser any longer!).

But first, here's a brief digression to the movie itself, and its FlixML review.

B Alert!

**Johnny Guitar
(1954, Republic Films)**

Flamboyantly mannish saloon owner Vienna (Joan Crawford) has never gotten along with dully mannish Emma.
And when Vienna has a fling with The Dancin' Kid, whom
Emma covets, Emma will stop at nothing to get revenge—
including driving the Kid out of town.

Into this mix rides gunslinger Johnny "Johnny Guitar"
Logan (Sterling Hayden). He and Vienna had a relationship
years ago, and now she's brought him into her present to
help defend her interests as she prepares to make a killing
from the coming railroad boom. Unfortunately, she's at the
bank, withdrawing money, when the Dancin' Kid's gang
pulls one last heist—and Emma, convinced that Vienna was
in on the robbery, wants her hanged….

Johnny Guitar has been tremendously popular in Europe.
(Do a Web search on the film title and you'll find as many
sites in French, Italian, Spanish, and German as in English.)
Truffaut was especially crazy about it. In one scene from his
Mississippi Mermaid (1969), Catherine Deneuve and Jean-
Paul Belmondo emerge from a theater where they've just
seen *Johnny Guitar.* Deneuve says, "You were right. It's not
just a film about horses." Reportedly, director Ray was so
taken with the Joan Crawford wardrobe in this film that he
cribbed from it when costuming James Dean in his later
Rebel Without a Cause.

Johnny Guitar's FlixML review

```
<flixinfo author="John E. Simpson" copyright="2001"
    xml:lang="EN"
    xmlns:xlink="http://www.w3.org/1999/xlink/namespace/">
    <title role="main">Johnny Guitar</title>
    <genre>
      <primarygenre>Western</primarygenre>
    </genre>
    <releaseyear role="initial">1954</releaseyear>
    <language>English</language>
```

```xml
<studio>Republic Pictures Corporation</studio>
<cast id="castID">
  <leadcast>
    <female id="JCrawford">
      <castmember>Joan Crawford</castmember>
      <role>Vienna</role>
    </female>
    <male id="SHayden">
      <castmember>Sterling Hayden</castmember>
      <role>Johnny Guitar</role>
    </male>
    <female id="MMcCambridge">
      <castmember>Mercedes McCambridge</castmember>
      <role>Emma Small</role>
    </female>
    <male id="SBrady">
      <castmember>Scott Brady</castmember>
      <role>The Dancin' Kid</role>
    </male>
    <male id="WBond">
      <castmember>Ward Bond</castmember>
      <role>John McIvers</role>
    </male>
  </leadcast>
  <othercast>
    <male id="EBorgnine">
      <castmember>Ernest Borgnine</castmember>
      <role>Bart Lonergan</role>
    </male>
    <male id="JCarradine">
      <castmember>John Carradine</castmember>
      <role>Old Tom</role>
    </male>
  </othercast>
</cast>
<crew id="crewID">
  <director>Nicholas Ray</director>
  <screenwriter>Philip Yordan</screenwriter>
  <cinematog>Harry Stradling, Sr.</cinematog>
  <sound></sound>
  <editor>Richard L. Van Enger</editor>
  <score>Victor Young</score>
  <speceffects></speceffects>
  <proddesigner>Edward G. Boyle</proddesigner>
  <makeup></makeup>
  <costumer>Sheila O'Brien</costumer>
```

```
    </crew>
    <plotsummary id="plotID">Flamboyantly mannish saloon owner
Vienna (Joan Crawford) has never gotten along with dully mannish
Emma. And when Vienna has a fling with The Dancin' Kid, whom Emma
covets, Emma will stop at nothing to get revenge -- including
driving the Kid out of town.<parabreak/>Into this mix rides
gunslinger Johnny "Johnny Guitar" Logan (Sterling Hayden). He and
Vienna had a relationship years ago, and now she's brought him into
her present to help defend her interests as she prepares to make a
killing from the coming railroad boom.<parabreak/>Unfortunately,
she's at the bank, withdrawing money, when the Dancin' Kid's gang
pulls one last heist -- and Emma, convinced that Vienna was in on
the robbery, wants her hanged.</plotsummary>
      <reviews id="revwID">
        <flixmlreview>
          <goodreview>
            <reviewtext></reviewtext>
          </goodreview>
        </flixmlreview>
        <otherreview>
          <goodreview>
            <reviewlink
xlink:href="http://www.entertainmentnutz.com/movienutz/movie
reviews/johnny_guitar.htm">MovieNutz (Brian W.
Fairbanks)</reviewlink>
          </goodreview>
          <goodreview>
            <reviewlink
xlink:href="http://film.guardian.co.uk/Century_Of_Films/Story/
0,4135,37234,00.html">Guardian Unlimited (Derek
Malcolm)</reviewlink>
          </goodreview>
          <goodreview>
            <reviewlink
xlink:href="http://members.aol.com/michaemann/jgmain.html">
The "Johnny Guitar" Society</reviewlink>
          </goodreview>
          <goodreview>
            <reviewlink
xlink:href="http://www.pifmagazine.com/vol23/v_Johnny_Guitar.shtml"
>Remote Control (Nick Burton)</reviewlink>
          </goodreview>
        </otherreview>
      </reviews>
      <distributors id="distribID">
        <distributor>
```

```
      <distribname>Reel.com</distribname>
      <distribextlink>
        <distriblink
xlink:href="http://www.reel.com/movie.asp?MID=5001"/>
      </distribextlink>
    </distributor>
    <distributor>
      <distribname>Amazon.com</distribname>
      <distribextlink>
        <distriblink
xlink:href="http://www.amazon.com/exec/obidos/ASIN/6303391931"/>
      </distribextlink>
    </distributor>
    <distributor>
      <distribname>Yahoo! Video Shopping</distribname>
      <distribextlink>
        <distriblink
xlink:href="http://shopping.yahoo.com
shop?d=v&amp;id=1800083797&amp;clink=dmvi-ks/johnny_guitar"/>
      </distribextlink>
    </distributor>
    <distributor>
      <distribname>BlockBuster</distribname>
      <distribextlink>
        <distriblink
xlink:href="http://www.blockbuster.com/mv/
detail.jhtml?PRODID=117675&amp;CATID=1100"/>
      </distribextlink>
    </distributor>
    <distributor>
      <distribname>MovieGallery</distribname>
      <distribextlink>
        <distriblink
xlink:href="http://www.moviegallery.com/vhs_info.cgi?product
_id=REP2127.3"/>
      </distribextlink>
    </distributor>
  </distributors>
  <dialog>Johnny: How many men have you forgotten? Vienna: As many
women as you've remembered.</dialog>
  <remarks>Tremendously popular in Europe. In one scene from
Truffaut's "Mississippi Mermaid" (1969), Catherine Deneuve and
Jean-Paul Belmondo emerge from a theater where they've just seen
"Johnny Guitar." "You were right," says Deneuve, "It's not just a
film about horses."</remarks>
  <mpaarating id="rateID">NR</mpaarating>
```

```
    <bees b-ness="&BEE5URL;"/>
</flixinfo>
```

Creating the basic result tree

There's not too much to add to what you already know. The idea—just as when transforming to XHTML or Open eBook, for example—is to begin with the root of the source tree and create a corresponding "root structure" in the result.

In this case, the result tree will be a print publication that at first simply re-creates a portion of the contents of a FlixML document. Eventually, this print publication will be one of those little "playbill"-type handouts you get when attending a play, and it might conceivably include reviews of more than one film (for a hypothetical "FlixML B-Film Festival"). But we'll work up to that.

Laying out the page

For now, let's just start with the information shown in Table 9–2, defining the look of an extremely simple page. Dimensions are given in points, a unit of measurement often used by print designers; there are approximately 72 points in an inch.[4]

Table 9-2   General Layout/Structure of a Simple Document Page

Item	Dimension (in points)
Page size (total)	200 W × 200 H
Page size (printable)	100 W × 100 H

Note that, for this simple example, we won't start out specifying any of the regions *around* the body, just the body region itself.

From layout to result

With the dimensions provided in Table 9–2 we have the rudiments of a simple page master. So we can start to build the XSLT stylesheet like this:

---

4.   Although you *can* use points to express both vertical and horizontal dimensions, technically they're for use only in specifying an object's height. As a unit of measurement for demonstrations, though, they're an ideal size, especially when dealing (as we will be) with Adobe's Acrobat Reader software.

```
<xsl:template match="flixinfo">
   <fo:root
     xmlns:fo="http://www.w3.org/1999/XSL/Format">
     <fo:layout-master-set>
       <fo:simple-page-master master-name="page-review"
         page-width="200pt" page-height="200pt"
         margin="50pt">
         <fo:region-body region-name="reg-body"/>
       </fo:simple-page-master>
       <fo:page-sequence-master
         master-name="seq-mast-cover">
         <fo:single-page-master-reference
           master-name="page-review"/>
       </fo:page-sequence-master>
     </fo:layout-master-set>
     <xsl:apply-templates select="title"/>
   </fo:root>
</xsl:template>
```

The layout master set constructed by this template rule has a single simple page master, which is assigned the name page-review (via its master-name attribute). The width and height are assigned as in Table 9–2; the margin is set to 50 points all around, which will make the "printable" area 100 points square. The page-review simple page master contains a single region—the body, which is assigned a name of reg-body.

Having defined the general layout of the page with the simple page master element, we need to indicate how pages which use this layout will be sequenced in the resulting document. This is accomplished with a page sequence master, named seq-mast-cover. It contains a single child, a single-page-master-reference whose master-name attribute does *not* name this reference, but rather points back to a page master which has this name—that is, in this case the page-review simple page master previously set up.

Note the way these elements and attributes are named. Yes, the names are confusingly (almost maddeningly) alike. However, their names are built up in a logical manner. For instance, as I mentioned, when an element name ends in "-master," that element will serve not to hold actual content but to describe a general class or type of objects (such as a type of simple page, defined by a simple-page-master element).

So far, all this does is instantiate the skeleton of an XSL-FO document. However, there is an xsl:apply-templates element to process title elements in the source tree. Here's what the corresponding template rule looks like:

```
<xsl:template match="title">
    <fo:page-sequence master-name="seq-mast-cover">
     <fo:flow flow-name="reg-body">
      <fo:block font-size="20pt"
        border-style="solid" border-width="1pt">
        <xsl:value-of select="."/>
      </fo:block>
     </fo:flow>
    </fo:page-sequence>
</xsl:template>
```

This template rule instantiates in the result tree a page sequence—that is, a flow object which actually contains some content. There's a `master-name` attribute, whose value asserts that the layout of this page sequence's contents is defined by the `page-sequence-master` element in the preceding template rule. (See the way the `master-name` attribute here ties back to the `master-name` attribute there?)

Within the page sequence, we're going to flow content into the body of the page. This portion of the page layout was previously defined by a region named `reg-body`, so that's the value we give to the `flow-name` attribute. Within the `fo:flow` element, we'll set up a block FO using 20-point type and surrounded by a narrow box. The contents of this block FO will be supplied by the value of the `title` element we're currently processing, per the `xsl:value-of` element in the template.

When applied to the *Johnny Guitar* FlixML review, this stylesheet creates the following result tree:

```
<fo:root xmlns:fo="http://www.w3.org/1999/XSL/Format">
    <fo:layout-master-set>
     <fo:simple-page-master
       master-name="page-review"
       page-width="200pt" page-height="200pt"
       margin="50pt">
       <fo:region-body region-name="reg-body"/>
     </fo:simple-page-master>
     <fo:page-sequence-master
       master-name="seq-mast-cover">
       <fo:single-page-master-reference
         master-name="page-review"/>
     </fo:page-sequence-master>
    </fo:layout-master-set>
    <fo:page-sequence master-name="seq-mast-cover">
     <fo:flow flow-name="reg-body">
```

```
    <fo:block font-size="20pt" border-style="solid"
      border-width="1pt">Johnny Guitar</fo:block>
  </fo:flow>
  </fo:page-sequence>
</fo:root>
```

Again, notice—now that the surrounding XSLT stuff has been removed—how the attributes in later elements refer back to those identifying earlier elements.

Viewing an XSL-FO Document

Now we come to a critical juncture: How do you actually look at one of these XSL-FO documents? (Or, heck, what can you do with one, period—look at it or otherwise?)

I'm not going to get into the details of using XSL-FO software at this point. But I do want to explain how I'm going to be showing you the effects of producing XSL-FO documents.

Step 1: Generate the XSL-FO document

To "generate" an XSL-FO document you can, of course, create one by hand. As I've mentioned, though, that's not a recommended course of action, and it's certainly not the one I'm using.

I'll use the Saxon XSLT processor to produce my XSL-FO result trees. I won't always show you (as I did above) the XSLT which transforms a given FlixML document in a given way; but understand that when you see blocks of XSL-FO code here, I've almost *never* hand-authored it.

Step 2: Convert the XSL-FO to PDF

Huh? Why go to all the trouble of generating XSL-FO result trees if you're just going to convert them to another Adobe format?

Granted, this seems at first glance to be kind of silly (if not downright perverse). There are a few reasons for it:

• Almost no native XSL-FO processors are available at the time I'm writing this. (And the one or two that are out there aren't particularly stable.) However, a number of solid XSL-FO-to-PDF converters *are* available.

- …and, of course, there's one extremely good PDF renderer widely available: Adobe's own free Acrobat Reader product. Note that Adobe's product for *creating* PDFs, Acrobat Exchange, is *not* free.
- Finally, I've got to convert the XSL-FO to *something* if I'm going to show you the effects of the vocabulary on output. Just as with the FlixML-as-XHTML MSIE screen shots in the first part of the book, screen shots of an Acrobat Reader window will make immediately obvious how a given result tree "works."

What I'll use

The specific package I'll use for Step #2 is the enigmatically named Xep, a product of RenderX. I had a couple of choices, but Xep is easily the most advanced product in terms of compliance with the XSL-FO standard.

On the other hand, Xep has a couple of disadvantages. First, its full-featured version is *very* expensive. (Anyone used to spending a couple hundred dollars for software, if that, will have the breath knocked out of her by Xep's price tag.[5]) Second, although Xep *is* available in a time-limited evaluation version, this version is functionally crippled in some ways. For instance, it stamps every page with a watermark-like indication that the page was created using a RenderX product; and after page 11, every page is *blank*.

Making do

Neither of these limitations will be crippling for my purposes (I'll just use the evaluation version), but they may be for yours. If you're interested in purchasing the uncrippled version of Xep, contact RenderX's sales unit at sales@renderx.com. The evaluation version can be downloaded from the company's Web site, www.renderx.com.

In terms of sheer numbers of users, probably the most popular XSL-FO-to-PDF package is FOP, originally developed by James Tauber but

---

5.   Not to imply that it's necessarily *over*-priced. The XSL-FO standard is undoubtedly enormous, and implementing a package that complies with it is an amazing achievement for RenderX. But it's not a product that will help drive XSL-FO's acceptance among the masses. (Among the masses of publishers with deep pockets, maybe.)

now supported by the Apache open-source project. Currently at version 0.16, FOP's greatest virtues are that it *is* open source and it's free. Unfortunately, both of those virtues combine to generate its biggest current weakness: It simply doesn't support enough of the current spec to be useful as a tool for *demonstrating* the current spec.

If you've got any application-development skills at all and would like to make a mark on the history of both the XML world and the open-source movement, I strongly urge you to get involved in bringing FOP up to snuff.

The XSL-FO result tree I reproduced earlier resides in a file called playbill.fo. (Other common filename extensions for XSL-FO documents are .fob and .xfo. However, if you use the .fo extension, Xep will automatically name the resulting file—in this case—playbill.pdf. Otherwise it simply tacks the .pdf extension onto the full XSL-FO document's filename.) When I run Xep (which is a command-line utility) against playbill.fo, it displays various status messages as it works its way through the XSL-FO code and then writes out a playbill.pdf file.

Figure 9–2 illustrates how playbill.pdf looks. I've turned Acrobat's "forms grid" on, and set it to display the grid in points (using a 10-point grid size) rather than inches. This makes it easier to understand the relationship between the PDF output and the XSL-FO that went into it. Note that the box surrounding the film's title starts at 50 points down, 50 points in from the left, and extends to the right margin—also 50 points in, per the margin settings for this simple page master. However, the vertical size of the box simply extends only to the bottom of the enclosed content, not to the bottom margin. This would allow further content to be added within the box, if so desired.

Other Regions

In general, the content to be transferred from your source tree will go into the body region of your XSL-FO result tree. In the other regions, you'd typically insert static text that would repeat from one page to the next. (This is enforced by a requirement that a page sequence may have only one `fo:flow` child element, but several `fo:static-content` children.) Let's add a couple of simple examples to the simple result tree we've got so far.

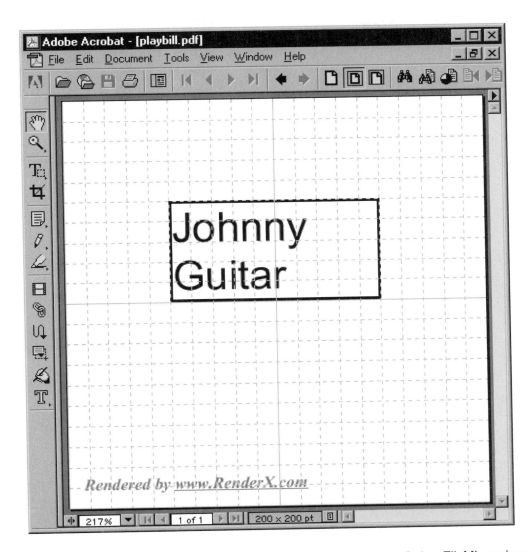

Figure 9-2 A simple XSL-FO rendering of part of the *Johnny Guitar* FlixML review, converted to PDF by RenderX's Xep processor. (Note the RenderX plug inserted at the bottom left; in the registered commercial version of Xep, this tagline does not appear.) The page size displayed in the status bar (200 × 200 pt.) is consistent with the page-width and page-height settings established for this simple page master in the XSL-FO code.

Adding a header: `region-before`

The first thing you've got to do before adding any actual text content to another (non-body) region in the result tree is establish the region's existence in the first place. This occurs in the simple page master's definition, immediately following the `fo:region-body` element.

The size of one of these "side regions," as they're called, is specified using an attribute named `extent`. For the before and after regions, this attribute defines their *height*; for start and end, their *width*.

So let's take a stab at declaring a before region. The result tree containing the simple page master will now look like this:

```
<fo:simple-page-master
   master-name="page-review"
   page-width="200pt" page-height="200pt"
   margin="50pt">
   <fo:region-body region-name="reg-body"/>
   <fo:region-before region-name="reg-before"
      extent="20pt"/>
</fo:simple-page-master>
```

The only change so far is the addition of the `fo:region-before` element. It specifies an extent of 20 points in size, which means that the before region will be 20 points high.

Now, to insert some static text in this before region, we also need to make a corresponding addition to the page sequence (which, again, is where the actual content appears):

```
<fo:page-sequence master-name="seq-mast-cover">
   <fo:static-content flow-name="reg-before">
    <fo:block font-size="10pt"
      background-color="silver">
      A FlixML Review
    </fo:block>
   </fo:static-content>
   <fo:flow flow-name="reg-body">
    <fo:block font-size="20pt"
      border-style="solid" border-width="1pt">
      Johnny Guitar
    </fo:block>
   </fo:flow>
</fo:page-sequence>
```

The addition is the `fo:static-content` element. Its contents will appear in every "reg-before" region created by this result tree—that is, in the `region-before` just added to the simple page master. Here, I've set the contents to the phrase "A FlixML Review," which will appear in 10-point type on a silver background.

A final reminder

I'm not going to belabor the issue further, but remember that what I'm showing you is the result tree of an XSLT transformation, from FlixML to XSL-FO. If this were a fragment of XSLT code, the words "Johnny Guitar" wouldn't be there—in their place would be the `xsl:value-of` element I showed you earlier.

All excited, we crank this through Xep and see Figure 9–3. Uh-oh. Looks like we've got something scrambled, hmm?

The "problem" isn't really a problem; it just requires a little more thought about what we've declared the document's layout to be at this point.

Remember first that the printable page area (defined by the `fo:simple-page-master` element's `height` and `width` attributes) was set to 200 by 200 points. The `region-before` has an extent of 20 points, and this seems to have rendered correctly. But there's no "automatic shoving-down" of the `region-body`; we've got to arrange that ourselves.

Typically, this is done by adding a `margin` attribute to the `fo:block` element enclosing the `region-body`'s contents. For instance,

```
<fo:flow flow-name="reg-body">
   <fo:block font-size="20pt"
     border-style="solid" border-width="1pt"
     margin-top="20pt">
     Johnny Guitar
   </fo:block>
</fo:flow>
```

Now (see Figure 9–4) the results are much more in line with expectations!

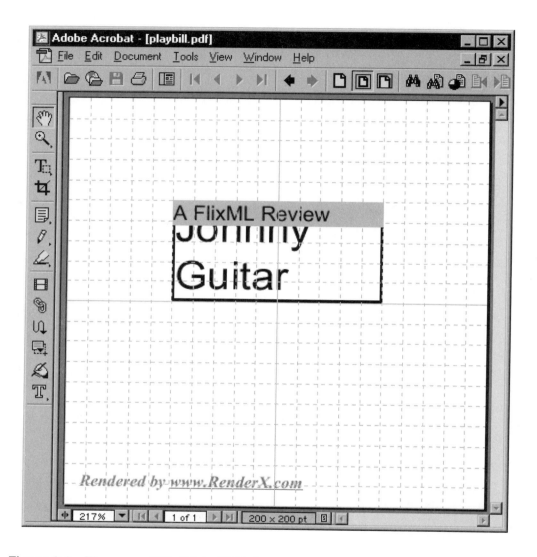

Figure 9-3 The same XSL-FO-to-PDF document as shown in Figure 9–2, here "en-hanced" by the addition of a before region. But this doesn't look like it's following any standard definition of "before," does it? (Looks more like "on top of.") See the text for an explanation.

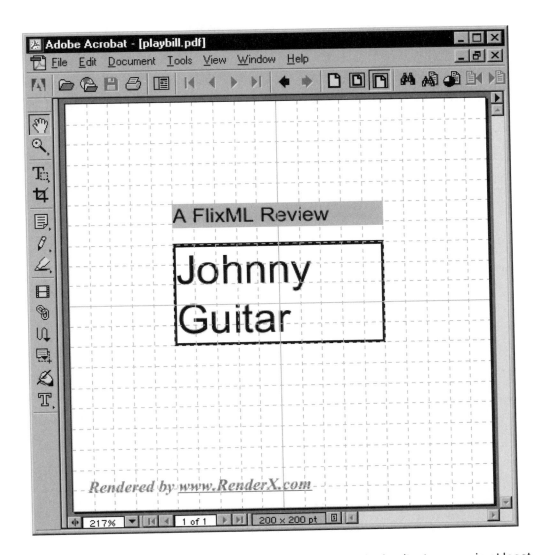

Figure 9-4   The body region of Figure 9–3 fixed up, by assigning it a top margin at least as large as the before region's extent. Notice the silver background to the before region, which is not 20 points high (the size of the region's extent). Rather, it's *10* points high (the height of the `fo:block` element within which the text is enclosed).

Things look like they're starting to shape up in some reasonable fashion now, so let's add code for the other three regions: after, start, and end. First, add them to the simple page master itself:

```
<fo:simple-page-master master-name="page-review"
   page-width="200pt" page-height="200pt"
   margin="50pt">
   <fo:region-body region-name="reg-body"/>
   <fo:region-before region-name="reg-before"
    extent="20pt"/>
   <fo:region-after region-name="reg-after"
    extent="20pt"/>
   <fo:region-start region-name="reg-start"
    extent="5pt"/>
   <fo:region-end region-name="reg-end"
    extent="5pt"/>
</fo:simple-page-master>
```

Note that this sets the extents for both the start and end regions to 5 points. (And recall that for these two regions, the extent attributes establish *width*.)

There's no need to make any further changes to the general structure of the page (which is what the simple page master defines), so we can move on to actually putting some content in those regions. As with the before region, we'll use static content; the fo:page-sequence element (as set up in the XSLT stylesheet) now looks like this:

```
<fo:page-sequence master-name="seq-mast-cover">
   <fo:static-content flow-name="reg-before">
    <fo:block font-size="10pt"
     background-color="silver">A FlixML Review</fo:block>
   </fo:static-content>
   <fo:static-content flow-name="reg-after">
    <fo:block font-size="8pt"
     background-color="silver" text-align="center">
     Copyright <xsl:value-of select="../@copyright"/>
    </fo:block>
   </fo:static-content>
   <fo:static-content flow-name="reg-start">
    <fo:block font-size="8pt"
     background-color="silver"
     height="60pt">S</fo:block>
   </fo:static-content>
   <fo:static-content flow-name="reg-end">
    <fo:block font-size="8pt"
     background-color="silver"
```

```
        height="60pt">E</fo:block>
    </fo:static-content>
    <fo:flow flow-name="reg-body">
      <fo:block font-size="20pt"
        border-style="solid" border-width="1pt"
        margin-top="20pt"
        margin-left="5pt"
        margin-right="5pt">
        <xsl:value-of select="."/>
      </fo:block>
    </fo:flow>
</fo:page-sequence>
```

As you can see, the `region-after` will contain the copyright date of the FlixML review, and the `region-start` and `region-end` will contain the literal characters "S" and "E," respectively. Notice, too, that the latter two regions' heights have been set to an arbitrarily large 60 points. (In theory, this should extend silver bars to the left and right down the length of the body region.)

After cranking this revised stylesheet through an XSLT processor, and the resulting XSL-FO document through Xep, we see the results in Figure 9–5.

What happened to the silver bars at left and right?

What happened to them is the same thing that happened to the silver bars at the top and bottom: They take up only as much space as required by the `font-size` attribute of the `fo:block` element, regardless of the value of the corresponding `height` attributes.

This is one of your first lessons in a, well, I don't want to say *nasty* reality about using XSL-FO... let's just settle for a *surprising* reality. Which is this: There may be not just one element or attribute you need to look at, but *several*.

In this case, it helps to know that `fo:block` elements can have not only `font-size` and `height` attributes but also a `line-height` attribute. This specifies the "vertical space taken up by a line of type," no matter how large or small the actual `font-size`. Replacing the `height` attributes in the corresponding `fo:block` elements in the page sequence with `line-height` attributes (with a value of 60) instead, this portion of the result tree now looks like the following:

```
<fo:static-content flow-name="reg-start">
    <fo:block font-size="8pt"
      background-color="silver"
      line-height="60pt">S</fo:block>
</fo:static-content>
<fo:static-content flow-name="reg-end">
```

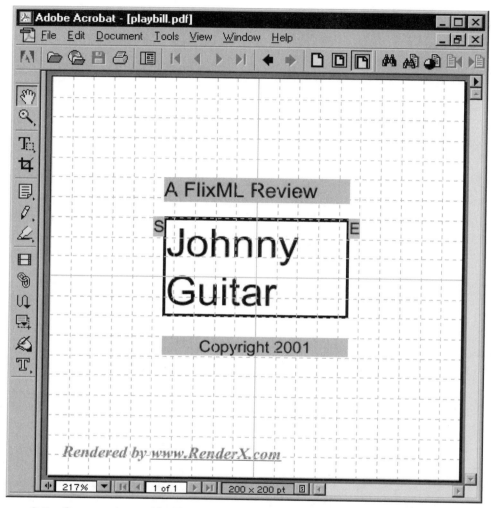

Figure 9-5   Same output as in Figure 9–4, "enhanced" by the addition of start, end, and after regions (left, right, and bottom respectively). Look back at Figure 9–4, and observe not only that the new regions have been added but that the *existing* ones have "shrunk" to accommodate the new ones, by 5 points at the left and right. The body has also shrunk by 20 points to accommodate the region-after, but that's not obvious here because the text in the body doesn't fill the entire region.

```
    <fo:block font-size="8pt"
      background-color="silver"
      line-height="60pt">E</fo:block>
</fo:static-content>
```

And the outcome of the usual XML-through-XSL-FO-to-PDF cycle now produces a document like the one shown in Figure 9–6.

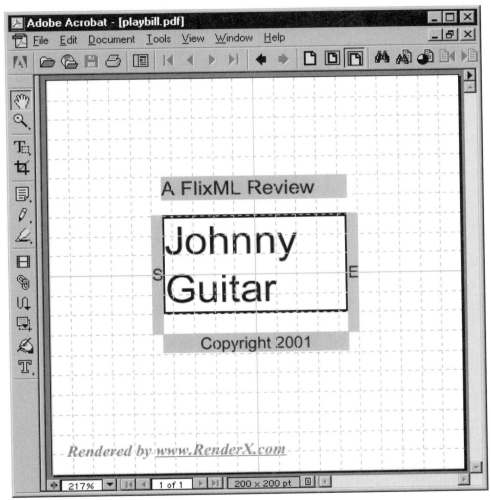

Figure 9-6 Full-length silver backgrounds added to the start and end regions (left and right, respectively), using the `line-height` instead of the (simpler and more intuitive) `height` attributes to the corresponding `fo:block` elements.

Getting the Word Out: XSL-FO Basics

Whatever else you can say about computers, the things certainly have (at least momentarily) secured the place of the written word in human affairs. Just when sound recording, radio, television, and films (yes, *B* films among them) seemed to be ushering in a new age of illiteracy, along came these marvelous devices to reaffirm the importance of placing one word after another and then picking them up the same way.

The primacy of words *per se* aside, we often need to place the words in contexts that, well, *look good*. The literate human eye has been trained to recognize the meaning of the *appearance* of sentences, words, individual letter-forms. This isn't just a matter of esthetics—style for style's sake—but also a practical device to strengthen the connection between words and what they mean and to enhance the ability of the reader to *get to* that meaning. Headings in printed materials announce the topic in advance, giving the reader's brain a split-second to adjust to a new (or nuanced) context. Running headers and footers constantly remind him, *Here's where you are.* If there's a lot of text to be displayed in a small font, laying it out in a multi-column format increases the odds that her eye will not tire (and wander) before reaching the end of the line of type—and, more importantly, that she can easily find the beginning of the *next* line. Even the tiny little strokes—the serifs—on the letters in a certain class of font aid in getting at the meaning: When viewed from a distance, or even close up in a small font, they cue the eye subtly that a given letter is not a *different* one. And so on.[1]

The material in this chapter does not presume to teach you typography. It's also not going to detail the use of some of the more esoteric page-layout features available within the XSL-FO vocabulary. Still, it's going to dwell on some things about page layout that your unconscious mind, at least, has always known—drag them, as it were, kicking and screaming into your conscious mind. Once they're there, I'll try to establish connections between them and certain fundamental XSL-FO syntax.

Area Trees, Area Models

You've probably seen at least one of those "cosmic zoom" movies, right? These are the documentary things that begin with a view of a galaxy spinning in space, then the "camera" comes in closer and closer to an individual solar system, then the third planet, and a land mass on that planet, down to a blade of grass, a molecule of chlorophyll, an atom.

Conceptualizing the structure of a printed document is something like that (on nowhere near so hypnotic and grand a scale, unfortunately). XSL-FO codifies this view of a document as something called an *area tree*.

Area trees

I don't know why they chose a tree metaphor for this (other than a desire to link XSL-FO in the user's mind to the same metaphor in its common XML/XPath/XSLT sense, the tree of nodes). In fact, most of the discussion of the area "tree" in the XSL-FO spec sounds more like a discussion of an area *box*. Or, even better, an area *grid*—with boxes not only nesting within but placed alongside one another.[2]

The core of this area tree notion is, of course, that of an *area* itself. In XSL-FO terms, an area has several key traits:

---

1.   Boy, once you start thinking about this stuff it's hard to stop. Meaning is at the heart of just about every typographical device you encounter, from the use of color, through the size of margins and "gutters" between columns, down to spaces and punctuation between words and, indeed, the space between each pair of letters *within* a word.

- It has a position on the page.
- It has something inside it.
- It *may* have a background (color or image), borders on any or all of its four sides, and a padding specification.

P a d d i n g   v e r s u s   m a r g i n

To some extent, XSL-FO follows the terminology of CSS when it comes to describing areas (although what the former calls "areas" are called "boxes" in CSS).

Working from the inside out: At the center of an area is the *content*, which may or may not be surrounded by a border. The space between the content and the inner edge of the border is the *padding*. The space between the outer edge of the border and the edge of the area itself is the *margin*. Thus, the distance between the rectangle in which the content itself resides and the outermost edge of the area itself is the sum of the padding, the thickness of the border, and the margin.

All of this has a couple of implications. First, you put a border around content, but not around an area. (You can, though, simulate the latter by putting a border around the content and setting the margin to 0.) Second, you don't specify the size of the "content rectangle" directly. (You specify the size of the area, the margin, the border thickness, height and width, and the padding. The size of the "content rectangle" is whatever remains.)

What's interesting about these three characteristics of a given area is that they may be applied to *any* area—not just the larger-scale ones such as the regions of a simple page master or the blocks of text within them, but even the individual characters. (There's an `fo:character` element, for instance, which lets you place a border around an initial large capital letter. You can do this

---

2. Historically, the Mother of All Models for print layout is indeed a series of nested or abutting boxes—originally, *literal* boxes in which type was set by hand. Connections to this history still lie behind much layout terminology. (For example, "uppercase" and "lowercase" originally referred to the locations of wooden racks where letters of that kind were kept until being placed in the printing press frame.) Newer technologies, like CSS and XSLT, have simply layered their own terms on the old. So you end up with a crazy quilt of language, over time.

because each character is assumed to implicitly occupy the "content rectangle" within its own area, as made explicit by the fo:character element.)

Somewhat crucially, not every FO causes an area to be created on the page. For example, a number of FOs are used primarily (or solely) as containers for others, and it's these other FOs that generate areas. The upshot of this is that although such container-type FOs certainly have content, they do not themselves have a position, and they may or may not have a background.

Types of area

The last chapter classified FOs as block, inline, "neutral," or out-of-line, depending on what kind of FO they can be contained by. There's a similar way of classifying *areas*, one that uses some of the same language.

Block areas   Block areas are what typically come to mind when you think of a page layout. They're rectangles arranged on the page above, below, to either side of, or within other rectangles on the same page. For the most part, block areas get placed on the page—stacked—vertically, one atop another, but sometimes it's possible to explicitly position a block.

Inline areas   Inline areas typically represent subsections of block areas, and they typically get placed on the page—stacked—horizontally, one alongside another. (Again, though, you may also explicitly position some inline areas.) The general idea is represented by Figure 10–1.

Figure 10-1   A single block area containing three inline areas. In this example, the inline areas are not contiguous, but there's no requirement that this be the case. Likewise, each inline area here occupies a rectangular shape, but this is almost incidental, a chance result of the size of the block; any of the inline areas could "wrap" within the overall block (simply by expanding or shrinking the block's width) and still be considered a single area.

Line areas   Figure 10–1 can be a little misleading, in that it may seem to imply that a block area—the overall area represented by the figure—can have both block and inline children (the big word BLOCK, somehow interrupted by occasional instances of the word inline). In fact, although any block or inline area can have block or inline children (depending on the formatting object defining the parent area), a given area will have *only* block *or* inline children— never a mixture.

A special kind of block area, called a *line area*, is a block whose children are all inline areas. Each of the inline areas can have its own characteristics, as shown in Figure 10–2.

INLINEinline**INLINEINLINEINLINE**
INLINEINLINE_inline_**INLINEINLINE**
inline**INLINEINLINEINLINEINLINE**
INLINE_inline_

Figure 10-2   A line area. The overall block (signified by the thin box surrounding the whole figure) contains only inline children. Here, most of these inline areas have the same display characteristics, but every now and then one of them breaks out in rebellion, as it were, with a look of its own.

Glyph areas   A *glyph* is a single character—not just the concept the letter represents but its physical representation as well, the way it *looks*. Thus, a capital Y is a different glyph than a lowercase y; and an uppercase Y in a given proportional font is a different glyph than an uppercase ʏ in a monospace font, or than an uppercase Y in a different proportional font, or (for that matter) than a bold italic *Y* version of itself.

Every single character of text content in an XSL-FO document implicitly occupies its own *glyph area*. Unlike the other kinds of area, a glyph area can never have as its content another area; it always contains one glyph, and one glyph only.

Thus, glyph areas are subsections of inline areas, just as inline areas are subsections of block areas (or larger, containing inline areas). Like inline areas, they "stack" horizontally, one alongside another.

W e s t e r n - c e n t e r e d ,   a g a i n

As a reminder, I'm continuing to use Western languages and writing systems as my default frame of reference in this chapter. These languages/writing systems start displaying content in the top left of an area and move "top to bottom, left to right" thereafter. So when I say "left-to-right," for instance, I really mean "in the direction in which one glyph normally follows another in the language/writing system under consideration." For other writing systems, this may be bottom-to-top/right-to-left, or bottom-to-top/left-to-right, or top-to-bottom/right-to-left, or even bi-directionally one way or the other.

This is yet another reason for the XSL-FO spec's length and apparent complexity: The spec's authors were determined to stay neutral regarding writing systems. For instance, they almost never just say "top to bottom" and "left to right"; rather, they use invented, inscrutable locutions like "block-stacking-strategy" and "inline-progression-direction." It's like the old radio comedy: You dread knowing that the spec's authors are approaching a closet door labeled, say, simply "Start"—because you know when they open it, a horrible avalanche of pots, pans, Tupperware, Grandma's china, tennis racquets, and screeching household pets is going to come crashing to the floor.

I'll trust you, the reader, to make the necessary adjustments to your own frame of reference.

Introduction to Formatting Objects

As I said in Chapter 9, a formatting object (FO) is pretty much anything *to which* formatting may be applied or *which* applies formatting itself. Let's take a look at some specific characteristics of these beasts.

Formatting objects classified by purpose

In the previous chapter, I mentioned that some FOs could be classified based on the contexts in which they appeared. For instance, some can appear only within block FOs, some only within inline FOs, and so on.

They can also be classified by *purpose*, or the general role they play in controlling the presentation of content. Each of the following sections summarizes one of these purposes. Each section also lists the various formatting objects that fall into this classification (and, where appropriate, indicates the context in which each may appear). I won't be detailing the use of every single FO, but I'll try to give you a sense of where to use it and what it does.

Declaration, pagination, and page layout FOs

This group of FOs controls the overall structure of a document to be presented using the XSL-FO vocabulary. In general, they also function as the high-level "wrappers" that provide structure to the XSL-FO document/result tree itself. Table 10–1 summarizes these FOs.

Table 10-1   Declaration, Pagination, and Page Layout Formatting Objects

Formatting object	Child of...
`fo:root`	N/A
`fo:declarations`	`fo:root`
`fo:color-profile`	`fo:declarations`
`fo:page-sequence`	`fo:root`
`fo:layout-master-set`	`fo:root`
`fo:page-sequence-master`	`fo:layout-master-set`
`fo:single-page-master-reference`	`fo:page-sequence-master`
`fo:repeatable-page-master-reference`	`fo:page-sequence-master`
`fo:repeatable-page-master-alternatives`	`fo:page-sequence-master`
`fo:conditional-page-master-reference`	`fo:repeatable-page-master-alternatives`
`fo:simple-page-master`	`fo:layout-master-set`
`fo:region-body`	`fo:simple-page-master`
`fo:region-before`	`fo:simple-page-master`
`fo:region-after`	`fo:simple-page-master`
`fo:region-start`	`fo:simple-page-master`
`fo:region-end`	`fo:simple-page-master`
`fo:flow`	`fo:page-sequence`
`fo:static-content`	`fo:page-sequence`
`fo:title`	`fo:page-sequence`

Because an XSL-FO document can't really do without most of these elements, I covered most of them in Chapter 9. The ones I didn't address are these:

- `fo:declarations`: This acts as a wrapper for global declarations to be used in an XSL-FO document. The only such declaration in the XSL-FO namespace is `fo:color-profile` (next bullet); the spec says that declarations from other namespaces can be included, without providing any examples.

- `fo:color-profile`: This element declares the International Color Consortium (ICC) "color profile" to be used in generating colors used by this XSL-FO document. A color profile is basically a table of numbers used to translate the colors that can be rendered by one class of devices to colors that can be rendered by a different class of devices. Its most important attribute is `src`, whose value is the URI of the color profile to be used. (For more information on ICC color profiles, see the ICC home page at www.color.org.)

- `fo:conditional-page-master-reference`: In discussing different kinds of page sequences in Chapter 9, I described the "one and only one page like this" case, the "repeating pages like this" case, and the "alternating pages like this" case represented by the `fo:single-page-master-reference`, `fo:repeatable-page-master-reference`, and `fo:repeatable-page-master-alternatives` FOs, respectively. This FO is a special form of the latter, which enables you to do simple kinds of alternation such as, "If this is the first page, lay it out in one manner; otherwise, lay it out in another."

Block-level FOs

As the name implies, block-level FOs are used for establishing block-type FOs—block *areas*—that can be filled with content and then moved around on the page as a unit (or simply "stacked" in their default arrangement).

In addition to other block-level FOs, inline-level FOs, and so on, block-level FOs can contain simple #PCDATA (text) content. Consequently, you'll use them often when transferring source-tree content to the result tree with the XSLT `xsl:value-of` element. Table 10–2 lists the block-level FOs.

Table 10-2   Block-Level Formatting Objects

Formatting object	Child of...
`fo:block`	Block FOs, `fo:flow`, `fo:static-content`
`fo:block-container`	Block FOs, `fo:flow`, `fo:static-content`

The `fo:block-container` element, says the spec, may be used to make blocks within blocks behave differently. For instance, the area it defines may contain multiple `fo:block` elements in alternating "writing modes" (e.g., left-to-right and right-to-left). It also can be used to assign common characteristics (such as height) to the block FOs it contains.

Blocks within an `fo:block-container` can also be "rotated" using an optional `reference-orientation` attribute. This attribute takes a numeric value, in (positive and negative) increments of 90: `-90`, `0`, `90`, `180`, and so on, through (positive or negative) `270`. Note, though, that this doesn't cause *text* to be rotated by 90 or however many degrees. Instead, it simply changes the definitions of "left," "right," "top," and "bottom"—moving them around the compass, as it were.

Inline-level FOs

As you can probably guess from the term, which is used in several XSL-FO contexts but always means pretty much the same thing, an inline-level FO is intended to effect some temporary change in the presentation of the content in which the inline-level FO's content appears. Thus, for example, a paragraph as a whole might need to be presented in thus-and-such a font, but you want to *interrupt* that treatment of the content with a different one. Table 10–3 lists the inline-level FOs.

Table 10-3 Inline-Level Formatting Objects

Formatting object	Child of...
`fo:bidi-override`	Inline, block
`fo:character`	Inline, block
`fo:initial-property-set`	`fo:block`
`fo:external-graphic`	Inline, block
`fo:instream-foreign-object`	Inline, block
`fo:inline`	Inline, block
`fo:inline-container`	Inline, block
`fo:leader`	Inline, block

Table 10-3   Inline-Level Formatting Objects (continued)

Formatting object	Child of...
fo:page-number	Inline, block
fo:page-number-citation	Inline, block

Some of these inline elements will function like the XHTML span element, as wrappers for text content which is to be presented differently than the content which surrounds it. Some of them, however, represent *non*-text content that simply appears amid the regular flow of text.

I'm going to spend more time detailing most of these FOs later in this chapter. The exceptions are these:

- fo:bidi-override: The term "bidi" (pronounced "bye-dye") refers to *bi-directional* text. This is text which, in certain writing systems, flows (for example) left-to-right on the first line, then drops down to the next line and flows right-to-left, then drops down to go left-to-right again, and so on. This element is used to force certain behaviors when the processor's Unicode algorithm for processing bi-directional text breaks down.
- fo:initial-property-set: This FO is used within an fo:block to specify the formatting properties of the block's first line of text.
- fo:inline-container: Like fo:block-container in relationship to block-type FOs, this is used as a wrapper for inline-type FOs, allowing you to assign common properties to the contained inline FOs.

Table FOs

Table 10–4 lists the FOs used for creating tables in an XSL-FO document/result tree.

Table 10-4   Table Formatting Objects

Formatting object	Child of...
fo:table-and-caption	Block
fo:table	Block, fo:table-and-caption
fo:table-column	fo:table
fo:table-caption	fo:table-and-caption

Table 10-4   Table Formatting Objects (continued)

`fo:table-header`	`fo:table`
`fo:table-footer`	`fo:table`
`fo:table-body`	`fo:table`
`fo:table-row`	`fo:table-header, fo:table-footer, fo:table-body`
`fo:table-cell`	`fo:table-row`

If you want your table to have a caption, use the `fo:table-and-caption` FO. The contents of this FO are an `fo:table` and an `fo:table-caption`; their placement relative to each other, when formatted, depends on the value of the `fo:table-caption` element's `caption-side` attribute. This value may be `before` (the default), `after`, `start`, `end`, `top`, `bottom`, `left`, or `right`.

Whether you're using a caption or not, the `fo:table` contains the bulk of the individual table-related elements. The XSL-FO table model differs in some interesting ways from that of XHTML; I'll cover table handling at the end of this chapter, in the section titled "Table-Type FOs Revisited."

List FOs

As you might guess, these FOs are used for presenting content in list (typically, but not necessarily, "bulleted") form. Table 10–5 lists the FOs of this kind.

Table 10-5   List Formatting Objects

Formatting object	Child of...
`fo:list-block`	Block
`fo:list-item`	`fo:list-block`
`fo:list-item-body`	`fo:list-item`
`fo:list-item-label`	`fo:list-item`

The root of any XSL-FO list is the `fo:list-block` element. Within that appear any number of `fo:list-item` elements, whose contents are—in this order—an `fo:list-item-label` and `fo:list-item-body` element.

Using the *Johnny Guitar* FlixML review from Chapter 9 as our source document, we could write an XSLT transformation to produce the following partial result tree showing how to use these elements together as a list of other reviews of the film:

```
<fo:flow flow-name="reg-body">
  <fo:block font-size="8pt" font-weight="bold">
   Read more about "Johnny Guitar":
  </fo:block>
  <fo:list-block>
    <fo:list-item font-size="8pt">
      <fo:list-item-label font-weight="bold">
        <fo:block>&#182;</fo:block>
      </fo:list-item-label>
      <fo:list-item-body>
        <fo:block margin-left="8pt">
          MovieNutz (Brian W. Fairbanks)
        </fo:block>
      </fo:list-item-body>
    </fo:list-item>
    <fo:list-item font-size="8pt">
      <fo:list-item-label font-weight="bold">
        <fo:block>&#182;</fo:block>
      </fo:list-item-label>
      <fo:list-item-body>
        <fo:block margin-left="8pt">
          Guardian Unlimited (Derek Malcolm)
        </fo:block>
      </fo:list-item-body>
    </fo:list-item>
    <fo:list-item font-size="8pt">
      <fo:list-item-label font-weight="bold">
        <fo:block>&#182;</fo:block>
      </fo:list-item-label>
      <fo:list-item-body>
        <fo:block margin-left="8pt">
          The "Johnny Guitar" Society
        </fo:block>
      </fo:list-item-body>
    </fo:list-item>
    <fo:list-item font-size="8pt">
      <fo:list-item-label font-weight="bold">
        <fo:block>&#182;</fo:block>
      </fo:list-item-label>
```

```
    <fo:list-item-body>
      <fo:block margin-left="8pt">
        Remote Control (Nick Burton)
      </fo:block>
    </fo:list-item-body>
  </fo:list-item>
 </fo:list-block>
</fo:flow>
```

As an aside...

A few notes about the code fragment above:

First, the entity reference ¶ is for a so-called "pilcrow" character or paragraph mark, ¶. You could, of course, use any other character representable in Unicode and whatever font the bullet will be displayed in, including any of the exotic characters available in so-called "dingbat" fonts for the XSL-FO processor and output device in question. You can also use an image instead of a character-based bullet.

Second, the fo:list-item-body elements all specify a margin, whereas the fo:list-item-label elements do not. As you can see, both of these FOs are being placed in the page's region-body. If you don't "force" the list-item-body over to the right like this, both FOs begin printing at the region-body's left edge—not at all a desirable result!

And third, note one important difference in transforming to a print document, as opposed to a Web page—no hyperlinks. If the target vocabulary were XHTML, it would have been entirely natural to enclose the names of the other reviewers in anchor (a) elements, transforming the corresponding xlink:href attributes in the source tree to href attributes in the result. Creating a hyperlink from a printed document, on the other hand, doesn't make a lot of sense.

Of course, if you're transforming to XSL-FO as an intermediate step on the way to transforming to a PDF document or other form of electronic output with which the user may interact, hyperlinking may make perfect sense. I'll show you how to do this in the next section, "Link and multi-formatting FOs."

The general idea here is to create a "bulleted" list in which the bullets are paragraph marks. The result is as shown in Figure 10–3.

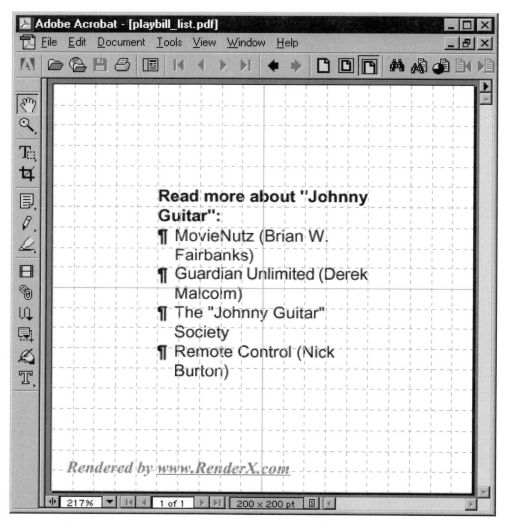

Figure 10-3 A bulleted list created from XSL-FO list-formatting elements and then transformed to PDF using RenderX's Xep processor. Converting the list items' text to hyperlinks (in the manner of the link to the RenderX home page) requires an additional bit of code, as shown in the next section.

Link and multi-formatting FOs

The FOs in this category are lumped together by the XSL-FO spec as those that handle "dynamic effects." Before I explain what this means, take a look at Table 10–6, which lists the FOs in question.

Table 10-6   Link and Multi-formatting Formatting Objects

Formatting object	Child of...
`fo:basic-link`	Inline
`fo:multi-switch`	Neutral
`fo:multi-case`	`fo:multi-switch`
`fo:multi-toggle`	Inline
`fo:multi-properties`	Neutral
`fo:multi-property-set`	`fo:multiple-properties`

Okay, now, about those "dynamic effects." Based on its name alone, the purpose of the `fo:basic-link` seems obvious enough. It becomes even more obvious when you consider that it takes one of two attributes—internal-destination or external-destination—whose values are URIs. (I'll show you an example of how to use this in a moment.)

Obvious though its purpose is, think for a second about the implication of having a hyperlinking FO in a document. Right: How do you hyperlink from a hard-copy paper document—or, more importantly, how can you *follow* such a link? And if you can't, why include such a bizarre FO in the spec?

The answer seems to be that the spec's authors are anticipating a day when XSL-FO documents are viewed as XHTML documents are now. (We're already there, sort of, in that PDF documents—the ultimate destination for most XSL-FO documents, at least as of mid-2001—can include hyperlinks.)

The ability to follow a hyperlink is a very rudimentary sort of "dynamic" effect. Much more elaborate are the effects expressed in the FOs whose names include the string "`multi-`."

Using `fo:basic-link`   The `fo:basic-link` serves the same purpose in an XSL-FO document that the a element serves in XHTML: to hyperlink to some target resource within this document or elsewhere.

The element has a number of attributes, but the most important are the previously mentioned internal-destination and external-destination.

The internal-destination attribute takes as its value the value of an ID-type attribute somewhere in the XSL-FO document/result tree in which the `fo:basic-link` itself appears.

Long on theory?

One can see how this works in theory. The practice may seem some-what tricky, though, since an ID-type attribute requires use of a DTD *declaring* the attribute to be of the ID type. That is, in this case you might think you have to include a DOCTYPE declaration in the XSL-FO result tree. Luckily, this doesn't seem to be the case; you just have to point to the value of an attribute *named* id, somewhere in the current document. I'll be looking more closely at this sort of "ID-type but not *really* ID-type" attribute later in this chapter, when I discuss the `fo:page-number-citation` FO.

The value of the `external-destination` attribute is the URI of some target document, but this URI is represented in a special way:

```
external-destination="url(target_uri)"
```

(This `url("target_uri")` notation is actually XSL-FO's way of expressing a datatype called a *uri-specification*.)

In discussing the XSL-FO example above, which created list-type FOs, I mentioned that the list items would be most usefully shown as hyperlinks, rather than as plain text. You could achieve this effect by modifying the XSLT code slightly to include `fo:basic-link` "wrappers" to the `fo:list-item-body` elements in the result tree:

```
<fo:list-item-body>
  <fo:block margin-left="8pt">
    <fo:basic-link
external-destination="url('{reviewlink/@xlink:href}')"
    text-decoration="underline" color="blue">
    <xsl:value-of select="."/>
  </fo:basic-link>
  </fo:block>
</fo:list-item-body>
```

Remember: You're not in Kansas anymore

Note that you have to specify how you want a link to "look" in XSL-FO, such as with the underlined/blue style specification for the text above. Without such a specification, the link is still active and can be clicked on or otherwise followed, but there's no indication that there is in fact a link *there* to be clicked on or followed. Unless the user just happens to pass her mouse cursor over the linked text, she'd never know it's an option!

Running this transform against the *Johnny Guitar* review produces a result tree which looks, in part, like the following:

```
<fo:list-item-body>
  <fo:block margin-left="8pt">
    <fo:basic-link
external-destination="url('http://www.entertainmentnutz.com/
movienutz/moviereviews/johnny_guitar.htm')"
      text-decoration="underline" color="blue">
      MovieNutz (Brian W. Fairbanks)
    </fo:basic-link>
  </fo:block>
</fo:list-item-body>
```

When you convert this XSL-FO result tree to PDF, you get the document shown in Figure 10–4.

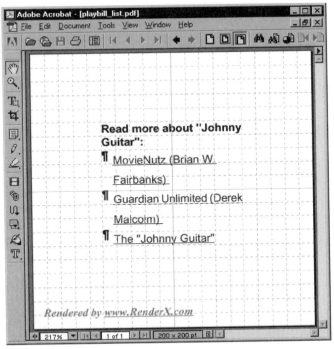

Figure 10-4 Hyperlinked version of the same XSL-FO result tree shown in Figure 10–3. Unlike with an XHTML document, there's no built-in way in which hyperlinked text is displayed. Although I've specified "blue underlining" for hyperlinks, they *stay* blue/underlined even after their target sites have been visited. Additional attributes to the fo:basic-link element can be employed to make these XSL-FO links behave in ways closer to their XHTML counterparts.

Unwanted side-effects

Figure 10–4 also (inadvertently) illustrates a danger familiar to anyone who uses leading-edge software (like Xep, in this case): Sometimes things just, well, *happen*...even though they're not supposed to.

Here, I've uncovered a bug in the evaluation version of Xep 2.21. (It was also a bug in the previous *commercial* version of the product; it's been corrected there, but RenderX hasn't gotten around to fixing it in the evaluation product.) What's gone wrong here is that the default line-height for the `fo:basic-link` element is *larger* than the font size being used in Figures 10–3 and 10–4. (It should acquire whatever line-height is in effect at that point.) This bumps all the `fo:block` elements within the `fo:list-item-body` elements down a little bit—compare Figure 10–4 to Figure 10–3 and you can see the effect clearly.

A bit more subtly, also note that the pilcrows in Figure 10–4 are clearly raised *above* their corresponding `fo:list-item-body` elements. This is another limitation of Xep 2.21, having to do with the way in which vertical alignment is handled for `fo:list-item-label` element content (the pilcrows, in this case).

RenderX is aware of both problems and says they will be fixed in the product's next release.

Using "multi-formatting" FOs   All those FOs containing "`multi-`" in their names are meant to control alternate ways of viewing the same content, based on some choice made by the user. Examples provided by the XSL-FO spec illustrate (a) how to build a collapsing/expanding menu of choices and (b) how to switch the coloration of an `fo:basic-link` FO while the user is in the process of traversing the link (typically by clicking on it), and then switching back.

Let's take a look at one of these two cases, the situation in which you want to show/hide content based on user action. (This is the more complicated, dynamic/interactive type of FO.) For this case, the root element of the relevant portion of the result tree is `fo:multi-switch`. Each of the alternative content displays is enclosed within an `fo:multi-case` element; specifically, within each `fo:multi-case` is an `fo:block` with these two children:

- `fo:multi-toggle`: This FO tells the processor which display to switch to when this case is activated.
- The actual content to be presented when this case is activated: This might be an `fo:basic-link`, or some regular text content.

Suppose we wanted to turn the list of hyperlinks to external *Johnny Guitar* reviews into an expandable/collapsible list of links. We might achieve this using an XSL-FO result tree like this:

```
<fo:multi-switch>
  <fo:multi-case
    case-name="collapsed"
    case-title="collapsed" starting-state="show">
    <fo:block>
      <fo:multi-toggle
        switch-to="expanded">+</fo:multi-toggle>
      <fo:basic-link
external-destination="url('http://www.entertainmentnutz.com/
movienutz/moviereviews/johnny_guitar.htm')">
        MovieNutz (Brian W. Fairbanks)
      </fo:basic-link>
    </fo:block>
  </fo:multi-case>
  <fo:multi-case
    case-name="expanded"
    case-title="expanded" starting-state="hide">
    <fo:block>
      <fo:multi-toggle
        switch-to="collapsed">-</fo:multi-toggle>
      <fo:basic-link external-destination="url('http://
www.entertainmentnutz.com/movienutz/moviereviews/
johnny_guitar.htm')">
        MovieNutz (Brian W. Fairbanks)
      </fo:basic-link>
    </fo:block>
    <fo:block start-indent="2pt">
      <fo:basic-link
external-destination="url('http://film.guardian.co.uk/
Century_Of_Films/Story/0,4135,37234,00.html')">
        Guardian Unlimited (Derek Malcolm)
      </fo:basic-link>
    </fo:block>
    <fo:block start-indent="2pt">
      <fo:basic-link
external-destination="url('http://members.aol.com/michaemann/
jgmain.html')">
        The "Johnny Guitar" Society
      </fo:basic-link>
    </fo:block>
    <fo:block start-indent="2pt">
```

```
     <fo:basic-link
external-destination="url('http://www.pifmagazine.com/vol23/
v_Johnny_Guitar.shtml')">
        Remote Control (Nick Burton)
     </fo:basic-link>
   </fo:block>
  </fo:multi-case>
</fo:multi-switch>
```

Let's walk through what's going on in this code:

- The overall structure is an `fo:multi-switch` block with two `fo:multi-case` children—that is, it defines two *cases*.
- The first `fo:multi-case` element is assigned a `name` attribute whose value is "collapsed." (This `name` attribute will be referenced later in the `fo:multi-switch` block.) There's also a `case-title` attribute that will be used as a label for the corresponding `fo:multi-case` element (perhaps as a "tool-tip" pop-up). Finally, there's a `starting-state` attribute. This attribute may take either of two values, `show` or `hide`, indicating whether the case defined is displayed or hidden, respectively. Here, with a value of `show`, we'd expect the little expandable menu to display in its collapsed form at first.
- The `fo:block` child of the first `fo:multi-case` element itself has two children: an `fo:multi-toggle` and an `fo:basic-link`.
- The `fo:multi-toggle` provides something for the user to interact with, to change the content's presentation from whatever is described here to some other presentation. Note that it has a `switch-to` attribute with a value of `expanded`, and #PCDATA content consisting of a simple plus sign (+). What this means is that when the user activates the toggle—the plus sign here— the content as presented by *this* `fo:multi-case` element will be replaced by the content as displayed by an `fo:multi-case` element with a `case-name` attribute whose value is `expanded`.
- The `fo:basic-link` element you've already seen. In this situation, in other words, when this page is first opened, the user sees only one link, to the left of which is a plus sign. He can follow the link, or activate the "expanded" case by interacting with the plus sign (probably by clicking on it).
- The alternate content presentation is defined by the second `fo:multi-case` element. Much of this block of code is analogous to the earlier one, but notice especially the differences. In general, they ensure that this presentation is *hidden* at first, and that when it's activated the plus sign in the earlier version is replaced with a minus sign. Below the link accompanying

the minus sign appear three more links. Clicking on the minus sign reverts the presentation to its "collapsed" state (per the `switch-to` attribute to the `fo:multi-toggle` element).

Well, that's the theory, anyway. To my knowledge, though, no XSL-FO processors (including Xep) actually support this "interactive document" behavior— or the somewhat simpler "multi-properties" behavior. Until they do, you should consider this class of FOs pretty speculative (except, of course, for the `fo:basic-link` element, which works fine).

Out-of-line FOs

The out-of-line FOs listed in Table 10–7 all describe what are, effectively, blocks of content positioned somewhere other than in the "normal" flow of content represented by block and inline FOs.

Table 10-7   Out-of-Line Formatting Objects

Formatting object	Child of...
`fo:float`	Any inline or block FO (but may not be a descendant of an out-of-line FO)
`fo:footnote`	Any inline FO (but may not be a descendant of an out-of-line FO)
`fo:footnote-body`	`fo:footnote`

The `fo:float` element is used to create a block-like structure around which text on the page flows. (Normally, blocks are stacked one atop the other or side-by-side.) It takes an attribute, `float`, used to indicate where (relative to the "wrapping" text) the floating content will appear; this attribute takes any of the values `left`, `right`, or `none`.[3] Within the `fo:float` can appear an image, other text, a table, and so on.

Unfortunately, only the `float="before"` option is nominally supported by the current version of Xep...and I haven't been able to get even that to work.

---

3.   The "none" value would seem to have limited usefulness, or maybe I'm just missing something; the spec's description of this value's behavior is, "The box is not floated."

The other popular FO-to-PDF processor, the open-source Apache Project's FOP, doesn't support it at all. So I can't demonstrate this feature to you here.

Footnotes, of course, can be useful in almost any print publication—for purposes ranging from the critical to the trivial.[4] In XSL-FO, you place an fo:footnote element at the point where you want the footnote reference to occur. This element takes two children: an fo:inline whose content is the character or number to appear at that point (typically in a tiny font, and raised above the line as a "superscript"); and an fo:footnote-body, whose content is the actual text of the footnote.

A few pages back, I showed you how to place the "other" (non-FlixML) reviews of *Johnny Guitar* in a list. I said there that if you're outputting to print, you can't really take advantage of hyperlinking to those reviews. However, you *can* put their URIs in footnotes. Here's a general XSLT approach to creating an XSL-FO document like this; as a footnote reference—the little raised number—it uses the value of the review's position among the list of all external reviews:

```
<xsl:for-each select="otherreview/goodreview">
  <fo:list-item>
    <fo:list-item-label font-weight="bold">
      <fo:block>&#182;</fo:block>
    </fo:list-item-label>
    <fo:list-item-body>
      <fo:block margin-left="8pt">

      <!-- Footnote reference will be placed at end of
        next line. -->
      <xsl:value-of select="."/><fo:footnote>
        <!-- Note the special attributes which make
          the footnote references look the way we're
          used to seeing them: raised above the main
          line of text, in a smaller font. -->
        <fo:inline baseline-shift="super"
          font-size="smaller">
          <xsl:value-of
            select="position()"/>
        </fo:inline>
        <fo:footnote-body>
          <fo:block
            font-size="4pt">
```

---

4.   Case in point.

```
        <!-- The footnote itself, like the
          reference, typically begins with a small
          superscript. -->
        <fo:inline baseline-shift="super"
          font-size="smaller">
          <xsl:value-of
            select="position()"/>
        </fo:inline>
        <xsl:text> </xsl:text>
        <xsl:value-of
          select="reviewlink/@xlink:href"/>
      </fo:block>
    </fo:footnote-body>
  </fo:footnote>

    </fo:block>
  </fo:list-item-body>
 </fo:list-item>
</xsl:for-each>
```

The comments placed inline in this XSLT fragment pretty much describe what's going on in the creation of the footnotes.[5] The result tree from this transformation appears, in part, as follows:

```
<fo:list-item-body>
  <fo:block margin-left="8pt">
    MovieNutz (Brian W. Fairbanks)
    <fo:footnote>
      <fo:inline
        baseline-shift="super"
        font-size="smaller">1</fo:inline>
      <fo:footnote-body>
        <fo:block font-size="4pt">
          <fo:inline
            baseline-shift="super"
            font-size="smaller">
            1
          </fo:inline>
```

---

5.   The one uncommented exception is the xsl:text element, whose contents consist of a single space. Its purpose is to force a slight separation between the superscripted number in the footnote body and the footnote's text itself. The Xep documentation points out that this can also be achieved by building a list within the footnote, but I didn't want to overwhelm you with a list-inside-a-list structure.

```
http://www.entertainmentnutz.com/movienutz/moviereviews/
johnny_guitar.htm
      </fo:block>
    </fo:footnote-body>
  </fo:footnote>
  </fo:block>
</fo:list-item-body>
```

And the PDF resulting from Xep's processing appears in Figure 10–5.

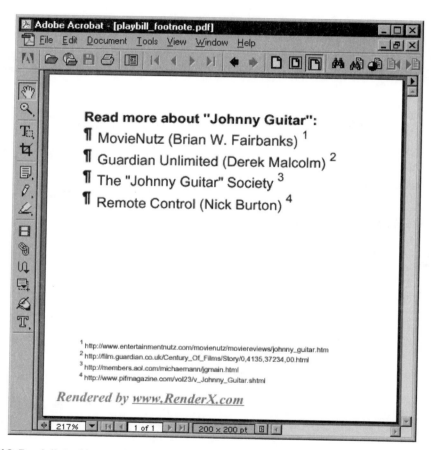

Figure 10-5   A list of items (the names of Web sites where you can find *Johnny Guitar* reviews, in this case), each of which has a corresponding footnote (the URI of that Web site). Note the up-shifted pilcrow characters, a minor Xep bug I mentioned in an earlier example. Also note that I've shut off the grid display within Adobe Acrobat, which would otherwise be very distracting when working with small font sizes; I'll pretty much *leave* it off, now that you have the idea.

Other FOs

Even the most obsessively categorizing specification always seems to have a hand-ful of miscellaneous items that don't fit neatly into one pigeonhole or another. The XSL-FO spec is no exception; it contains three such items, as listed in Table 10–8.

Table 10-8   Other Formatting Objects

Formatting object	Child of...
fo:wrapper	Neutral
fo:marker	Neutral
fo:retrieve-marker	Neutral

Using `fo:wrapper`   The `fo:wrapper` element serves one simple pur-pose: to pass on to its descendants any presentation or other properties they share in common. This simplifies their coding, obviously, and makes it much eas-ier to create consistent and easily maintainable display properties for large, con-tiguous chunks of an XSL-FO document.

One interesting thing about `fo:wrapper` is that it's effectively "invisible" to the document's structure. On its own terms, it may take any kind of children at all—block, inline, or #PCDATA. However, the allowable children of any given instance of the `fo:wrapper` element are always constrained by *that instance's* par-ent. For instance, look at this XSLT fragment:

```
<xsl:template match="cast">
  <fo:page-sequence master-name="seq-mast-cover">
    <fo:flow flow-name="reg-body"
      font-family="Helvetica" font-size="8pt">
      <fo:block>
        <fo:block>
        Lead cast of
        <fo:inline font-style="italic">
          <xsl:value-of select="//title"/></fo:inline>:
        </fo:block>
        <fo:wrapper font-family="serif">
          <xsl:for-each
            select="leadcast/female | leadcast/male">
            <fo:block>
              <xsl:value-of select="castmember"/>
              <xsl:text> </xsl:text>
```

```
        <fo:inline font-style="italic">
          (<xsl:value-of select="role"/>)
        </fo:inline>
      </fo:block>
    </xsl:for-each>
  </fo:wrapper>
    </fo:block>
  </fo:flow>
  </fo:page-sequence>
</xsl:template>
```

This template rule for processing a FlixML review's cast element (particularly that element's leadcast child) creates a series of fo:block elements in the result tree, one for each male or female element in the leadcast. The overall "look" of each of those blocks of text is established by an fo:wrapper element which establishes the font in which that cast member's information will be presented.

Now, this fo:wrapper is itself a child of an fo:block element. I mentioned some time ago that a given block FO may have either block or inline children, but cannot mix the two. Therefore, in this case the fo:wrapper is constrained by two facts: First, its parent is an fo:block; second, the parent has another child—an fo:block in which the words "Lead cast of *[movie title]*" will appear. Thus, even though fo:wrapper itself is "allowed" to have an fo:inline child, here it may not. In terms of the structure of the enclosing fo:block element, it's like the fo:wrapper didn't exist at all.

A portion of the result tree from this transformation appears as follows:

```
<fo:block>
  <fo:block>
    Lead cast of
    <fo:inline
      font-style="italic">Johnny Guitar</fo:inline>:
  </fo:block>
  <fo:wrapper font-family="serif">
    <fo:block>
      Joan Crawford
      <fo:inline font-style="italic">
        (Vienna)
      </fo:inline>
    </fo:block>
    ...
  </fo:wrapper>
</fo:block>
```

After processing by Xep 2.21, this XSL-FO result tree displays as in Figure 10–6.

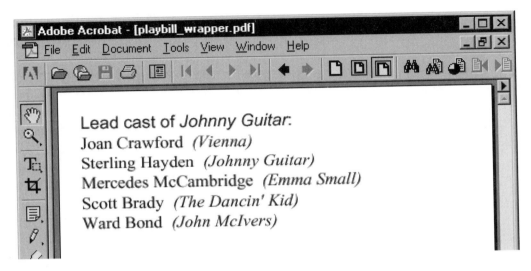

Figure 10-6 Using `fo:wrapper` to pass display characteristics (here, just the `font-family`) on to its children. These characteristics can be overridden as desired. For instance, in this case the role played by each cast member is italicized.

Using "markers" The `fo:marker` and `fo:retrieve-marker` elements are used together to put running headers and footers on a page of output. The `fo:marker` element declares the content of the header/footer; the `fo:retrieve-marker` actually creates an instance of that content.

Language decisions

Your curiosity about the term "marker" would certainly be justified. I don't know how they came up with that bit of terminology as a name for these common components of a page's makeup. While I can see the need for *some* umbrella term to encompass both headers and footers, "marker" seems a bizarre choice. I'm guessing it's a bit of jargon carried over from typesetting or from word-processing or page-design/ publishing software.

By the way, note that these "headers and footers" can actually be placed in *any* of the page's side regions, not just the body-before and -after.

You indicate where a header or footer is to be inserted using the `fo:retrieve-marker` element (which can appear only within an `fo:static-content` element). The `fo:retrieve-marker` has several attributes, the most important of which is `retrieve-class-name`. The value of this attribute matches the value of the `marker-class-name` attribute to some `fo:marker` element. (That's the only attribute `fo:marker` takes.)

Where to place the `fo:marker` element is—take your pick—either a simpler or a more complex decision. It can be a child of any block or inline FO, which is certainly easy to remember. However, most logically you should make it a child of the block or inline FO that will provide its content. Regardless of where you place it, it must be the *first* child of its parent.

Here's a portion of an XSLT stylesheet to be applied to a FlixML review, with a discussion following:

```
<xsl:template match="plotsummary | remarks">
  <fo:page-sequence master-name="seq-mast-contents">
    <fo:static-content flow-name="reg-before">
      <fo:block font-size="5pt"
        background-color="silver"
        text-align="center"
        line-height="10pt">
        <fo:retrieve-marker
          retrieve-class-name="head"/>
      </fo:block>
    </fo:static-content>
    <fo:static-content flow-name="reg-after">
      <fo:block font-size="5pt"
        border-top=".5pt"
        text-align="center">
        <fo:retrieve-marker
          retrieve-class-name="foot"/>
      </fo:block>
    </fo:static-content>
    <fo:flow flow-name="reg-body">
      <fo:block>
        <fo:marker marker-class-name="head">
          Playbill:
          <fo:inline font-style="italic">
            <xsl:value-of select="//title"/>
          </fo:inline>
        </fo:marker>
        <fo:marker marker-class-name="foot">
          Copyright <xsl:value-of select="../@copyright"/>
```

```
        by <xsl:value-of select="../@author"/>
        / Page <fo:page-number/>
      </fo:marker>
      <fo:wrapper font-size="6pt">
        <fo:block font-weight="bold" text-align="right"
          border-style="solid" border-width="1pt"
          padding="3pt" margin-top="12pt">
          <xsl:value-of select="name()"/>
        </fo:block>
        <fo:block text-indent="3em"
          margin-bottom="12pt">
          <xsl:value-of select="."/>
        </fo:block>
      </fo:wrapper>
    </fo:block>
  </fo:flow>
 </fo:page-sequence>
</xsl:template>
```

The result tree created by this stylesheet will include, in the region-before, the contents of the fo:marker whose marker-class-name attribute has a value of head; and, in the region-after, the contents of the fo:marker whose marker-class-name attribute has a value of foot. The former will contain (as you can tell by tracking down the appropriate fo:marker) the word "Playbill:" followed by the italicized title of the movie, and this content will be placed in a silver-colored block. The latter will contain copyright information and the current page number in a block, at the top of which is a thin border.

Within the region-body will appear the contents of the source tree's plotsummary and remarks elements. Each is preceded by a boxed block, labeling the text as appropriate (just using the element names in this example, for convenience).

A portion of the result tree (here, just the part pertaining to the running page footer) looks as follows:

```
<fo:page-sequence
  master-name="seq-mast-contents">
  ...
  <fo:static-content flow-name="reg-after">
    <fo:block font-size="5pt"
      border-top=".5pt"
      text-align="center">
      <fo:retrieve-marker
```

```
          retrieve-class-name="foot"/>
    </fo:block>
  </fo:static-content>
  ...
  <fo:marker marker-class-name="foot">
    Copyright 2001
    by John E. Simpson
    / Page <fo:page-number/>
  </fo:marker>
  ...
</fo:page-sequence>
```

Figure 10–7 shows the result of feeding the above through Xep and viewing the PDF output in Acrobat's "facing pages" mode.

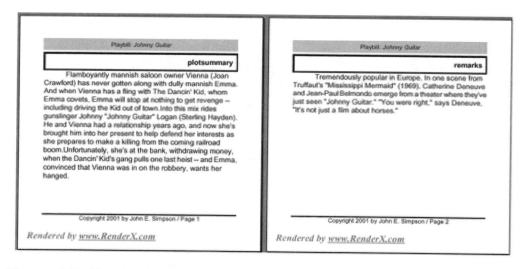

Figure 10-7 Running headers and footers, added to the page layout using XSL-FO "markers." Note that the first line of the `plotsummary` and `remarks` elements contents is indented slightly, using the `text-indent` attribute with a value of "3em." (An em is a printer's unit of measurement; its exact size varies depending on the size of the font at that point, equal to the width of a lowercase "m"—hence the name.)

Inline-Type FOs Revisited

One of the most important categories of formatting objects includes those classified as *inline* FOs. These elements were listed, more or less without comment, in Table 10–3, and I've demonstrated a couple of them already. In this section I'll look in detail at some of the most important of the remaining inline FOs.

Using `fo:character`

Handling text a character at a time isn't something you'll want to do on every page. In general, it's useful only for creating a large initial capital letter, in "drop-cap" or other form, such as at the beginning of a chapter. The way you'd accomplish this in an XSLT stylesheet, transforming a FlixML review's remarks element to XSL-FO, might look something like this:

```
<xsl:template match="remarks">
  <xsl:variable name="init"
    select="substring(., 1, 1)"/>
  <xsl:variable name="rest"
    select="substring(., 2)"/>
  <fo:flow>
    <fo:block>
      <fo:character [initial caps style attributes]
        character="{$init}"/>
      <fo:inline [remaining text style attributes]>
        <xsl:value-of select="$rest"/>
      </fo:inline>
    </fo:block>
  </fo:flow>
</xsl:template>
```

Note that the `fo:character` element, somewhat surprisingly, is *empty*—you don't place the character to be represented by the element between start and end tags. Instead, you supply it as the value of the `character` attribute.

Demonstrating this FO fully is a bit complicated. Xep doesn't support it at all.[6] The Apache Project's open-source FOP product does support `fo:character`; however, it still doesn't support many other language features. Nonetheless it's possible at least to demonstrate `fo:character` in isolation, as it were, using FOP. We can use a template rule like the one above to generate a result tree looking something like the following:

---

6.   The Xep documentation says, "The element is not very useful for PDF formatting." This is kind of unconvincing, though, since the `fo:character` element is used to ascribe certain properties to a single character/glyph—and where would such properties be useful, if not in print?

```
<fo:flow flow-name="reg-body">
 <fo:block>
 <fo:character
    font-family="serif"
    font-style="italic"
    font-size="18pt"
    font-weight="bold"
    character="T"/>
 <fo:inline
    font-family="sans-serif"
    font-size="10pt"
    font-weight="normal">remendously popular in Europe. In one scene
from Truffaut's "Mississippi Mermaid" (1969), Catherine Deneuve and
Jean-Paul Belmondo emerge from a theater where they've just seen
"Johnny Guitar." "You were right," says Deneuve, "It's not just a
film about horses."
  </fo:inline>
 </fo:block>
</fo:flow>
```

Running this XSL-FO document through FOP, we get the result shown in Figure 10–8.

T remendously popular in Europe.
In one scene from Truffaut's
"Mississippi Mermaid" (1969),

Figure 10-8   Large initial capital letter, created using the `fo:character` FO as converted to PDF by FOP 0.18. This isn't terribly sophisticated initial-cap layout. For one thing, the space between the capital T and lowercase r is way too big. This effect could be minimized if you could add style characteristics like background-color and borders to the `fo:character` element, but you can't (at least with FOP, although the XSL-FO spec asserts that it should be possible). A better solution would be to set the initial cap in its own `fo:float` element, with the text wrapping around it. But then you've got another problem: `fo:float` is supported only minimally in Xep, and not at all in FOP. The software will catch up to the spec someday.

Pulling in non-XSL-FO content

Words aren't the only things you need to place on a page, of course. Often you need to enhance the words with images—either in the form of familiar JPEG and other bitmap formats or expressed in XML vocabularies other than XSL-FO. These are handled using two inline-type FOs: `fo:external-graphic` and `fo:instream-foreign-object`, respectively.

Using `fo:external-graphic`

References to images can be included in your XSL-FO documents with the empty `fo:external-graphics` element, the most important attribute of which is `src`. Just as in an XHTML `img` element, the `src` attribute's value is the URI of an image to be included at that point.

Using it is pretty straightforward. I've got a logo for my flixml.org Web site, which I could include on the "cover page" of a FlixML-based XSL-FO document using an XSL-FO result tree something like the following:

```
<fo:page-sequence master-name="seq-mast-cover">
  <fo:static-content flow-name="reg-start">
    <fo:block
      margin-top="20pt"
      height="50pt">
      <fo:external-graphic
        src="images/flixml_logo_rotate.jpg"/>
    </fo:block>
  </fo:static-content>
  <fo:flow flow-name="reg-body">
    <fo:block font-size="20pt"
      border-style="solid" border-width="1pt"
      margin-top="20pt"
      margin-left="25pt"
      margin-right="5pt">
      Johnny Guitar
    </fo:block>
  </fo:flow>
</fo:page-sequence>
```

This drops the (rotated) logo into the region-start of the cover page—that is, at the left of the region-body (where the title of the film, in this case, will appear inside a boxed area).

Converting the XSL-FO to a PDF document using Xep, we see results as shown in Figure 10–9.

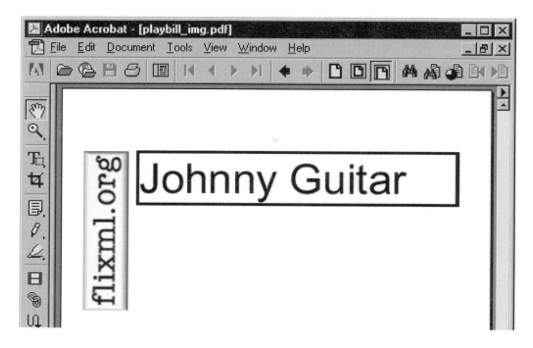

Figure 10-9   An image inserted into an XSL-FO document (conversion to PDF by Xep), using the `fo:external-graphic` FO. This formatting object has quite a broad array of attributes, including those dealing with scaling, alignment, and so on; I encourage you to experiment with these attributes yourself, as they can make all the difference between acceptable and dreadful image quality and placement.

Using `fo:instream-foreign-object`

One of the more interesting XML-related developments in the last year or two has been the creation of XML vocabularies to represent non-text content.[7] The `fo:instream-foreign-object` FO explicitly allows you to include such XML-based content in your XSL-FO documents, even though (obviously) it's from a non-XSL-FO namespace.

One such vocabulary is the W3C-recommended Scalable Vector Graphics language. SVG allows you to describe various geometric shapes in a way which (unlike using bitmapped graphics) ensures their image quality will not degrade at smaller or larger sizes.

---

7.   Well, *I* think it's interesting, anyway.

Now, I'm no SVG guru by any means. But even *I* can create a simple circle with it. To do so, I'll need to supply the following:

- A namespace declaration for the SVG namespace prefix (`svg:`, by convention): The correct URI to use is http://www.w3.org/2000/svg.
- The root element of an SVG document: With the namespace prefix, this is `svg:svg`.
- An element to define the circle's characteristics: This is the empty `svg:circle` element, whose `style`, `cx`, `cy`, and `r` attributes define the circle's general "look," center on the X (horizontal) axis, center on the Y (vertical) axis, and radius, respectively.

To embed this SVG code in a XSL-FO document, just place it between the start and end tags of an `fo:instream-foreign-object` element. As I've done within the second `fo:block` in the following code fragment, for instance:

```
<fo:page-sequence master-name="seq-mast-cover">
  <fo:flow flow-name="reg-body">
    <fo:block font-size="20pt"
      border-style="solid" border-width="1pt"
      margin-top="20pt"
      margin-left="20pt" margin-right="5pt">
      Johnny Guitar
    </fo:block>
    <fo:block
      margin-top="30pt">
      <fo:instream-foreign-object>
        <svg:svg>
          <svg:circle
            style="fill:silver"
            cx="100" cy="75" r="50"/>
        </svg:svg>
      </fo:instream-foreign-object>
    </fo:block>
  </fo:flow>
</fo:page-sequence>
```

Restating the obvious

The above, again, is just a code fragment. Elsewhere in the XSL-FO document, at a point above this in the document tree, you'd need to include the namespace declaration:

```
xmlns:svg="http://www.w3.org/2000/svg"
```

Now—as with a few of these other off-the-mainline FOs—Xep doesn't support the creation of PDF documents using embedded SVG…but FOP does. So again we turn to the Apache product. Converting the above XSL-FO code to PDF with FOP produces results as shown in Figure 10–10.

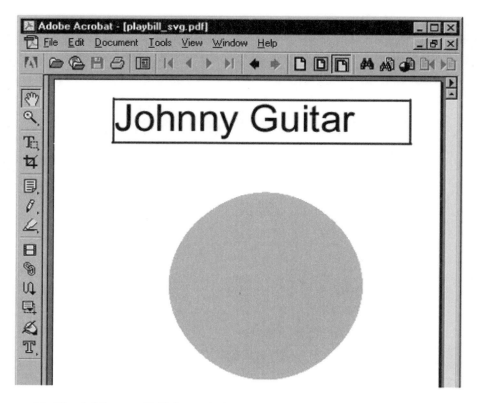

Figure 10-10   Adding an SVG-based circle to a PDF document (by way of the XSL-FO `fo:instream-foreign-object` element). FOP takes the SVG code and converts it to the necessary PostScript equivalent.

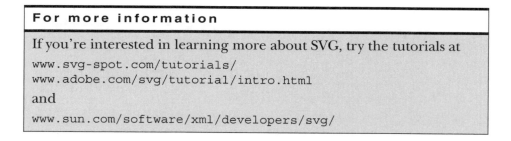

For more information

If you're interested in learning more about SVG, try the tutorials at

`www.svg-spot.com/tutorials/`
`www.adobe.com/svg/tutorial/intro.html`

and

`www.sun.com/software/xml/developers/svg/`

Creating leaders

Leaders (pronounced "LEEDers") are typically those rows of dots you might see in a table of contents connecting (say) each chapter number and title at the left to the corresponding page number at the right. In XSL-FO, a leader can also be a horizontal rule placed on the page before or after some other inline content (as you might do for creating a "signature block" on a contract, for example).

The fo:leader element is used to create a leader in an XSL-FO document. It can take numerous attributes; among the most important for its own purposes (as opposed to those which can apply to other inline FOs, too) are these:

- leader-pattern: values space, rule, dots, or use-content. This attribute specifies how exactly the leader will be represented. The space, rule, and dots values should be pretty obvious. The use-content value specifies that the content of the fo:leader element will be used as the "leader charac-ter(s)." (Note that unless you specify leader-pattern="use-content", the fo:leader element should be empty.)
- rule-style: values none, dotted, dashed, solid, double, groove, and ridge. This attribute defines the type of horizontal rule to use as a leader, and obviously makes sense only if you've set leader-pattern to rule.
- rule-thickness: value is a typical CSS-style dimension; the default is 1pt. As with rule-style, this applies only when you're creating a horizontal rule.

As an example, we could create a "lead cast" listing for *Johnny Guitar* using an XSLT stylesheet that includes the following fragment:

```
<xsl:for-each
  select="leadcast/female | leadcast/male">
  <fo:block
    text-align="center">
    <fo:inline>
      <xsl:value-of select="castmember"/>
    </fo:inline>
    <fo:leader leader-pattern="dots"/>
    <fo:inline font-style="italic">
      <xsl:value-of select="role"/>
    </fo:inline>
  </fo:block>
</xsl:for-each>
```

This sets up an `fo:block` for each member of the movie's lead cast. Within the block are three inline-type FOs: the name of the cast member, a string of leader dots, and the name of the character played by that actor or actress. The portion of the result tree for Joan Crawford's character, for example, looks like this:

```
<fo:block text-align="center">
  <fo:inline>Joan Crawford</fo:inline>
  <fo:leader leader-pattern="dots"/>
  <fo:inline font-style="italic">Vienna</fo:inline>
</fo:block>
```

Together with some other formatting you can by now easily add on your own, you might thus end up with a page looking something like Figure 10–11.

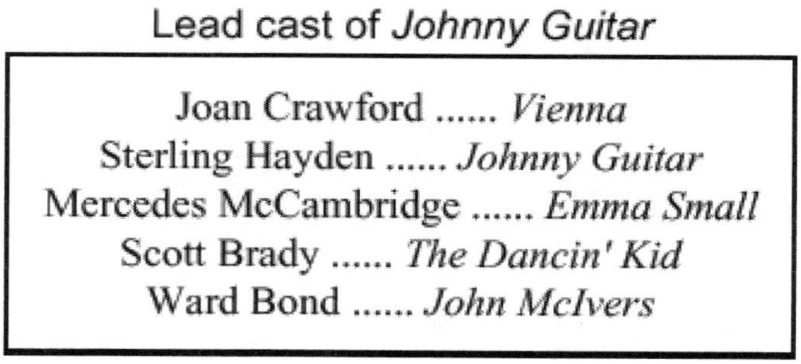

Lead cast of *Johnny Guitar*

Joan Crawford ...... *Vienna*
Sterling Hayden ...... *Johnny Guitar*
Mercedes McCambridge ...... *Emma Small*
Scott Brady ...... *The Dancin' Kid*
Ward Bond ...... *John McIvers*

Figure 10-11 *Johnny Guitar*'s lead cast, presented here in a box with leader dots (the result of the `fo:leader` FO) separating each cast member's name from his or her role. Note the width of the `leader-dot` pattern; the default for this is 12 points, but you can adjust it with a `leader-length` attribute to the `fo:leader` element.

XSL-FO document page numbers

In any print publication, you typically need to do two things with page numbers: You need to place them on a page, and you need to *refer* to the page number on which a particular piece of content appears.

You've already seen the solution to the first of these two problems several times: Use the `fo:page-number` FO at the point where you want the current page's number to appear (typically in a running heading or footing). Like other block and inline FOs, this one may be styled pretty much any way different from (or the same as) the FOs surrounding it.

Page-numbering limits

By default, page numbers display as simple integers—1, 10, 2027, and so on. However, you can override this default format using various attributes to the corresponding `fo:page-sequence` element. Among these attributes are `format`, `grouping-size`, `grouping-separator`, and `letter-value`; their allowable values are the same as those of identically named attributes to the XSLT `xsl:number` element. This permits you to use Roman numerals to number the pages in a book's front matter, for example.

The one thing you cannot do, though, is try to get around this problem using the XSLT `format-number()` function, with or without the `xsl:decimal-format` element. That's because the number to be formatted in this case—the page number within the XSL-FO or PDF document—is simply not available at the time the XSLT processor runs.

A little trickier to handle is task #2—getting a page *reference* to appear. The general approach requires that you use attributes named `id`[8] on any FO whose page number you might need to refer to. Then, where you need to refer to this content, drop in an `fo:page-number-citation` element with a `ref-id` attribute whose value matches that of the desired content's `id` attribute.

And don't forget...

These attributes named "id" are also potentially useful as the targets of `fo:basic-link` elements using an internal-destination attribute, as I mentioned earlier.

For instance, omitting a lot of extraneous details for the moment, you might have something like this in your XSLT stylesheet:

```
<xsl:template match="[something in source tree]">
  <fo:page-sequence
    master-name="[page-seq-master name]"
    id="[unique value for referred-to page]">
    [remainder of page sequence, including
    fo:flow elements, fo:static-content elements, etc.]
```

---

8.   These aren't necessarily ID-type attributes in the formal XML sense, although they function similarly. Each one is assumed to be unique.

```
  </fo:page-sequence>
</xsl:template>
```

This sets up a page sequence whose start we'll want to reference somewhere. Now, to actually instantiate the reference, you'd do something like the following:

```
<xsl:template match="[something else in source tree]"
  <fo:page-sequence
    master-name="[page-seq-master name]">
    <fo:flow flow="[region name]">
      . . .
      <fo:block>
        An interesting section starts on page
        <fo:page-number-citation
          ref-id="[unique value for referred-to page]"/>.
      </fo:block>
      . . .
    </fo:flow>
  </fo:page-sequence>
</xsl:template>
```

See the way the value of the `ref-id` attribute cross-references the value of the `id` attribute in the preceding code fragment? This will cause the XSL-FO processor to replace the `fo:page-number-citation` element with the number of the page on which that "bookmark" appears.

More performance anxiety

Note that this means that the XSL-FO processor must build internally a list of all pages tagged with an `id` attribute—at least, it must do so if it detects any `fo:page-number-citation` elements in the XSL-FO document. For *big* documents, this is likely to be a memory-expensive feature.

How Do I...
Create a basic table of contents using XSL-FO?

I've got a real example of these page numbers and citations to show you, but it's a little involved to present in one big chunk of code. In this section, I'm going to break down the most important steps to show you one at a time. (This will also be a good refresher course in how to build an XSL-FO document in its entirety.)

Define the page masters

This example includes two `fo:simple-page-master` elements in the layout master set:

```
<fo:simple-page-master master-name="page-toc"
  page-width="200pt" page-height="200pt"
  margin="20pt">
  <fo:region-body region-name="reg-toc"/>
</fo:simple-page-master>

<fo:simple-page-master master-name="page-review"
  page-width="200pt" page-height="200pt"
  margin="20pt">
  <fo:region-body region-name="reg-body"/>
  <fo:region-before region-name="reg-before"
    extent="10pt"/>
  <fo:region-after region-name="reg-after"
    extent="10pt"/>
</fo:simple-page-master>
```

The first one sets up a page to be used as a table of contents for the resulting XSL-FO document; it contains only a single region, the body. The second will be used for all other pages in the document and includes not only the body but before and after regions as well.

Establish page sequence masters

Given the above simple page masters, the example establishes a page sequence master corresponding to each, as follows:

```
<fo:page-sequence-master
  master-name="seq-mast-toc">
  <fo:single-page-master-reference
    master-name="page-toc"/>
</fo:page-sequence-master>

<fo:page-sequence-master
  master-name="seq-mast-contents">
  <fo:repeatable-page-master-reference
    master-name="page-review"/>
</fo:page-sequence-master>
```

As you can see, with the `fo:single-page-master-reference` and `fo:repeatable-page-master-reference` elements, these page sequence masters declare that the table-of-contents page will be just a single page long, whereas the contents themselves will simply repeat the same page structure indefinitely, until all content is exhausted.

Note that both of these first steps take place within an `fo:layout-master-set` element; like the rest of the general structure of the result tree, these portions of the content are instantiated by an XSLT template rule that processes a FlixML document's root `flixinfo` element. Here's the general form of that template rule:

```
<xsl:template match="flixinfo">

  <fo:root
    xmlns:fo="http://www.w3.org/1999/XSL/Format">

    <fo:layout-master-set>
      [page masters and page sequence masters, as above]
    </fo:layout-master-set>

    <xsl:apply-templates select="title"/>
    <xsl:apply-templates
      select="plotsummary | remarks"/>

  </fo:root>

</xsl:template>
```

After the basic page layouts and sequence masters have been established, the template rule invokes others for the children of `flixinfo` named `title` (the first `xsl:apply-templates`) and `plotsummary` or `remarks` (the second one).

Build the title/table of contents page

We're going to do this when we locate the review's `title` element in the source tree:

```
<xsl:template match="title">
  <fo:page-sequence master-name="seq-mast-toc">
    <fo:flow flow-name="reg-toc">
      <fo:block
        font-size="24pt"
        font-weight="bold"
        text-decoration="underline"
```

```
        text-align="center">
        Table of Contents
      </fo:block>
      <fo:wrapper
        font-size="12pt"
        font-weight="normal"
        text-align="center">
        <fo:block>Plot Summary:
          <fo:page-number-citation
            ref-id="plotsummary"/>
        </fo:block>
        <fo:block>General Remarks:
          <fo:page-number-citation
            ref-id="remarks"/>
        </fo:block>
      </fo:wrapper>
    </fo:flow>
  </fo:page-sequence>
</xsl:template>
```

(Note that this works for the simple example of *Johnny Guitar*, which has only one `title` element. To make this truly robust, we'd need to fine-tune the match criteria.[9])

This builds a page sequence which maps back to the "seq-mast-toc" page sequence master. In the body of that page (i.e., in the region named "reg-toc"), it instantiates two `fo:page-number-citation` elements in the result tree: one corresponding to the element with an `id` attribute value of "plotsummary" and one to the element with an `id` attribute value of "remarks."

To me, the most interesting thing about this code is what it says about an XSL-FO processor, which is this: Your reference to a page (the `fo:page-number-citation`) can appear in the document *before* the page is actually generated. There's only one practical way for a processor to do this, which is to generate all the pages internally and then go back and replace all the page *references* with the corresponding page *numbers*. As I said before, processing such an XSL-FO document is probably quite a memory hog!

---

9. You *do* know how to do this fine-tuning, right?

Build the document itself

For this portion of the XSLT stylesheet, I've pretty much followed the pattern I suggested above, under the "XSL-FO document page numbers" section. It looks like this:

```
<xsl:template match="plotsummary | remarks">
  <fo:page-sequence
    master-name="seq-mast-contents"
    id="{name()}">
    [fo:static-content and fo:flow elements for
    filling pages with content from source tree]
  </fo:page-sequence>
</xsl:template>
```

As you can see, for simplicity I've just assigned the name of the element in question to be the page sequence's identifier. Therefore, we'll end up with one page sequence with an `id` of `plotsummary` and one with an `id` of `remarks`. The fact that these names are associated with `id` attributes enables them to be associated with the `fo:page-number-citation` elements constructed earlier.

More side-effects

This template rule creates one page sequence for the `plotsummary` element and a separate one for `remarks`. Remember that, in the XSL-FO world, each page sequence begins on a new page. Thus, the above code will *not* cause the plot summary to appear on one page, followed immediately—if there's room—by the remarks. The remarks will always start on a fresh page of their own.

Check Your Results

Now we've got a complete XSLT stylesheet, in this case laying out a document consisting of a one-page table of contents, followed by at least one page of output for the plot summary from a FlixML review and at least one page of output for the review's `remarks` element.

After running this stylesheet through an XSLT processor like Saxon, then feeding *its* output to Xep, we end up with the PDF version of the *Johnny Guitar* review's `plotsummary` and `remarks` elements, as in Figures 10–12 and 10–13.

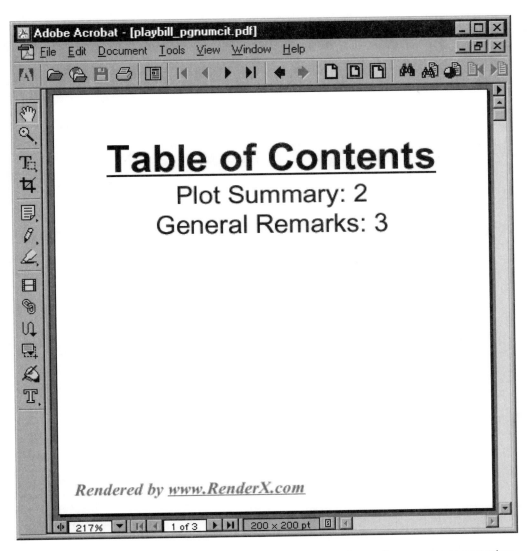

Figure 10-12 A "table of contents" page, with page-number references generated using the `fo:page-number-citation` FO. This is pretty elementary layout; if I'd wanted to make it more like a traditional table of contents, I'd probably have used leader dots between the page title and page number. Also, there's no particular reason to restrict yourself to using this feature with tables of contents. You can use it for in-text cross-references, of the form "For more information, see page *[fo:page-number-citation]*."

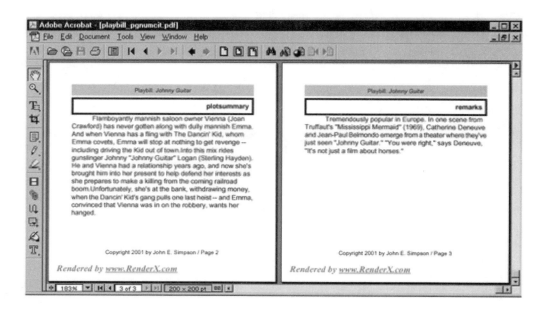

Figure 10-13 The two pages referenced by the `fo:page-number-citation` elements which constructed Figure 10–12. Again, the layout is no great shakes; I'm just trying to demonstrate how the page numbers, and their references, work out in practice.

Table-Type FOs Revisited

Way back in Table 10–4, I listed without explanation the FOs used to construct XSL-FO tables. These constituent table-type FOs are arranged in a hierarchy; some of them are completely optional. Figure 10–14 illustrates this tree model of table FOs.

Each of the formatting objects in an XSL-FO table has a corresponding area in the XSL-FO area tree. Consequently, each FO can be styled differently, or you can style the parent and let the effects trickle down to the children and other descendants. However, as you can see, *none* of these elements takes #PCDATA content directly. And interestingly, the contents of a table cell are not an inline-type but a *block*-type FO—which may include other tables, if desired. (Although the figure doesn't show it, the contents of the `fo:table-caption` element, too, are one or more block-type FOs.)

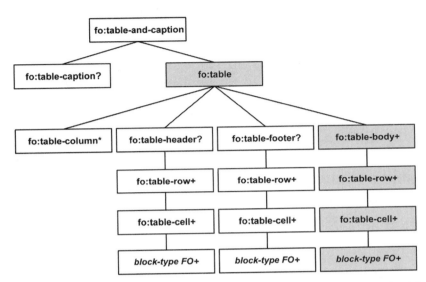

Figure 10-14 The tree model of XSL-FO table elements. The only required "path" in this tree is the one shown with shaded backgrounds; thus, you don't need to include a caption, any `fo:table-column` elements, headers, or footers. Note, too, the "occurrence indicators"—the familiar, regular-expression markers ?, *, and + characters, indicating "0 or 1," "0 or more," and "1 or more," respectively. Although this figure is adapted from one in the XSL-FO spec, note that the arrangement of table rows and table cells shown here is common, but not required; you can omit the `fo:table-row` elements, as explained in the text.

Basic tables

As you can see from Figure 10–14, at a bare minimum an XSL-FO table consists of an `fo:table` element with one or more `fo:table-body` children; within the latter are one or more (optional) `fo:table-row` elements and one or more (required) `fo:table-cell` elements; and within each table cell are one or more block-type FOs (`fo:block`, `fo:table`, and so on). Let's take a look at each of the core table-type FO elements in detail.

The `fo:table` element

In addition to many of the usual sorts of formatting properties, such as `back-ground-color` and `text-align`, the `fo:table` element takes a number of attributes that either are specific to it or have aspects or values of interest when you're building a table. I've assigned these attributes to several categories, depending on whether they control the size of the table, its "keeps and breaks," or its unique identity.

Non-standard categories

The spec itself doesn't group these attributes to the `fo:table` element in this way. It's just a convenient way to discuss them here.

Attributes affecting table size   Naturally, one of the first things you need to consider when laying out a table is how much "real estate" it's going to spread across in your document. Attributes in this category serve to define this important characteristic of a table.

- `table-layout`: values `auto` or `fixed`. This attribute controls the way the table's width is determined. The `auto` value says, "calculate the width based on the space taken up by the content of the individual columns." The `fixed` value requires that the XSL-FO processor "draw" the table according to specific column sizes and/or the value (if provided) of the `width` attribute.
- `height`, `width`: values usually expressed in familiar CSS-style number-and-units terms, such as `6in`, `200pt`, `25em`, and so on. Percentages can also be used; in this case, the size is relative to the size of the block that contains the table, not to the width of the entire page.

Attributes affecting "keeps and breaks"   A *keep* is a specification of how to retain content on the same page as some other content appearing before or after it. A *break* is the flip side—is specifies a point where content must begin on a separate page.

- `keep-together`, `keep-with-next`, `keep-with-previous`: values `auto`, `always`, or an integer indicating the "strength" of the keep. These attributes define keep conditions to be applied to a table. The `keep-together` attribute says to keep the entire table on a single page, if possible; `keep-with-next`, to keep the table on a page with the area that *follows* it; and `keep-with-previous`, to keep the table on a page with the area that *precedes* it. You can use more than one of these attributes, but be prepared for unpredictable behavior if all of their conditions can't be met simultaneously. The integer representing the keep's "strength" is used by the processor to resolve conflicts when more than one adjacent area specifies a keep—the higher the number, the more weight the processor will accord to this keep. (A value of `always` functions like an infinite strength, overriding any keeps with numeric strengths.) The `auto` value effectively tells the processor to do the best job it can.

- `break-after`, `break-before`: values `auto`, `column`, `page`, `even-page`, or `odd-page`. These two attributes and their values are used for forcing page or column breaks at specific points, depending on where the table falls. (The term "column" here applies to one of the vertical columns on a multi-column page layout, not to *table* columns.) The values indicate the context in which you want the table to be considered when placing the break. For `break-after`, the table will be considered to *end* within that context; for `break-before`, to *begin* within it. Thus, for example, `break-after="even-page"` forces the next page following the table to be an odd-numbered page (possibly generating a blank page in the process, if the table itself ends on an odd-numbered page). Similarly, `break-before="odd-page"` forces the table to begin at the top of an odd-numbered page (possibly generating a blank page, if the area before the table itself ends on an odd page).

- `table-omit-header-at-break`, `table-omit-footer-at-break`: values `true` or `false`. These attributes and their values control whether table headers and footers are repeated at the top or bottom of the page, respectively, when the table is too long to fit on a page. For both attributes, the default value (if none is specified) is `false`: Headers and footers are not repeated after/before page breaks in the middle of a table.

More useful than you'd think

Except for the attributes described in the last bullet above, the attributes in this category can be applied to FOs other than tables. Keeps and breaks can both be applied to block-type FOs, `fo:table-row`, and `fo:list-item`; for inline-type FOs, any list-type FO, and `fo:title`, you can use the keeps only. Thus, these can be extremely useful as general-purpose attributes—as much as or even more than such display properties as fonts and backgrounds.

Of course, if you do use these attributes for non-table FOs, substitute the appropriate term in place of "table" in any of the discussion of keeps and breaks.

Uniquely identifying a table   There's no surprise here: To tag a table with a unique identifier, assign the desired unique value to an `id` attribute. This attribute can be applied to any FO in the document, not just to tables. But it's especially important for tables because of the frequency with which tables are *referred to* in a document's text. For instance, you could generate a list of all tables in a document, together with the page numbers on which they start, using this attribute in concert with the `fo:page-number-citation` element described earlier.

The `fo:table-body` element

This element acts primarily as a container for the table rows and cells, and thus has no attributes uniquely its own. (It does, of course, accept an `id` attribute and the usual array of display/presentation properties.)

In fact, this element is so simple you may wonder why bother with it at all. Why not just include the rows/cells in the `fo:table` element directly? For the answer, look back to its representation in Figure 10–14—particularly, to the occurrence indicator that comes with it: a plus sign, for the "one or more occurrences" condition.

What this means is that a given `fo:table` element may contain one or more `fo:table-body` children. Now, I won't kid you—the notion of a table with more than one table body sounds mostly like a solution in search of a problem. But it *can*, in theory, be useful in some circumstances. For instance, you can assign certain inheritable properties to the overall table, which will then be automatically assumed by the separate table bodies.

The `fo:table-row` element

This FO has no attributes unique to it. Its purpose is to contain `fo:table-cell` FOs within a single horizontal "thing." You can use it to ascribe various presentation properties to the constituent table cells.

Figure 10–14 notwithstanding, you don't absolutely need to include an `fo:table-row` for each row in the table. I'll discuss the alternative next, under `fo:table-cell`, as well as why you might want *not* to choose the alternative.

The `fo:table-cell` element

The "table tree" depicted in Figure 10–14 shows that for each table body, header, or footer, there are one or more table-row children.

That's not necessarily true, though. The `fo:table-row` element is actually an *optional* child of `fo:table-body`, `fo:table-header`, and `fo:table-footer`.

The cells themselves can be made immediate children of the table body, header, or footer; the rows in this case are defined implicitly, using some of the attributes in the following list:

- `starts-row`, `ends-row`: values `true` or `false` (the default). These are the "row-defining" table-cell attributes, used in place of an `fo:table-row` wrapper. The first cell in the row would have a `starts-row="true"` attribute; the last, `ends-row="true"`. There are undoubtedly applications for which omitting the table row is desirable; in general, though, it seems to me that you should avoid this approach of declaring rows-without-rows. Awfully error-prone, I'd think, and also conducive to possibly erratic XSL-FO processor behavior should you end up with an inconsistent number of cells in each row.
- `number-rows-spanned`, `number-columns-spanned`, `column-number`: value for each is an integer. All of these attributes pertain to cells that span rows and/or columns. The `number-rows-spanned` and `number-columns-spanned` attributes work just as the `rowspan` and `colspan` attributes in XHTML do, respectively; if you don't specify one of them, the cell behaves as if the corresponding value was 1. The `column-number` attribute specifies the number of the first column to be spanned by the cell, with the default being whatever the current column number is. (If this is the first cell in the row, the current column number, obviously, is 1; if this is some other cell, the current column number is the previous cell's column number plus the value of the `number-columns-spanned` attribute for that cell.)
- `empty-cells`: values `show` (the default) or `hide`. This attribute instructs the XSL-FO processor how to treat cells with no value, in terms of their borders. If the cell is empty and `empty-cells` is `show`—and, of course, if there *is* a border declared for the cell—the border will appear around the cell; if the cell is empty and `empty-cells` is `hide`, there will be *no* border around the cell.

Building a basic table: An example

Using the above fundamental building blocks to construct an XSL-FO table similar to the XHTML counterpart is no more difficult than that task, and the general approach is the same.

- Instantiate the general, overall structure of the table in an XSLT template rule which matches the parent (or other convenient ancestor) of the data to be used to fill in the rows.
- Instantiate a row for each occurrence of some kind of content, using either an xsl:for-each loop or an xsl:apply-templates to invoke some subordinate template rule.
- Instantiate a cell within the row for each data point for that occurrence, using simple xsl:value-of elements to transfer source to result tree.

I'll show you these three steps in the context of building a table of a B film's crew members, using the *Johnny Guitar* review as my demonstrator.

Build the general structure

A convenient place to build the XSL-FO table's overall structure (at least, for demonstration purposes!) would be in the template rule for processing the source tree's crew element. This template rule might look something like the following:

```
<xsl:template match="crew">
  <fo:page-sequence master-name="seq-mast-contents">
    <fo:flow flow-name="reg-body">
     <fo:block
       font-family="sans-serif"
       font-size="14pt"
       font-weight="bold"
       font-style="italic"
       background-color="silver">
       <xsl:value-of select="//title"/>
     </fo:block>
     <fo:table
       margin-top="5pt">
       <fo:table-body>
         [table rows go here]
       </fo:table-body>
     </fo:table>
    </fo:flow>
  </fo:page-sequence>
</xsl:template>
```

There's nothing particularly exotic about the table; I'm not trying to force breaks or keeps, for instance, and I'm accepting the default table size. Note that, just before the table, I've included an fo:block element to contain the movie's title; because I haven't specified any margins or padding for this fo:block, it will span the full width of the page's body region, and this will give us some idea of how the XSL-FO processor determines the table's default width (by comparing it to the width of the fo:block, in other words).

Building the table rows

As I've said, you can do this with either an xsl:for-each loop or—if the content to be repeated is a child of the source-tree element you selected for the preceding step—an xsl:apply-templates with a corresponding template rule for processing that child.

Again, because I'm just trying to demonstrate basic principles here, I'll keep the XSLT structure as simple as possible. Thus, I'll replace the italicized "*[table rows go here]*" in the above code fragment with an xsl:for-each:

```
<xsl:for-each select="*">
  <fo:table-row
    font-family="serif"
    font-size="8pt"
    font-weight="normal">
    [table cells within a row go here]
  </fo:table-row>
</xsl:for-each>
```

Again, this is very much in line with how you build a table with XHTML. I'm using the fo:table-row just to assign some inheritable display-attribute properties that will be in effect (unless overridden) in the individual cells.

Build the cells

I'll set up each row with two cells: one for the crew member's position (as captured in the name of each given child of the crew element) and one for his or her name. The following code would thus replace the "*[table cells within a row go here]*" placeholder in the preceding fragment:

```
<fo:table-cell>
  <fo:block
    font-weight="bold">
    <xsl:value-of select="name()"/>
  </fo:block>
</fo:table-cell>
<fo:table-cell>
  <fo:block>
    <xsl:value-of select="."/>
  </fo:block>
</fo:table-cell>
```

The crew member's position will display in bold; the name inherits the font-weight assigned to the fo:table-row element.

Results of the above transformation, after being cranked through Xep to a final PDF format, appear as in Figure 10–15.

Johnny Guitar

director	Nicholas Ray
screenwriter	Philip Yordan
cinematog	Harry Stradling, Sr.
editor	Richard L. Van Enger
score	Victor Young
proddesigner	Edward G. Boyle
costumer	Sheila O'Brien

Figure 10-15   A basic XSL-FO table. Note that the width of a table, by default, is 100% of the width of its container—in this case, the `fo:flow` FO that constitutes the page's body region. We can see this by comparing the alignment of text in the table to the width of the `fo:block` containing the movie's title. Less obvious is that the XSL-FO processor has automatically assigned 50% of the table's width to each *column*, based on the fact that there are two cells in each row.

The whitespace (or gutter) between the two columns is a bit too wide. We've got two choices for getting rid of it: Shrink the overall table width itself or reduce the size of the left-hand column. If we shrink the table's width to 85% of its containing FO (by applying a `width="85%"` attribute to the `fo:table` element), we get the results shown in Figure 10–16.

Johnny Guitar

director	Nicholas Ray
screenwriter	Philip Yordan
cinematog	Harry Stradling, Sr.
editor	Richard L. Van Enger
score	Victor Young
proddesigner	Edward G. Boyle
costumer	Sheila O'Brien

Figure 10-16   Same content and formatting as in Figure 10–15, but with a table width explicitly set to 85%. Note that without any explicit setting of the *column* widths, the XSL-FO processor still automatically calculates the width of columns at 50% of the overall table width, causing some of the names to wrap within their cells.

Probably a better solution—at least with this content and this page size—is to leave the table at 100% the width of its container and narrow the first column to, say, 40% of the width of the table. The result is shown in Figure 10–17.

Johnny Guitar

director	Nicholas Ray
screenwriter	Philip Yordan
cinematog	Harry Stradling, Sr.
editor	Richard L. Van Enger
score	Victor Young
proddesigner	Edward G. Boyle
costumer	Sheila O'Brien

Figure 10-17   Same table, same contents, but with the first column explicitly reduced to 40% of the overall table's width. If you do this yourself, be sure you're shrinking the `fo:table-cell` element, *not* the `fo:block` containing the crew members' titles. If you do the latter, the content is crammed into a block 40% of the width of the *cell*, which will remain at 50% of the width of the table itself. The results aren't pretty: Letters run into letters like a row of double-timing soldiers crashing headlong into the brick wall represented by the `fo:block`'s right edge.

Tables with optional components

The XSL-FO table model includes a number of optional pieces you can use, or not, as your needs dictate. These were the elements depicted in Figure 10–14 in white (unshaded) boxes.

As you can see from that figure, I've already covered some of this material, because the lower-level table FOs can be children/descendants of either the required or the optional "container" table-type FOs.

Most of the optional components serve purposes you can pretty much guess at from the corresponding element names. And there's not much new in the way of attributes, either. I'll cover the exceptions in this section.

Using `fo:table-and-caption` and `fo:table-caption`

The `fo:table-and-caption` FO—which serves as a container for a table that you want to supply a caption for—comes with one attribute of note: `caption-side`. This attribute takes a value of `top`, `bottom`, `left`, or `right` and is used for positioning the caption relative to the table itself.

If you think about it, this can be a little tricky—especially when you're positioning the caption to the left or right on a fairly narrow page.

Unfortunately, I can't demonstrate this complication with either Xep or FOP. The former supports only the `top` and `bottom` values for the `caption-side` attribute; as for FOP, it doesn't yet support either `fo:table-and-caption` *or* `fo:table-caption`.

However, I can use Xep at least to demonstrate *a* table caption. To do so, I'll use the XSL-FO table that produced Figure 10–17. This requires only that the `fo:table` element be wrapped in an `fo:table-and-caption` and preceded by the `fo:table-caption` you want to use. So the XSLT template rule for processing a FlixML `crew` element will now be structured like this:

```
<xsl:template match="crew">
  <fo:page-sequence master-name="seq-mast-contents">
    <fo:flow flow-name="reg-body">
      [fo:block containing film title, as before]
      <fo:table-and-caption>
        <fo:table-caption
          width="90%">
          <fo:block
            font-size="4pt"
            font-style="italic"
            background-color="#D8D8D8"
            padding="3pt"
            margin="3pt">
            Here's the crew of the movie. There's not
            really any point to this caption, except to
            DEMONSTRATE a caption.
          </fo:block>
        </fo:table-caption>
        <fo:table
          margin-top="5pt">
          [remainder as before, except wrapped in
          fo:table-and-caption element]
        </fo:table>
      </fo:table-and-caption>
    </fo:flow>
  </fo:page-sequence>
</xsl:template>
```

The table formerly depicted in Figure 10–17 now looks like Figure 10–18.

Johnny Guitar

Here's the crew of the movie. There's not really any point to this caption, except to DEMONSTRATE a caption.

director	Nicholas Ray
screenwriter	Philip Yordan
cinematog	Harry Stradling, Sr.
editor	Richard L. Van Enger
score	Victor Young
proddesigner	Edward G. Boyle
costumer	Sheila O'Brien

Figure 10-18 Table with a caption placed at the top. Compare to Figure 10–17, on which this one is based. As an aside, note the way Xep has collapsed all that whitespace in the `fo:block` element contained by the `fo:table-caption`. (Which is quite okay: That whitespace was there just for formatting purposes within the XSLT stylesheet itself.) This is a side-effect of an attribute, `white-space-collapse`, that can be applied to any FO that might contain multiple consecutive occurrences of whitespace; the default value of this attribute is `true`, meaning that such whitespace is collapsed to a single space. And yes, for what it's worth, Saxon retained the whitespace—as it should have—when it created the result tree from the above template rule.

Using `fo:table-column`

The XSL-FO table model, like XHTML's, is row-oriented: Table cells belong to rows; properties assigned to rows are inherited by their cells; and the properties of columns, by default, are simply *implied* by the properties of the cells making up the columns.

But the ability to assign characteristics to an entire column of data at a time is a useful feature. Furthermore, using this feature can make your XSL-FO documents more concise, by eliminating the need to assign display and other attributes to every cell in the column. Enter the `fo:table-column` element.

This is an empty element—you don't wrap cells in `fo:table-column` parents—so XSL-FO retains its row-primacy nature. Besides the usual attributes for styling content, `fo:table-column` takes a few others of interest:

- `column-width`: value is one of the usual CSS-style dimension specifications, such as `100px`, `1.5in`, `25mm`, and so on. This attribute specifies the width of the column identified by the `column-number` attribute.
- `column-number`: an integer value, identifying the column to which this column specification applies.
- `number-columns-repeated`: an integer value. This attribute is used to assign identical features to more than one column at a time—as the XSL-FO spec says, "with the same effect as if the `fo:table-column` formatting object had been repeated *n* times in the result tree." This provides the same functionality to the `fo:table-column` element as that provided inherently by XHTML's `colgroup` element.[10]
- `number-columns-spanned`: value is an integer. For table cells, I've already covered the purpose of this attribute. For table columns, it's used to define how many columns are spanned by table cells that may use the built-in XSL-FO function `from-table-column()`. (XSL-FO functions are covered in the next chapter.)
- `visibility`: values `visible`, `hidden`, and `collapse`. This "feature" can be used to show, hide, or collapse a table column, respectively. This is useful only in the case of dynamic/interactive XSL-FO documents; for print, why would you ever want to hide or collapse a column?

We can easily add a couple of `fo:table-column` FOs to our XSL-FO table, which displays information about a film's crew members. To do so, just add those elements (which are empty, remember) to the XSLT template rule which processes the `crew` source-tree element. For example,

```
<fo:table-column
  column-number="1" column-width="52pt"
  background-color="silver"/>
<fo:table-column
  column-number="2" column-width="88pt"/>
```

(Remember that the `fo:table-column` elements must appear as children of the `fo:table` element, *before* the `fo:table-body` itself. This turns out to be another advantage of the strange concept of a table with two table bodies: If you're using

---

10. Not a lot of Web sites out there use `colgroup`, which is a fairly recent addition to the (X)HTML vocabulary. But for the same purposes served by this FO—consistency and concision—I encourage you to try using it if you have the opportunity.

fo:table-column elements to define the columns' widths and other properties, you're doing so for *all* table bodies within the table.)

Results of adding these column specifications to the existing display of the *Johnny Guitar* crew appear as in Figure 10–19.

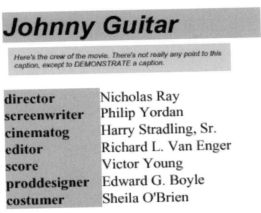

Figure 10-19   Defining common properties for whole table columns, in XSL-FO's row-oriented world, using fo:table-column. Note that the first column has been assigned both background-color and column-width attributes; the second, column-width only. The column widths I chose for this demonstration are not the same as the 40%–60% split previously assigned to the columns; here, column 1 is somewhat narrower than that (and column 2 is wider), making the table as a whole appear narrower than it does in Figure 10–18.

Using fo:table-header and fo:table-footer

There's no real trick to adding a header or footer to a table; simply include an fo:table-header or fo:table-footer element, respectively, in the XSL-FO result tree. These elements must appear as children of the fo:table element, following the fo:table-column element(s), if any, and before the fo:table-body.

One interesting feature of XSL-FO table headers and footers is that they're like mini-table bodies themselves, able to contain multiple rows and cells. The other thing to bear in mind is that—unlike XHTML's th element—an fo:table-header (or -footer, for that matter) does not have any inherent display properties. Text within an fo:table-header will not be automatically bold-faced, for instance. This makes headers and footers purely structural concepts in XSL-FO.

We could set up a table header for our table of *Johnny Guitar*'s crew members something like this:

```
<fo:table-header>
  <fo:table-row>
    <fo:table-cell
      number-columns-spanned="2">
      <fo:block
        padding="3pt" margin="1pt"
        border-style="solid" border-width=".5pt"
        text-align="center"
        font-size="8pt" font-weight="bold">
        Crew Members
      </fo:block>
    </fo:table-cell>
  </fo:table-row>
  <fo:table-row>
    <fo:table-cell>
      <fo:block
        padding="3pt" margin="1pt"
        border-style="solid" border-width=".5pt"
        text-align="center"
        font-size="8pt" font-weight="bold">
        Title
      </fo:block>
    </fo:table-cell>
    <fo:table-cell>
      <fo:block
        padding="3pt" margin="1pt"
        border-style="solid" border-width=".5pt"
        text-align="center"
        font-size="8pt" font-weight="bold">
        Name
      </fo:block>
    </fo:table-cell>
  </fo:table-row>
</fo:table-header>
```

This establishes a header two rows high. The first row contains a single table cell, spanning two columns; the second, two cells at one column each. This creates a display something like that shown in Figure 10–20.

It turns out that the content depicted in Figure 10–20 just about fills the available space on the artificially small page size we've been using so far. At this point, I'm going to return the caption to the table and also add a table

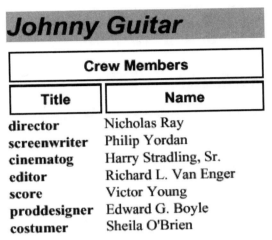

Figure 10-20 Adding a two-row table header. For this example, I also eliminated the silver shading of column 1 *and* the table caption shown in earlier figures. I'll re-introduce the caption in a moment.

footer—a note to the effect that the titles shown are, for now, just the names of elements from the source tree. These changes should force the table to break across pages.

The footer looks like this in the XSLT template (or in the XSL-FO result tree, for that matter):

```
<fo:table-footer>
  <fo:table-row>
    <fo:table-cell
      number-columns-spanned="2">
    <fo:block
      padding="5pt" margin="1pt"
      border-style="solid" border-width=".5pt"
      font-size="4pt" font-style="italic">
    * Note: Titles shown here are not "official"
    titles taken from the film's credits. They're
    just the names of elements taken from the XML
    source tree.
    </fo:block>
  </fo:table-cell>
  </fo:table-row>
</fo:table-footer>
```

When you view Xep's conversion of the XSL-FO to PDF in Acrobat Reader's "facing pages" mode, what you see resembles Figure 10–21.

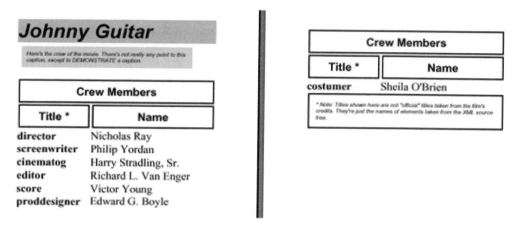

Figure 10-21   XSL-FO table with caption (light silver box), two-row header, and footer, as rendered to PDF by Xep 2.21. The table now crosses a page boundary. Xep has repeated the table header by default, but not the footer; in this version of Xep, repeatable table footers aren't supported. (A table footer appears only once, at the very end of the table.)

If for some reason you wanted *not* to repeat the headers on pages beyond the table's first, you could set the `fo:table` element's `table-omit-header-at-break` attribute to `true`. (Its default value is `false`—meaning, "Do *not* omit the header at the break.")

Advanced XSL-FO

With what you already know about XSLT and XSL-FO, you can lay out a reasonably sophisticated print publication from an XML source tree.

This chapter will introduce you to some of the more exotic features of the XSL-FO specification. The purpose here, as in Chapter 6 (which did the same for XSLT), is not to cover every remaining square millimeter of the standard with a fine-tooth comb; nor is it to promise that you'll have attained XSL-FO guruhood by its completion. No, the main thing I'm trying to do is make you aware of how much more there is to know about XSL-FO.

This chapter concludes with the biggest "How Do I...?" project in the book: producing a complete "FlixML B-Movie Film Festival" playbill-style brochure. That project doesn't use all the techniques from XSLT or XSL-FO, but it uses a fair proportion of them. It also will show you some of the major considerations you need to weigh in producing your own full-sized print publications from XML source documents.

XSL-FO Functions

Functions in an XSL-FO document work just as they do in an XSLT stylesheet: You pass them an argument or two, they do something with the arguments, and they return a value. Indeed, some of the XSL-FO functions have exactly the same names and do exactly the same things as certain XSLT functions. The only difference is that an XSLT function returns its value when the stylesheet is processed. An XSL-FO function, on the other hand, returns a value which cannot be processed (usefully, or perhaps at all) until "run time" for the XSL-FO document itself.

A slight conflict in terminology

There *is* one other difference to be taken into account when comparing the two standards' treatment of their functions. What XSLT calls "arguments," XSL-FO sometimes calls "arguments," and sometimes calls "parameters." The latter seems a pretty unfortunate word choice. It's not that hard. after all, to think of contexts where the word "parameter" might mean either an XSLT-type parameter *or* an XSL-FO-type parameter.

I'm going to use "argument" rather than "parameter" for the values you pass to XSL-FO functions. Just be prepared to deal with the potential confusion if switching back and forth between the two specs on your own.

XSL-FO expressions

Before diving into the details—how to call each function and what it returns—I think it'd be a good idea to consider how, exactly, you use *any* function in an XSL-FO document.

Think about the XPath and XSLT functions you already know. Pick one at random...or, heck, I'll pick one for you. Let's consider the `substring()` function. Can I do the following in a template rule in an XSLT stylesheet that is transforming to XHTML?

```
<p>substring("John", 1, 1)</p>
```

Does this place a capital "J" in an XHTML `p` element?

No, of course not.[1] What this places into the result tree (into a p element, in particular) is not the value returned by the `substring()` function call but simply the text string s, u, b, s, t, r, and so on, up through the closing `)`. If you want a function to behave like a function, and not like a string of literal characters, you need to use it in a context in which XSLT will recognize it as something other than a string. For instance,

---

1.   And if you answered "yes," well, I'm speechless.

```
<p><xsl:value-of
  select="substring('John', 1, 1)"/></p>
```

The value of an XSLT `select` attribute here is called an *expression*. Where an expression is expected, you can use a number, a literal string, a function call, and so on.

So it is with XSL-FO functions. You can't simply use them willy-nilly where you'd like to display the values they return. (Indeed, the problem is even more acute in XSL-FO than in XSLT: There's no equivalent of the `xsl:value-of` XSLT element.) As a rule, you can use these function calls only in very limited contexts—in place of literal text in attribute values.

Weak software support

No matter how useful these functions may seem, bear in mind that XSL-FO processing software, as a class, is nowhere near as mature as XSLT software. Support for these so-called "core" functions seems particularly weak.

Whatever this means for your own work right now, it certainly means you won't be seeing a lot of screen shots in this section of the book!

Numeric functions

Functions in this category, like numeric functions in XSLT, operate on numeric arguments and return numeric values. In fact, a few of these functions duplicate the work of XSLT functions exactly.

The `floor()`, `ceiling()`, and `round()` functions

These functions do just what the XSLT functions of the same names do. To refresh your memory:

- `floor(number)`: Returns the integer with the highest value less than or equal to the argument passed to it.
- `ceiling(number)`: Returns the integer with the lowest value greater than or equal to the argument passed to it.
- `round(number)`: Returns the integer closest in value to the argument passed to it. If there are two such integers (i.e., if *number* includes a fractional part of .5), the function "rounds up" to the larger of the two.

The `min()` and `max()` functions

Both of these functions accept two numeric arguments. The `min()` function returns the lower of the two arguments passed to it; the `max()` function (surprise!) returns the higher of the two values.

The XSL-FO spec doesn't establish any limits on nesting these functions, which—if you use that fact carefully—may permit you to determine the minimum or maximum of *more* than two values.

For instance, consider an XSLT stylesheet that has defined four variables, called a, b, c, and d. Their values are 10, 25, 15, and 8, respectively. The XSL-FO document could display the largest value if the stylesheet has a template that looks something like this:

```
max(<xsl:value-of select="$a"/>,
   max(<xsl:value-of select="$b"/>,
   max(<xsl:value-of select="$c"/>,
   <xsl:value-of select="$d"/>)))
```

See? This will produce a result tree that looks like the following:

```
max(10, max(25, max(15, 8)))
```

The processor will resolve the nested `max()` functions from the inside out, like this:

- The maximum of 15 and 8 is 15; when you pass this result to the next `max()` function...
- the maximum of 25 and 15 is 25; when you pass this result to the next `max()` function...
- the maximum of 10 and 25 is 25, which is the final result.

Something like this might be useful if you needed to allocate a large enough area to contain any of several possibilities. For instance, you could make all the columns in four separate tables the same size simply by ensuring that the four tables all had the same number of columns—that is, the largest number of columns needed by *any* of the four.

The `abs()` function

As you might guess, this function returns the absolute value of the argument passed to it.

Most of the numbers you'll be using in an XSL-FO context represent two things: units of measure and pages. It's hard to imagine a case in which one of those kinds of numbers should suddenly become negative—but, of course, if it *does* do so, you'll need to use this function to handle the number.

An exercise in frustration

That's what reading the XSL-FO spec is, in a lot of cases. As far as I can tell from simply reading the spec *and* from doing an automated text search, there's exactly one reference to the `abs()` function—which occurs in the heading to the brief, two-sentence description of the function's purpose. There are no examples of its use—or, indeed of its *usefulness*—anywhere.

One correspondent from the XSL-FO mailing list suggests that the function's purpose is to evaluate not simply the absolute value of *a* number but the absolute value of the *difference between two numbers*. In an XSL-FO context, for instance, this could be used to determine the distance between any two arbitrary points on a page, without worrying about which value is larger. This still seems kind of a stretch to me, but it's the best rationale for `abs()` that I can think of, or that anyone else has suggested to me!

Color functions

Each of the functions in this group returns a color value. The color value so returned can be used in contexts where color is meaningful—for example, as the value of a `background-color` attribute.

Depending on the processor, such a value may be representable as a *name* (e.g., `silver`, `orange`, `cyan`, `teal`). Regardless of the processor, though, colors may always be represented in a form that should be familiar to you if you've worked with colors on the Web, such as `#000000` for black and `#0000FF` for pure blue. It's the latter values which are returned by these functions.

- `rgb(`*red_value*`, `*green_value*`, `*blue_value*`)`: Pass this function three separate color values (amount of red, amount of green, and amount of blue—a so-called RGB color, hence the function's name), and you get back a single, hex-based color value. For instance, `rgb(255, 255, 255)` (pure white) returns #FFFFFF, and rgb(192, 192, 0) (a kind of mustard yellow) returns #C0C000.[2]

- icc-color(*fallback_red, fallback_green, fallback_blue, color_prof, specific_color...*): If you're using ICC color profiles[3] in your application, you can use this function to select a color from a given profile. Probably the most important argument is color_prof; its value is the name of a color profile defined in an fo:color-profile FO for this XSL-FO document. (If the color profile isn't available for some reason, the processor will fall back to the RGB value defined by the first three arguments.) Following the name of the color profile is a comma-separated list of one or more specific color values; what you actually use for these values depends on the color profile in question.

- system-color(*color_name*): While Xep and FOP are pretty good about recognizing the names of the most common colors from the Web palette, you may not be able to rely on this level of intelligence from *every* XSL-FO processor. The system-color() function affords you a certain amount of protection in this respect; rather than using the name literally, pass it to the function to get back a hexadecimal #rrggbb color.

Internal inconsistencies

See the flaw here? Why would a processor intelligent enough to support the translation of a color's name to its hex value not also be intelligent enough to support the plain old name by itself—converting it internally to the right hex value?

---

2. Those of you who are mathematically inclined may have already seen how this works: Each six-digit hexadecimal number returned as a color by any of the XSL-FO color functions actually consists of three *pairs* of hex digits. The first pair represents the color's red component; the second, the green; and the third, the blue. Thus, because 192 in decimal equals C0 in hex, an RGB value of 192, 192, 0, translates to a full six-digit hex color value of C0C000.
3. Briefly discussed in Chapter 10, under the discussion of the fo:declarations FO.

Font functions

There's only one such function, the "s" in "functions" notwithstanding. This is the `system-font()` function.

You pass up to two arguments to `system-font()`. The first is the name of a font on the system running the XSL-FO processor; the second, which is optional, is the name of some font-related property, such as `font-size`, `font-weight`, and so on. The `system-font()` function then returns the value of that property for the system font in question.

Do not mistake the term "system font" for something like Arial, Univers, Garamond, or even one of the more generic fonts such as serif and monospace. What "system font" refers to are fonts in use in various widgets and gimcracks in the user interface. The XSL-FO spec names six such fonts: `caption`, `icon`, `menu`, `message-box`, `small-caption`, and `status-bar`. Thus, if the user has selected 10-point Garamond as the font used for displaying menu choices on her system, the function call

```
system-font(menu, font-family)
```

returns `Garamond`, whereas

```
system-font(menu, font-size)
```

returns `10pt`.

If the second argument is missing, it is derived from the context in which the function call is being made. For instance, consider this portion of an XSL-FO document:

```
<fo:block
  font-family="system-font(caption)">
  A caption goes here!
</fo:block>
```

The call to `system-font()` behaves here as if you'd explicitly used instead

```
font-family="system-font(caption, font-family)"
```

Why would you want to use the `system-font()` function to assign these properties to print documents? You probably wouldn't. I'm guessing this function will find most use when and if XSL-FO documents ever become truly interactive. For example, you could build an `fo:multi-switch` structure (as explained in Chapter 10) that closely mimicked a user's "home interface"—to the point that he didn't even know he was interacting with an XSL-FO document instead of a real menu, dialog box, or whatever.

Aural Stylesheets

XSL-FO incorporates about the same level of support for so-called "aural" stylesheets as CSS does. Of course, to a great extent this is conjectural; there's very little software that supports (X)HTML-rendered-aurally, and to my knowledge there's absolutely *no* software that supports XSL-FO-rendered-aurally.

That said, it's a responsible consideration to bear in mind: How do you allow for the fact that someone "looking at" your XSL-FO document may, in fact, be blind or profoundly sight-impaired? Is it possible to make your content available to her, as well as to someone sitting there physically turning the pages? (Note that this is a separate issue from producing Braille editions of printed matter.)

Aural properties—such as volume, speech rate, the "voice" with which text is rendered, whether punctuation should be read, and so on—are outlined in Section 7.5 of the XSL-FO spec. Essentially, this section quotes from (and links to) CSS's explanations of the same properties.

Another alternative for accessibility

If you really need to make content accessible for aural presentation—in the text-to-speech sense—I strongly urge you to consider one of the XML vocabularies explicitly developed for that purpose, rather than piggybacking on XSL-FO. (Or on CSS, for that matter.) Languages I know of that address this problem go by the names VoiceXML, VoxML, and SABLE.

As is the way of the world, of course, each of these standards is embraced by some organizations and software/hardware vendors, and none of them is embraced by all. Nevertheless, a solution that was built from the ground up with aural accessibility in mind is almost bound to be more comprehensive—more *useful*—than something like the aural features sort of bolted onto the side of a general-purpose language like XSL-FO.

There's one other option for making your documents accessible, even if you want to stick to XSL-FO. This involves the use of pre-recorded sound and other multimedia representations of the text in the document. You can accomplish this with the `fo:instream-foreign-object` FO—annotating (as it were) each bit of crucial *text*

> with a corresponding bit of speech or other sound. Because this FO accepts, as descendants, markup from other XML namespaces, you can in effect embed (say) SMIL code in your XSL-FO documents.
>
> The catch, of course, is then finding *software* that can handle both XSL-FO and whatever embedded vocabulary you've selected. One of the packages covered in Chapter 12, called X-Smiles, does just that.

Writing Modes and Internationalization

I've alluded to this elsewhere: The XSL-FO spec is almost obsessively language-neutral. Although it often accepts property values such as "left" and "bottom" out of deference to CSS, with which it shares most properties, whenever possible the XSL-FO spec assumes you know the *writing mode* of the language in which the document will be reproduced.

In XSL-FO, this is expressed in terms like "start" and "end" (rather than "left" and "right"), but also in a property (i.e., attribute) named `writing-mode`. This attribute takes the following values:

- `lr-tb`: left-to-right, top-to-bottom. This is the writing mode familiar to users of most Western languages. Text begins at the top left and proceeds to the right; each new line begins anew at the left, below the preceding one.
- `rl-tb`: right-to-left, top-to-bottom. This is used in Arabic and Hebrew text. Text begins at the top right and proceeds to the left; each new line begins at the right, below the preceding one.
- `tb-rl`: top-to-bottom, right-to-left. This is used in Chinese and Japanese text. Text begins at the top right and proceeds to the bottom; each new line begins at the top, to the left of the preceding one.
- `lr`: Shorthand for `lr-tb`.
- `rl`: Shorthand for `rl-tb`.
- `tb`: Shorthand for `tb-rl`.

This greatly over-simplifies XSL-FO's support for internationalized presentation. (For instance, the language also provides for rotated glyphs in certain languages and writing systems, and for bi-directional writing modes.) If you are preparing documents for an audience for whom this is an important consideration, you should refer to section 7.26 of the XSL-FO spec.

How Do I...
Create a B-movie festival "playbill" from a FlixML review?

I'm not going to reproduce here the entire XSLT stylesheet I built to do this (let alone its entire XSL-FO result tree). Instead, I've selected three problems you might come face-to-face with in doing something like it yourself:

- How do I create a "watermark" effect with XSL-FO?
- How do I use leader dots with justified text?
- How do I build a document with space for binding down the center of two facing pages?

Before looking at those three specific questions, though, I'll give you a general sense of how these playbill-type things are set up and the way the code works.

Layout of the playbill

In general, the pages of the flixml.org playbill are 5.5 x 8.5 inches in size—that is, like an 8.5 x 11 paper size, landscape format, divided in half. Each playbill covers one showing of one movie, and consists of these kinds of pages:

- the front cover
- advertisements
- table of contents
- list of sponsors
- the playbill proper
- an "about flixml.org" page
- the back cover

The bulk of the playbill, of course, comes from a FlixML review and goes into the "playbill proper" section. Material on the other pages comes from a variety of sources. For instance, the main title of the film appears in several places besides the playbill proper (notably, the cover); ads are external JPEG images; and some of the content is kept in an external "parameters file," whose contents are read into a variable in the XSLT stylesheet and used as needed.

There's nothing particularly exotic about the design of any of these pages. For example, the "about flixml.org" page looks like Figure 11–1.

Figure 11-1   The "about flixml.org" page at the back of the B-movie film festival playbill. Of course, there's nothing I can add to *your* knowledge of that topic; this is for the benighted film audience who doesn't know anything about FlixML or, for that matter, XML itself.

Little bits of code

I mentioned before that one of the resources tapped for building each playbill is an external file which contains some "driver parameters." This file has grown and shrunk as I've needed one thing or the other not actually included in the FlixML review itself. The current version of the file looks like this:

```
<params>
  <date>June 18, 2001 - 8:00 pm</date>
  <ads>
    <half src="half.jpg"/>
    <qtr src="qtr_l.jpg"/>
    <qtr src="qtr_r.jpg"/>
  </ads>
</params>
```

The date element provides date and time information to be displayed on the playbill's cover. Each child of the ads element defines one of the advertisements that appear on page 2 (the inside front cover). I access these parameters, of course, using the XSLT document() function. For instance,

```
<xsl:variable name="params"
  select="document('params.xml')/params"/>
...
<fo:block font-size="14pt" font-weight="bold"
  margin-top="1.25in" text-align="center">
  <xsl:value-of select="$params/date"/>
</fo:block>
```

If you look back at the list of sections in the playbill, you'll see that much of the content (as I said) doesn't come from a FlixML review at all. Structurally, in respect to the XSLT stylesheet, what this would normally mean is that the root element's template rule would be *enormous*, including within it the templates for everything *but* the review proper. I didn't like this idea—it was too hard to find what I was looking for—so I wanted to break out each of those sections into its own template rule. But if they don't correspond to content, how do you do that?

The way I do it is with, well, I guess you could call them almost-bogus template rules. They all key off the review's title element, and each is invoked with a different *mode*. (The title element is processed for real by a couple of unmoded template rules—one for the main title, one for any alternate titles.) Thus, the body of the template rule for processing the root flixinfo element looks like this:

```
<xsl:template match="flixinfo">
  <fo:root
```

```
xmlns:fo="http://www.w3.org/1999/XSL/Format">
<fo:layout-master-set>
  ...simple page masters, page sequence masters...
</fo:layout-master-set>

<!-- Build the front cover (odd page) -->
  <xsl:apply-templates select="title" mode="cover"/>

<!-- Build the ads page (even page) -->
  <xsl:apply-templates select="title" mode="ads"/>

<!-- Build the table of contents (odd page) -->
  <xsl:apply-templates select="title" mode="toc"/>

<!-- Build the sponsors page (even page) -->
  <xsl:apply-templates select="title"
    mode="sponsors"/>

<!-- Build a "movie info" section for tonight's film
  (starts on odd page) -->
<fo:page-sequence master-name="seq-mast-movie">
  ...
  <fo:flow flow-name="reg-body">
    <fo:block-container
      margin-bottom=".5in">
    <!-- Build top of first page of review -->
    <xsl:apply-templates
      select="title | genre | releaseyear | studio |
        mpaarating"/>
    <!-- Build rest of review -->
    <xsl:apply-templates
        select="cast | crew | plotsummary | remarks"/>
    </fo:block-container>
  </fo:flow>
</fo:page-sequence>

<!-- Build the "about" page (odd page) -->
  <xsl:apply-templates select="title" mode="about"/>

<!-- Build the back cover (even page) -->
  <xsl:apply-templates select="title"
    mode="back_cover"/>

</fo:root>

</xsl:template>
```

There's really not much very complex going on in the stylesheet. I use some named attribute sets and some named templates, which helps simplify a lot of the code (both *per se* and as something I need to maintain from time to time).

One feature I've toyed with but not yet implemented is a playbill for a double- or triple-feature, incorporating reviews of more than one film.

Total length of the XSLT stylesheet is more than 700 lines.

Now, finally, let's take a look at those three specific problems: building a watermark, creating a justified leader block, and constructing alternate left- and right-hand page layouts.

Creating a watermark

On its own, XSL-FO is capable of creating borders of only the plainest kind: solid lines, double lines, grooved, ridged—like that. You can put a border around selected sides of an area, but the border's main characteristic will remain unchanged—it will be relentlessly *dull*.

One gimmick for putting a fancier border around an area is to find a clip-art border suitable for the area's content, and add the image to the page layout not with an `fo:external-graphic` FO but using the `background-image` attribute to an `fo:block` element. The general syntax of this attribute is this:

```
background-image="url(uri_of_image)"
```

In the case of the flixml.org B-movie film festival playbill, I've used several blocks of code in preparing the cover. One of them looks like this:

```
<fo:block font-size="36pt" font-weight="bold"
  font-family="serif" text-align="center"
  width="3in" height="1.5in"
  line-height="1.5in" margin-left=".75in"
  background-image="url(watermark.jpg)">
  playbill
</fo:block>
```

The important piece here, of course, is the `background-image` attribute I just described. The entire block area has that background image behind it; if the block is bigger than the image's actual size, the image will be tiled; if smaller, the image will be clipped. That's why I've specified both `width` and `height` here.

The `line-height` attribute is important because it ensures that the text "playbill" will be properly vertically aligned within the area (and, hence, on top of the background image).

Image scaling and resizing

The XSL-FO spec provides for *scaling* images to a particular size...but only so long as the image is being incorporated via the `fo:external-graphic` element. When used as an area background, an image is basically stuck at whatever its native size is.

The Xep vendor, RenderX, justifiably terms this "a nasty hole in the specification." If you're using Xep, you can take advantage of a handful of "extension properties" provided by RenderX to plug the gap: `rx:background-content-height`, `rx:background-width`, and `rx:background-scaling`. To use these extension properties in your Xep-processed XSL-FO document, you must declare the `rx:` namespace prefix as follows:

```
xmlns:rx="http://www.renderx.com/XSL/Extensions"
```

I've got several properly sized background images and borders I use for this purpose, selecting whichever seems most suitable for the film in question.

Figure 11–2 shows a typical front cover for one of these playbills, using a "wooden frame" motif, in keeping (as such things go) with the *Johnny Guitar* Western theme.

Using leader dots with justified text

When I covered the `fo:leader` inline-type FO in the last chapter, I showed you how to use it with no options. This produced acceptable results for some purposes (as shown in Figure 10–11).

More often, though, when you see leaders in the real world they're set up in a block of justified text. Items to the left of the leader are left-justified, and those to the right are right-justified. The leader itself—usually just the typical string of dots—fills all available space between the end of the text preceding the leader and the start of the text after it.

What I didn't tell you in Chapter 10 is that, with `fo:leader`, you can specify the *length* of the leaders. In fact, you can specify not just an absolute length but also the leader's minimum, maximum, and optimum lengths. The syntax for doing so looks kind of odd at first:

```
leader-length.minimum="min_length"
leader-length.maximum="max_length"
leader-length.optimum="opt_length"
```

(The defaults for these three lengths are `0pt`, `100%`, and `12pt` respectively.)

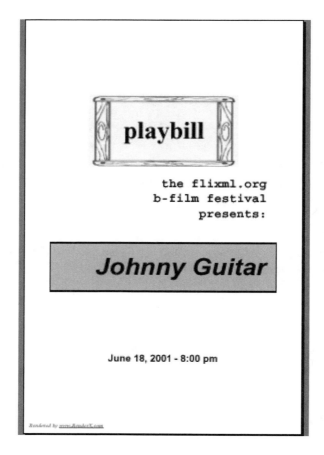

Figure 11-2 Cover of a film-festival playbill, using a background image instead of a plain old rectangular border around the word "playbill." As usual in this XSL-FO portion of *Just XSL*, don't think too hard about the specific layout/design—I'm not trying to bowl you over with a gorgeous product. (I'm probably not *capable* of bowling you over with one, come to that.)

Now, plain text by default in XSL-FO is considered to be an inline area, implicitly. Likewise, `fo:leader` is an inline FO. And so is `fo:page-number-citation`. So, you might conclude you could do something like the following to produce a traditional justified-style table of contents block:

```
<fo:block text-align="justify">
  Chapter 1
  <fo:leader leader-length.minimum="12pt"/>
```

```
<fo:page-number-citation
  ref-id="identifier"/>
</fo:block>
```

The idea here is to force the chapter number to the left, followed by a leader at least 12 points long, followed by the page number forced to the right.

Alas, this doesn't work in practice. The reason? Look at any single line of justified text, or for that matter the last line of any block of justified text, like this:

> Justified text isn't *always* justified. Justified text isn't *always* justified. Justified text isn't *always* justified. Justified text isn't *always* justified. Justified text isn't *always* justified. Justified text isn't *always* justified. Justified text isn't *always* justified. Justified text isn't *always* justified. Justified text isn't *always* justified.

Any line in our hypothetical table of contents will be in exactly the same situation. It won't automatically fill the margin-to-margin space; the only lines that will do so (if any of them do!) are the ones that take up *more* space than the margin-to-margin distance allows.

You can simulate the effect with XSL-FO, though, using a "poor man's justified leader block" coded something like the following (just showing the first line in detail):

```
<fo:table>
 <fo:table-body>
  <fo:table-row>
   <fo:table-cell>
    <fo:block margin="2pt" text-align="right">
     Sponsors
    </fo:block>
   </fo:table-cell>
   <fo:table-cell>
    <fo:block margin="2pt" text-align="center">
     <fo:leader leader-pattern="dots"
      leader-length.optimum="100%"/>
    </fo:block>
   </fo:table-cell>
   <fo:table-cell>
    <fo:block margin="2pt" text-align="left">
     <fo:page-number-citation ref-id="sponsors"/>
    </fo:block>
   </fo:table-cell>
  </fo:table-row>
  ...other rows as above...
```

```
    </fo:table-body>
</fo:table>
```

Right: Use a plain old table, with each row consisting of three cells. The first cell contains the chapter title or other text aligned right; the second, the leader; and the third, the page number aligned left.

Converted to PDF, this structure resembles Figure 11–3.

Sponsors 4

Cast 5

Crew 5

The Plot 6

Remarks 6

flixml.org 7

Figure 11-3   The "poor man's justified leader block" described in the text. It's actually a three-column table with (in this case) section titles in column 1, the leaders in column 2, and the corresponding page numbers in the last column. There really ought to be some way to do a rich man's version of this—the real thing, without using a table. Maybe there is. But the spec (and/or Xep, and/or FOP) has stubbornly refused to yield up that secret to me so far![4]

Building a document with different left- and right-page layouts

I alluded to this in earlier chapters, without showing you how to achieve it. There are a number of pieces to this puzzle.

Setting up the simple page masters

First, you need to construct separate simple page masters for the left- and right-hand pages. These are nearly identical:

---

4.   Of course, using table columns as alignment devices is no great revolutionary hack. It's been around for years, not only in Web-page design but in SGML and non-markup-based layout systems. It's still disappointing to have to resort to it in the context of a brand-spankin'-new spec, though.

```
<fo:layout-master-set>

  <!-- Left-hand pages -->
  <fo:simple-page-master
    master-name="page-movie-info-l"
    page-width="5.5in" page-height="8.5in"
    margin-top=".75in" margin-bottom=".75in"
    margin-left=".5in" margin-right=".75in">
    <fo:region-body region-name="reg-body"/>
    <fo:region-after region-name="reg-after"
      extent=".5in"/>
  </fo:simple-page-master>

  <!-- Right-hand pages -->
  <fo:simple-page-master
    master-name="page-movie-info-r"
    page-width="5.5in" page-height="8.5in"
    margin-top=".75in" margin-bottom=".75in"
    margin-left=".75in" margin-right=".5in">
    <fo:region-body region-name="reg-body"/>
    <fo:region-after region-name="reg-after"
      extent=".5in"/>
  </fo:simple-page-master>

  ...other page and page-sequence masters...

</fo:layout-master-set>
```

In fact, these two page masters are identical in every respect but one. Look at the `margin-left` and `margin-right` attributes to the `fo:simple-page-master` elements. See? They're simply switched, with left-hand pages bumped slightly leftward and right-hand ones, slightly to the right.

Associating the simple page masters with odd and even pages

Once you've got the layouts shifted to the outside of each two-page spread, as I just described, the next step is to tell the processor which layout to use on odd-numbered and which on even-numbered pages. You do this with a form of page sequence master you haven't seen before. Instead of a page sequence master defining *single* or *repeatable* sequences of pages, you set up one defining *alternative* sequences, like this:

```
<fo:page-sequence-master master-name="seq-mast-movie">
  <fo:repeatable-page-master-alternatives>
    <fo:conditional-page-master-reference
```

```
      odd-or-even="even"
      master-name="page-movie-info-l"/>
    <fo:conditional-page-master-reference
      odd-or-even="odd"
      master-name="page-movie-info-r"/>
  </fo:repeatable-page-master-alternatives>
</fo:page-sequence-master>
```

The heart of this structure is the `fo:repeatable-page-master-alterna-tives` element, which acts as a wrapper for the `fo:conditional-page-master-reference` elements—each of which makes a connection between a page layout and a condition in which to use that layout. The `master-name` attributes of the latter point back to the simple page masters established in the preceding step, and the `odd-or-even` attribute (with values, obviously, of `odd` or `even`) tells the processor when to use that layout.

Other considerations

The preceding steps describe all you need to do for most purposes when laying out alternating left- and right-hand page designs.

If you look at most books, newspapers, and other publications, though, you'll see that the left and right sides differ in ways other than just their offsets from the center. For instance, in this book's manuscript form (as I've actually keyed it in), even-numbered pages have a header consisting of the page number, the chapter title, and the chapter number (in that order); odd-numbered pages show the most recent level-1 heading and the page number (in that order).

You could accomplish the same thing fairly easily with XSL-FO, since each separate simple page master can have its own `region-before` in which to put those customized headers.

My flixml.org playbill doesn't use headers on any pages, but I do use page *footers*; these simply contain the word "Page" and the page number, created with code like the following:

```
<fo:static-content flow-name="reg-after">
  <fo:block font-size="10pt"
    border-top=".5pt solid" padding-top="2pt"
    text-align="inside">
    Page <fo:page-number/>
  </fo:block>
</fo:static-content>
```

This code is unremarkable except for one little bit: the value of the `fo:block` element's `text-align` attribute. Typically, of course, you use values like `left`, `right`, `start`, and `end` for this element. However, the XSL-FO spec also provides two special values, `inside` and `outside`; these apply to exactly the situation we're dealing with now. A value of `inside` aligns the text with the margin closest to the *inside* of a two-page spread; a value of `outside`, obviously, with the margin closest to the *outside*.

Once again, though, we're pretty much in the realm of theory rather than practice here. Xep 2.21—at least, the evaluation version—consistently equates `inside` with a value of `left` and `outside` with a value of `right`.

Figure 11–4 shows you how a couple of facing pages (in this case, from the playbill for *When Dinosaurs Ruled the Earth*) look when rendered to PDF by Xep.

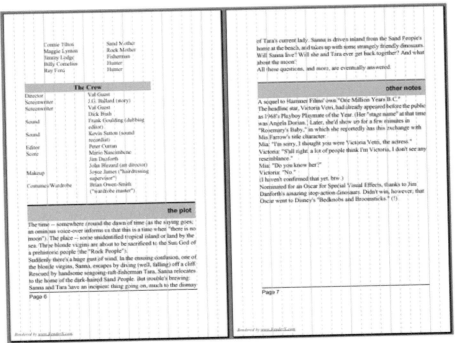

Figure 11-4   Alternate left- and right-hand page layouts. I've shut off the Acrobat Reader vertical form grid here, but turned on the horizontal, with major divisions of an inch and minor ones at each quarter-inch. Note how the page on the left is left-shifted a quarter of an inch, and the one on the right, right-shifted the same amount. Also notice the stubborn page number placement.

CHAPTER 12

XSL-FO Software

What if a tree falls over in a forest and there's no one to hear it: Is there a sound? The status of software to support XSL-FO reminds me of that tired old war-horse of college-dormitory "philosophy."

Not that the release of XSL-FO software is the event going unnoticed. No— the thud in the forest is the sound of the massive XSL-FO spec itself hitting the ground. And all around, so it may seem, is silence. There *is* very little XSL-FO software (yet) to celebrate the spec.

I can think of a few reasons why this might be so. Maybe the most obvious is that the standard isn't a final Recommendation yet; given its size and the complexity of the issues it's dealing with, the surprising fact may be that *any* vendors have bet on it so far.

More subtly, though, there may be a problem with what XSL-FO is attempting to do. It's like an open-source PDF. Why would this present a problem? First, vendors may be reluctant to bet on what they perceive as a dead-trees publishing platform. With all the talk of e-books, electronic ink, high-resolution digital reading hardware, and so on, why sink resources into something that's not the wave of the future? Second, I think software vendors, as a rule, simply don't *understand* what I'll loosely term "print." With some exceptions,[1] makers of com-

---

1. Among them Adobe, obviously (not just because of PDF, but also because of their PageMaker and FrameMaker products); Quark; and maybe (*maybe*) the makers of leading word processors.

puter software simply aren't comfortable with—or don't even know—the concepts of even basic typography and design. It's a black art (so they seem to think), practiced by ink-stained wretches who still worship at the feet of Gutenberg.

(To the extent that this perception of typography and design is held, it seems particularly shortsighted. After all, there may be truly practical reasons why "good" typography and design are considered good in the first place—having to do with the efficiency, comfort, and *pleasures* of reading rather than the ease of producing software for profit.)

Whatever the reasons, software developers for the most part haven't leapt to experiment with (let alone embrace) XSL-FO. In general, the limited offerings so far fall into two categories: XSL-FO-to-PDF conversion engines and native XSL-FO "readers."

What about XSL-FO authoring tools?

We probably won't see any of these for a while, if ever.

Over the short term, at least, XSL-FO is likely to remain a kind of esoteric subject, well-suited for people who aren't scared off by the terrors of building XSLT stylesheets but inaccessible to Plain Folk. This almost guarantees it won't be of interest to tool makers—at least the ones who intend to *sell* their products.

And, indeed, the language itself is so verbose and jargon-laden that creating it even by hand (rather than from an XSLT transformation) is a task almost no one will want to do. (For sure, if *I* had had to create it manually, you'd never be reading an XSL-FO section of *Just XSL.*)

Third, even if you wanted to create an XSL-FO document by hand-editing it, the effort would be literally meaningless—devoid of semantics, of *meaning*. Even a plain old word processor calls headings *headings* and paragraphs *paragraphs*. In XSL-FO, they're not even graced with that much intelligence. They're just block or inline FOs of a certain font family, font size, and font weight. This isn't just hard to do right manually, page after page, it's also almost unbearably boring.

Eventually, someone will endeavor to build a GUI-based XSL-FO editor. (A couple of the tools I'll show you later in this chapter are verging in that direction.) When they do, maybe editing raw XSL-FO documents will become practical.

Converting XSL-FO to PDF

This was the original approach to doing something useful with XSL-FO, and it's probably still the most popular. (It's certainly the one I've demonstrated throughout Part 3 of this book.)

For a potential developer of XSL-FO software, the idea is fairly simple, even if putting it into practice requires great skill and patience:

- Start with the assumption that an XSL-FO document exists. You don't care where it came from—manually created, auto-generated as an XSLT result tree, or (who knows?) maybe even as a "Save As…" output from a word processor. But you, the developer, don't have to build *editing* software.
- Also start with the premise that you don't need to develop *viewing* software. A user who wants to see or print an electronic document already has a de facto standard platform for doing so: Adobe's well-documented Portable Document Format (PDF).
- So then, what's left for your XSL-FO processor to do is something like what an XSLT processor does: Translate an XML source tree (always in the XSL-FO vocabulary, in this case) to some other form—that of a PDF document.

A big deal: Inside a PDF document

To get an idea of the magnitude of the problem of converting a straight-text XSL-FO document to PDF, use a simple text editor to open a PDF file. You'll see something like this (corresponding to the hyperlink enclosing "Rendered by www.RenderX.com" footer on every page produced by the Xep evaluation version):

```
18 0 obj
<</Type/Annot
/Subtype /Link
/Rect [50.307 8.739 113.433 14.441 ]
/BS <</Type/Border
>>
/Border [0 0 0]
/C [0 0 0]
/A <</S /URI /URI (http://www.renderx.com)>>
>>
endobj
```

And that's just the *legible* part. What makes this even harder to understand is that, not only are the contents inscrutable, so is the very *structure* of the document.

I don't want to belabor this too much, because it is off the main subject. But in the course of preparing this chapter, I learned of a couple of products that at least reveal the inner structure of a PDF document (even if they don't teach you much about the contents).

One of these is called PDF Explorer ($39 direct from the publisher, Mapsoft, at www.mapsoft.com; time-limited trial version available for download). Figure 12–1 shows you the bit of PDF above, rendered by PDF Explorer. (To help orient you, what's highlighted in this screen shot is the /URI piece from the above PDF code.)

Anyhow, as you can see, the decision to automate creation of even a moderately complex PDF document can't be one for a software maker to take lightly. We should probably consider ourselves lucky that *any* of them have!

Getting the software

As I delve into each of the four packages covered in this chapter, remember that you can find them—as well as others—at the same software sites I mentioned in Chapter 7:

```
www.xmlsoftware.com
www.xml.com/resourceguide
xml.coverpages.org
```

The Apache Project: FOP

FOP was originally developed almost as a proof-of-concept exercise by developer James Tauber.[2] The concept he was trying to prove was what he *did* prove—that converting XSL-FO to PDF was even doable in the first place. After he'd taken FOP through a couple of revisions, he turned the package over to the open-source Apache Project for future work.

Currently, FOP is still not at a full-fledged 1.0 version; at this writing, it's "only" at 0.18. (Still, that represents a lot of work for an open-source product based on a complex and still not final specification.)

---

2.   Tauber is the proprietor of the aforementioned xmlsoftware.com Web site, and several others including the new (at this writing) xslinfo.com site.

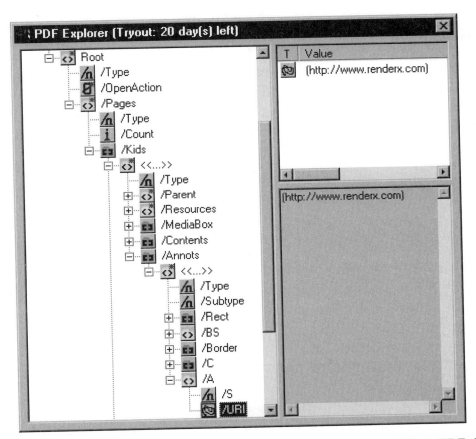

Figure 12-1 A portion of the *When Dinosaurs Ruled the Earth* playbill—a PDF document (created from my XSL-FO by RenderX's Xep) viewed here by Mapsoft's PDF Explorer. This makes it obvious that a PDF document has a structure, a fact not easily discernible from reading the raw document contents. As in many "Explorer"-type applications, in PDF Explorer you drill down into a tree structure by clicking on one of the little plus signs, and collapse it by clicking on a minus sign. The /Parent branch is particularly unproductive to drill down into; it shows the structure of the parent of the current node (the current node here being the first page of the review; that is, the first /Kid—clever, eh?—node of the /Pages node for the document). What makes this an unproductive exercise is that looking down at the /Parent node shows you *its* parent, and so on, until you've effectively traversed the entire `ancestor::` axis (in XPath terms).

Although FOP implements most of the features of the XSL-FO spec, sometimes it does so in limited ways. For example, XSL-FO defines a `margin` property (attribute) that can be placed on any block or inline FO. It's actually a shorthand property—allowing you to specify the top, bottom, left, and right margins simultaneously, without using separate `margin-top`, `margin-bottom`, `margin-left`, and `margin-right` properties. FOP doesn't (yet) support `margin` itself—you've got to use `margin-top`, and so on—and it does so only on page and region FOs.

The Apache Project released FOP 0.18 while I was working on the earlier chapters in this part of *Just XSL*. I'd experimented with FOP 0.17 till then, been frustrated by things that I *couldn't* show you with it, and switched to Xep. Rather than change horses in mid-stream (and potentially delay completing the chapters even longer), I continued to use Xep, despite FOP 0.18's advances. In a few cases, FOP supported features which Xep didn't, and in those cases I did use FOP.

Installing and running FOP

You can download FOP from the Apache Web site, at xml.apache.org/fop/. Installing it is like installing most other Java-based packages: Simply extract the contents of the compressed file into its own directory, and make that directory "visible" to the Java processor by including it in your CLASSPATH.

Sometimes easier said than done

Like many non-Java programmers, I suspect, I'm regularly frustrated by someone's claim that "all" I have to do to run some Java application or another is un-Zip it and set the CLASSPATH. FOP's installation was no less frustrating in this respect; on the other hand, it was no *more* frustrating. Trust me—eventually it's possible to make it work!

Included with FOP are the Apache Project's Xerces XML parser and Xalan XSLT processor. (Although not directly used in the XSL-FO-to-PDF conversion, Xalan can be used in the optional XML-to-XSL-FO preliminary step.)

You can run FOP from a Web server or from the command line of whatever operating system you're using. The general command-line syntax is this:

```
fop basic_opts in_opts in_doc out_opts out_doc
```

The only required argument on the command line is *in_doc*—the name of the input XSL-FO document. Given this command line,

```
fop playbill.fo
```

FOP simply translates the given XSL-FO code to its PDF equivalent, and places the output in a document named (in this case) playbill.pdf. If, for some reason, you wanted it to create a differently named PDF document, you'd supply that name as the *out_doc* argument.

There are three sets of optional arguments that can be used with FOP. I'll discuss them briefly next.

basic_opts Regardless of other options you might use, you can also employ any of the following. Note that each option is preceded by a hyphen.

- `-d`: Use debug mode (not documented further).
- `-x`: Dump configuration settings (not documented further).
- `-q`: Use quiet (non-verbose) mode (not documented further).
- `-c` *userconfig.xml*: Use settings established in an external configuration file whose name is *userconfig.xml*. This configuration file comes with the FOP installation; it's a well-formed XML document that drives certain kinds of FOP behavior. Currently, you can control only two kinds of behavior: hyphenation of text content and custom font installation.
- `-l` *lang*: Display user informational messages in the language indicated by *lang* (not documented further).

in_opts These options are used to signal various conditions about the nature of the input.

- `-fo` *infile*: The input file is an XSL-FO document. (This is the default if you supply no other *in_opts*.)
- `-xml` *infile*: The input file is raw XML and, before being converted to PDF, must be transformed to XSL-FO using the stylesheet identified by the `-xsl` option, discussed next (which must be included when you use the `-xml` option).
- `-xsl` *stylesheet*: This names the stylesheet to be used for transforming the raw XML document to XSL-FO.

As an example, if you had a raw XML document named crisscross.xml which you had not yet transformed to a particular XSL-FO document, you could use this command line:

```
fop -xml crisscross.xml -xsl playbill.xsl
```

As before, FOP will carry the file *name* forward, adding only an extension. In this case, as output you'd end up with a crisscross.fo and a crisscross.pdf document.

out_opts   Predictably, these command-line options control the nature of FOP's *output*. By default, FOP writes to a PDF file, but you've also got a few alternatives.

- `-pdf` *outfile*: The input document is converted to PDF. (This is the default, obviously.)
- `-awt`: The input will be displayed on screen. This makes FOP behave like an example of the other category of XSL-FO products—native XSL-FO viewers—although (as you'll see in a moment) the results are decidedly mixed.
- `-mif` *outfile*: The input will be converted to MIF. This is the file format used by Adobe FrameMaker documents.
- `-pcl` *outfile*: The input will be converted to Printer Control Language (PCL) format. PCL is the "language" understood by Hewlett-Packard printers and plotters, and is therefore sometimes called HP-PCL. If you've got an HP printer/plotter on a Windows computer, you can create an HP-PCL file yourself by selecting that output device in the Print dialog, then checking the "Print to file" checkbox.
- `-txt` *outfile*: The input will be converted to a text file. Boxes are drawn using hyphens and vertical bar (or pipe, |) characters.
- `-print`: The input file will be converted and sent to the printer as a print file, with no intermediate file being preserved. This command-line option includes other options that allow you to specify page ranges, whether to print only the odd or only the even pages, and so on. (For details, use `-print help`.)

I confess I'd never tried any of these output options before. Some of them were pretty interesting, though.

For example, the `-awt` option formats the output and opens up a Java Abstract Window Toolkit (AWT) window displaying it. Figure 12–2 depicts this window, in this case displaying the "about flixml.org" page of a full FlixML filmfest playbill. (Compare this to Figure 11–1, whose output came from Xep and Adobe Acrobat Reader.)

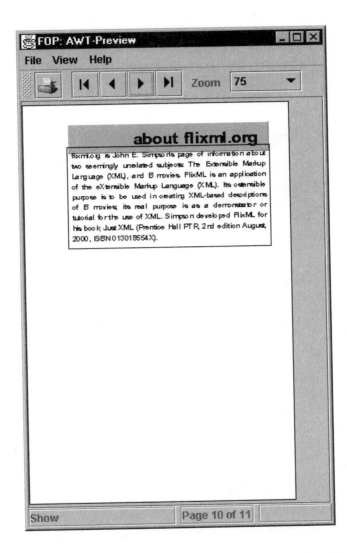

Figure 12-2 The FOP AWT output window. Getting to this point was kind of complicated; it required removing from the XSL-FO document a bunch of properties FOP doesn't support, hand-tweaking those it *does* support, and finally deciding that this was good enough for a screen shot. To some extent, this figure reflects limitations in FOP. For example, the external graphic elements that would otherwise appear here were rejected because, FOP said, it had no "protocol" for JPEG images—whatever *that* means. It probably also reflects limitations in Java/AWT. The PDF version of this page, created when I used FOP's default settings, still didn't display the images but also didn't include that weird overlapping of areas at the top.

FOP features

Certainly, the various input and output options available to a FOP user qualify as features.

The other big area in which FOP shines is its support for SVG images. I covered this in Chapter 10, during the discussion of the `fo:instream-foreign-object` FO.

Finally, if you're using the Apache Project's Cocoon Web publishing platform (covered in Chapter 7), you should be aware that the Cocoon package comes with FOP. Thus, Cocoon can generate PDF and other forms of output as well as XHTML for the Web. Often, when a print document is available for download, the download page includes links to several physical files, of different formats, stored on the server. If you're running Cocoon, though, the links can simply point to the FOP processor, passing it the correct parameters to generate the correct file type on the fly.

RenderX's Xep

This is the command-line package I used to create almost all the PDF output used in examples throughout this part of the book. So you already know some things about it.

First, you know that it's highly compliant with the XSL-FO spec. I encountered very few features described by the spec which weren't implemented by the product, once I took into account the "Non-Conformance Issues" and other notes provided with the Xep documentation.

Second, in that documentation RenderX has been very forthcoming about the things Xep *doesn't* do—and (quite impressively and convincingly, I thought) about *why* it doesn't do those things. For example, one of the non-conformance issues identified has to do with border and padding properties on regions. Xep doesn't follow the spec, says the documentation, because

> ...In the XSL FO CR, border and padding properties are permitted on region elements (fo:region-body, fo:region-before, fo:region-after, fo:region-start, and fo:region-end); but the spec says they only may accept values of 0 (sic!). In XEP, we dare give a natural interpretation to non-zero values of these properties—draw a border around the respective region area, and pad its content rectangle by the specified amount.

Makes sense, doesn't it? So it goes with most of RenderX's handling of spec ambiguities and confusion.

And third, RenderX has provided many valuable services to the XSL-FO community. For instance, they've come up with a DTD for XSL-FO documents which is very hard to argue with—and which can be invaluable when you're trying to figure out which element may contain which other elements, which attributes may go with which elements, and so on.

As impressed as I am with Xep, however, it's hard for me to recommend the retail (non-crippled) version. The RenderX Web site shows a sliding "server-based" price schedule, wherein the exact amount for a license depends on how many processors the server is running. This ranges from $3,000 *per CPU* for servers with 11 or more CPUs up to $5,000 *per CPU* for servers with 1 to 4 CPUs. To say that this puts Xep out of reach of 90% of potential developers of PDF documents is kind of an understatement.

The word from inside

The $5,000 single-CPU pricing was so hard for me to understand that I got into an email exchange about it with RenderX's CEO, Roman Kagarlitsky.

As Kagarlitsky explained it, RenderX is in a tricky position. It's a small company—one of those engineering firms that's top-heavy with developers and light on sales- and technical-support personnel. Its flagship product, Xep, is in something of a niche market, at least so far. Customers who want the features of the commercial product—those who aren't simply trying to learn XSL-FO but who *need* XSL-FO—tend to be corporate customers who don't blink at the license price: joint ventures, OEM accounts, and so on. (The license is a "perpetual license" and includes technical support for six months.) The number of such customers seems to balance nicely with RenderX's current staffing levels; selling, say, 10,000 copies of the package, at greatly reduced prices, would put the company in an untenable position. (As Kagarlitsky says, RenderX isn't in the business of selling software; it's in the business of selling service and support. Maybe a good analogy would be Red Hat, which "sells" the free, open-source Linux by selling Red Hat's support and value-added features.)

As an example of the kind of customer RenderX might hope to attract, consider a vendor of document-management software and services for the public sector. Government agencies are huge consumers and producers of paper forms. (This comes as a surprise, right?) If the content with which these forms' fields are populated is XML-based, Xep's ability to produce a PDF that "locks in" a given form provides a good fit for a gap in the vendor's product line. So $5,000 is cheap, compared to the cost of hiring a developer to create essentially the same product.

On the other hand, RenderX also is affected by the "benign self-interest" motive: The more people who know XSL-FO and have learned it using Xep, the more of those $5K licenses RenderX will eventually be able to sell.

Meanwhile, at some distance behind but still making progress, there's the slower-moving but free and open-source FOP. At what point will FOP catch up with Xep sufficiently to knock the latter's pricing completely out of whack? Will the fact that FOP is open source, dependent for support on the volunteer community, be a sufficiently strong incentive for customers to continue to pay for Xep?

I worry about the fate of companies like RenderX. (And, needless to say, so do the Roman Kagarlitskys of the world.)

Pricing aside, here's some information about using Xep. Note that the following applies to the evaluation version only; there may be some differences for the commercial one—but I wouldn't know, not being in a position to spring for $5K myself!

Installing and running Xep

Like FOP, Xep is Java-based. Unlike FOP, though, the Xep setup went very smoothly—I don't think I've ever had fewer problems installing a Java application on my Windows machine.

Running it is also simple; it's got many fewer command-line options than FOP:

- -DROOT *root*: Sets the (relative) path to certain kinds of optional files used by Xep; the default value of *root* is `.`, meaning that Xep will look for these files, if needed, in the directory where Xep itself is running.
- -DGCLEVEL *gc_switch*: Possible values for *gc_switch* are 0, 1, 2, or 3. What this switch controls is the so-called *garbage-collection* strategy used by Xep. ("Garbage collection" is the process whereby a computer program frees up memory as it's done with it, rather than hanging onto all memory used until the program itself terminates.) The default value is 0, which means no

garbage collection is performed—leading to the possibility that if your input file is very large, you may run out of memory. If you set it to 3, the garbage-collection routine is invoked after formatting each page; this slows Xep down quite a bit, but also helps ensure that you won't hit an out-of-memory wall. (Values of 1 and 2, obviously, are intermediate values favoring less and more garbage collection, respectively.)

- -DVALIDATE *trueorfalse*: By default (i.e., with a *trueorfalse* value of true), Xep validates the input XSL-FO document against the RenderX-supplied DTD for the XSL-FO vocabulary. This increases the likelihood that the actual "render to PDF" portion of the Xep code will be dealing only with legitimate XSL-FO documents—and hence XSL-FO documents with no lurking surprises. Although validation adds a few seconds to execution time, RenderX recommends against tampering with this switch. So do I.

Xep features

I think I've pretty much covered this territory throughout Part 3 of the book. Xep does a great job complying with the XSL-FO spec.

Native XSL-FO "Viewers"

XSL-FO is a vocabulary suited primarily for defining print documents. That's the primary reason why I think most of the early XSL-FO software has focused on translating XSL-FO documents to print-friendly PDF.

But then of course...

...there's also the other motivation: If a vendor can create unambiguously "correct" PDF documents from XSL-FO input, the vendor needn't be concerned with how to render the result. The renderer, of course, is the ubiquitous Adobe Acrobat Reader.

A handful of software developers have opted to ignore PDF as an output medium, though. Let's look at some reasons why this is the case, and then look at a couple of the packages in question.

Why *not* PDF?

Maybe the most obvious (although not necessarily most important) reason why a developer wouldn't want to output to PDF is that the format is *owned*, by Adobe.

Of course, Adobe makes the internals of the PDF format available to interested developers and gives away the Acrobat Reader program to boot. And the company isn't likely to change the internals radically, or even unilaterally, unless it wants to ignite a firestorm of protest. Still, the fact that such an important standard could be owned—and hence controlled—by a corporate entity just bothers a lot of people.[3]

Everyday needs versus legal needs

When you're considering this "Why not PDF?" question, you always need to bear in mind that what's sufficient for many (perhaps most) purposes is insufficient for one: legal documents.

I've alluded to this elsewhere—that not only the content but the exact placement and look of the content constitutes a legal document. If the layout and appearance of content in one instance of a document is only slightly different from that in another instance, you can't have much confidence at all that the content itself is unchanged. On the other hand, there's the "see-through" test of authenticity: If you can lay one instance on another and, while holding them up to a window, determine that everything lines up exactly, you've just established that they are exactly the same document—actually irrespective of their "content." Using this test, the placement of dots on a laser-printed page *proves*, by any measure, that the two documents are the same (even though neither may be the "original").

Adobe recognized this need early on in the development of electronic document management, and satisfying it is one of PDF's principal reasons for being. Although a PDF document—at least in unlocked form—can be edited, this results in a document for which the printed appearance is measurably different.

No matter how uncomfortable you may be at Adobe's control of PDF, this is probably the main reason why the format is not going away anytime soon (if ever).

---

3.   This mirrors the discomfort that many developers express with Sun's ownership of Java. (And all of Sun's efforts to convince developers of the company's good intentions have left many unswayed. There may be a lesson here for Adobe as well.)

As a practical rather than philosophical matter, on the other hand, binding XSL-FO input to PDF output may—almost certainly *will*—mean that XSL-FO will never grow beyond whatever features Adobe deigns to include in the PDF format. (For instance, it seems awfully unlikely that PDF will ever support aural properties for FOs. What do you think the odds are of any software's actually making use of those properties, if the only thing to "do" with XSL-FO is turn it into PDF? Right: zilch.)

Third, PDF is not markup—no matter how structured it is. It's a dead end. What can you convert PDF *into*? You can easily develop an XSLT stylesheet or two for running raw XSL-FO documents through second, third, and more transformations if needed. There's nothing like it for manipulating a PDF document.

Again, remember...

...PDF does exactly what it's supposed to do: Lock down the physical structure of a document as well as its content. The fact that you can't—easily or at all—convert a PDF document into something else is what enables it to meet this goal. So, "dead end," sure; but that's just what the doctor ordered in this one respect.

Related to the preceding argument, it must also be conceded that PDF documents are readable to an even narrower segment of the human population than XSL-FO documents (inscrutable though *those* can be). Like the preceding argument, this isn't so much "XSL-FO versus PDF" as it is "*XML* versus PDF."

All of these, I think, add up to a pretty substantial case that, as valuable as PDF may be as a destination medium, a far better world would be one in which—at the very least—we weren't locked into accepting PDF as the *only* "good" end for XSL-FO documents.[4]

---

4.   While I haven't mentioned it here, there *is* another text-based standard (sort of) for representing the physical appearance of a document as well as its content. This is Microsoft's Rich Text Format, or RTF. RTF's problem is in some ways the opposite of XSL-FO's: It's *under*-specified. It's also notoriously difficult to work with when you need to tweak something by hand. And finally, not even Microsoft's own products support it consistently. All that said, if you're interested in learning more, check the Microsoft Web site: support.microsoft.com/support/kb/articles/Q269/5/75.ASP. The version of RTF which is current as of this writing is 1.6.

Antenna House's XSL Formatter

This is a quite popular tool among the XSL-FO developer community. It's a Windows- and Windows-only-based product, but is very useful as a testing environment.

If you're using XSL Formatter, you can forget about juggling physical XSL-FO documents. XSL Formatter works with the raw XML document and XSLT stylesheet (as you can see in Figure 12–3). It builds the XSL-FO tree in memory only, and there's no "save as XSL-FO" option.

Figure 12-3 The initial Antenna House XSL Formatter window. Actually, when you first open the program it's even plainer than this: Both the Document and Stylesheet pick lists are empty. Here, I've simply prepared XSL Formatter for a possible rendering, but I haven't actually initiated anything yet. Until actually running the transformation (which can be performed in a number of ways, including simply clicking on the toolbar button labeled "F"—for "run Formatter"), the main area of the window remains blank. Well, not counting the product vendor/name in the center.

XSL Formatter comes with a reasonably good range of options that you can set at your pleasure. Figure 12–4 shows you the "Default Fonts" tab in the options dialog. In the absence of other font characteristics on a given FO, the settings shown here will be in effect in this particular transformation.

As always, what software does with an XSL-FO document at this stage in the spec's history is subject to a certain amount of variety (to put it politely). As you can see in Figure 12–5, XSL Formatter does a reasonably good job with many XSL-FO features...while glossing over some others. (Interestingly, by the way, XSL Formatter uses the MSXML 3.0 parser and XSLT processor.)

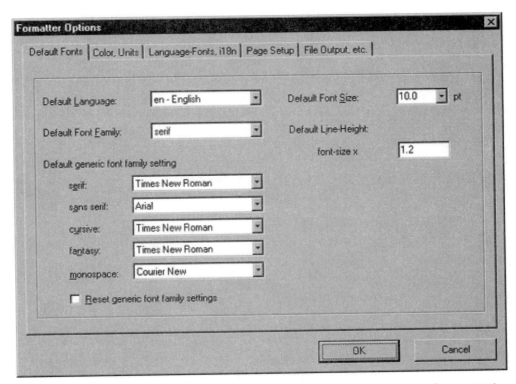

Figure 12-4 XSL Formatter's options dialog. One of the most interesting aspects of XSL Formatter, to my mind, is the presence of the "Language-Fonts, i18n" tab. That tab lets you customize fonts to be used on a *language-by-language* basis—invaluable if your application requires multi-language support. (Note that Antenna House is a Tokyo-based corporation.) XSL Formatter is notable for its support of non-Western writing modes (e.g., top-to-bottom/right-to-left).

In terms of debugging an XML-to-XSL-FO transformation, one useful feature offered by XSL Formatter is the display of *borders* around formatting objects. These aren't real borders, just pale blue guidelines showing you the limits, as explicitly sized or simply defaulted, of each object on the page, as shown in Figure 12–6.

The version of XSL Formatter depicted here is 1.1E (English-language evaluation version); it can be downloaded from the Antenna House site at www.antennahouse.com. The Japanese-language version is not free (currently listed at a little over ¥200,000), nor will the English-language one be free once Antenna House feels that it's of production quality. There is no word on whether a (crippled and/or time-limited) free evaluation version will still be available at that point.

Figure 12-5 The cover of the *Johnny Guitar* playbill, as rendered by XSL Formatter. Compare this with Figure 11–2. A couple of observations: First, XSL Formatter doesn't support the `background-image` property, so the "watermark" technique discussed in Chapter 11 (which provided a graphic frame around "playbill") doesn't work here. Also note that XSL Formatter's default fonts are different than Xep's—and that Antenna House, like RenderX, stamps every page generated by its product's evaluation version with a corporate tag line.

Figure 12-6 The same page as that depicted in Figure 12–5, but with XSL Formatter's "show borders" option turned on. Note that each word, but not each character, is bordered separately. This is functionally very useful. For example, note the two borders around the word "playbill": one immediately surrounding it, one marking the limits of the `fo:block` element containing the word. The distance between these two borders represents the padding and/or line height established by properties on the FOs in question. It would be even more useful in debugging if there were an option to display a ruler along the page edges, or to display a regularly spaced grid, or both.

> ## A caveat about XSL Formatter
>
> Although the package supposedly runs on all flavors of Windows, from
> 95 up, I have had trouble with it on both Windows 95 and 98 machines.
> The trouble is unpredictable, but when it happens the symptoms are
> always the same: Windows Explorer crashes. Not the Internet Explorer
> browser—Windows Explorer itself. This results in horribly fouled-up
> icons and system tray, and other programs start behaving erratically.
>
> Although many other users swear by XSL Formatter, and although
> its features and XSL-FO support are very good, its instability on my sys-
> tem has meant that I never run it unless I'm trying to demo it, such as
> for the screen shots above. No doubt there's something specific about
> my setup, or the particular combination of software, that's causing XSL
> Formatter to be this erratic, but I did want to mention it to you, in any
> case. When you experiment with it, begin by opening *only* XSL Format-
> ter, and go on from there.

X-Smiles

X-Smiles is a Java-based, open-source browser of XML files. (Explicitly, one of its
objectives is *not* to be an HTML browser, although its developers have stated that
XHTML support may be added at some point.) Originally developed by students
at Helsinki University of Technology (www.hut.fi/English/), the project is still
maintained there.

The overall goals for the project are summed up in a heading on its home
page. (That's either www.xsmiles.org or www.x-smiles.org. Be sure to get that
".org" top-level domain right, though.) On that home page, currently, the heading reads like this:

```
X-SMILES
an open xml-browser for exotic devices
```

Specifically, as you can learn by delving into other pages at the site, X-Smiles
is out to support XSLT, XSL-FO, SVG images, and Synchronized Multimedia
Integration Language (SMIL)—all of them W3C-specified XML vocabularies.[5]

---

5.   There's also an interesting array of "secondary priorities," not all of which have
     been addressed yet: mixing different XML vocabularies in a given document; sup-
     port for multimedia content and streaming; support for forms in XML documents
     (possibly using the XForms standard); and ECMAScript support. By any measure,
     the X-Smiles project's goals are very ambitious!

Installing and running X-Smiles

Because it's Java-based, installing X-Smiles requires only that you un-Zip a compressed file in a convenient location and point your CLASSPATH to the X-Smiles location.

Running the program depends, slightly, on which version of Java you're running on your machine. If you've got Java 2, you just enter this command line from the installation directory:

```
java -jar xsmiles.jar
```

(If you've got an earlier version of Java and are running on a Windows platform, X-Smiles comes with an xsmiles.bat file which you can easily edit once and then run from the command line thereafter.)

Now, just based on the name alone, you might think that X-Smiles "specializes" in displaying SMIL documents. Although that may be true at some level, at another, very different level the program is quite comfortable with XSL-FO too.

Consider Figure 12–7, which is what you see when you first fire up X-Smiles with the above command line. Note that this looks in some ways like an XHTML document viewed in a normal Web browser, including images, hyperlinks, and so on. Also note, though, the name of the currently open file—demos.xml. More importantly, note the top right corner of the display: Is that a page header there?

Indeed that is a page header. What you're looking at in Figure 12–7 is not a raw XML file, or even an XSL-FO document in any real sense, but rather an on-the-fly *transformation* of XML to XSL-FO. If you pull down the View menu in this initial window, you can select a "View XSL Source" option. Then you see what's shown in Figure 12–8.

X-Smiles comes with a number of configuration options—three pages of them, in fact. You can see the first page of them in Figure 12–9.

As I mentioned above, X-Smiles does *not* support viewing of (X)HTML files at this time. Whether you try to open an actual document of that type or an XML document transformed via XSLT to that type, you'll see an error message, as in Figure 12–10.

X-Smiles can open and display true XSL-FO documents, as long as the XSL-FO features in them don't exceed FOP's capabilities. Figure 12–11 shows the "about flixml.org" page from a FlixML playbill. As you can see, this looks strikingly like (indeed, pretty much identical to) FOP's view of this page (shown in Figure 12–2).

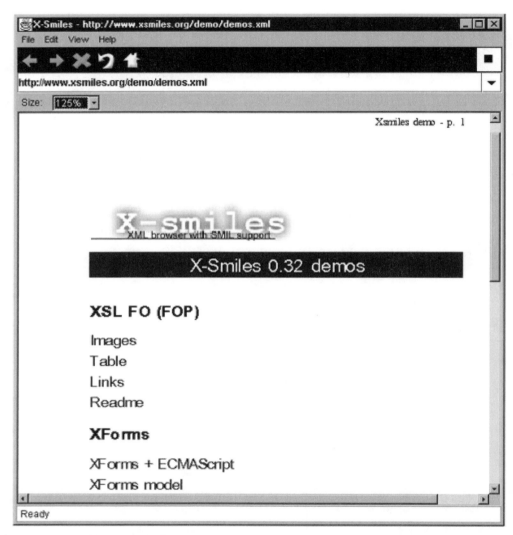

Figure 12-7 The initial X-Smiles display. If this were a Web page, it would be functional enough but nothing (as the saying goes) to write home about. Each of the items displayed in the lists below the "demos" heading is a hyperlink to a demonstration of one feature or another. Although you can't see it in this screen shot and it doesn't seem to be listed among the official X-Smiles goals, one of the features apparently supported is something called SIP videoconferencing. (I can hear you now: "*Videoconferencing*? In an *XML* document?" Yeah. X-Smiles uses something called the Java Media Framework [JMF] to achieve this.)

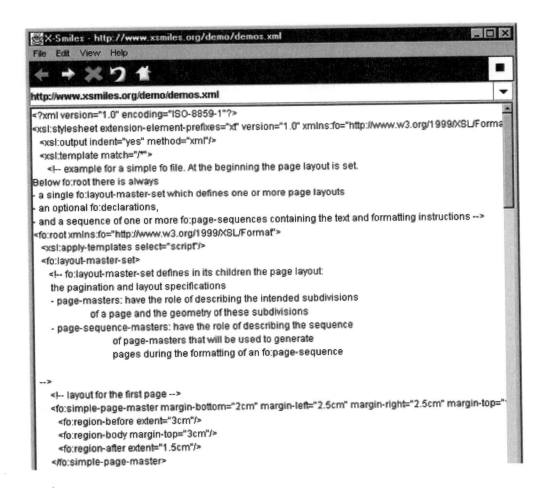

```
<?xml version="1.0" encoding="ISO-8859-1"?>
<xsl:stylesheet extension-element-prefixes="xt" version="1.0" xmlns:fo="http://www.w3.org/1999/XSL/Forma
  <xsl:output indent="yes" method="xml"/>
  <xsl:template match="/">
    <!-- example for a simple fo file. At the beginning the page layout is set.
Below fo:root there is always
- a single fo:layout-master-set which defines one or more page layouts
- an optional fo:declarations,
- and a sequence of one or more fo:page-sequences containing the text and formatting instructions -->
<fo:root xmlns:fo="http://www.w3.org/1999/XSL/Format">
  <xsl:apply-templates select="script"/>
  <fo:layout-master-set>
    <!-- fo:layout-master-set defines in its children the page layout:
    the pagination and layout specifications
    - page-masters: have the role of describing the intended subdivisions
            of a page and the geometry of these subdivisions
    - page-sequence-masters: have the role of describing the sequence
            of page-masters that will be used to generate
            pages during the formatting of an fo:page-sequence

    -->
    <!-- layout for the first page -->
    <fo:simple-page-master margin-bottom="2cm" margin-left="2.5cm" margin-right="2.5cm" margin-top="
      <fo:region-before extent="3cm"/>
      <fo:region-body margin-top="3cm"/>
      <fo:region-after extent="1.5cm"/>
    </fo:simple-page-master>
```

Figure 12-8 The start of the XSLT stylesheet used by X-Smiles to display its home page. As you can see from the location bar at the top of the window, you're still nominally looking at the XML source tree, not at an XSL-FO result tree. In fact, there *is* no XSL-FO result tree in this case, except the one built in memory by X-Smiles.

Main:

Homepage:

http://www.xsmiles.org/demo/demos.xml

XML Parser:

Xerces   ▼

XSL Processor:

Xalan ▼

GUI:

Initial GUI:

New GUI   ▼

☑ **Skin Look and Feel**

☑ **Virtual Prototype mode**

Figure 12-9   Some of the configuration options available with X-Smiles. Note that you can swap in different parsers or XSLT processors, but the defaults are those that come with Apache: Xerces and Xalan, respectively. If you look back at Figure 12–7, you may also observe that the XSL-FO processor used by X-Smiles is FOP. There's no way to change this at present, which means you're restricted to whatever XSL-FO features FOP supports. (I'll show you an example of this in a moment.)

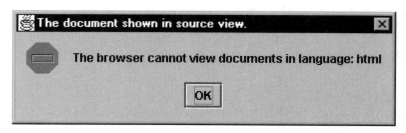

Figure 12-10   An X-Smiles error message—the one you see when you try to open a (real or virtual) (X)HTML document...or one in any other unsupported vocabulary, for that matter.

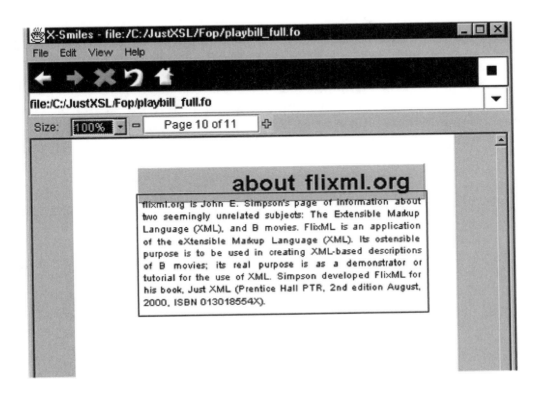

Figure 12-11 The X-Smiles view of an XSL-FO document page with an embedded JPEG image. As with FOP's view of the page (presented in Figure 12–2), the absence of the image has to do with the undefined "protocol" for JPEG images, while the overlapping block FOs are artifacts of the page's being displayed with the Java AWT.

Epilogue

It's fitting, I think, that *Just XSL* concludes here: at the tail end of a chapter about a tentative technology, following a description of an open-source, far-sighted, but still tentative *application* of that technology.

I hope you'll agree with me at this point that XSLT is, without question, an important weapon in the arsenal of anyone who wants to "do XML." The jury may still be out on XSL-FO; but as long as we're stuck with paper documents, the pressure will remain (I believe) for its adoption. And beyond that, well, who knows? Why wouldn't an eBook work just as well when driven by XSL-FO as it does when driven by the OEB vocabulary?

The best of luck to you in your own transformational experiences with the two languages. And as I did at the end of *Just XML*, I want to close with an invitation: Stop by at flixml.org sometime—and let me know you did! And remember, always, to reserve part of your attention not for all the 1s and 0s inside silicon-based chunks of hardware—no matter at how high a level those 1s and 0s are dealt with—but for the real world. Maybe it's not (okay, okay, it's *probably* not) B movies. But *something* out there constitutes real life for you—life apart from computers and the Internet. Keep in touch with that side, okay?

A P P E N D I C E S

For More XSLT Information...

Naturally, I'd like nothing more than to know that Part 2 of *Just XSL* covers every possible eventuality you'll encounter in using XSLT. Unfortunately, although I cover the standard there, I know in my heart of hearts that I can never really cover everything you'll ever need to know about XSLT. Particularly,

- How nice for me that I can use FlixML, a tightly controlled source tree vocabulary of my own invention. But I'd be astounded if that turns out to be the vocabulary you use in your own everyday XML/XSLT life. In your own work with XSLT, you're almost certain to encounter data structures some part of which is accessible only using a really long, and/or really complex, XPath expression. (And that part, of course, is the part that your work will require you to access.) Or maybe finding the source node-set is easy, but you need to do something especially bizarre with it. I can only show you the XPath and XSLT atoms here, and the most common molecules. I can't document all possible compounds. So I know you'll need to look elsewhere, as well.
- Other than offering what are, really, fairly superficial demonstrations of selected XSLT software, I can't cover the universe of *all* XSLT software. Not only will you need to know about other software, you'll probably need to know more about using the software I've demonstrated.

So you'll need some other resources to back you up. Luckily, XSLT's been such a success that there are plenty of them at hand.

A.1 General Information About XSLT

Got a question about how best to solve a particular XSLT problem? Confused by some nuance in the spec? Just looking for commiseration with others who, like you, have tried (and frustratingly failed) to make their variables vary? Start with these resources—I do.

A.1.1 Web sites

Relevant W3C specifications

W3C specs are all posted to the same general location on the Consortium's site: www.w3.org/TR. If you enter just that much of the URI into your browser's address/location field, you see a list of pointers to all available W3C specs. Here are URIs for specific specs covered in Part 2 of *Just XSL*:

- **XPath 1.0: Recommendation**
  www.w3.org/TR/xpath
- **XSLT 1.0: Recommendation**
  www.w3.org/TR/xslt
- **XSLT 1.1: Working Draft**
  www.w3.org/TR/xslt11
- **XSLT 2.0 Requirements: Working Draft**
  www.w3.org/TR/xslt20req

Other sites devoted to XSLT

Although the W3C specs are the last word on anything relevant to XPath or XSLT, they're not necessarily the place to turn when you need general information in an easily digestible form. Try the following in addition to the official documents.

- **XSL Frequently Asked Questions** (started and maintained by Dave Pawson)
  www.dpawson.co.uk/xsl/xslfaq.html
  Dave Pawson, a regular contributor to the XSL-List mailing list (more information below), has set up this site as a means of looking up answers to questions someone else has probably already asked. The questions—and, of course, the answers—were posted on XSL-List, and are here grouped into categories (e.g., "Where to Start," "Special Characters," "External Issues")

and subcategories ("Design Patterns," "Employment," "Apple Mac," "Date and Time"). Many questions have multiple answers, just as they do on the list, each augmenting or shading in useful ways the ones coming before it. This site has some information about XSL-FO, but it's primarily focused on XSLT.

- **Jeni's XSLT Pages**

  www.jenitennison.com/xslt

  Like Dave Pawson's XSLT FAQ, above, the content here is largely culled from the questions and answers posted to the XSL-List mailing list. Jeni Tennison generally provides the most exhaustive answers to a given question, not simply answering the question but walking you through all the steps necessary to arrive at the answer. Along the way, completely unbidden, she stops to point out other features of the landscape you may have missed, such as how the structure of your source tree is particularly inefficient or how you'd benefit by using a different XSLT processor. Not every imaginable XSLT question is answered here; but if Tennison provides an answer you don't understand, chances are the problem (alas) is *yours*.

- **XML.com's XSLT resource guide**

  www.xml.com/pub/rg/XSLT

  XML.com is one of the best sites for XML-related information of all kinds, including both original content (updated monthly or weekly) and copious links to other resources. The "resource guide" is particularly valuable. Although the overall site links to a number of XSLT-related resources (including XSLT software and so on), this one is best for keeping apprised of general XSLT information.

- **The XML Cover Pages guide to XSL**

  xml.coverpages.org/xsl.html

  Robin Cover manages somehow to track, seemingly, every single bit of information on the Web which has anything vaguely to do with XML—including XSLT and XSL-FO. Updated daily, sometimes more often, this is a huge collection of links to articles and white papers, corporate sites, press releases, FAQ lists, software vendors, you name it.

- **Crane Softwrights Ltd. resource library**

  www.cranesoftwrights.com/resources/index.htm

  This Canadian XML/XSLT/XSL-FO consultancy offers a broad range of services, including a number of popular courses and seminars at XML-related conferences and trades shows. The "Resource Library" is a collection of free tools and information of interest to users of stylesheet languages—not only the XML-based variants but also their DSSSL precursor. I'm especially fond of SHOWTREE, an XSLT stylesheet for transforming a given XML source document into an outline-style version of itself (e.g., with element nodes numbered 1, 1.1, 1.1.1, 1.1.2, 1.2, and so on), and thereby showing the complete XPath-reachable tree of nodes. SHOWTREE's application itself may be of limited use, but *as a stylesheet* it's a nice demonstration of quite a number of XPath/XSLT features. As the SHOWTREE page mentions, if you'd like a more graphical rendering of the same thing, you can use Mike Brown's "Fancy XML Tree Viewer." The correct URI for that stylesheet is skew.org/xml/stylesheets/treeview/ (note no "www." prefix).

• **Mulberry Technologies quick references**
  www.mulberrytech.com/quickref/index.html
  This SGML/XML consulting firm has a special interest in transformational stylesheet languages, and hence supports both the amazing XSL-List mailing list (below) and its companion DSSSL-List list, for those working with XSLT's predecessor for transforming SGML documents. They've also produced an excellent, concise PDF summary of XPath and XSLT syntax, available (free for the download) from the above page. (If you're feeling especially geeky, you might also want to check out the page of "SGML/ XML Songs" at the site. Aside to the composers and librettists: Don't quit your day jobs!)

A.1.2 Mailing lists/Newsgroups

• **"XPath Comments"** list at
  lists.w3.org/Archives/Public/www-xpath-comments/
  This is the official W3C mailing list for commenting on and asking questions of the editors of the XPath spec. There's not a lot of activity on most of these W3C lists. That said, the list *is* read by the editors, the XPath Working Group, and other interested parties; so if you see traffic here, pay attention—it's probably authoritative. To subscribe to the mailing list, rather than just reading the archived messages, send an email to www-xpath-comments-request@w3.org with the word `subscribe` in the message's subject field.

• **"XSL-Editors"** list at
  lists.w3.org/Archives/Public/xsl-editors/

As above, but this one is for questions about the XSLT and XSL-FO specifications (particularly the former). To subscribe to the mailing list, rather than just reading the archived messages, send an email to xsl-editors-request@w3.org with the word `subscribe` in the message's subject field.

- **XSL-List** archives and subscription information at www.mulberrytech.com/xsl/xsl-list/

This is, without a doubt, *the* resource for anyone using XSLT, whether on a casual or an intensive basis. I can't say enough good things about it. Rarely—when someone asks a question whose answer could have been easily located in the list archive, Dave Pawson's FAQ, or another online resource—you may see an irritable response. But as a rule, contributions to the list are civil and good-natured and completely helpful. Solutions (often two, three, or more) to a given problem range from the simple and straightforward to the arcane but effective. The list is frequented by developers of XSLT processors, practitioners, authors, and so on. One caveat: The scroll rate is tremendous, often getting up in the range of 75 to 100 messages a day. If this sounds overwhelming to you, consider subscribing to the list's daily digest rather than the whole thing.

- **XHTML-L** archives and subscription information at groups.yahoo.com/group/XHTML-L

I include this mailing list—ostensibly devoted to the XML-ized flavor of HTML—here among the XSLT information resources for two reasons. First, XHTML is arguably the most common result tree for XSLT transformations; if it will be your result tree, the more you know about it, the easier the transformations will be. And second, often the conversation centers not around XHTML but specifically how to "do XHTML" by way of an XSLT transformation. The tone on the list is occasionally argumentative but never nasty. And unlike some Yahoo!-based mailing lists, XHTML-L is free of advertisements (thanks to the generosity of its maintainer, Simon St. Laurent).

- **XML-L** archives and subscription information at listserv.heanet.ie/xml-l.html

Although this list ostensibly handles "general discussion of XML" only, you'll find that much of that discussion centers around XSLT, XPath, and other non-core XML standards. The volume of postings is easy to handle—some days none at all, on busy days perhaps a dozen—and the tone is businesslike: questions asked and questions answered. One of the most

venerable XML mailing lists, with archives going back to 1997. (For what
it's worth, this is the list you'll most likely find me monitoring on a regular
basis.)

• **exslt** archives and subscription information at
  lists.fourthought.com/mailman/listinfo/exslt
  I mentioned EXSLT briefly in Chapter 8. This is the grass-roots community
  effort to build a library of extension "functions" coded entirely in XSLT.
  (These are actually just pre-built named templates, identified with an EXSLT
  namespace prefix.) Of course, the measure of any grass-roots effort's success
  is not only how many lives it affects but how many people are actually
  involved in making it happen. By all means, consider making a point of
  reading and contributing to the conversations on this wonderful list.

• **news://comp.text.xml**
  There is not, to my knowledge, any newsgroup devoted to discussing XSLT
  only (or XSL-FO, for that matter)—not counting those devoted to particular software packages or platforms. (I'll cover these in section A.2.) However, as with the XML-L mailing list, the comp.text.xml newsgroup regularly
  deals with questions about how to achieve a particular goal with XSLT. And
  as with XML-L, the tone is straight to the point. The traffic on
  comp.text.xml is a little more brisk than on XML-L, and you may find the
  level of expertise—even among the questioners—higher as well.

A.2 XSLT Software

As I said in Chapter 7, the best way to locate specific software to download is
from a general-purpose, "XSLT software"-type portal, such as xmlsoftware.com.
In this section of the appendix, I wanted to list some software-specific resources
unrelated to the download, as such.

A.2.1 Web sites

Although the following are all product-specific sites, they provide a wealth of
material on XSLT as well as on the products in question.

• **Microsoft Developer Network (MSDN)**
  msdn.microsoft.com
  At least for the time being, most questions about client-side scripting of
  XML and XSLT are answerable in a single word: Microsoft. There's plenty

of information here about such scripting, of course, but if you're transforming to XHTML on the server, you'll also want to make this a regularly visited waystation. Even if you don't use Microsoft products at all, the XSLT Developer's Guide and XSLT Reference are worth bookmarking. Some information therein is Microsoft-specific, but they're generally good guides to understanding the spec. These specific sub-sites are located at msdn.microsoft.com/library/psdk/xmlsdk/xslp8tlx.htm and msdn.microsoft.com/library/psdk/xmlsdk/xslr1vad.htm, respectively.

- **VBXML.com**

  www.vbxml.com

  Unabashedly Microsoft-centric—even more than MSDN, above—this site is a terrific reference site for developers working with XSLT on either the client or the server side.

- **The Apache XML Project**

  xml.apache.org

  Of course, this is the place to visit if you're looking to use any of the Project's XML- or XSLT-related products (like the Xalan XSLT processor). However, it's also a fine resource for general information about the technology. This is especially true in the code samples included with the various products' downloads. Unfortunately, there doesn't seem to be anywhere on the site that collects all these code samples in any structured repository. As with the EXSLT initiative mentioned in Chapter 8 and section A.1.2 above, the Apache XML Project is completely volunteer-dependent. Don't be shy about offering assistance of any kind, as well as (or in exchange for!) downloading the available applications.

- **Sun Microsystems XML Site**

  www.sun.com/xml/

  If you're a Java developer, you need to spend a lot of time snooping around this site. For XSLT, perhaps the main point of interest will be the XSLT Compiler. This application takes an XSLT stylesheet as input, producing as output a Java class file that does everything the stylesheet does. This can result in quite large performance gains over processing raw stylesheets with a generic XSLT processor. For more general Java/XML resources, see the companion site at java.sun.com/xml/.

A.2.2 Mailing lists/Newsgroups

Like many people who've been involved with XML for a couple years, I generally *like* answering people's questions. So it's always excruciating to see someone in a panic post a message to a general-purpose mailing list such as XML-L or comp.text.xml, along the lines of "I'm using the XMLHaste parser and transforming with the DOMinator XSLT processor, and I CAN'T GET IT TO WORK! Please please please help me, my boss is really breathing down my neck...!"

This is excruciating because the odds are virtually nil that subscribers to such a general list will be able to help with such a specific problem. What you want to do, if you find yourself in such a panicky situation, is locate a mailing list or newsgroup devoted to your particular package(s) and ask *there*. Here's a sampling, in alphabetical order by the name of the software product or vendor in question.

- **4Suite** (Python-based, open-source XML product suite, including 4XPath, 4XSLT, and others)
  lists.fourthought.com/mailman/listinfo/4suite
- **Apache** XML Project-related:
  xml.apache.org/mail.html
- **LotusXSL** (IBM XSLT processor; basis for Apache Xalan)
  www.alphaworks.ibm.com/aw.nsf/discussion?ReadForm&/forum/
  lotusxsl.nsf/discussion?createdocument
- **MSMXL** (including using it client- or server-side, with ASP pages, and so on)
  news://microsoft.public.xml
- **Sablotron** open-source XSLT processor
  www.gingerall.com/charlie-bin/get/webGA/act/mlists.act
- **Saxon** XSLT processor
  saxon.xsl.listbot.com/
- **Transformiix** (Netscape/Mozilla XSLT processor)
  news://netscape.public.mozilla.layout.xslt
- **XML::XSLT** (Perl XSLT processor)
  lists.sourceforge.net/lists/listinfo/xmlxslt-discuss
- **XT** XSLT processor
  www.4xt.org/list/

Although I didn't spend any time discussing this XSLT processor in Part 2 of the book, its history is quite interesting. It was written by James Clark, editor of the XSLT 1.0 spec and a hugely influential researcher and developer of XML software. (His expat C-based non-validating XML parser processes XML data in near real-time, and, as a result, has found its way into many other products including Netscape/Mozilla.) Because of Clark's position as the spec's editor, XT is widely regarded as the "reference" by which all other XSLT 1.0 processors should be measured. However, Clark ceased working on it a few weeks before the spec was finalized…so XT does *not* implement some features of the final spec, particularly keys. (XT is still among the fastest and most stable XSLT processors, and is highly recommended as long as you don't need keys or any other features introduced since early November 1999.) It's currently maintained by the nonprofit, open-source group known as 4xt.org. As of this writing, the 4xt.org site itself—not counting the still active mailing list—hadn't been updated for several months.

For More XSL-FO Information...

Moving from XSLT to XSL-FO, as of mid-2001, is like falling asleep in Florida on a spring evening and waking up the next morning in Alaska. It's hard to get used to the idea of so few young flowers and blades of grass barely poking their heads out—especially after the green excess of the day before.

I'm certain that, given time, the situation will change. In the meantime, the following seem to be the best resources for information on XSL Formatting Objects. (Note, too, that many of the XSLT resources listed in Appendix A support XSL-FO as well. If what you're looking for isn't provided by one of the individuals or organizations listed here, flip back to Appendix A.)

B.1 General Information About XSL-FO

This is the area currently lacking the most outside help for XSL-FO aficionados—information about the standard that's not tied to specific products.

B.1.1 Web sites

W3C specifications

The W3C XSL-FO spec is in the same general area of the Consortium's site as the XSLT-related specs: www.w3.org/TR.

- **XSL 1.0: Candidate Recommendation**
  www.w3.org/TR/xsl

  Note that this is a much bigger document than the XSLT standard. The page listed here is just the table of contents, linking you to 14 separate Web pages (called "slices") where specific sections of the standard are housed. At the very top, under the "This version" heading, you can find links enabling you to download it in alternative formats, including "HTML (one large file)." If you choose this option, be prepared for a certain amount of confusion if you're working offline: Images are not included with the HTML document. This standard is relatively dependent on the presence of images displayed inline in order to make sense of things like page structure; so, if you're going to be using the HTML version offline, you'll find it full of placeholder-type empty boxes where the figures belong. Probably a better option is the .zip compressed version of the standard, available from another one of these links. This compressed file includes not only the HTML form of the XSL-FO standard but also the raw XML form, the 14-slice version...*and* all the images.

- **Scalable Vector Graphics (SVG) 1.0 Candidate Recommendation**
  www.w3.org/TR/SVG/

  If you plan to create XSL-FO documents with embedded SVG images (as discussed in Chapter 10), you'll need to understand at least the rudiments of the SVG vocabulary.

Other sites devoted to XSL-FO

As I mentioned several times in Part 3 of *Just XSL*, I found the XSL-FO spec spectacularly unreadable—even allowing for the general unreadability of official standards documents. (Maybe it's just me.) Here are some of the other resources you can call on as needed.

- **XSL Frequently Asked Questions** (FO section)
  www.dpawson.co.uk/xsl/sect3.html

  I mentioned Dave Pawson's XSL FAQ in Appendix A as an excellent resource for general XSLT information. This portion of that FAQ is devoted exclusively to questions and answers about formatting objects. It includes an aptly titled "Gentle Introduction to XSL-FO." Pay special attention to the "Jargon" section of the latter, which is indispensable in demystifying the XSL-FO spec.

- **Elliotte Rusty Harold on XSL-FO**

   www.ibiblio.org/xml/books/bible/updates/15.html

   Harold's *XML Bible* has been, since its publication, a justifiably best-selling survey of just about everything to do with XML. He's posted several chapters of the book (translated to HTML) at his Web site, updating them as the need arises. This is Chapter 15, devoted to XSL-FO.

- **Norm Walsh's XSL Tutorial**

   nwalsh.com/docs/tutorials/xsl/xsl/foil40.html (basic XSL-FO)

   nwalsh.com/docs/tutorials/xsl/xsl/foil71.html (advanced XSL-FO)

   This tutorial (which Walsh presented at the XML Europe 2000 conference in Paris) is structured like a slide show, each "slide" explaining or illustrating some feature of XSL-FO. The full tutorial includes information on XSLT; the URIs provided here are for the XSL-FO portions (although they naturally include some XSLT code, as well). If you're interested in the complete tutorial, go to nwalsh.com/docs/tutorials/xsl/, instead. Note that this is available either as a single big file, or in a frames-based version with a linked table of contents in one frame.

- **XML.com: "Using XSL Formatting Objects"**

   www.xml.com/pub/a/2001/01/17/xsl-fo/index.html

   J. David Eisenberg provided this clear quick-start guide to building a simple XSL-FO document.

- **RenderX's XSL-FO DTD**

   www.renderx.com/Tests/validator/fo.dtd.html (HTML format)

   www.renderx.com/Tests/validator/fo.dtd (pure text DTD format)

   Part of the key to understanding any XML vocabulary in depth is being able to see how its content model is formally expressed, as a DTD or XML Schema. RenderX (publisher of the Xep XSL-FO processor used throughout Part 3 of *Just XSL*) has offered this interpretation of the XSL-FO content model, in lieu of one from the W3C. Useful in any case, but if you're using Xep it's doubly so—since you can expect that processor to fully conform to this version of the DTD. This site also includes a handful of Xep-specific extensions to the XSL-FO vocabulary, using an rx:-prefixed namespace.

- **XML-DEV on "The Future of Formatting Objects"**

   lists.xml.org/archives/xml-dev/200006/msg00110.html

   The XML-DEV mailing list—nominally for developers of XML software, hence the name—has been so wide-ranging and influential since its founding that singling out a single discussion is kind of like pointing to a star on a clear night and averring, "There. That one. That's the most beautiful thing up there." That said, the discussion to which the above URI is the root message was enormously important to my own thinking on this and related subjects. (I especially liked the offshoot discussion whose subject was changed to "The problem with typography [with or without flow objects].")

B.1.2 Mailing lists/Newsgroups

- **"XSL-Editors"** list archives at
  lists.w3.org/Archives/Public/xsl-editors/
  I mentioned this in Appendix A. It's the "official mailing list" for questions about both the XSLT and XSL-FO specifications. As I said in the previous appendix, this isn't a very active list; but if one of the spec's authors/editors has something to say here, it's worth paying attention to. To subscribe to the mailing list, rather than just reading the archived messages, send an email to xsl-editors-request@w3.org with the word `subscribe` in the message's subject field.

- **"XSL-FO Editors"** list archives at
  lists.w3.org/Archives/Public/www-xsl-fo/
  In January 2001, the W3C started this list specifically for discussion of XSL-FO, independently of XSLT. The same general comments apply here as for the XSL-Editors list (above): If you see a post from someone whose name appears on the XSL-FO spec masthead, listen up. To subscribe to the mailing list, rather than just reading the archived messages, send an email to www-xsl-fo-request@w3.org with the word `subscribe` in the message's subject field.

- **XSL-FO mailing list** archives and subscription information at
  groups.yahoo.com/group/XSL-FO
  Established in January 2001, this Yahoo!-hosted mailing list (founded by Andrew Watt) has already become a good source of shared information about XSL-FO in general and the products that support it.

B.2 XSL-FO Software

As with XSLT, the XSL-FO spec is supported by a number of vendors whose Web sites offer not only product-specific details but also valuable general information about the standard itself. (In some cases, this general information is not available from the Web site itself but is included in the form of HTML pages, Windows Help files, Javadocs, and so on, included with the product distribution.)

B.2.1 Web sites

Here are the sites of vendors of products which I've found particularly useful not just for processing XSL-FO but for *learning* it.

- **The Apache XML Project: FOP**

  xml.apache.org/fop/index.html

  This is the open-source XSL-FO to PDF product. Most of the information at the Web site is FOP-related, understandably, but don't ignore the contents of the docs/examples directory created when you install the processor.

- **RenderX: Xep**

  www.renderx.com/FO2PDF.html

  The URI above takes you directly to the Xep product page. (The processor's original name was FO2PDF, hence the page name.) But the RenderX site includes a generous dollop of other information that will be useful to you, no matter what processor you use. These include an XSL-FO DTD (described above in Section B.1.1), an XSL-FO test suite, a tutorial, and other resources.

- **Antenna House: XSL Formatter**

  www.antennahouse.com

  Documentation (at least for the English-language version of the application) is rather limited, restricted to showing which features of the XSL-FO spec are supported by the product.

- **X-Smiles**
  www.xsmiles.org
  www.x-smiles.org (alternative URI)
  This open-source XML browser supports not only XSL-FO but also SMIL, SVG, and other XML-based multimedia formats. Very little information on XSL-FO (or the other standards) *per se* at the site or included with the download, although links are provided to official standards pages.

B.2.2 Mailing lists/Newsgroups

- **Apache (FOP)**
  Subscribe to the FOP developers mailing list by sending an email message to fop-dev-subscribe@xml.apache.org. (Subject and message body are irrelevant for the subscription request; it's probably a good idea to leave them blank, though.)
- **Xep mailing list**
  To subscribe to the mailing list for product discussion and support, send an email message to majordomo@renderx.com. The body of the message should consist of the following:

  ```
  subscribe xep-support
  ```

  There's also a broadcast-only mailing list just for new product announcements and so on. You can receive messages from this list by sending an email to the same mailing address as above; in this case, though, the body of the message should read:

  ```
  subscribe xep-announce
  ```
- **X-Smiles mailing lists** archives and subscription information at
  www.xsmiles.org/xsmiles lists.html

For More B-Movie Information...

Since writing *Just XML* and springing FlixML on the world, I've found lots of stuff about B movies on the Web and elsewhere—and I've had lots more stuff forwarded to me by readers and visitors to flixml.org.

This appendix is in no way meant to be final. (Information about second-tier movies seems to be proliferating like Pod People, making it hard to nail down in anything remotely resembling final form.) And Internet resources, as you know, have a way of coming and going, leaving no trace of where they might have relocated to. That said, the sites and other resources listed here seem to have at least a modicum of permanence.

One other note, by the way: The term "B movies" seems to be synonymous for many with "cheesy, campy movies," "movies with no redeeming value other than their casts' anatomical dimensions," and so on. I'm not a big fan of such truly awful movies; of those discussed in *Just XSL*, the closest to awful is *When Dinosaurs Ruled the Earth*. (But that film's hilariously wooden pretentiousness redeems it.) Some of the resources—particularly the Web sites—listed in this appendix celebrate cinematic badness *per se* rather than the gold-hidden-among-the-dross nuggets that I tend to prefer.

C.1 Books about B Movies

Books are listed here in alphabetic order by first significant word in the title.

- *The Devil Thumbs a Ride (and Other Unforgettable Films)* by Barry Gifford (Grove Press, 1988). ISBN 0-8021-3078-X. ($7.98) Now out of print, sadly. I found my copy via Amazon.com's out-of-print book search; it took them four months to come up with it!
- *A Girl and a Gun: The Complete Guide to Film Noir on Video* by David N. Meyer (Avon Books, 1998). ISBN 0-380-79067-X. ($14.00)
- *Mondo Macabro: Weird & Wonderful Cinema Around the World* by Pete Tombs (St. Martin's/Griffin. 1998). ISBN 0-312-18748-3. ($18.95) I don't think I've ever seen any of the films discussed in this book. (The Indian *Tarzan Comes to Delhi*, anyone? Or the Turkish *Yor—The Hunter from the Future*?) It seems fairly certain I'd have remembered them if I *had* seen them.
- *Second Feature: The Best of the Bs* by John Cocchi (Citadel Press/Carol Publishing Group, 1991). ISBN 0-8065-1186-9. ($16.95)
- *VideoHound's Complete Guide to Cult Flicks and Trash Pics* by various contributors (Visible Ink Press/Gale Research, 1996). ISBN 0-7876-0616-2. ($16.95) If the main VideoHound guide (listed below) is the encyclopedia of movies, you might consider this the "B" volume. The films herein are rated using the same 1- to 4-bone scale (including "WOOF!" for 0 bones) as in the main guide. However, the ratings here seem to have been arrived at independently, so a film rated poorly in the general guide may get a couple or three bones in this cult-films edition.
- *VideoHound's Golden Movie Retriever (1998 ed.)* by various contributors (Visible Ink Press/Gale Research, 1998). ISBN 1-57859-024-8. ($19.95 for nearly 1800 pages—a bargain.) This is just the most recent edition I've got, but the Hound updates it annually. Of course, if you're interested primarily in movies made before 1980, you don't *need* the most up-to-date edition. Amazingly well-cross-referenced and indexed. VideoHound also publishes specialty titles, such as one on science-fiction films, one on horror films, and the one described above.

C.2 Web Sites Devoted to B Movies

I've broken these down into two categories: Those I've spent a lot of time on and those I haven't. Within each category, sites are listed in alphabetical order by the site name.

C.2.1 Regular stops

For general information about B films, I think the following sites are tops.

- **The Astounding B-Monster**

  www.bmonster.com/

  For original content about B films *only*, this is a great place to start. The design of the site is kind of jarring—I think they're striving for the garish look of a cheaply made, color, science-fiction film of the late 1950s or so. But it's a great site to browse through. The one thing I wish they'd include is a page of links to other sites.

- **Internet Movie Database (IMDB)**

  www.imdb.com

  I described the VideoHound guide above as an encyclopedia of film. And so it is—the *print* form. IMDB is unquestionably the best *online* source of information about just about any film, though. One thing I especially like to do with it is look up some B film by title, then click on a cast member's name. This takes you to a filmography of that actor's entire, er, *oeuvre*. (If that's not too pretentious a word in this context!) Once there, notice the menu down the left side of the page—particularly the one labeled "External Links." Follow those links to find sites devoted to a particular B-film cast member. For example, using this technique I located "*Silent Scream*: The Unofficial Barbara Steele film site" with news about, interviews with, and other information about Barbara Steel, who played the warden in *Caged Heat* (home.earthlink.net/~gershom/steele.html).

- **The Joe Bob Report (Joe Bob Briggs):**

  www.joebob-briggs.com/

  Those of you in the United States may remember Joe Bob Briggs from his Saturday late-night show "MonsterVision," on the TNT cable-TV channel. Well before that show, though, he'd already endeared himself to B-film aficionados with his so-called "Drive-In Movie Reviews." (Historically, B movies may have been born in Saturday-afternoon matinees. But they reached adolescence in the drive-in movie theaters of the 1950s and 1960s.) Note that the guy's not shy about his politics, which tend to the liberal and libertarian; if you think that might offend you, you might want to go straight to his collected reviews of hundreds of films, starting at www.joebob-briggs.com/bmovieguide/index.html.

- **Oh, The Humanity! The Worst Movies on Earth**

  www.ohthehumanity.com/

  Great domain name, huh? My favorite way to use the site is to go to the reviews page, www.ohthehumanity.com/reviews.html, and click on the Random Movie link on the left-hand menu. I've found quite a few winners that way. Not particularly comprehensive, though—at last count, it included reviews of only a few dozen films.

- **Open Directory/dMoz guide to B-Movie sites**

  dmoz.org/Arts/Movies/Genres/B-Movies/

  You may know about the general Open Directory/dMoz project already. It's kind of an open-source, non-commercial Yahoo! The page listed here includes links to more than 20 sites (including some of those listed here, as well as others) the last time I visited. The page's guide has included a brief description of B movies that covers the usual—low budgets, often painful to sit through, and so on. But then it adds, "There are also, however, some truly killer Bs. Good-bad and good-good mingle together under the B-Movie mantle." Well said.

- **Pat LaRosa's Old B-Movies site**

  www.oldb-movies.com/

  Primarily a nostalgia-oriented site, concentrating on Bs from the 1930s and 1940s. What I find most interesting is its focus on B-movie *studios* rather than on the films themselves. This site also includes a good collection of stills captured from the films and lobby cards used to promote them in theaters.

- **TerribleMovies.com**

  www.terriblemovies.com/

  Subtitled "B-Movies, B-Lifestyles, and the C.H.U.D.s who love them." The reviews here are pretty good, even if there aren't a lot of them. But the "Essays" section is great, currently including musings on (among other subjects) the history of Bs, plague films, and "B Movies & Coping with Life."

C.2.2 Occasional stops

I haven't spent much time visiting any of the following sites (and, hence, haven't provided any information on them, other than their URIs); they may be incredible resources or duds. Consider this just a sampling, the proverbial tip of the iceberg; I might have listed 50 or more others in place of these. Some of these sites are devoted to particular genres, some to particular actors or studios, and some to nothing at all—except the lure of the B film in general!

- **Bad Movie Planet**
  www.badmovieplanet.com/
- **The Bad Movie Review Website**
  www.badmovies.org/
- **The B-Movie Guide**
  finvarra.www1.50megs.com/
- **B-Movie Section at VideoFlicks.com**
  www.videoflicks.com/bmovie/
- **Bruce Campbell Online**
  www.bruce-campbell.com
- **Dr. Squid's Smorgasbord of Terror**
  www.proaxis.com/~sherlockfam/drsquid.html
- **Foiled Productions ("low-to-no-budget movies")**
  www.foiled.co.uk/
- **Grand Central Rocket**
  sfstation.members.easyspace.com/rocket.htm
- **Jabootu's Bad Movie Dimension**
  www.jabootu.com/
- **Like Television - Movies**
  tesla.liketelevision.com/liketelevision/search/movies.php?
  q=Movies&theme=guide
- **Midnight Marquee Press/Cool Links**
  www.midmar.com/links.html
- **Sandman Cinema**
  www.sandmancinema.com/
- **Science Fiction Matinee**
  tatooine.fortunecity.com/herbert/305/sfm1.htm

C.3 Other Resources

Just a couple of other places for you to check for B-film information:

- First, there's at least one public mailing list devoted to the Bs. It's one of the TopicA discussion groups. Subscription information and archives are at www.topica.com/lists/B-Movies/.

- Second, although not related to B movies in particular, make it a point to visit the movie-mistakes.com site every now and then. An excellent, enjoyable, extended lesson in how even A-list films sometimes tremble on the brink of B-ness!

Index

Symbols

! (exclamation mark), as negation operator in Boolean expressions, 56, 57,
59, 75

#default, keyword for default namespace,
104

( ) (parentheses), grouping separator,
61-62

* (asterisk), wildcard in node test, 46

. (period/full stop), shortcut for self, 31,
51

.. (double period), shortcut for parent, 31,
49

/ (slash), used to separate steps, 30-31
not used as division operator, 78

// (double slash)
avoiding leading, in XPath location
paths, 80
JavaScript comment marker, 164-166
shortcut for descendant-or-self axis, 52

:: (double colon), separator between axis
and node test, 43, 47

?xml-stylesheet? PI
description, 85-88

pseudo-attributes
alternate, 87, 88-89
charset, 87
href, 86, 98-99
media, 87
title, 86-87
type, 86
and XSLT processors, 95

@ ("at sign"), shortcut for attribute axis, 55

[ ] (square brackets), delimiters for predicate, 62

{} ("curly braces"), delimiters for attribute
value template (AVT), 128

| (pipe/vertical bar), union operator, 330

A

abs() function(XSL-FO), 514-515

absolute location paths, 30

advanced XSLT problems
grouping, 331-339
table structures, 327-331
validating (Schematron), 340-345

alternate pseudo-attribute (?xml-
stylesheet? PI), 87, 88-89

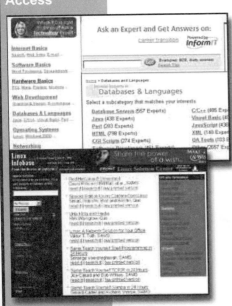

tice Hall: Professional Technical Reference

Back | Forward | Reload | Home | Search | Guide | Images | Print | Security | Stop

PH PTR

http://www.phptr.com/

P R E N T I C E   H A L L

Professional Technical Reference
Tomorrow's Solutions for Today's Professionals.

Keep Up-to-Date with
PH PTR Online!

We strive to stay on the cutting edge of what's happening in professional computer science and engineering. Here's a bit of what you'll find when you stop by **www.phptr.com**:

@ **Special interest areas** offering our latest books, book series, software, features of the month, related links and other useful information to help you get the job done.

☞ **Deals, deals, deals!** Come to our promotions section for the latest bargains offered to you exclusively from our retailers.

$ **Need to find a bookstore?** Chances are, there's a bookseller near you that carries a broad selection of PTR titles. Locate a Magnet bookstore near you at www.phptr.com.

! **What's new at PH PTR?** We don't just publish books for the professional community, we're a part of it. Check out our convention schedule, join an author chat, get the latest reviews and press releases on topics of interest to you.

✉ **Subscribe today! Join PH PTR's monthly email newsletter!**

Want to be kept up-to-date on your area of interest? Choose a targeted category on our website, and we'll keep you informed of the latest PH PTR products, author events, reviews and conferences in your interest area.

Visit our mailroom to subscribe today! **http://www.phptr.com/mail_lists**